Economic Development from the
State and Local Perspective

Economic Development from the State and Local Perspective

Case Studies and Public Policy Debates

David J. Robinson

This publication has been created to provide you with accurate and authoritative information concerning the subject matter covered. However, this publication was not necessarily prepared by persons licensed to practice law in a particular jurisdiction. The author is not engaged in rendering legal or other professional advice, and this publication is not a substitute for the advice of an attorney. If you require legal or other expert advice, you should seek the services of a competent attorney or other professional.

First published in 2014 by
PALGRAVE MACMILLAN®
in the United States—a division of St. Martin's Press LLC,
175 Fifth Avenue, New York, NY 10010.

Where this book is distributed in the UK, Europe and the rest of the world, this is by Palgrave Macmillan, a division of Macmillan Publishers Limited, registered in England, company number 785998, of Houndmills, Basingstoke, Hampshire RG21 6XS.

Palgrave Macmillan is the global academic imprint of the above companies and has companies and representatives throughout the world.

Palgrave® and Macmillan® are registered trademarks in the United States, the United Kingdom, Europe and other countries.

ISBN 978-1-137-32067-4   ISBN 978-1-137-31749-0 (eBook)
DOI 10.1057/9781137317490

Library of Congress Cataloging-in-Publication Data

Robinson, David J., 1966–
    Economic development from the state & local perspective : case studies and public policy debates / by David J. Robinson.
        pages cm
    Includes index.

    1. United States—Economic policy—21st century. 2. Economic development—United States. 3. State governments—United States. 4. Local government—United States. I. Title.

HC106.83.R635 2014
338.973—dc23   2014010221

A catalogue record of the book is available from the British Library.

Design by Newgen Knowledge Works (P) Ltd., Chennai, India.

First edition: September 2014

10 9 8 7 6 5 4 3 2 1

This book is dedicated to my wife, Julie Dorrian, and son, Hugh, for the love and support they gave me in the endeavor to research and write this book.

CONTENTS

ILLUSTRATIONS

Figures

Tables

PREFACE

Restarting the American economy is today's number one public policy priority. Public and private sector organizations across the United States are struggling with how to revive the American economy to not only employ people and create wealth but also to keep America on top of the global economy. Most of the action creating jobs and wealth occurs at the state and local levels. The federal government is primarily a funder of economic activity and regulator of money supply, global trade, labor laws, provider of national defense, and an overall social safety net.

Economic development is a game played at the state and local levels. This book is a discussion about that game, how it is played, and how it is won. This book is not meant to be a treatise on the topics covered in economic development and is certainly not a complete discussion of any of the topics. Instead, this book attempts to cover the major issues facing economic development practitioners. To keep the approach practical, economic development strategy, public policy, and real estate development issues are covered.

No single formula exists for successful economic development. Regions and states have different assets and liabilities that mandate certain strategies and make others impractical. Successful economic development is not the result of one major real estate project or even a series of it. Successful economic development happens where regions and states focus on building block strategies and then move onto more advanced drivers of economic development. Nearly all communities implement some or all the building blocks of economic development. These strategies focus on zoning land for development as well as gaining land for development through annexation and eminent domain. These elementary strategies include the use of tax policy to retain and attract companies and the development of workforce programs. Infrastructure development is a pivot strategy for economic development practitioners. The building blocks of economic development finally address quality-of-life issues such as making neighborhoods safe, ensuring families have good schools, creating a base of affordable housing, and providing cultural and entertainment options people desire.

Those quality-of-life issues are the starting line for economic development. The next step is implementation of the five drivers of economic development. These more advanced strategies of economic development center on technology, energy, globalism, service, and advanced manufacturing. Regions and states leading the nation in economic growth follow one or more of these proactive strategies. They go far beyond the traditional building blocks of economic development and create advanced strategies around core regional strengths in growing industry segments.

Focus of the Book

The beginning chapters introduce core economic development concepts and a case study that will be used throughout the class. The book proceeds to fundamental issues impacting the economic development, defined as "building blocks." Finally, the book discusses the more advanced proactive economic development strategies, defined as the five drivers of economic development. It utilizes a common-class case study throughout the book and examines the issues facing local and state economic developers, starting with the most basic and moving up to the more complex and advanced.

Chapter 1 introduces core economic development and lays a foundation for the rests of the book. Chapter 2 outlines how regions and states prepare and implement a strategic economic development plan. It discusses the process, issues, and theories regions and states face when planning to increase wealth creation. Chapter 3 outlines the roles of local, state, and federal governments and the growing role of the private sector in the business of economic development. This chapter discusses how American regions and states approach and implement economic development.

Chapter 4 introduces the case study to readers, which will be used throughout the book. A case study approach brings the real-life issues facing local and state economic development leaders and introduces the reader to all the players involved in an economic development project. It also helps the reader develop critical thinking, speaking, writing, and advocacy skills needed for successful economic development. The book's case study creates a mythical city project that has the traditional complexity facing big urban economic development projects and illustrates how economic development is much more than tax incentives. Stories on crime, zoning, workforce, tax, eminent domain, infrastructure development, annexation, smart growth, housing, sustainable development, technology-based economic development, and globalism fill the book's case study.

Following the chapters that introduce basic concepts of economic development and the case study, the book explores the first level of sophistication for local and state economic development, defined as the "building blocks." The introduction of the book's true substance begins in chapter 5—the preparation of a site for development that must have a use permitted typically by local government zoning rules. This chapter digs into the first land use issue related to economic development, and this is zoning.

Chapter 6 continues the land use discussion with an examination of the role of eminent domain in economic development. Eminent domain is a land use issue impacting the economic developer's ability to assemble land for wealth creation purposes. Policy makers and courts impact eminent domain. Multiple states' approaches to eminent domain will be examined, and the readers will find themselves arguing in a city council meeting regarding the good and bad of eminent domain. Chapter 7 concludes the discussion of land use issues by examining how growth laws and policies impact economic development through annexation policy. This discussion center on annexation (adding land to a municipality) and examines how states like Arizona and Texas use annexation as an economic development tool.

Infrastructure is the next economic development "building block" the book discusses. Chapter 8 examines how various public finance tools and government programs are utilized to develop the roads, highway, bridge, water, sewer, telecommunication, and other infrastructure necessary for all economic developments to happen. Particular attention is paid to the role of tax increment financing to develop infrastructure tied to economic development.

Chapter 9 addresses how workforce issues impact regional and state economic development. Hot topics such as workforce training and impact of immigration are covered in this chapter. Chapter 10 looks to the use of tax policy as a tool for developing jobs and wealth. Again, as with all the chapters, the reader will go through the case study to feel all the issues impacting the use of tax incentives as a company retention and attraction tool.

Chapter 11 examines the quality-of-life issues of safety, education, and housing that dominate and impact company location decisions. No economic development can happen where there is a perception of high crime. The book examines the policy issues facing communities that are working to address the challenge of crime. Hot topics such as gun control, conceal carry, and code enforcement are discussed. The chapter discusses how communities have addressed the challenge of crime to redevelop a neighborhood. The successful redevelopment of Times Square in New York City is used as a national model for addressing crime control. In addition, the book's case study will take readers through the challenges of controlling crime at the local level. Chapter 11 discusses how states and regions are entering an age of education reform in their efforts to address shortcomings in the quality of secondary and primary schools. This chapter also discusses how the national housing market impacts economic development and the role the federal government plays in subsidizing this industry.

The book proceeds to inform how more advanced regions and states utilize modern economic development strategies, known as the five drivers of economic development. Chapter 12 reviews how a sustainable development model based on smart growth, historic preservation, and brownfield redevelopment can move growth more inward and less outward. This model is built around a new approach to land use policies and working to attract high-wage companies in the energy sector. Chapter 13 addresses the growing technology-based economic development model that many regions and states are using to transform their economy. Chapter 14 outlines the emerging strategies to help regions and states succeed in a growing global marketplace. Topics such as export and foreign direct investment success are discussed.

Chapter 15 outlines the challenges and solutions of today's advanced manufacturing sector. Successful state policy moves to enrourage the manufacturing industry to grow are discussed, which include many of the building block issues and the controversial Right to Work legislation. Chapter 16 outlines the creation of a high-wage regional service economy well beyond the low-wage retail jobs many would associate with the service sector. The dependence of these industries on a quality workforce and unique infrastructure, such as global airports, is discussed. Finally, the book concludes with a discussion of what the future holds for America's economic development at the state and local levels. The range of topics includes higher education, regionalism, new transportation funding models, green buildings, emerging global giants such as Brazil, India, and China, and cutting-edge smart growth tactics to grow more in than out.

Economic Developers Are Problem Solvers

Economic development involves problem solvers and starters. Both these roles are often played by policy makers, lawyers, community leaders, developers, labor unions, central city activists, business leaders, educators, and regular citizens. Policy makers are the ultimate decision makers who must address economic issues. The struggles, strategies, policies, and laws facing economic development leaders are the focus of this book.

Economic development strategy and planning matter; however, success lies in the execution of that strategy and plan. Economic developers are typically problem solvers. They identify the challenges as to why a region or state is not succeeding in the global economy, take stock of what resources they have to work with, and go to work solving the challenges before them.That approach of identifying challenges and providing solutions is the format of this book. This challenge to solution model may involve public policy, business, legal, or other issues, but to keep the reader in the real world, each chapter will revolve around the identification of problems and a discussion of solutions policy makers, legislators, courts, business leaders, and others have used to build successful economies.

Multidisciplinary Approach

Private sector developers, Fortune 500 CEOs, and small business leaders alone do not hold the answer to a region or state's economic challenges. Local government planners, lawyers, judges, city council members, state legislators, governors, teachers, police officers, chamber of commerce executives, and government-funded economic development staff working collectively hold the key to economic success at the state and local levels.

Economic development is not just about good government planning. Land use planning makes a difference in the creation of quality neighborhoods. However, many community problems are not just the result of poverty but often are the results of a planner's idea of a paradise 50 years ago. As an example, Euclidian zoning approach of land use planning and massive interstate highways that extend suburbs as far as a car can be driven are now out of favor with the majority of current urban thinkers and can be blamed as part of the reason why urban sprawl has occurred. The more popular "modern" approach is geared toward mixed uses, getting people out of their automobiles, and creating walkable neighborhoods. No doubt, 50 years from now, planners and economic development practitioners will be "fixing" the infill approach of today. A study of economic development limited to planning, community development or housing, land use issues, and in silos may fail to address the broad array of issues the local and state economic developers face on a daily basis.

Holistic Economic Development Strategy

The view of this book is that successful stragetic economic development is about more than the use of tax incentives to lower the cost of doing business at a specific site. Instead, this book addresses a broader approach to economic development that not only ensures sites are ready for development but also addresses broader issues such as crime, workforce, and infrastructure. This book is grounded in the actual practice of economic development.

While this broader, holistic approach is essential to successful economic development, this book does not lose sight of the fact that retention of existing business, development of an innovation-based economy, embracing globalism, and attracting foreign direct investment are the building blocks to twenty-first-century economic success. Studies prove that retention creates 80 percent of new jobs and that companies that export or are technology-based or a part of a global firm all pay higher wages on average. The holistic economic development strategy is centered on the retention and attraction of high-wage jobs of the future, which can achieve community success for decades to come. In addition, this book will promote a sustainable development model because it is important to not just create jobs but to create quality development that serves as magnets for future investment.

An additional bias of this book is that the private sector is the key to successful economic development. Post–World War II, the focus of most private sector development has centered on the suburbs. While an upward urban trend was starting to gain movement, the current financial services and real estate–based economic recession has halted that movement. The long-term solution to economic development, no matter where it is, does not lie in government programs or dollars but in attracting massive private investment.

In an age of declining government revenues, the federal government alone lacks the resources to address the challenges of economic development. Successful economic development happens most often because of private sector risk taking and regions and states creating a positive business climate and utilizing target incentives. Most successful development stories have a strong element of the public sector harnessing the power and capital of the private sector. This book discusses how the government uses the law and public policy to create incentives for private sector investments to create a quality sense of place by tacking crime, schools, and infrastructure.

Economic development is clearly the topic of our time. A national recession has everyone looking for ways to transform their economy. This book outlines the road to economic recovery through regional and state action.

DAVID J. ROBINSON

Acknowledgments

I acknowledge the support, work, and wisdom of a number of individuals without which this book would have not made it to publication. First, my friend and colleague, Steve Brennen, provided invaluable perspective and research for this book. Steve's career in economic development at the federal, state, and local levels provided great insight. Much thanks go to the leadership of The Ohio State University John Glenn School of Public Affairs—Director Trevor Brown and Professor Rob Greenbaum—for their support and for giving me the opportunity to teach an Economic Development Policy course. That teaching experience is the basis for this book. Thanks also go to Bowling Green State University economics professor and Director of the Center for Regional Development, Michael Carroll, for his wisdom and support for this book. Finally, the team at Porter Wright Morris & Arthur, LLP, Andy Emerson and Dan Massey in particular, provided friendship and wisdom as well on a range of topics.

CHAPTER ONE
DEFINING ECONOMIC DEVELOPMENT

Chapter Goals

1. Understand the elements of economic development
2. Recognize the difference between economic development, real estate development, and community development
3. Understand who implements economic development policy and why
4. Identify the basic "building block" economic development strategies
5. Identify the advanced "five drivers" economic development strategies

Economic Development Is a Public Policy Solution

Economic development is a public policy solution to the challenges of a global, high-tech economy in the age of a jobless economic recovery. Economic development takes the form of government incentives and subsidies to encourage private sector wealth creation.[1] The federal government impacts the economy but does not dictate a national economic development strategy. Instead, vibrant regional and state economies are created through local and state public-private partnerships.

The United States faces economic problems based upon a new global, high-tech economy that impacts wealth and job creation. The United States has the largest economy in the world—constituting more than 20 percent of the world's gross national product (GDP).[2] However, by 2030, the Chinese economy will represent well over 20 percent of global GDP and will be larger than the US economy as Figure 1.1 shows.[3]

On top of new global economic challenges, America is facing a jobless economic recovery. The unemployment rate even during the current period of economic growth does not reflect the traditional rate of decline followed in previous recessions. Traditionally, the American economy follows a V-shaped recovery from recessions. A steep collapse is followed by a steep recovery back up. However, the last three economic recessions have not followed this pattern, and Americans are facing a jobless recovery with above-average unemployment rates.[4]

Technology transformed the American economy. The expansion of global markets and explosion of technology in all industries put America through a great period of "creative destruction."[5] The process of creative destruction argues that greater economic gain comes from the new industry and innovation killing the old.

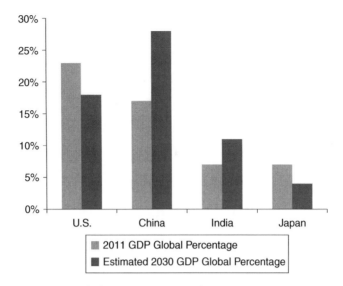

Figure 1.1   Emergence of Chinese economy over the American economy.

Source: Asa Johansson, et. al. "Looking to 2060: Long-Term Global Growth Prospects: A Going for Growth Report", *OECD Economic Policy Papers*, No. 3 (2012), p. 22.

Creative destruction explains the constant evolution and success of capitalistic mar-kets, but the ride along the creative destruction roller coaster is not fun for everyone. It now takes only 170 workers to produce what it used to take 1,000 workers to produce in 1950.[6] Nationally, with only 10 percent of Americans working in the high-wage manufacturing sector, down from 33 percent in 1950s, a large number of American workers are searching for high-paying jobs.[7]

The economic challenges of the state of Michigan illustrate the public policy problem the economic development policy is meant to solve. In the 1950s, Michigan was an economic miracle. In 1954, Michigan's per capita income was at 120 percent of the national average.[8] By the early 1960s, half the state's economy was based upon manufacturing.[9] From the 1950s into the early part of the twenty-first century, Michigan's economy experienced a dramatic decline as the high-paying manufac-turing sector dropped to just over 10 percent of the state's economy by 2009, and the per capita income for the state was just 87 percent of the national average.[10] The once-powerful city of Detroit is being evacuated. Detroit had 1,849,568 residents in 1950 and now is hovering near 700,000.[11] American public policy makers are work-ing to avoid Michigan's challenges.

Economic Development Is Played at the Local and State Levels

To address the challenges of wealth creation, government in partnership with the private sector implements economic development strategies. Government devotes resources to economic development based upon the concept of public good. A public good can be defined as those things that all people can enjoy in common because their use does not subtract from others' use of the same good.[12] Examples of public goods include clean drinking water and air, quality medical care, sanitation systems and schools, safe streets, and successful economic development. Economic development is a public good because it creates the wealth people need to live. The more economic success individuals have, the larger the private market and government tax revenues grow to provide the resources everyone needs to succeed.

Local and state governments take the lead in the retention and attraction of jobs and companies. The federal government defines the legal and constitutional powers of government to regulate private industry and implements monetary, fiscal, trade, labor, and other laws at the national level. It funds a range of programs used by local and state governments and private sector companies to foster economic development. It adopts broad full employment goals but does not mandate a national economic plan. Instead, a federalist approach dominates where local and state governments take the lead in implementing economic development strategies.

Economic Development versus Real Estate Development versus Community Development

Economic development differs from real estate development and community development. Economic development creates a higher standard of living for its residents. Its focus on retaining and attracting higher-wage jobs and developing companies provides a stronger tax base for local government and schools. These essential public services help develop a world-class quality of life.

Economic development differs from real estate development and traditional notions of community development. At times they all overlap, but at their core the goals of each are different. Economic development involves the use of public subsidies to incentivize private sector wealth creation. Real estate development is the "continual reconfiguration of the built environment to meet society's needs."[13] It may or may not create high-wage jobs. Real estate development improves a parcel of land to increase its value. Real estate developers turn a cornfield into a housing project or an abandoned factory into a shopping center. Houses and shopping centers are part of a strong regional economy, but often they do not contain high-wealth jobs. While not always focused on attracting high-wage jobs, real estate developers can be a part of a team focusing on economic development.

Community development is the opposite of real estate development. It focuses on equality of opportunity. The goal of community developers is to address poverty through affordable housing, workforce training, and small business financing strategies. Many of their outcomes are aligned with economic development, but community developers are looking to improve the quality of life of a targeted neighborhood. They focus on locating regional resources in a neighborhood struggling with crime, inadequate housing, unemployment, and aging infrastructure. Community and economic development may overlap. Everyone wants high-wage jobs of the future. But, high-crime neighborhoods with residents with low educational attainment are not attractive sites for the location of high-wage jobs.

Economic Development: Regional, State, and Industry Winners

In a nation with wage rates and government regulatory burdens far above China and unemployment above normal levels, American engagement in economic development policy is a fact of life. As Washington continues to debate, posture, and argue, regions and states are incentivizing wealth creation through economic development strategies. Not every place in the United States is Detroit. Success stories of regional and state economic development can be found in the four corners of the United States.

Using per capita income as a measure of economic development success, Connecticut, New Jersey, Massachusetts, New York, and Maryland dominate.[14] The East Coast benefits from substantial population density, high college education rates, large presence of global corporate headquarters, and an urban renaissance of America's largest cities. New York City drives much of this economic development. With 8,200,000 residents, New York City is not only the nation's largest city, but its population grew by over a million since 1980.[15] New York City's 3,200,000 private sector jobs is near an all-time high.[16] The Big Apple operates a modern service economy, with financial services and real estate constituting 12 percent of the regional economy and professional services and health care constituting 15 percent and 16 percent, respectively.[17] New York City's economic renaissance is linked to quality-of-life improvements matched with financial incentives to retain and grow the financial services industry. New York City is an example that a high-wage, high-cost city can serve as success story of economic development.

Per capita income is not the only measure of economic success. A measure of only income ignores the high cost of living many of these regions endure. Figure 1.2 illustrates wage and employment rates and their overall growth are also measures of economic development.

Industry sectors influence the economic success of a region. Recent economic winners from employment and wage perspective are dominated by energy and agriculture markets. The energy-oriented economies of North Dakota, South Dakota, Wyoming, Louisiana, and Iowa illustrate the most growth in per capita income from 1990 to 2012. The North Dakota boom is remarkable and based upon the exploration of oil and natural gas from once-dominant shale deposits. In 2012, North Dakota's GDP led the nation with a 13.4 percent increase.[18] This rate of growth is larger than China and more than twice the growth rate of second-place Texas. Policy

Figure 1.2 State employment and wage winners.

Source: United States Bureau of Labor Statistics, Retrieved from http://www.bls.gov/home.htm.

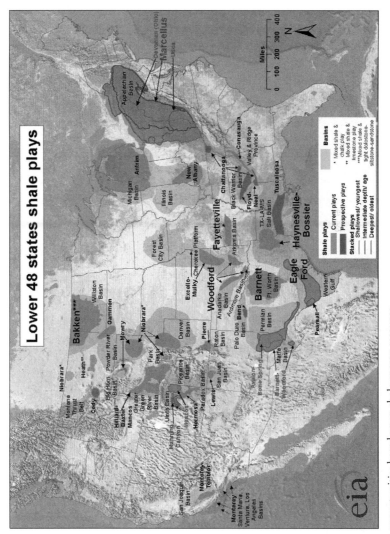

Figure 1.3 Growth opportunities based upon shale energy resource.

Source: U.S. Department of Energy, Energy Information Agency, Lower 48 Shale Map, retrieved from http://www.eia.gov/oil_gas/rpd/shale_gas.pdf.

makers and business leaders make decisions impacting the region's ability to grow an energy market. The availability of a low-cost energy source in North Dakota positions this state and others for future industrial growth. North Dakota is only starting to gain energy-related jobs and yet they still lead the nation in GDP growth.

As Figure 1.3 illustrates, North Dakota is not alone in gaining from the development of energy and jobs from shale gas. Regions across the United States are benefiting from the use of new technology to extract domestic energy. A handful of regions and states blessed with an energy resource takes that advantage to new heights. Texas offers one such example. The economic development story of Texas is well known. The lone star state is booming. Texas' real GDP grew 13 percent from 2009 to 2012.[19] While Texas grew, major states such as California struggled. California's share of the American economy shrank from 13.1 percent to 12.9 percent during 2009–2012.[20] Texas' portion of the American economy increased from 8.2 percent to 9 percent during this same timeframe.[21] Again, Texas is benefiting from the energy boom, but the state uses a $300,000,000 economic development incentive to retain and recruit companies across the globe, operates without a state income tax, and offers manufacturers' labor policies they like.

Energy is not the only source of economic success in the United States. The birth of the American manufacturing industry in the south is another example of an economic winner. The southern region of the United States is experiencing an economic renaissance around the recruitment of global manufacturing facilities. States such as Alabama, Tennessee, and Mississippi landed global auto, steel, and aerospace factories producing billions if not trillions of dollars in economic impact. As the auto and steel industry jobs evacuated the industrial midwest over the past 40 years, these jobs landed in southern states. Alabama has as many auto assembly plants as Ohio with half the population. Again, this global economic success did not happen by accident. The Southern American manufacturing industry was recruited by low-wage costs and business-friendly tax and labor policies.

Other economic development lists exist as well. These lists are of the economic losers. The industrial midwest is struggling, but even these states show prospects of success. Ohio's $1,600,000,000 technology commercialization program is building a new generation of high-tech companies. Cleveland is becoming the center of an emerging medical device industries attracting millions of dollars of investment. Ohio is also benefiting from an explosion of shale oil and natural gas that is starting the Buckeye State on the path North and South Dakota blazed. State policy makers and business leaders push Ohio in this economic direction by making investment decisions with government resources and adopting policies friendly to business.

Regional and State Economic Development Strategies Build Success

How do these regions and states find their own path to economic development success? Regional and state economic development strategies are either basic "building block" or more advanced, proactive strategies, known as the "five drivers" of economic development. All regions and states implement building block economic development strategies, preparing sites for development through land use planning, annexation, and eminent domain. Building block strategies also address infrastructure development, workforce, tax policy, and quality-of-life issues. These fundamental economic development strategies are the floor and not the ceiling. They cannot be overlooked. Larger, proactive efforts to retain and attract high-wage jobs center around the use of building block economic development strategies but targeted toward high-wage industry clusters.

A number of select industries provide high-wage jobs, wages above the national average. Manufacturing has long led the list of high-wage industries in many parts of the United States. More recently, high-tech and service industry occupations have led an economic renaissance in many regions of the country. Also, firms that participate in the global economy through foreign ownership or exports pay above-average wages.[22] Finally, companies in the energy industry are current economic leaders.[23] High-wage energy, technology, manufacturing, global, and service industries constitute the five drivers of successful economic development. Regions and states truly succeeding in developing high-wage jobs implement strategies around the five drivers of economic development that include energy, technology, globalism, advanced manufacturing, and service. The five drivers of economic development happen in regions and states that offer all the benefits of basic economic development but succeed at attracting high-wage jobs in targeted industries. The five drivers of economic development focus on high-wage energy, high-tech, global, advanced manufacturing, and service industries. Figure 1.4 provides an outline of specific examples of both the building blocks and five drivers of economic development strategy.

Strategic Economic Development Plan	• Oregon and Green Jobs
Land Use Planning	• Houston and No Zoning
Annexation	• Texas Annexation
Eminent Domain	• Tennessee Emiment Domain Law
Infrastructure	• Chicago and Tax Increment Financing
Workforce	• RTP and Bio Work Program
Tax Policy	• Alabama Economic Development Incentives
Quality of Life	• Utah Ski Industry
Energy-led Economic Development	• North Dakota Shale Gas
Technology-based Economic Development	• Silicon Valley
Globalism	• Tulsa Export Strategy
Advanced Manufacturing	• The South
Service	• Columbus, Ohio

Figure 1.4 Primary state and local economic development strategies.
Source: Self Created.

Oregon and Economic Development Strategic Planning

Fundamental to success in economic development is the implementation of a strategic plan to promote the creation of jobs and wealth. The essential elements of a strategic economic development plan start with reaching consensus on community economic goals; creating measurable objectives that define the plan's success; developing economic development strategies that fit a region's strengths, weaknesses, opportunities, and threats; and finally creating a list of action steps to make the economic development goal a reality. Policy makers and business leaders use economic development organizations, both public and private sector, to implement economic development strategies. Oregon is an economic winner based in large part on implementing an effective economic development plan. Oregon went after green jobs and they are getting them. Oregon's strategies to gain green jobs involved more than their traditional smart growth land use tactics, but it also included regulatory approaches supporting renewable energy and tax incentives targeted at alternative energy companies. Portland, as Oregon's economic center, uses a public-private partnership to drive its economic development strategy with strong participation of both local government and private industry leadership. Oregon is a leader in green jobs and, in particular, grew manufacturing jobs in the alternative energy industry.

Land Use and Houston

The regulation of land use is central to building block economic development strategies. Successful economic development is not possible without a stable and predictable legal process to purchase and develop real estate.[24] Local government manages the growth and development through a comprehensive plan that sets the overall goals, objectives, and policies to guide the local legislative body's decision making regarding the development of a region or community. Zoning is the prime tool local governments use to regulate land use and implement their comprehensive plan. Zoning divides the land within a jurisdiction into districts with varying restrictions on uses (such as size and location of buildings, yard areas, and intensity). As zoning approaches its hundredth birthday in America, its use is being challenged. Houston stands out not only as a twenty-first-century global economic success story but also as a national model for prodevelopment land use regulation. Houston has long been the only major city in the United States not using traditional zoning. Houston's land use regulation is a modified version of zoning that creates only two types of zoning in a much simplified but understandable process, which has helped this mega-city grow into a global powerhouse. While Houston's strength in the energy industry is given much credit for its growth, Houston's prodevelopment land use regulatory model also deserves credit for the city's impressive growth of high-wage jobs.

Arizona Annexation Policy

The availability of land ready for improvement and development is another essential building block required for economic development. Government enables that land is ready and available for development through annexation. Annexation is the legal process by which a municipality brings land into its boundaries to ensure development occurs.[25] Annexation ensures that potential areas of development have essential public services often larger municipalities have to offer. Arizona and its mega-city, Phoenix, offers a prodevelopment annexation policy worthy of note. All states permit municipalities to annex land tied to economic growth and the extension of city services to unincorporated territories. Few are as aggressive as Arizona in their use of annexation to grow regional economies. Phoenix offers a model for aggressive annexation policies in practice. Phoenix is over 500 square miles in size. This is gigantic even for the fifth largest city in the United States. State law drives Phoenix's growth through one word—water. This desert-based region lacks water, and development cannot happen without a long-term guarantee of available water. Thus, Phoenix with a large municipal water system is the place to be.

Eminent Domain Surviving in Tennessee

Eminent domain is the power guaranteed by the Fifth Amendment to the US Constitution that provides for just compensation when government takes land for a public purpose. The US Supreme Court extended eminent domain for economic development projects. The Court determined that a local government could take a person's property, provide them just compensation, and give that property to another private owner if the local government liked the land use plan of the latter. The Supreme Court decided to let state governments and state courts determine if this decision applied at the state level. States across the union rejected the Supreme Court's decision. In fact, eminent domain has become a dirty word when linked to economic development. Tennessee is no different than all the other state governments that examined how eminent domain and economic development would coexist. They rejected the blanket application of the Supreme Court decision. However, Tennessee made an important exception for the state's industrial park program. Tennessee, like many other states, operates a series of industrial parks tied to the retention and growth of their manufacturing and distribution industry. While rejecting the Supreme Court's interpretation of eminent domain and economic development, Tennessee did permit its industrial parks to continue its use of eminent domain. This small move sets the volunteer state apart from the rest of the nation.

Chicago and Public Infrastructure

Government's provision of infrastructure is the most traditional public subsidy provided by local and state governments to incentivize economic development. Infrastructure includes roads, water, sewer, rail, power, and telecommunication services needed to facilitate the use of property. Government uses its own resources and public finance tools such as industrial revenue bonds, special assessments, transportation improvement districts, and tax increment financing (TIF) to fund infrastructure for economic development. Chicago is a national leader in using public finance tools such as TIFs to foster economic development. Chicago is America's second largest city and a global powerhouse. However, aging neighborhoods, high cost of living, crime, and a struggling urban school system threaten its economic future. Chicago answered this threat through the aggressive use of TIFs to build public infrastructure essential for economic development projects. Chicago already has a substantial population base, world-class airport, and strong corporate headquarters base, but to attract new companies, Chicago has developed hundreds of TIF districts and property taxes created are poured back into the infrastructure needed at that site.

Workforce and the Research Triangle Park

Land and infrastructure are just the start for what is needed to retain and attract high-wage jobs. Economic development demands qualified workers. What those jobs are and what skills they require will differ with each region. However, all regions have a common need for a quality workforce ready to work. Workforce strategies take advantage of the regional workforce pool and existing industry clusters. Also, a quality workforce is created through a range of workforce development programs that focus on turning residents into workers industry in the region can employ. Regions and states launch successful industry-based training programs that prepare workers for service in particular industries. Finally, regions and states are building a workforce by attracting immigrants. North Carolina's Research Triangle Park (RTP) is a global economic powerhouse, but it is built not just on the backs of three major research-oriented universities but also through a national model for workforce development. Bio Work is a partnership between business and university leaders, which prepares RTP residents to become workers in the bio or pharmaceutical manufacturing industry. RTP is filled with global biomanufacturers in large part because the region developed qualified workers for the high-wage and high-skilled jobs in this industry. North Carolina, like much of the industrial midwest, answered a crisis for former textile mill and tobacco laborers with a program to position these residents to gain high-wage jobs in the bioindustry.

Tax Policy and Alabama's Global Recruitment Campaign

Tax policy is another prime building block economic development strategy. The federal government has a range of tax credits and other incentives to promote economic development. Regions and states use economic development incentives as a tool for business retention and attraction. Economic development incentives include tax credits, tax abatements, grants, or loans a public entity provides to a private entity in reward for locating a job-producing facility in their community. Tax credits are awarded competitively depending on the number of jobs and capital investment created by a given project or business and they act as a deduction for taxes a company otherwise would pay. The award of tax abatements prevents the payment of taxes based upon the location of a company at a designated site. A range of grants for workforce training, equipment purchases, and Brownfield remediation is awarded by local and state governments across the nation. Finally, government provides access to capital through low or no-interest loans. Local and state incentives are awarded through a formal site selection process conducted in stages, starting with the choice of a general region and ending with the selection of a specific site within that region. Alabama is a global manufacturing powerhouse in part due to its aggressive and successful use of tax incentives to lure auto and airplane assembly plants to their state. Alabama recruited Honda, Mercedes, Hyundai, and Airbus assembly facilities, constituting billions of dollars in investment and thousands of jobs not just with these facilities but with the supply chain manufacturers and distributors that follow these factories. Alabama gained these jobs through tax incentive packages exceeding $100,000,000 in value.

Quality of Life and Utah Skiing

Quality of life is something every community argues it has, but it involves much more than sunshine and palm trees. Companies and their executives are looking for high-quality schools and health-care institutions, safe streets, affordable workforce housing, and ample recreational activities. Successful primary and secondary schools exist in America, but legal, societal, and funding issues create a complex route for many regions and states to educate children. In addition, many communities have proved that streets once crime-ridden can be transformed into highly productive neighborhoods attractive to high-wage workers. Health care is a major quality-of-life factor as well. Health-care institutions are not only major employers, but access to high-quality health care makes regional workers more productive. Recreational amenities also impact a region's quality of life, and they matter for economic development purposes. Finally, affordable workforce housing impacts economic development. Not every region has mountains, an ocean, or perfect weather; however, those regions that do need to capitalize on it. Utah used their mountains to the advantage of strategic economic development. Utah's strategy to set their mountain-based region apart was the hosting of the Winter Olympics. The Salt Lake City games and the development of the Downtown Park City and their ski resorts led to hundreds of millions in economic gain, not just during the Olympics but for decades to come. Recruiting and funding the Winter Olympics for Salt Lake City was no easy task, but it continues to pay big dividends by highlighting the great quality of life this region offers.

North Dakota and Energy-Led Economic Development

Fostering the growth of the energy industry is the nation's leading economic development strategy. Energy-led economic development grows regional economies through the retention and recruitment of traditional and alternative energy companies. Energy is a growth industry. Electricity demands will grow 28 percent from 2011 to 2040.[26] The exploration, production, and distribution of energy to meet this demand builds successful regional and state economies. A boom in domestic energy production related to shale deposits beyond traditional oil producing and refining states creates substantial economic benefits beyond traditional energy industry regions. Midstream and downstream energy and energy-related chemical companies plan to invest $346,000,000 in the United States from 2012 to 2025.[27]

Industrial production should increase 3.5 percent by the end of the decade due to shale, and US manufacturing output is expected to grow by $258,000,000 for the same reason.[28] Jobs in the energy industry, whether traditional or alternative energy, pay above-average wages. No region is benefiting more from energy than North Dakota. The exploration and development of shale gas from deposits once thought dormant is amazing. North Dakota's growth last year was more than China's and more than double of Texas'—the state that finished second. North Dakota and other regions in the shale boom are adopting regulatory policies permitting this exploration, recruiting companies with targeted incentives, ensuring the infrastructure is in place to spur this investment, and developing the workers needed for a booming industry in towns previously nearly unoccupied.

Silicon Valley Is the Technology-Based Economic Development Model

The birth of the computer launched the beginning of the Information Age and the creation of technology-based economic development. Commercializing research and development is big business for companies large and small. From 1996 to 2007, university licensing agreements based on product sales contributed $47,000,000,000 to $187,000,000,000 to the US GDP.[29] Research and development in total generates $1,238,000,000,000 for the US economy.[30] High-tech jobs also are high-wage jobs. A regional technology-based economy centers around the creation of jobs and companies in the science, technology, engineering, and math fields (STEM). STEM jobs pay 26 percent higher annual average wages.[31] Silicon Valley is the unquestioned "King" of technology-based economic development. The strong marriage between leading research universities such as Stanford University and Cal-Berkley and the information technology industry is the origin of Silicon Valley, starting after World War II. Stanford's Research Park is a world-class example of land use policies, wherein the creation of research parks offers a new twist on retaining and attracting high-tech companies. Public policies to promote capital access also illustrate the strength of Silicon Valley. Access to venture capital is the lifeblood for high-tech, early-stage companies. Silicon Valley has half the pool of all the US venture capital. Everyone else is far behind.

Going Global in Tulsa

Globalism represents access to growing markets. In fact, 70 percent of the world's customers are outside of the United States, and workers of firms that export or are owned by global parents earn higher-than-average wages.[32] To address these opportunities in global markets, regions and states work with existing businesses to enhance their export opportunities and launch attraction campaigns to promote foreign direct investment (FDI). Export strategies improve advocacy and trade promotion efforts on behalf of domestic companies through trade missions and direct linkage between small and medium-sized US companies and global trade partners. They increase access to export financing through the import-export bank, reinforce efforts to remove trade barriers to ensure fair trade, and promote sustainable and balanced growth. FDI campaigns first define what constitutes a FDI, next focus on a group of core regional clusters, then define the benefits of FDI, and finally market the region globally. New York City and Los Angeles are not the only global winners in America. Mid-sized regions such as Tulsa prove they can compete on a global scale. Tulsa through the support and development of the aviation industry is a national export leader and is home to global aviation companies. Tulsa built a globalism strategy around being the intellectual research and development center and a strong supplier of workers for the aviation industry as well as working to promote the region globally for domestic companies and international leaders.

The South Has Risen Again with Manufacturing Jobs

Manufacturing jobs are not just high paying but they do not require an advanced professional or college education. Manufacturing workers earn more than those in other industries, measured on a weekly basis. Manufacturing workers from 2008 to 2010 averaged $943.06, 19.9 percent more than the nonmanufacturing average of $786.40.[33] Due to productivity gains and lower regional wages, manufacturing jobs in many parts of the United States are in a state of decline. However, advanced manufacturing facilities are central to regional and state economic development. Regions and states use labor policies such as Right to Work laws to slash the cost of doing business in their markets as well as retain and attract advanced manufacturing jobs. Regional and state initiatives for advanced manufacturing include tax incentives, lower power costs through regulatory policies or market forces, and land use strategies to prepare sites to manufacturers' needs. These initiatives also center around bringing research wisdom to the benefit of local manufacturers. Finally, regional advanced manufacturing efforts are tied to logistics programs, providing additional jobs but also lowering the transactional costs of local manufacturers. No part of the nation has benefited more from new advanced manufacturing facilities than the southern part of the United States. The number of southern states growing in advanced manufacturing is too large to pick just one. Tennessee is now home to multiple global autoassembly plants. South Carolina is still benefiting from an investment from BMW in Spartanburg. Georgia is a leader in reshoring projects back from global markets. Texas is winning nearly every economic category. Advanced manufacturing is an economic force throughout the nation, but the south is the leader in new manufacturing growth and development.

Columbus, a Service Leader in the Industrial Midwest

The service sector now dominates the American economy. Service sector industries are a link between producers and consumers, are information-intensive, and depend on workers with college and university degrees. Regional and state economies are dominated by the service industry. The real question is whether that region or state will attract the high-wage or just the low-wage service jobs. America is full of successful regional service-based economies. These regions focus on the retention and recruitment of corporate headquarters facilities and professional service firms. Regions attracting high-wage service jobs develop infrastructure such as global airports and offer low corporate tax rates and headquarters-specific tax incentives.

Regions also link companies in business services, develop a high number of college-educated workers, and focus on a common industry cluster. Columbus is a national leader in high-wage service industry jobs. Columbus uses aggressive land use tactics built around an annexation policy that spurs growth in the central city and ensures financial health and growth of the region. Columbus also takes advantage of the 100,000 college and university students, which creates an educated workforce pool attractive to corporate headquarters and professional service firms alike. Finally, Columbus benefits from being a lower cost alternative compared to New York City, Chicago, and other larger markets. Columbus, like Tulsa, illustrates that mid-sized regions can compete even if located in the struggling industrial midwest.

Economic Development Case Study 1.1: Baltimore's Harbor Development

Baltimore offers an example of the successes and failures of implementing an economic development strategy. Baltimore is a major American city with a direct link to the Atlantic Ocean connected to the eastern US population base. In 1950, Baltimore provided 75 percent of all jobs offered to workers in the state of Maryland, but over the next 35 years, Baltimore lost over 100,000 manufacturing jobs or 75 percent of its industrial employment.[34] As the city struggled, the business community came to the rescue. In 1955, the Greater Baltimore Committee was formed to bring together a group of influential business leaders to work with city government to develop civic programs.[35] The Greater Baltimore Committee did not solve the loss of manufacturing jobs, but instead turned into a real estate development machine focused on the downtown Baltimore waterfront.[36] Responding to a decline in business at the Baltimore Harbor, the business community in partnership with the local government launched a series of projects to save the city built around an area known as the Inner Harbor.

Harborplace Mall opened in 1980 in the Inner Harbor to create a center for retail in the once-bustling Port of Baltimore.[37] Harborplace resulted from decades of work on related projects that led to this retail initiative.[38] The Inner Harbor received shoreline improvements starting in 1948; the Charles Center office complex was built in the 1960s, Maryland Science Center, World Trade Center, and Convention Center were all built in the 1970s; and the National Aquarium and Hyatt Regency Hotel opened in the same timeframe as Harborplace followed, of course, by two major league sports stadiums.[39] Downtown Baltimore's once-busy harbors, which employed thousands of workers who made middle-class wages, have been replaced with high-rise, high-rent condo projects. Hundreds of millions of dollars in public funding have been used for these developments in downtown Baltimore.

There is no doubt the Inner Harbor transformed into a national tourist attraction that creates convention, conference, and other businesses that were not there before. This approach by Baltimore has been replicated all over America. High-wage, working-class jobs have been replaced by low-wage tourist and entertainment jobs. The question is whether this economic transformation is a good one for Baltimore and other regions' residents and whether it has turned the city and region around. No one can claim Baltimore has not been fighting urban decline in the past 60 years, but the question is whether their strategy has been working. The answer appears to be a no. First of all, the evacuation of Baltimore has continued, as the 2010 census illustrates that the city has now lost nearly one-third of its residents from its peak population and even lost 4.6 percent of its population from 2000 to 2010.[40] As with many other aging urban centers, the population is evacuating the city and the redevelopment of the Inner Harbor has not stopped that trend.[41]

Second, replacing high-wage union longshoremen jobs with retail-oriented positions is not a good trade for area workers. The average salary in the Baltimore-Washington-Northern Virginia area is $26 an hour.[42] The mean salary for retail-oriented workers such as food preparation workers is below $10 an hour and for retail sales workers is $11.53 an hour compared to over $18 an hour for freight and material movers who dominate a busy port.[43] It is unlikely these workers are buying a downtown condo at the Inner Harbor because the trade down to retail from logistics is cutting the average wage of the working class nearly in half. As proof that this retail for industry trade is not working for Baltimore, 2010 data indicate the average per capita income in Baltimore was just over $23,000 while the national average was nearly $40,000.[44]

Finally, Baltimore may be struggling economically because like many other urban centers it has struggled to address crime in the streets. Baltimore still has over 200 murders per year, which is a decline over past years but still illustrates struggles with public safety. In fact, Baltimore was recently cited as having the fifth highest murder rate per 100,000 residents in the nation.[45] High crime areas have no chance of locating a grocery store or gas station than a factory or office building. One bright spot for Baltimore appears to be some success on the urban school front. Recently, Baltimore city schools reached an 87 percent high school graduation rate, which puts them high above many of their urban counterparts.[46]

Projects such as the Inner Harbor illustrate that isolated real estate development does not solve the challenges of economic development such as addressing crime, creating a low-cost business-friendly regulatory environment, transitioning to high-paying research and development–oriented or global jobs, and opening new markets for area businesses. It creates a location for tourist and suburbanites to visit for a couple of hours rather than building high-wage jobs and creating true wealth for its residents. The transition Baltimore is making from a center of trade and manufacturing to a retail/service-based economy illustrates a national struggle. Civic and political leaders failed to see economic development, particularly in downtown, in terms of global competition, but instead they saw it as a battle with the dreaded suburbs.

Urban leaders also for the most part did not succeed on more complex issues such as addressing crime, educational quality of the public schools, growth of existing companies, development of high-tech jobs, and recruitment of new global companies to the region. Instead, they focused on the precious resources of money, time, and political energy on real estate projects and ribbon cutting, which have created popular tourist spots and transformed many urban centers' economy to lower-paid, retail-oriented jobs. In addition, all the energy and resources Baltimore has placed into turning their waterfront from a logistics center into a tourist attraction involves a major opportunity cost. Imagine that in the 1950s and 1960s the same energy, wisdom, and resources of the business community had been focused on fighting crime, holding urban schools accountable, building a global research and development center, and figuring out how to make the Port of Baltimore a logistics center once again. Communities, even successful ones like Baltimore, have a finite level of resources and leadership energy to use. This large focus on building a national tourism center as an apparent lynchpin for economic success sacrificed other efforts that could have created high-wage jobs and wealth for the region.

Baltimore is trying to move in the right direction. It has a strategic economic development plan engaging the public and private sectors. Baltimore's current economic strategy seems to focus on mass transit, housing, and other community development issues and not as much geared toward creating a technology-based economy, succeeding in the world of global trade or redeveloping its urban core through traditional tactics such as reducing the cost of doing business in the city.[47] In fact, Baltimore's comprehensive economic development strategy makes no mention of the region's most important asset, Johns Hopkins University Hospital System, which could be the region's largest economic asset and a strong link to the growing health sciences research and development.[48] Community development without economic development is just as doomed to fail as a real estate–based approach. Many urban centers are rightly focused on their constituents, receiving quality social services and gaining access to area jobs. However, if the streets are not safe and the schools are not producing quality workers, no company will stay or locate in the region. It takes a broad, holistic economic development plan to make it all work.

The balance of this book is about implementing effective economic development strategies to encourage wealth creation. That link between strategy and wealth creation is a key to regions and states succeeding in the twenty-first century or shrinking and collapsing into economic chaos.

Big Questions

1. Is wealth creation the best measure of economic success?

2. Is poverty rates a better measure of economic success?

3. Is the level of unemployment a better measure of economic success?

4. Should the focus of economic development really be about key quality-of-life measures?

5. Can communities focus on the building blocks of economic development and the more advanced strategies at the same time?

Class Writing Assignment

Baltimore needs your help. The mayor has asked you for a brief memo outlining what economic development strategy they should develop. Your analysis will need to include a brief description of the Baltimore economy, which includes strengths and weaknesses and recommendations for moving in a new direction based upon building block and at least one advanced economic development strategies.

Additional Reading

Comprehensive Economic Development Strategy for Alabama, 2012, retrieved from http://ceds.
alabama.gov/.

David Birch, *Job Creation in America: How Our Smallest Companies Put the Most People to
Work* (New York: Free Press, 1987).

Economic Development Strategic Plan for Martin County, North Carolina (September 2011),
retrieved from http://www.townofwilliamston.com/NewSite/News/Strategic per-
cent20Pl percent20Exc percent20Summary percent20Final.pdf.

Greater Baltimore Committee, 2004–2005 Annual Report, retrieved from http://www.gbc.
org/reports/AnRpt05/GBC2005AnnualReport.pdf.

Harvey M. Jacobs and Kurt Paulsen, "Property Rights: The Neglected Theme of Twentieth
Century Planning," *Journal of American Planning Association*, 75, 2 (2009) 134–143.

Marie Howland, "Planning for Industry in a Post Industrial World," *Journal of American
Planning Association*, 77, 1 (2010) 39–53.

Paul A. Samuelson, "The Pure Theory of Public Expenditure," *Review of Economics and
Statistics*, 36, 4 (1954) 387–389.

Robert E. Lang and Jennifer LeFurgy, *Boomburbs: The Rise of America's Accidental Cities*
(Washington, DC: Brookings Institution Press, 2009).

Timothy Besley, *Public Goods and Economic Development* (London, England: London School
of Economics, 2004).

Thomas A. Dillon, Richard K. Lee, and David Matheson, "Value Innovation: Passport to
Wealth Creation," *Research-Technology Management*, 2, 48 (March–April 2005) 22–36.

Chapter Two
Strategic Economic Development Planning

Chapter Goals

1. Recognize the role of economic development planning and its importance in the ultimate success of a region's efforts to create wealth
2. Understand the distinction between economic development strategies and tactics
3. Be prepared to discuss how industry cluster strategy is a starting point for economic development planning and not an end point
4. Be able to identify the various economic development theories and argue which one fits the twenty-first century

Strategic Planning and Economic Development

Successful economic development starts with a good plan and strong local leadership. The plan could be based upon a company launching a new product, or service or public and private sector community leaders working to promote their region or state as a world-class economic destination. A strategic economic development plan recognizes the assets a region begins with and that the key players in economic development are the public and private sector partners at the local and state levels. To be successful, strategic economic development planning should be based upon a range of economic theories. Strategic economic development planning sets priorities through consensus on economic goals, objectives, strategies, and specific tactics.

Portland's (Oregon) use of an economic development plan illustrates how a thoughtful strategy built a strong regional economy. Oregon for decades was growing, but the state fell behind as the tech boom hit California and Washington. From 1997 to 2009, Portland was nearly last in new, private sector job creation compared to other Western regions.[1] This region, which constitutes the thirtieth largest city in the United States, adopted a strategic economic development plan in 2009 to be the world's leading sustainable economy.[2] Portland developed three core economic development strategies to generate job growth; to produce and sell products and services for existing, emerging, and relocating businesses;

maintain leadership in sustainability through an innovative urban setting; and promote economic growth throughout the city.[3] Portland also developed an industry cluster strategy for clean tech, software, athletic and outdoor, research and development, and advanced manufacturing industries.[4] Portland's economic development plan is implemented by a Portland Economic Cabinet. This group includes public and private sector leaders, and the status of implementing the strategic plan is noted every year. Portland's economic development plan is succeeding. Portland reports gaining or retaining nearly 5,000 jobs from 2009 to 2012 and gaining nearly $800,000,000 in capital investment related to this job growth.[5]

Policy Arguments for Strategic Economic Development Planning

A smart strategic planning drives successful economic development. Cities implementing effective economic development strategies lower their unemployment rates.[6] Effective strategic economic development planning involves public policy issues as well as traditional economic development tactics such as retention and attraction campaigns. Local, state, and federal policies, regulations, and budget priorities impact the success or failure of a region, state, and nation's economic development. Public policy issues such as taxes, labor, trade, infrastructure, technology creation, and protection impact economic development planning. However, public policy solutions alone are not the total basis for effective strategic economic development planning. Region's economic development plans start with the assets of the region, identify the policy solutions to build success, and then outline those traditional tactics that will move the region in the right direction.

Strategic Planning as an Economic Development Tool

Strategic economic development planning is not only about public policy but includes real estate development issues. In simple terms, economic development cannot happen unless sites are ready for development. Few companies want to tackle complex issues related to contaminated sites, angry neighbors, or politicians with a list of requests related to a simple zoning change. Strategic economic development planning is also about quality. Also, economic victory is not just about housing. Strategic economic development planning needs to focus on wealth creation and not just economic growth. High-wage jobs are the goal.

Strategic economic development planning develops the quality of place. Quality of place creates world-class neighborhoods through good schools, safe streets, and decent housing. Strategic economic development planning involves the power of government. This power ranges from the power of the purse to spend taxpayer dollars on tax incentives, infrastructure, and other government programs to the regulation of land use all the way to the government actually seizing private property to enable development. Economic development success lies not with one program or project but a broad initiative that creates a quality place where people want to live, work, and raise a family.

Strategic economic development planning is not easy. Global trade agreements made domestic labor forces overpaid for traditional manufacturing jobs as compared to developing countries. The global market provides challenges for a region's economic development plan. In addition, economic development planning involves large constitutional battles and small legal fights among neighbors over what they are doing with their land. In short, strategic economic development planning focuses on incentivizing the creation of high-wage jobs and growing private sector companies that have a multiplier effect for the larger benefit of the community.

Theories of Economic Development

Philosophy drives economic development policies and impacts strategic economic development planning. The philosophies range from a full-fledged market approach to location theory, economic gardening, product cycle, growing markets, to more modern approaches such as the creative class approach. Economic development philosophies have a direct impact on what strategies work best to incentivize high-wage job creation. Believers in certain philosophies may not be open to certain strategies and tactics other philosophies embrace.

Market-Oriented Economic Development

The market or neoclassical theory of economic development states that the aggregate output of a region, state, or nation is based upon the labor, capital, and technology impact of its economy.[7] The market theory of economic development involves the most limited role for the government. Under the market-oriented approach, the role of government in the private economy is limited to the essentials of providing a national defense, administering justice, and development of public infrastructure. Based upon the neoclassical view of economics, a market-oriented approach to economic development dictates that economic systems will reach a natural balance if capital can flow without restriction from high-cost areas to low-cost areas. Poor communities will naturally draw business away from high-cost, rich areas based upon the cost of doing business.

Adam Smith's famous book *An Inquiry into the Nature and Causes of the Wealth of Nations* acts as the intellectual basis for a market-oriented economic development approach. Smith's gospel cautions against government controls of the private economy as they will have a harmful impact on wealth creation. Instead, Smith trusts the individuals and their free will to navigate the marketplace to reward winners and punish economic losers. Smith's "invisible hand" of the market acts as the spur for innovation and better products and services. Those failing to provide quality services and products or irrationally rising their prices will feel the negative impact of the market.

A market-oriented economic development approach identifies government programs as at best a well-intentioned waste of taxpayer dollars and at worst an intrusion in the marketplace for a select few companies that will cause a harmful market disruption. Supporters of this "laissez-faire" approach to economic development point to the explosion of jobs and companies during the Industrial Revolution and the Information Age as caused by the private sector and not by any government program. The "free market" crowd supports little action by government and focuses on undoing government regulation of private activity in the environment, labor, and other regulatory issues and reducing taxes on corporations to create an attractive environment to start and grow a business. The market-oriented approach rejects the notion of tax incentive programs to retain and attract business at the local and state levels. No government role would be the goal of a market-oriented approach to economic development.

Of course, market-oriented economic development purist could be accused of ignoring the role of a national immigration policy played in providing a low-cost workforce and federal government tariffs on foreign goods during the "free market" boom of the Industrial Revolution. The early growth of the Silicon Valley is also tied to a series of federal military contracts awarded to these tech companies. Free market purists struggle to keep government and business leaders from proactive economic development activities.

Location Theory of Economic Development

The location theory of economic development focuses on what factors lead companies to choose a specific location and how this impacts a region or state's economic development. Early thinking on location theory focused on infrastructure as key element to impacting the location of jobs. As an example, it is no accident that New York City developed into a global leader because it started over 200 years ago with a deepwater port essential for the global trade of the nineteenth century. The Great Lakes states is another example. The Industrial Revolution grew up in northeastern Ohio, southern Michigan, and western Pennsylvania and New York because these locations had the natural resources needed to operate steel, auto, and oil factories, and a logistics and distribution network enabled by the strategic location along the Great Lakes, Ohio River, and a rail network built to fight the Civil War. Location is a prime factor that determines the economic development of a region.[8]

The definition of infrastructure is very different to a nineteenth-century factory than it is to an early-stage high-tech start-up company of the twenty-first century. Traditionally, infrastructure is the roads, water, sewer, and power services a company needs to operate. As the Information Age launched, advanced telecommunications and broadband services became essential infrastructure. A survey of corporate location consultants indicates a list much broader than traditional infrastructure that impacts where their clients locate facilities (Table 2.1).

Location theory led communities and states to launch business retention and attraction programs. This approach involves efforts by both the public and private sectors to develop and implement government programs, policies, and tax incentives to reward specific economic activity by a private sector company. Private companies are rewarded for making economic investments in a specific location.

Location theory forces regions and states to address issues of cost of doing business. Higher costs for groceries, housing, utilities, transportation, health care, and services make a region less attractive to new investment. Lower-cost regions and

Table 2.1   Top ten corporate site selection factors

Ranking	Site Selection Factor
First	Highway accessibility
Second	Labor costs
Third	Proximity to major markets
Fourth	Availability of skilled labor
Fifth	Available land
Sixth	Energy availability and cost
Seventh	State and local incentives
Eighth	Occupancy or construction costs
Ninth	Tax exemptions
Tenth	Expedited or "fast track" permitting

Source: 25th Annual Corporate Survey and 7th Annual Consultant Survey Complete Results, Area Development Magazine, Winter, 2011 retrieved from http://www.areadevelopment.com/AnnualReports/jan2011/corporate-consultants-survey-site-selection2011-39290.shtml.

states are more attractive to new economic development. Table 2.2. illustrates a cost of living comparison of select major urban centers across the U.S. Public policy debates impacting economic development come back to the location theory for its intellectual basis. Regions such as the southern part of the United States are building a global manufacturing economy based in large part on low cost of living matched by lower wage rates. However, midwestern urban centers that have transformed from industrial to regional service economies are also highly competitive from a cost-of-living standpoint.

Challengers to the location theory point out that the approach is really a drive to the economic bottom creating a focus on low-wage jobs and low-cost sprawling development patterns. They also note that an overreliance on the factors of cost of doing business ignores many of America's most successful regional economies, such as New York, Washington, DC, and Los Angeles. These regions consistently rank the highest cost markets in the United States, but all three operate successful global economic centers with above-average wages. Location theory finally fails to acknowledge more modern economic development approaches such as industry clusters and creative class approaches that illustrate how regions develop high-wage jobs in what may be higher-cost markets.

The answer to location theory challenges is somewhere in the middle. Midwestern regions such as Columbus gained 20,000 financial services jobs in part from JP Morgan Chase from midtown Manhattan. Columbus offers a large pool of young, college-educated workers willing to work for far lower wages than their New York City counterparts. Their ability to work for lower wages is only possible because Columbus costs far less than New York City to buy or rent housing, food, and other services. However, New York City remains the nation's global financial services hub with an unquestioned cluster of investment banking and related financial services firms.

Table 2.2 Cost of living composite index of major US cities

Metropolitan Area	Composite Index
Indianapolis, IN	87.2
Louisville, KY	87.7
Memphis, TN	88.2
Nashville-Franklin, TN	88.9
St Louis, MO-IL	90.4
Des Moines, IA	90.9
Pittsburgh, PA	91.5
Oklahoma city, OK	91.7
Dallas, TX	91.9
Houston, TX	92.2

Source: "Cost of Doing Business," *Destination Kansas City*, Ingram's Kansas City Business Magazine, 2013–2014, p. 20.

Economic Cluster Analysis

A challenge to location theory is industry economic cluster strategy. Michael Porter is the "father" of modern economic cluster analysis. Under an economic cluster strategy, regional economic development initiatives begin with identifying a region's business strengths. The global economy rarely permits a region to be all things to all people. The competition across the globe for jobs is simply too fierce. An economic cluster comprises a geographic concentration of firms within a particular industry.[9] It includes core firms and other organizations that can contribute to the industry's competitive success. A cluster includes economic development staff, supplier firms, university researchers, consultants, lawyers, accountants, and other organizations that support a particular industry.[10] Those supporting players are essential for the creation and operation of an industry cluster. They provide the business operation expertise that helps companies grow and succeed. Regions without that cast of professional service providers suffer when attempting to grow an economic cluster.

Successful economic clusters require joint action of the impacted organizations, a common geographic district, and an analysis to define the core industries of that district.[11] This core industry analysis utilizes census and business data from reporting services or direct surveys, and economic data in a defined geographic area are reviewed to identify potential cluster members.[12]

Successful initiatives of economic development cluster have several common characteristics, including:

- a shared understanding of the role of clusters in competitive advantage
- a focus on removing obstacles and easing constraints to cluster growth
- a structure that embraces all clusters
- clear definition of cluster boundaries
- comprehensive involvement of cluster participants and related institutions
- private sector business leadership

- focus on the personal relationship among the cluster participants
- a belief in action focused on results
- creation of the cluster as an institution in the region or state[13]

Next, a supply chain analysis is conducted of the potential cluster members to expand the list of cluster participants. A market analysis is then performed on each of the region's specific industry clusters to determine where growth markets exist. A strengths/weaknesses/opportunities/threats (SWOT) analysis is performed to identify where a region's industry strengths match up with potentially growing markets. A SWOT analysis is essential for a community when it comes to setting an overall goal for their strategic economic development plan. Based upon global benchmarks, a community or state must make an honest assessment of how they compare to their real competition. A true SWOT analysis compares this community or state to who they want to be. If they want to be a global leader in technology-based economic development, models for comparison are the RTP and not the community ten miles down that road. Finally, a cluster team of industry leaders is formed to implement the planned growth of the identified industry clusters.[14]

Economic cluster strategy permits regions to focus on high-wage jobs in which the region has strengths in a growing industry. It permits high-cost and low-cost regions to succeed with less of an emphasis on the issues of cost of doing business.

Economic Gardening Theory of Economic Development

The economic gardening theory advocates a concentration of economic development resources on a specific class of companies, known as "gazelles." Economic gardening is about cultivating and nurturing local growth-oriented companies by giving them the tools they need to succeed. Decades ago, MIT's David Birch advocated that a majority of American jobs were being created by growing companies that are between 10 and 99 employees.[15] It is these small to medium-sized "gazelles" that, Birch advocates, regions focus on for economic success.

Economic gardening identifies high-growth companies and works more as a coach with targeted businesses than giving away tax incentives. Economic gardening develops tactical and strategic information; nurtures connections to trade associations, think tanks, academic institutions, and similar companies; and creates a region's quality of life and intellectual infrastructure.[16]

The Internet and technology explosion create an array of tools needed for an effective economic gardening program. Examples of economic gardening tools provided by economic developers to help grow local businesses include geographic information systems, databases that develop marketing lists and industry trends and answer custom business questions, and training and seminars dealing with business, management, and customer strategies.[17] Again, nothing new about these data-based services, but many small businesses do not have the staff or expertise to utilize this information.

The second element of an economic gardening program is infrastructure—including the physical but also the quality of life and intellectual infrastructure in a community.[18] Economic gardening brings a community's infrastructure to the benefit of gazelles. This not only acts as a justification for public investments in hard and soft infrastructure but also brings to the benefit of gazelles the "smart" people in a community who understand marketing, legal, management, and accounting issues facing growing companies.

Connections are the final element of economic gardening. Not all successful CEOs learn from a class or a meeting. Connecting to other more experienced business leaders is the most important element.[19] Economic gardening initiatives socially network the gazelle executives with the university, finance, legal, and other business leaders. Local connection programs develop customers through structured "buy local" or export programs that link gazelles with larger company customers and global markets.[20]

Product Cycle Theory of Economic Development

Raymond Vernon developed the product cycle theory of economic development. Product cycle argues that regions with the wealth to fund research and innovation will first develop products and services that can be standardized and distributed to other markets.[21] It is the early market entry of this innovation that enables job and company creation ahead of the competition that provides an economic benefit for a region or a state. A technology-based economic development strategy is an example of the product cycle theory. Regions such as Northern California and Raleigh-Durham (North Carolina) launched technology-based economic development initiatives in the 1940s and 1950s and are today global economic powerhouses. Industrial states such as Pennsylvania, Ohio, and West Virginia are running fullsteam ahead trying to catch up in the development of a technology-based economy.

Product cycle initiatives start with intellectual infrastructure, that is, universities and public or private research laboratories that generate new knowledge and discoveries and mechanisms for transferring knowledge from one individual or company to another and physical infrastructure such as a skilled technical workforce.[22] Product cycle initiatives need sources of risk capital, good quality of life, and an entrepreneurial culture.[23] Regions and states creating a product cycle initiative promote entrepreneurship, turning universities into economic engines, as well as create a capital access fund and workforce training programs targeted at high-tech industries. This multifaceted strategy develops a deep and long-term approach to building high-tech start-ups and larger established companies.

Growing Markets as Economic Development

Another theory of economic development is to grow external markets for goods, services, and products outside of a region or state. Growing industries produce more goods, services, and products that create wealth for local companies and workers. Known also as the economic base theory, growing markets strategy is illustrated by export campaigns that support company efforts to sell local goods and services in global markets and promote local sites with those same foreign markets as a prime location for global company location. Exports and FDI campaigns illustrate using globalism as an economic development strategy. Globalism represents access to growing markets. According to the US Department of Commerce, 70 percent of the world's customers are outside of the United States.[24]

Growing markets strategies also involve business retention and attraction campaigns. Locating a major autoassembly plant or research and development center from out of a state or around the globe is frontpage news. However, successful regional economic development organizations need to recognize that business attraction is only 20 percent of the typical job growth in the region and can become a giant consumer of time and resources. Business attraction campaigns are divided up into marketing and sales.

As the term indicates, marketing in the economic development context is the general promotion of a region to create brand identity. Business marketing efforts promote a region to a targeted audience through paid advertisements in trade publications or Websites. Regions participate in trade shows across the nation and globe with trade booths and social networking events. Regions coordinate with state and regional partners, such as major university alumni and governor and mayor's trade missions, to promote the region and specific sites.

Economic development sales are the specific promotion of a region to a select group of companies and organizations. Direct sales occur through briefings with targeted stakeholders, who are known to impact the global site location process, such as accountants, lawyers, and corporate location consultants. The economic benefits of the region such as a low cost of living, high quality of life, and a strong link to an industry supply line are promoted. The availability of essential workforce and infrastructure, favorable regulatory and tax climate, and a competitive economic development incentive package are also topics of conversation. Regions sell their community through coordinated sales calls with corporate headquarters and suppliers of a region's existing company base across the globe and cold calls on companies in targeted industries.

Creative Class Theory of Economic Development

Creative class is a modern theory of economic development created by Richard Florida. Florida studied successful regions around the globe and determined that the key to success in a modern, Information Age economy is the recruitment of highly educated and mobile workers. Florida defined these workers as the creative class. The basis for the creative class argument is that location does matter even in a new economy.[25] Florida argues that human capital is the key issue when studying how regions succeed on an economic basis. Factors such as reducing the cost of doing business pale in comparison to the quality and education level of a region's workforce. In essence, the more the people with college education and advanced degrees, the more successful the region will be.

The creative class theory of economic development values quality of life and openness and diversity that are appealing to this highly educated workforce. These "creative professionals," according to Florida, constitute 30 percent of the total US workforce and are moving away from traditional corporate life. Those challenging the creative class approach question its application to many regions across the United States. Florida's approach may well prove possible for regions with a large university student population but is not within the grasp of regions that lack a large pool of intellectual capital. The approach ignores the success of southern states in transforming their economies into manufacturing powerhouses winning the battle of global trade.

Economic Development Planning Toward Wealth Creation

Developing a strategic economic development plan centers around how a region or state can retain and gain higher-wage jobs and create a new breed of companies in emerging industries. Economic development planning reaches consensus on community economic goals; creates measurable objectives that define the plan's success; develops economic development strategies that fit a region's strengths, weaknesses, opportunities, and threats; and prioritizes action steps necessary to make the economic development goal a reality.

Economic Development Goal

An economic development goal is a vision statement for what a community is and wants to be. Many communities want to be everything to everybody. Built-in existing constituencies that are established leaders in most communities may not be the leaders in the industry of the future. The first step in developing an economic development goal is to document the condition of the local economy and available resources. Documenting the local economy involves a review of economic and demographic data and subjective impressions. Research of the local economy addresses what industries are growing, what industries are large, and what industries are in decline.[26] Communities consider demographic factors such as education and employment to measure key productivity and workforce issues.[27] This local data will be later compared to national trends as part of measuring success. In addition, an economic cluster analysis is helpful when a community or state is attempting to establish an overall goal for their strategic economic development plan.

The actual statement as to what the goal of a strategic economic development plan is short, direct, and concise. Clarity matters—as does consensus from the community leaders. A goal statement is based upon the data derived of the regions' strengths, weaknesses, opportunities, and threats. Finally, the goal statement should push the community to be a world leader in core industries that have a link to the region but also have bright prospects for growing in the future.

Economic Development Policy Case Study 2.1: Tipton County Economic Development Plan Goal Statement

Tipton County is a rural community located in the center of Indiana. Like many rural communities, Tipton County faces challenges in retaining its population base and offers "small town values with big opportunities." To address these larger economic development opportunities, Tipton County developed a strategic economic development plan through Ball State University. It starts with the important goal statement:

> In 2025, Tipton County's people are known for cooperation in improving their communities to residents of all ages and economic strata. Thoughtfully planned growth in business, agriculture, downtowns, and neighborhoods has resulted in amenities such as fine parks for recreation and leisure, good schools, libraries, and cultural activities. They are supported by a strong philanthropic and volunteer base that preserves these amenities with a minimum tax burden. The economy is vibrant and diverse, populated by businesses, large and small, local and international, engaged in manufacturing, agriculture, service, retail, construction, technology, trades, and the professions. People of all economic and social strata are attracted here for jobs, to start new businesses and especially to improve their economic conditions. Residents routinely take advantage of the wide range of housing, educational, and employment options to improve their quality of life. This able resident labor force is a strong attraction for employers.[28]

The Tipton County goal statement is positive and adopts a strategic direction for the future of the region. Quality of life and job creation are central issues. This goal statement starts where Tipton is now and moves it to where the community leaders would like it to be.

Measuring Economic Success for a Strategic Economic Development Plan

Metrics are essential to measure the success for a strategic economic development plan. Simple measures of success in a silo such as unemployment rate, poverty, and personal income without comparing a region's economy to others create a weak measure of success. Successful economic development is not redeveloping a community "eyesore" but creates additional community wealth. How do we measure wealth creation? Economists offer many alternatives for measuring wealth creation.

Per capita income is one measure. It is the mean money income received in the past 12 months computed for every man, woman, and child in a geographic area.[29] A geographic area's per capital income is derived by dividing the total income of all people 15 years and over by the total population in that area.[30] Money income is amounts reported separately for wage or salary income, net self-employment income, and interest, dividends, or net rental or royalty income or income from estates and trusts.[31] Funds from social security or railroad retirement income, supplemental security income, public assistance or welfare payments, and pensions constitute money income.[32]

A weakness of per capita income as a means to measure wealth creation is that receipts from capital gains, money received from the sale of property, and income "in kind" from food stamps, public housing subsidies, medical care, and employer contributions for individuals are not accounted.[33] So are withdrawals of bank deposits, money borrowed, tax refunds, exchange of money between relatives living in the same household, gifts and lumpsum inheritances, and insurance payments.[34]

Per capita income may underreport totals because the data rely on answers to questions based on memory.[35] Even the Census Bureau admits that underreporting tends to be more pronounced for income sources that are not derived from earnings, such as public assistance, interest, dividends, and net rental income.[36] However, the per capita income of a region or state remains one of the best measures of wealth creation related to economic development. Regions creating high-wage jobs not only can increase the wages paid to workers but those high-wage jobs have a high "multiplier effect," which enables them to fund a wider range of low-wage jobs that are the larger part of any regional and state economy.

Another measure of wealth creation is private, nonfarm employment totals. Private, nonfarm establishments are a single physical location where business is conducted or services or industrial operations are performed.[37] Two or more activities conducted at a single location under common ownership are grouped together as a single establishment, and establishments with paid employees include all locations with paid employees at any time during the year.[38] Paid employment measures both full- and part-time employees on the payroll, paid sick leave, holidays, and vacations; however, proprietors and partners of unincorporated businesses are not included.[39]

Private, nonfarm employment is a good economic development measure as it removes the economic benefit of government, university, school, and other public sector workers who operate based upon tax dollars. Economic development is the study of the use of public subsidies to incentivize private sector, high-wage job group that creates wealth. Government institutions are of importance, but they support economic development and do not create it. Private, nonfarm employment data measure the success or failure of a community to develop those nonpublic sector jobs.

Another measure of economic development success comes from the Payroll Survey.[40] The Payroll Survey is a monthly poll of 140,000 businesses and government agencies representing 410,000 US locations for the purposes of measuring employment, hours, and earning estimates for the nation, states, and metropolitan areas by industry.[41] The Payroll Survey identifies not only overall employment but which jobs and industries pay higher wages. The Payroll Survey identifies which jobs and industries create wealth. However, a weakness of the Payroll Survey is that is estimates only nonfarm wage and salary jobs and is not an estimate of all employed persons.[42] It can count an individual with two jobs twice and it excludes employees in agriculture and the self-employed.[43]

This and other federal government data sets enable regions and states to identify high-wage jobs and industries to prioritize their public subsidies for economic development purposes. Only 15 percent of all US jobs pay at least 50 percent more than the overall average wage.[44] However, these high-wage jobs on average pay about twice the overall average.[45] These high-wage jobs are concentrated in a minority of industrial sectors and high-tech scientific sectors.[46]

Shift-Share Analysis

Another model used to measure economic success is the shift-share analysis. This approach compares local economic success with national economic success in industries of interest or the market overall. A community's claim for economic success in the financial services market because of a 5 percent job growth rate is not as impressive if the financial services industry grew by a 10 percent nationally. Shift-share analysis analyzes a region's growth into segments by comparing the national economic growth rate with the growth or decline of employment in that industry at the local level.[47] Shift-share studies look at how regions impact growth or decline of employment in a specific industry. Shift-share analysis distinguishes between growth attributable to the growth of the national economy, growth attributable to the mix of faster or slower-than-average growing industries, and growth attributable to the competitive nature of the local industries.[48]

Measuring economic success based upon the shift-share model involves identification of at least two points of time to measure data, research of local industry employment data and national industry employment data typically from the federal government's Bureau of Economic Administration, and the comparison of the local versus the national economic data.[49]

The national growth share is calculated by multiplying the base year for each industry by the national average employment growth rate over the time period to be examined. Adding these results for each industry creates the national growth component for the local economy.[50] The growth rate equals employment in year of interest minus employment in base year divided by employment in base year.[51] This formula determines if a regional economy is growing at or below the national employment rate. The measure is against the national average of growth or decline. Critiques of shift-share analysis point to the unfairness of measuring the success or failure of a specific company or industry in a region.

Economic Development Policy Case Study 2.2: Measuring Economic Development Success in Nevada—A Primer on Economic Development Strategies

Nevada is working to diversifying its struggling economy. The booming 1990s were good for Nevada, but the collapse of the financial services and real estate market made Nevada the biggest loser in the nation. Nevada is facing double-digit unemployment rates, collapsing home values, and skyrocketing home foreclosures. The struggles are complicated further based upon the state's overreliance on the gaming and entertainment industry. Even these mostly low-wage service jobs are disappearing in this current market. To address these challenges, Nevada launched an economic diversification program and established metrics to measure success tied to job and wage creation. However, the public began to question the state's use of tax incentives to lure companies to the silver state. Nevada approved $87,600,000 in tax incentives to create only 2,900 jobs over the past several years.[52]

Table 2.3   Top ten Nevada tax incentive awards

Company	Tax Incentive	Jobs
Apple	$55,000,000	35
Quail Hollow	$6,200,000	44
Olin Corp	$2,700,000	5
Urban Outfitters	$2,600,000	110
SA Recycling	$1,700,000	27
Toys R Us	$1,600,000	51
Amonix Inc	$1,200,000	337
Patriot Precision Ammunition	$1,200,000	37
CC Landfill Energy	$1,200,000	2
Ken's Food, Inc.	$1,100,000	10

Source: Anjeanette Damon, "Economic development costs Nevada $30,000 per job in tax incentives," *Las Vegas Sun*, January 17, 2013 retrieved from http://www.lasvegassun.com/news/2013/jan/17/economic-development-costs-nevada-30000-job-tax-in/.

Nevada is spending $30,000 per job through its economic development incentive program.[53] As Table 2.3 indicates, Nevada is aggressive with its use of tax incentives. While national comparisons indicate Nevada does not spend as much as other states in the aggregate for economic development programs, a comparison of the number of jobs created with the incentives provides a metric to challenge the state's use of tax incentives.[54]

Economic Development Strategies

Once an economic development goal and clear objectives are established, the next step in creating a strategic economic development plan is adopting the strategies essential for success. Economic development tactics launched without a well-thought-out strategy dooms an effort to failure. Few communities adopt only a single economic development strategy. Often, communities adopt too many strategies. Strategies can embrace both the building blocks and five drivers of economic development to create both "offensive"- and "defensive"-oriented strategies to incentivize the creation of high-wage jobs.

Economic Development Policy Case Study 2.3: Florida's Strategic Plan and Economic Development Strategies

Enterprise Florida is a public-private partnership leading Florida's economic development in partnership with the Florida Department of Commerce. Enterprise Florida's strategic plan for economic development uses four strategies to achieve their economic vision and goals:

1. Strengthen collaboration and alignment among state, regional, and local entities toward the state's economic vision

2. Develop and implement a statewide strategy to develop regional talent and innovation clusters using global best practices
3. Strengthen Florida's economic regions and connect resources across regions to build Florida as a globally competitive mega region
4. Position Florida as a global hub for trade, visitors, talent, innovation, and investment[55]

Enterprise Florida established further area-specific strategies, such as leading the nation in student performance and market-relevant workforce skills, diversifying Florida's economy and growing in global markets, and modernizing Florida's infrastructure.[56] Florida's area-specific strategies also are developing the nation's leading business climate, customer-focused support services, creating strong partnerships to meet the state's economic development goals, and being a national leader in building communities to live, learn, work, and play.[57]

Strategic Economic Development Plan Tactics

The final piece of creating a strategic economic development plan is to identify specific action steps. These specific action steps are laid out along a calendar-based timeframe. This outline of action steps provides a detailed guide for how the overall goal is going to be met based upon the choice of economic development strategies.

Economic Development Policy Case Study 2.4: Sonoma County
Economic Development Plan Tactics

Even wine country needs an economic development strategy. As Table 2.4 indicates, Sonoma County's (California) economic development strategy contains tactics illustrating the specific action steps the region is taking to win the global economic battle.

Table 2.4 Sonoma county economic development tactics: Strategic objectives and action steps

Improve regulatory compliance	Appoint a business development and regulatory assistance liaison within the EDB to assist businesses through the regulatory processes and resolve obstacles to business development
	Staff a customer service ombudsman position within PRMD dedicated solely to resolving permitting issues for both home owners and business customers
	Form a multiagency task force to look for opportunities to simplify and streamline regulatory processes across jurisdictions
Deliver business development and outreach services	Staff a business retention and expansion program
	Develop a county-wide working group of public and nonprofit agencies to organize county-wide efforts in retaining businesses
Create a workforce development strategy	Develop an employer-driven, agency-inclusive workforce development plan focused on the current and future needs of county employers
Encourage business cluster development	Staff a cluster development program to facilitate expansion of targeted industry sectors

Table 2.4   Continued

Develop financial resources program	Develop a financial resources "toolbox" for local businesses, including development incentives and greater access to capital and explore new funding options
	Identify and apply for state and federal financial incentives in support of the local business community
Facilitate broadband deployment in rural parts of the county	Develop a strategic plan for broadband deployment in rural parts of the county and encourage new efforts around "middle mile" and "last mile" deployment
Engage in strategic asset development and branding	Take inventory of strategic assets and their producers, develop strategies to maximize value and image, and help coordinate marketing activities of the major industries and employers to provide a unified image of Sonoma county
Enhance coordinated economic development resources within the county	Form an interdepartmental economic development strategy committee to coordinate services and leverage resources among key departments involved in economic development activities
	Partner with and help coordinate county-wide economic development activities including local cities, chambers, BEST, and other organizations to reduce redundancy and increase efficiency of related services

Source: *Economic Development Strategy and Jobs Plan*, Sonoma County Economic Development Board, California, November 2011, retrieved from http://edb.sonoma-county.org/documents/2012/EconomicDevelopmentStrategy JobsPlan.pdf.

Big Questions

1. Who should be engaged in strategic economic development planning?

2. How do communities build a long-term competitive advantage?

3. What are the dangers of an overreliance on economic development cluster analysis?

4. How can communities address the need to diversify their economy?

5. What are the limits of the benefits of strategic economic development planning?

Class Writing Assignment

What economic theory do you think works? Where do you draw the line with government involvement? Should we just trust the marketplace or should government play a larger role in economic development? Write a 500-word op-ed story on which economic theory you believe is needed to achieve wealth creation.

Additional Reading

A Blueprint for Propelling a New Economic Development Direction for Michigan, Small Business Association of Michigan, prepared by Public Policy Associates, Incorporated, October 2010.
Christian Gibbons, "Economic Gardening," *Economic Development Journal*, 9, 3 (Summer 2010) 5–12.

Douglass C. North, "Location Theory and Regional Economic Growth," *Journal of Political Economy*, 63, 3 (June 1955) 243–258.

F. J. Arcelus, "An Extension of Shift-Share Analysis," *Growth and Change*, 15, 1 (1984) 3–8.

Gerald L. Gorden, *Strategic Planning for Local Government* (Washington, DC: ICMA Press, 2005).

Joel Kotkin, "Undying Creed, The Acceleration of Our Exceptionalism," *World Affairs*, January–February 2010, retrieved from http://www.worldaffairsjournal.org/article/undying-creed-acceleration-our-exceptionalism.

Mercedes Delgado, Michael E. Porter, and Scott Stern, *Clusters, Convergence, and Economic Performance*, submitted for publication, March 11, 2011, retrieved from http://www.isc.hbs.edu/pdf/DPS_Clusters_Performance_2011-0311.pdf.

Michael Porter, *The Competitive Advantage of Nations* (New York, NY: The Free Press, 1990).

Richard Florida, *TheRrise of the Creative Class: And How it's Transforming Work, Leisure, Community and Everyday Life* (New York: Basic Books, 2002).

Wassily W. Leontief, *Input-Output Economics*, 2nd ed. (New York: Oxford University Press, 1986).

CHAPTER THREE
ECONOMIC DEVELOPMENT ORGANIZATIONS

Chapter Goals

1. Recognize what economic developers do and how they do it
2. Understand what makes a successful public-private partnership
3. Recognize the different types of economic development organizations and be able to determine which one should be used in different situations
4. Acknowledge both the strengths and weaknesses of economic development organizations

Economic Development Organizations and Economic Development

Policy makers and business leaders are fortunate to have a broad array of tools at their disposal to implement economic development strategies. Economic development organizations is one of the tools. They use business retention, business attraction, and promotion of entrepreneurship as their prime tools to promote economic growth. Economic development organizations are in the business of creating successful public-private partnerships. These organizations are private sector led, public sector led, or a combination of both. Private sector–led economic development models are growing in popularity. Many major metro regions have created multicounty private sector–led groups, likely with public sector funding, charged to retain and attract jobs. In some states, the private sector is taking over economic development; however, the majority of state economic development efforts are directed by state government.

Success stories abound about how economic development organizations impact a region's growth and success. One such example is how a Nissan manufacturing facility ended up in Tennessee. Of course, Tennessee offered a site with needed infrastructure, a large pool of available skilled workers, and an array of tax incentives to Nissan. Tennessee was not the only state going after Nissan. However, the Nissan project actually got its start through a conversation years before between the state economic development leader for Tennessee and a Nissan official at a University of Tennessee alumni event in California. It was that personal connection between the company and the state, fostered by an economic development leader, that may have given the volunteer state a leg up in a highly competitive market.

Policy Arguments for Economic Development Organizations

Not all states are winners in the economic development game. Recent winners are a small number of states in the south and middlewest. While California is still the nation's largest state economy, the lone star state of Texas is making a strong play to move into the number one position.[1] They recently surpassed New York to be the nation's second largest state economy, and the industrial midwest, California, Massachusetts, New Jersey, and Georgia, have seen recent economic declines.[2] The federal government does not dictate what states and regions do and do not to promote economic success. They provide tax credits and programs that all regions can access. States and regions are left to their own efforts to be economic winners or losers. The creation of economic winners and losers across the United States and a lack of national coordination on economic development strategy turned economic development into a competitive business at the state and local levels. State governments operate economic development organizations to retain and attract high-wage jobs.[3] Competition dictates regions to not only create economic development strategies that focus on what industries to grow but also to focus on how best to retain and attract high-wage jobs.

The existence of regional economic winners and losers creates a strong policy argument for communities to utilize economic development organizations to play in this game. Multicommunity or regional development organizations is one strategy implemented by communities to promote economic success. Regional economic development organizations crossing local government boundaries are more effective as they increase budgets and staff and reduce local battles over existing companies.[4] Private sector economic development leadership brings new financial resources to business retention, attraction, and promoting entrepreneurism. Opponents of the use of economic development organizations question whether their programs really impact economic growth. They argue that regional companies' business decisions dictate economic success of a region much more than economic development groups promoting that region. The programs offered by these groups are argued to be "free money" given as an incentive to companies growing through their own efforts and not due to promotion of the region.

Economic Development Organization as an Economic Development Tool

Dating back to the 1920s, private sector companies started working together to form economic development organizations to further their business growth.[5] New York City hired its first economic development staff member in the late 1960s. Economic development organizations today focus on three core tools: job retention campaigns, job attraction campaigns, and promotion of entrepreneurship.

Existing companies produce 80 percent of a region's new jobs.[6] The economic success of a region starts with a successful existing job retention program. A job retention campaign is referred to as a business retention and expansion (BR&E) program. BR&E programs are broken down into multiple phases, all geared toward keeping and developing new jobs from a region's existing base of companies. Phase 1 of a BR&E program is organizing the efforts internally within an economic development organization to ensure proper funding and staffing is available.[7] Phase 2 is researching the companies that exist in a region, identifying the ones growing, and developing a common survey instrument for use with all the companies in which local economic development officials will visit.[8] Phase 3 is meeting with local company executives to gather information using the common business survey about what issues their company is facing and how local economic development officials can assist their company to grow in the region.[9] Phase 4 is solving any challenges the company identified.[10] Problem solving helps the company to gain access to capital, addresses a regulatory issue with state government, gain better transportation access, or other business and policy issues.

Business attraction campaigns promote a region through marketing to companies likely to have an interest or link to the region. A state or regional economic development marketing plan creates a community message, identifies prospect companies, and connects with these through a range of methods. The economic development marketing message communicates the strengths of the region or state that appeal to prospective companies. These strengths range from the existence of like industry clusters to a large workforce pool, special tax advantages, and links to markets. Once a message is developed, a list of company prospects is created. This is done through an industry cluster analysis that identifies local company strengths and connections to like or similar industries. Local companies are a source for prospective development as they provide key suppliers and others with an interest to be more closely connected with their business. Finally, a business attraction campaign is launched geared toward the targeted companies on a regional or state prospect list.

An economic development marketing campaign includes:

- Peer-to-peer campaigns: introduction to national company prospects by local company leaders
- Internet/Website and social media: advertisements and direct contact campaigns through social media sites such as LinkedIn, Google, and industry/trade association sites to drive traffic to the campaign's Website
- Award campaign: launch a campaign to gain high rankings in key awards given by groups of interest to the industries targeted
- Hosting special events: participation in targeted industry/trade association events such as the Industrial Asset Management Council, Site Selection Guild, and CoreNet events, which are populated by corporate site location consultants
- Media relations/publicity: a media story placement strategy that promotes a region to the targeted industries in key industry/trade publications and corporate site selection magazines
- Advertising in industry/trade publications: an advertisement strategy targeting select industry/trade publications

- Direct mail: a direct mail campaign communicating the region's benefits to the targeted companies
- Telemarketing: a telemarketing campaign to coordinate conversations between the targeted companies and local and state economic development leaders[11]

Global business attraction campaigns hope of landing a major FDI project. Finally, business attraction campaigns market and react to corporate site location consultants who represent big and small companies alike in their efforts to determine the best location for company expansion.

Promoting entrepreneurship is the final tool economic development organizations use. The explosion of the Information Age enabled local and state economic development groups to devote resources to fostering the growth of early-stage companies. Local and state economic development efforts spend nearly half their economic development spending on promoting entrepreneurship with the aim of becoming the next Silicon Valley.[12]

Successful regional and state entrepreneurship strategies encourage people with ideas to take the risk of starting their own business in the hope of creating wealth. Regional and state entrepreneurship programs develop a culture that nurtures and supports these small business owners. They build capital access, business services, and business opportunities for emerging small businesses. Entrepreneurship programs develop venture capital and other access to capital tools essential for the growth of emerging, early-stage technology companies. In addition, regional and state entrepreneurship programs create capital access programs for small and minority-owned firms that may struggle to gain capital from traditional sources. Business incubators and accelerators create homes for early-stage company start-ups. These facilities provide a low-cost real estate option matched with business services ranging from accounting to legal to marketing that many emerging small business need but cannot afford.

Entrepreneurship programs educate local businesses on export and government procurement opportunities and create "buy local" campaigns to grow small local businesses. These entrepreneurship programs support existing and successful small to mid-sized companies, often called middle market, that are growing and moving a region up the economic ladder.

The Role of an Economic Development Organization

Public or private economic development organizations develop public-private partnerships to leverage the resources and knowledge of the private sector for a public purpose. The prime role of the economic developer is to create, negotiate, and implement the public-private partnership to make the project vision a reality. Policy makers build them to create opportunities for public or private sector economic development organizations. Six critical elements are required for a successful public-private partnership:

1. The top political leadership supports and buys into the project.
2. The public sector is actively involved in the project or program from start to finish.

3. The public-private partnership is the result of a well-thought-out plan—typically in the form of an agreement.
4. The private partner provides the initial stream of income, but both the public and private sectors create a dedicated stream of revenue for the project.
5. Communications with all the stakeholders involved with the project occur.
6. Government picks the "best value" partner not necessarily the lowest bidder for the project to be successful.[13]

Public-private partnerships are criticized as a "government giveaway." However, policy makers see the public-private partnership as the framework or the agreement upon which most economic development projects are based. Success or failure may follow the public-private partnership formation. Public-private partnerships are essential for economic development in a global age.

In most states, established economic development organizations exist and operate with clear metrics and measures of success. Economic development policy makers assist communities in the creation of economic development entities that retain and attract business investment. Public-private partnerships are not organized or managed directly by government or a developer but by an economic development entity. These entities provide a method to memorialize a development agreement and to create a method for joint governance and management of a specific site. The entities carry on the goal of the public-private partnership to utilize some form of government funding or resources to benefit specific development projects. These public-private partnerships are so complicated that they need a separate entity to carry forward their tasks.

Table 3.1   Economic development organization metrics

Unemployment in the region
Number of jobs retained in targeted industry groups
Number of new businesses opened in targeted industry groups
Number of businesses closed in targeted industry groups
Number of businesses attracted in targeted industry groups
Number of business relocations from the region in targeted industry groups
Total number of FDIs
Ranking for exports of products and services
Total number of inbound global investments
Total inventory in the region by targeted industry
Available square footage by use and industry type
Amount of square footage leased during the measurement period by use and industry type
Cost per square foot of actual deals by use and industry type
Growth of the target retention companies
Growth of the target attraction companies
Number of building permits issued for targeted industries
Number of business visits conducted as part of a business retention program

Source: David Ammons and Jonathan Morgan, "State-of-the-Art Measures in Economic Development, *PM Magazine*, 93, 5 (June 2011).

High-quality regional economic development organizations start with clear, objective, and defined metrics that measure success or failure of the organization. The metrics need to be known by the leadership of the organization and the stakeholders and the results shared on an annual basis. As Table 3.1 shows, a wide range of metrics exists for regional economic development organizations.

Public Sector versus Private Sector Economic Development Organizations

Much is in debate about whether the public sector or the private sector should lead regional and state economic development. Local governments execute most economic development strategies, but multicounty, private regional economic development models are a growing trend. Most state-based economic development efforts rely upon state government to operate their economic development programs, but many states are considering the private sector model.

Public Sector Economic Development Organizations

The majority of regions and states rely on government officials to implement economic development policies. These state and local government officials focus on business retention and expansion efforts to retain and attract new jobs to a region. They bear the responsibility of implementing the process, with elected legislative bodies, to approve the company's tax incentives award.[14] Public sector–led economic development organizations at the state level are state executive agencies with a director who reports directly to the governor.

Texas operates a state government–run economic development program. The Texas economy is booming. Texas recently surpassed $1,000,000,000 in annual economic output and gained nearly a full percentage point in its share of the US economy during the decade.[15] This economic expansion has been only matched twice in 50 years—California in the 1980s and Texas during the oil boom of the 1970s.[16] Texas is the nation's most successful state economy, and Texas operates a state agency for economic development whose director reports to the governor. The Texas Economic Development and Tourism Division within the Office of the Governor focuses on domestic and international company expansion and recruitment and strategic initiatives centering around aerospace, aviation, military preparedness, small business development, and defense.[17] They provide basic business research services to companies in the site location process and offer an economic development bank to fund tax incentives such as Texas Product Business Fund, Texas Leverage Fund, Texas Industry Development Loan Program, Texas Enterprise Zone Program, and Industrial Revenue Bonds.[18] In 2012, the Texas Economic Development Bank provided incentives that generated 2,482 new jobs, retained 25,858 jobs, and helped support 47 new projects that produced more than $5,900,000,000 in capital investment.[19] Figure 3.1 illustrates the long term job growth of Texas as proof of their economic success.

Advocates of public sector–led economic development organizations point to Texas as an example of how government leads the retention and recruitment of

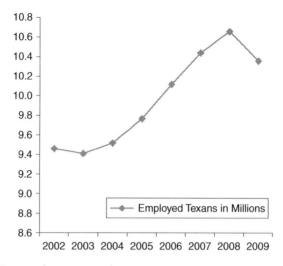

Figure 3.1 Texas employment growth 2002–2009.

Source: An Analysis of Texas Economic Development Incentives, EMSI Employment Data for Texas, 2002–2009, Texas Comptroller of Public Accounts, 2010, p. 4.

business from both an operational and an open government perspective. In states such as Texas, economic development leaders at the state level report directly to the governor. These economic development leaders are empowered to achieve success and held directly responsible for failures. Public sector–operated economic development organizations are more open to the public in their use of tax dollars as they comply with public record laws, file annual reports to state legislatures, and are audited by other state government officials.

Public sector–led economic development organizations at the local level exist in a variety of forms. The majority of local governments operate economic development as a city or county department reporting directly to the elected or appointed executive (mayor, county commissioner, or city/county manager).

Some local governments actually operate an independent commission to administer economic development strategies. Portland offers an interesting example of an independent local government commission that operates an economic development program. The Portland Development Corporation (PDC) was created by the voters in 1958 to focus on economic development and urban renewal.[20] The current PDC strategic plan focuses on a small group of goals: strong economic growth and competitiveness, development of healthy neighborhoods, social equality through promoting equal access to economic opportunities and a living wage, creating a vibrant central city by focusing on five urban renewal areas, and providing transparent and accountable stewardship of public resources.[21] The PDC is a creation of the Portland City Charter. The PDC is governed by a commission appointed by the mayor.[22] Just like its city department counterparts, the PDC has the authority to use city funds for economic development, urban renewal, and affordable housing initiatives, and it is part of the overall City of Portland budget.[23]

Economic Development Policy Case Study 3.1: Texas' Local Economic Development Resources

The state of Texas is not only a leader among the states in the retention and recruitment of companies, but it offers an innovative model for economic development at the local level. Texas' local economic development organizations have a funding model that provides them resources many of their counterparts in other states lack. Under the Development Corporation Act of 1979, Texas cities have the ability to finance new and expanded companies through the creation of economic development corporations (EDCs)—either type A or type B.[24] Type A EDCs fund industrial development such as business infrastructure, manufacturing, research and development, military base realignment, job training classes, and public transportation.[25] Type B EDCs fund all type A projects and, in addition, parks, museums, sports facilities, and affordable housing, but have stronger administrative restrictions.[26]

Texas' EDCs get special access to city sales tax revenues for economic development.[27] Sales tax revenues fund the acquisition of land, machinery and equipment, construction costs, planning, and professional services related to the project, financial transactions and reserve funds, and administrative and other necessary expenditures.[28] Texas does not have an income tax, and local and state governments look to sales and other taxes to operate. In addition, Texas' use of sales tax revenues for economic development purposes must be approved by the voters and used to retain and recruit jobs.[29] Texas municipalities using sales tax revenues for economic development must do so based upon a performance agreement with companies that export a majority of its products or services to markets outside the local industry sectors, such as agriculture, mining, manufacturing, and scientific research and development.[30]

In 2010, 698 EDCs existed throughout Texas, with a total revenue base of nearly $1,500,000,000.[31] In FY 2010–2011, sales tax constituted 73 percent of EDC revenues with bond proceeds following up as the second largest source of revenues and lease/user fees constituting the balance of revenue sources.[32] State law generally caps marketing and promotional expenditures by both type A and type B corporations at 10 percent of the EDC's annual revenues, but the limit is 25 percent for a type A city in limited circumstances.[33] Twenty-two of the 219 type A EDCs spent more than 10 percent of their revenues for marketing and promotion, and of the 470 type B EDCs, 57 exceeded the 10 percent threshold.[34] Texas EDCs use this sales tax revenue as a pool of funding for local economic development incentives to match the long list of state incentives utilized by the lone star state.

Challenges to Public-Funded Economic Development Organizations

While Texas and other regions and states offer positive examples, many other states such as Florida, Ohio, Wisconsin, and Michigan look to a private sector model for enhancing their economic development services. The privatization model began at locally delivered economic development services. This growth of private sector economic development is based upon concerns with the public sector–controlled economic development services. Prime negatives brought up against the public sector model for economic development are a lack of sufficient resources, requirements for public access, and lack of ability to operate at the speed of business.

Opponents of public-operated economic development organizations claim that private sector organizations are able to leverage additional private sector dollars to assist in the implementation of economic development work. The private sector resources act as an additional flow of money on top typically of public dollar contributed to the private sector economic development operation. Second, government-structured economic development organizations comply with state public records and auditing laws that may expose the salaries, tactics, and company targets to not only the public but also to competitors in other states. Opponents of public-operated economic development organizations claim they are not able to pay or hire high-quality staff compared to their private sector counterparts. Thus, they struggle to operate economic development organizations as efficiently as their private sector counterparts. Finally, opponents of public-operated economic development organizations point to the $5,000,000,000 in funding California redevelopment agencies were taking from other governmental functions for economic development and housing purposes at the local level.[35] These redevelopment agencies were recently abolished by the California legislature after building up funding through the use of tax increment financing constituting 12 percent of all property tax expenditures in the entire state.[36]

Private Sector–Led State Economic Development Organizations

A popular trend is the privatization of the economic development function at the state level. Public sector leaders are looking to harness the expertise, connections, and resources of the private sector to gain the public benefit of wealth creation. These state government leaders want an economic development initiative that moves at the speed of business with an organization that has few of public access challenges of government. The transition from a public state government agency to a private economic development corporation is not always easy. However, states are moving in the direction of privatizing economic development to gain larger marketing campaigns, ease entertainment and travel costs, and put a "business friendly" face on economic development matters. Opponents of the privatization of state economic development efforts call into question the use of public tax dollars by a private sector organization that may award tax incentives to companies that contribute to the organization or participate in its management.

Economic Development Policy Case Study 3.2: Wisconsin Economic Development Corporation

The Wisconsin Economic Development Corporation (WEDC) is the private sector–led organization operating the state's economic development and job creation efforts. The 90-plus employees of WEDC use five key metrics to measure the performance of the organization.[37] WEDC brings a substantial budget to the state's economic development program. Cash proceeds are nearly $40,000,000, tax credits $95,000,000, and bonding capacity recently available is at nearly $16,000,000.[38]

Advocates of privatizing state economic development functions point to the ability of the private sector to better market the state to private sector leaders. Current plans for the WEDC include generating assistance opportunities for more than 1,000 Wisconsin businesses and managing 400 business accounts and 150 community accounts to successful assistance engagements.[39] WEDC plans to expand extended enterprise capabilities, coordinate all regions of the state, and implement seven significant statewide economic development improvements.[40] WEDC also plans to deploy 13 account managers throughout the state to link businesses and communities throughout the state, provide ongoing training and tools for account managers, and implement tools to certify ten sites through the Ready Set Build! Program.[41] Deploying salesforce as a CRM tool with 50 partners to enhance business support coordination, a business retention and expansion tool, and Economic Modeling Specialist Inc. statewide utilizing the state's network of nine regional planning commissions are the final pieces of the WEDC program.[42] WEDC is just one state's effort to jumpstart a struggling economy by privatizing economic development.

Regional Private Economic Development Organizations

Many more major metro areas privatized the economic development function than state governments. Major metro regional economic development programs are private sector led and funded with both public and private sector funds. Privatizing local economic development forces local governments to work collectively. A private sector group can coordinate the retention and attraction of jobs for a region because it does not gain or lose tax dollars as a specific city does when a company decides a location in a specific place. Critics of privatizing local economic development point to the fact that local governments in many states have their own set of powers as political subdivisions, and their approval of tax incentives and other functions can only be played actually by local governments.

Charlotte (North Carolina) is an early adopter of a private sector regional economic development organization. The Charlotte Regional Partnership is a nonprofit, public/private economic development organization serving a 16-county region.[43] This multicounty regional economic development effort actually includes 12 counties in North Carolina and four counties in neighboring South Carolina.[44] This private sector regional economic development group serves communities in different states because that is the natural shape of their market, they are funded by public and private sector dollars, and elected officials are not in charge of the organization.[45] The Charlotte Regional Partnership implements economic development services of business retention and expansion marketing. These efforts include coordinating with corporate site location executives on existing and new company opportunities, promoting the region through global marketing, and news story placement on the success of the region. The Charlotte Regional Partnership is funded by 190 private sector companies and governments.[46] They benefit from both public and private sector funding opportunities. Whatever Charlotte is doing, economic development is working. The region and the states of North and South Carolina are clear economic winners. North Carolina is State of the Year for economic development purposes and Charlotte is Major Market of the Year.[47] Thus, even in the economic boom region of the south, the Charlotte region is a major economic leader. While how they do economic development is not the entire story, groups such as the Charlotte Regional Partnership are a major contributor to the region's success as company retention and attraction efforts are highly competitive among the regions and states.

Challenges for Private Sector–Led Economic
Development Organizations

Not all is perfect with private sector–led economic development organizations. The state of Ohio's effort to privatize its state economic development function has run into legal challenges and conflicts over whether the Auditor of State can audit the books of the privately run JobsOhio organization.[48] The battles in Ohio illustrate the political and policy conflict that opponents of privatizing economic development see as being created when government is taken out of the economic development frontline. Those concerns are how public money is being used and how open this private sector organization is willing to be. JobsOhio refunded the small amount of state government start-up funding it took and will not agree to be audited in the future. Supporters of JobsOhio point out that this organization markets the state for economic development, and local and state government officials still retain the ultimate authority to award or not award government funding.

Private sector regional and state economic development almost always operates with public dollars; however, they rarely want the public scrutiny that comes with those resources. Opponents of privatizing public functions such as economic development also argue that ethical challenges are posed by private sector organizations taking over the functions of government.[49] In addition, many economic development organizations are granted governmental powers not just to recruit businesses but to purchase property through eminent domain, award public dollars through grants, tax credits, tax abatements, and government-financed loans and government-backed tax exempt financing to support private ventures. Private companies empowered to award these government funds may be taking financial contributions from many of the same companies that would benefit from specific economic development projects. This sets up a potential conflict of interest for the private sector economic development organization and illustrates how a government body supervised by a publicly elected body ultimately has the people to answer to and local and state ethics laws to address conflict of interest issues.[50]

**Role of the Federal Government: Economic
Development Administration**

The federal government plays a secondary role in economic development due to a lack of funding and a very narrow scope for the US Department of Commerce's Economic Development Administration (EDA). With just over 200 employees and less than $300 million to cover the entire nation, the EDA is a small player in an economic development world where local and state governments spend $80 billion.[51] The EDA offers seven programs that typically operate as matching funds for public sector organizations to incentivize economic development. The public works program is the EDA's prime business retention, attraction, and expansion fund. A typical project from this program involves a grant to fund the improvement of a water and sewer system to support the expansion of an existing business.[52] To qualify for EDA funds, a region must be economically distressed based upon a per capita income level of no more than 80 percent of the national average or an unemployment rate that is just above or much above the national average.[53] In addition, the region must have adopted a comprehensive economic development strategy along very precise EDA guidelines.[54] Low funding levels and geographic limits impact the ability of EDA to participate in a large number of economic development deals.

Big Questions

1. What purpose does an economic development corporation serve?

2. Why cannot government or the private sector play that role?

3. Do you believe that economic development organizations are not worth the time or government funding?

4. California's extensive network of state government–funded economic development organizations has been attacked as an example of wasteful government spending. How would you defend their role?

5. How should economic development organizations have their success measured?

Class Writing Assignment

Debate is on whether the function of economic development should be "privatized." States such as Ohio have followed models created by Michigan and Florida to create private sector organizations to implement economic development corporations to market the state for economic development purposes. Write a 500-word op-ed piece for the local newspaper outlining whether the public or private model for economic development is best.

Additional Readings

Aaron N. Gruen, "Avoiding the Pitfalls of Public-Private Partnerships," *ED Now* International Economic Development Council, 13, 6 (March 18, 2013) 1–4, retrieved from http://www.ggassoc.com/publications/PublicPrivatePartnerships.pdf.

Brad Watts, "What Should EDA Fund? Developing a Model for Preassessment of Economic Development Investments," *Economic Development Quarterly*, 25, 1 (2011) 65–78.

David Ammons and Jonathan Morgan, "State-of-the-Art Measures in Economic Development," *ICMA Publications/PM Magazine*, 93, 5 (June 2011) retrieved from http://webapps.icma.org/pm/9305/public/cover.cfm?author=David percent20Ammons percent20and percent20Jonathan percent20Morgan&title=State-of-the-Art percent20Measures percent20in percent20Economic percent20Development&subtitle.

David Callies, Daniel J. Curtin, and Julie A. Tappendorf, *Bargaining for Development: A Handbook on Development Agreements, Annexation Agreements, Land Development*

Conditions, Vested Rights, and the Provision of Public Facilities (Washington, DC: Environmental Law Institute, 2003).

David Sloane, *Planning Los Angeles* (Chicago, IL: APA Planners Press, 2012).

Dwight Shupe and Misty Ventura, "Negotiating Development Agreements with Cities," *Texas Real Estate Business*, March 2006, retrieved from http://www.texasrebusiness.com/articles/MAR06/feature2.html.

Elizabeth Currid-Halkett and Kevin Stolarick, "The Great Divide: Economic Development Theory Versus Practice-A Survey of the Current Landscape," *Economic Development Quarterly*, 25, 2 (May 2011) 143–157.

Enterprise Florida Annual Incentives Report FY 2011–12, retrieved from http://www.florida-jobs.org/about percent20awi/open_government/2012_IncentivesReport.pdf.

Julie Cencula Olberding, "Diving into the 'Third Waves' of Regional Governance and Economic Development Strategies: A Study of Regional Partnerships for Economic Development in U.S. Metropolitan Areas," *Economic Development Quarterly*, 16, 3 (August 2002) 251–272.

Moira Quinn, *Envision Charlotte*, Urban Land Institute, April 12, 2012, retrieved from http://urbanland.uli.org/Articles/2012/April/ul/QuinnCharlotte.

Umut Toker, *Making Community Design Work, A Guide for Planners* (Chicago, IL: APA Planners Press, 2012).

Chapter Four
The Metropolis Case Study

Chapter Goals

1. Understand how a case study process works and its value as a learning tool
2. Learn about the role of an advocate and importance of negotiation skills in economic development
3. Recognize the players and the issues in the Metropolis case study
4. Understand the importance of comparing a region's economic characteristics

The Case Study Process

Case studies are often the best method to illustrate how the real world operates. The class will decide whether Metropolis Tech Expo 2020 happens or not. As in real life, ordinances must be drafted, debated, negotiated over, and voted on; strategic plans must address the issues of concern; and public policy issues must be debated. During city council debates, proponents will present their views, same with opponents, and then city council votes. Efforts will first focus on defining the project through the creation of strategic economic development plan for Metropolis. City council will then debate, negotiate, and ultimately vote on a series of ordinances focusing on specific aspects of the project. In addition, competing plans and documents will be produced for implanting this major economic development project.

The Economic Development Players

Before delving into the case study, it is important to gain a general understanding of the key players as it relates to the state and local economic development process.

Business Leadership. Business leaders, whether they have a financial interest or not, are dragged into major public policy debates over economic development issues. Part of the reason is economic self-interest. As leaders of companies serving the community, these businesses have a better chance of success if the region is successful. If the region has low unemployment, low crime, and big projects to show off and enjoy, it is easier to attract workers and sell goods and services to the region. Regional business leaders have an economic justification for involvement in local and state economic development strategy.

Developers. Developers in the context of economic development constitute the company or organization that wishes to change the use or reuse the property in question for a profit or not. They want to enhance the use of the property through constructing infrastructure and buildings and recruiting new users to the site. Developers are public sector organizations or private sector companies. Developers are the catalyst for change. They are often the visionary. The good ones never take their eye off the concept of economic profit while appearing not to care about the profit in the deal. Developers can also be driven by greed and short-term profit margin. They can lack the long-term vision to produce high-quality developments for business and the community.

Design Professionals and Land Planners. Design professionals and land planners give life and definition to the developer's vision. They are an interesting mix of artists and business persons. Working closely with the developers, they outline plans for the design and structure of a building and its surrounding environment. These professionals make a neighborhood happy or furious. They design a project that fits the neighborhood or a monster building that does not belong in the area. Land planners are government officials with an urban design background. They provide a roadmap for development in a neighborhood and fight to keep that vision alive against developers and neighbors.

Labor Unions. While the percentage of unionized workforce is on the steep decline, many regions and states are or were home to major industrial labor unions. Do not let the low percentage of workers in a union confuse you as to their political influence. In many states, a large number of retired union workers exist. Politicians seek the endorsements of these unions when they run for election. Labor unions impact economic development projects in many cities across the United States.

Lawyers. Lawyers are central to economic development. They represent clients before every imaginable tribunal—city council, city government regulatory agencies, county government, neighborhood civic associations, state legislative committees, state government regulatory agencies, development and planning commissions, congressional committees, federal government regulatory agencies, and even in the court room. Lawyers can be a productive force in economic development projects or a tool to obstruct the same.

Political Leadership. Politicians most often are decision makers' lawyers, developers, community and civic leaders, labor unions, government planners, design professionals, preservationists, business leaders, and the New Urbanists. Politicians may be mayors, city council members, county commissioners, state legislators, governors, development directors, congressmen, judges, and a variety of local, state, or federal agency government officials. Most politicians are not elected but are appointed.

Neighbors/Community Leaders. Neighbors may be for or against a new development and jobs in their neighborhood. Chances are the residents in support of the development rarely make their way down to city hall to complain. Opponents are more than willing to travel. Not in My Backyard (NIMBY) epitomizes the perspectives of many residents impacted by economic development projects. Neighbors impacted by economic development efforts use every weapon to fight a proposed development.

New Urbanists. New Urbanists want neighborhoods built around walkability and mass transit and bikes for longer trips. New Urbanists do not like "McMansions" built on three-acre plots where a cornfield used to be. They believe in sustainability by preventing sprawl and developing neighborhoods with maximum density that has homes built tightly together and linked with mass transit. New Urbanist has a different version of zoning in mind that builds mixed-use neighborhoods for long-term economic development.

Preservationists. Preservationists want to save old buildings and other structures. It is not that they are opposed to change, but historic preservationists want to see these old buildings restored. Cost does not typically matter to them because they often do not own the buildings. They spend other people's money, but their vision can often save some amazing buildings and facilities. Preservationists are typically organized, highly educated, and not afraid to go to court if necessary.

News Media. The news media, whether newspaper, television, radio, or the Internet, operates as an important check on the actions of the government and private sector. The news media calls attention to the plans of government and can be a "cheerleader" for development, or its biggest opponent. The news media gives a voice to the little guy in the neighborhood impacted by the development. The news media, with a business protected by the First Amendment to the US Constitution, always matters in economic development projects.

Tea Party. The Tea Party is a new force in public policy and economic development. They are fiscally conservative but more likely to align themselves with neighborhood leaders than with big business. They are not timid and are better at being in the minority than the majority. However, the Tea Party is a player in the economic development process. They have a base of members that impacts elections and gains media attention with relative ease. They support capitalism but not the use of government money to spur economic development.

Metropolis Case Study: Metropolis Tech Expo 2020

Metropolis sits in the center of Ohio and is like most mid-sized cities in the United States—it has had its share of successes and failures. This 200-year-old city has a population of 800,000, and the downtown is home to the state capital. Metropolis has a below-average unemployment and poverty rate and has seen the overall base of population grow through an aggressive annexation process in the 1960s. Metropolis' annexation policy is based upon the fact that it owns the regional water and sewer division and will not provide service to customers in a township unless they annex into the city. Major Fortune 500 companies call the city home, and the region has a growing base of logistics and technology companies to match its core of state government, insurance, banking, and professional service firms that follow all those organizations. The majority of the population are Caucasians, but African Americans make up about 25 percent of the city's population. The city is perpetually young because it is home to the nation's largest university, which creates a large pool of college students and young workers. Most people in Metropolis believe it is a nice place to live and raise a family. It is not New York City or Chicago but, for the most part, it offers a very nice suburban style of life.

Big University Neighborhood, Metropolis, and Competitor Demographics

While Metropolis in general is a twenty-first-century success story, many of its neighborhoods are not. In fact, the demographic information listed in Table 4.1 focuses on a neighborhood just east of the highly successful Big University. This demographic information illustrates the struggles Metropolis faces in the neighborhood east of Big University and provides some context for comparative communities.

Big University may be a shining star from an academic standpoint but is surrounded by a struggling neighborhood buried in poverty and searching for an economic development project to revitalize the area. The University of course is a major strategic asset being located in the middle of Metropolis.

Most people in Metropolis have not seen the urban blight that has taken over many neighborhoods, nor do they seem to understand the new threats created by global competition to the region's white-collar workforce. The downtown struggles to compete with the free parking and the convenient location of the suburban office park, and the city fathers were recently shocked when Metropolis had the highest downtown office vacancy rate in the United States. Many great buildings were torn down in the 1950s in the name of urban renewal and cheap parking.

Crime is a serious issue in the central city, and the urban school system struggles to meet the performance levels of its suburban counterparts. The once-great neighborhoods are divided by interstate highways, hit by the impact of forced school desegregation and busing, and killed by the invasion of crack cocaine and other drugs. These neighborhoods are the other side of Metropolis. Few in these neighborhoods went to college. Most did not finish high school, and few have two parents in the household. These neighborhoods had public sector investment over the years, but for the most part the private sector had stayed away. Politicians created public housing projects and built recreation centers, swimming pools, road improvements, and much more. However, the business base for private sector development of these neighborhoods is mostly gone. As people left and crime moved in, banks, restaurants, grocery stores, and dry cleaners evacuated as well. People living in these neighborhoods have to fight every day to go to work, take care of their children, and save their community. However, most feel it is an uphill task.

The newspaper in town, *The Metropolis Bugle*, recently launched a month-long series on the challenges the city faces as it enters its two hundredth year. The series discussed the good, the bad, and the ugly of Metropolis, outlined the history of the city's development efforts, why the schools are struggling, how global competition threatens its future and creates new opportunities, and demanded the politicians do something about it.

Metropolis Economy

Metropolis' diversified economy is balanced among services, trade, government, and manufacturing sectors. State government, education, banking, research, insurance, and data processing, in particular, have helped the city resist recession. Telecommunications, retailing, health care, and the military are other strong employment areas. Home to more than 70 insurance companies, Metropolis ranks

Table 4.1 Select demographic data for Big University neighborhood and select competitors

Demographic Measure	Big University Neighborhood	Metropolis Overall	Rest of Big University State	Raleigh, North Carolina	Nashville, Tennessee
Renter-occupied apartments	54%	51%	31%	48%	40.8%
Median house value	$69,441	$138,200	$134,600	$214,900	$166,400
Racial make-up	75% African American	25.7% African American	11.6% African American	29.6% African American	27.6% African American
Average adjusted gross income	$23,299	$41,370	$45,395	$51,969	$45,540
Median age	30.5 years	30.6 years	36.2 years	30.9 years	33.9 years
Residents with income below the poverty level	45%	22.6%	14.8%	15.9%	17.3%
Population growth since 2000	−5%	10.6 %	1.6%	47%	11%
Cost of living index with 100 as national average	95	96.2	102	95.4	89
Population over 25 with a college degree by percentage	6%	29%	26%	44.9%	29.7%
Unemployment rate	7.25%	7.1%	7.7%	6.7%	7.5%
Murders per 100,000 people	20	12.2	4.1	3.4	12.6

Source: US Census Bureau.

high among the US regional insurance capitals. The city is the corporate headquarters for many large firms such as Big Insurance Enterprise, Global Banc Corporation, The Clothier, Inc, The Electric Company, Hamburger's International, Big Stores Corporation, Chemical R Us, Research Memorial Institute, and Bob's Breakfast Place, Inc. Twenty of Metropolis' largest financial institutions operate more than 400 offices throughout the metropolitan region. The US government is the city's third largest employer. It operates the Supply Center, with 3,000 employees working in a massive central storehouse that ships up to 10,000 items a day to military posts around the world. Manufacturing comprises about 10 percent of the metropolitan area. Strategically located between the northeast and midwest regions and served by an excellent transportation system, Metropolis is a marketing, distribution, and warehouse center. Metropolis is an example of a successful service-based economy.

A link in the import/export shipping network is Ace's Air/Industrial Park, which has been designated a foreign trade zone. Twenty-one passenger and freight air carriers serve Metropolis International Airport; two passenger carriers and a number of freight carriers fly out of Ace; and Bolt's Field provides runway space and amenities for charter air services. Three major railroads operate through Metropolis; all provide piggyback and rail car shipping and two have export/import containerization facilities. Completing the ground transportation system are more than 100 motor freight companies. One of three inland ports in the United States, Metropolis, receives and ships US customs-sealed containers to the Pacific Rim. As Ohio's largest city, Metropolis is the only one whose population increased in the 1990s, and this trend continued in the 2000s. Eighty-three percent of the population aged over 25 years are high school graduates and 29 percent have college degrees; 71 percent of the population over the age of 16 is in the labor force. While the region has a more desirable workforce than the rest of the nation, the increase in average age is causing some concern.

Traditional economic mainstays such as government, the Big University, corporate headquarters, and large financial institutions lend stability to the local economy. The Metropolis area lost manufacturing jobs in the last decade but has added positions in services to create a net gain in jobs overall. Metro Metropolis has nearly 1,000,000 workers with an annual average wage for production workers at just under $20 an hour. Ohio's state income tax rate ranges from 0.743 percent to 7.5 percent with a basic state sales tax rate of 5.25 percent plus local levies (food and prescription drugs are exempt); a local income tax rate of 2 percent; taxes on real property are assessed on 35 percent of the property's total market value; and businesses with personal property valued at $10,001 or more must also pay personal property tax in the state of Ohio.[1]

An Economic Comparison: Raleigh

Metropolis is not alone. This region competes with successful job centers such as Raleigh (North Carolina) and Nashville (Tennessee). Raleigh and the RTP area consistently rank among the nation's best economies year after year. Unemployment remains low and per capita income remains high with the region's biggest industries of government, education, and health care surviving most recessions. The RTP is located in both Wake County (home of Raleigh) and Durham County (home of Durham). While Duke University is in Durham County, Wake County plays host to both the University of North Carolina–Chapel Hill and North Carolina State University. The Centennial Campus is a research and development center affiliated with North Carolina State University located in Raleigh. All of these organizations make this region a global, high-tech powerhouse with roughly 140 corporate, academic, and government agencies in the RTP alone employing more than 38,500 workers and providing an annual payroll in excess of $2,000,000,000.[2] Raleigh is both the state capital of North Carolina and a center of banking, industry, and commerce for much of North Carolina. Fueled by a highly educated workforce, companies find Raleigh an attractive market to locate. Items and goods produced by regional companies include pharmaceuticals, electronic equipment, electrical machinery, processed foods, and metal products.[3]

Recently, over 300 new industries expanded in Wake County, bringing in over 17,000 new jobs, and 400 expanded industries in Durham County, bringing 31,810 new jobs.[4] The landing of a major Google facility was a corporate site location win for the region. The area continues to be a global leader in high-tech jobs as evidenced by the amount of venture capital that is available. Raleigh benefits substantially from its close proximity to the RTP and the region's explosive growth of biotech firms. The RTP is globally ranked fourth in the 2010 International Ranking of Emerging Biotech Hubs by Business Facilities.[5] The Downtown Raleigh Renaissance, a revitalization process designed to create a stronger and more vibrant downtown, successfully completed three major projects totaling almost $250,000,000 to enhance the region's conventional business including a new 500,000-square-foot convention center, a 400-room Marriott headquarters hotel, and the reopening of Fayetteville Street to vehicular traffic.

Raleigh is at the crossroads of both Norfolk Southern and CSX rail service linking the east coast to midwest and Canadian markets. As Raleigh is within 500 miles of half the US population and North Carolina has a 78,000-mile highway network, it is not a surprise that more than 300 motor freight carriers operate in the area with over 40 motor freight terminals.[6] Raleigh boasts a skilled, educated, enthusiastic, and growing workforce. In fact, Raleigh was recently voted the number one city with the happiest workers by the Hudson Employment Index and the number one "hottest job market" by *Business 2.0* magazine.[7] The average hourly earnings of production workers in the Raleigh region's manufacturing sector is $14.45.[8] Raleigh has an impressive list of major employers within its borders and the RTP's list is even better. Major Raleigh employers include State of North Carolina, Wake County Public School System, North Carolina State University, WakeMed Health & Hospitals, Rex Healthcare, Progress Energy, Wake County government, City of Raleigh, First Citizens Bank, Allscripts Healthcare LLC, News & Observer, and Waste Logistics, Inc.[9]

An Economic Comparison: Nashville

Like Metropolis and Raleigh, Nashville (Tennessee) is a state capital of a large state, home to a world-class university, and an emerging location for high-tech companies and regional corporate and manufacturing facilities. Nashville's diverse economy brings strengths in finance and insurance, health care, music and entertainment, publishing, transportation technology, higher education, biotechnology, plastics, and tourism and conventions. Moody's Investors Service placed Nashville eighth in a ranking of the top ten most diversified local economies and ranked twenty-fifth in *Forbes* magazine's listing of top places for business and careers.[10] Health care is big business in Nashville. Over 20 health-care companies are based within the city, with a total 350 health-care companies having Nashville operations, and the region benefits as home to Vanderbilt University and their world-class hospital and research center.[11] Spinning off this base of health-care firms, Nashville is building a high-tech economy and has over ten investment and venture capital companies dealing primarily with health care, and the nearly 100,000 health-care workers in the Nashville metro area recently earned more than $4,000,000,000 payroll.[12]

The creative arts are also big business in Nashville. The city is a major southeastern US publishing center, home to a leading publisher of Bibles, and is growing as a distribution center for books and other print media.[13] Music is of course Nashville's most famous product. The 200-plus local recording studios, music-related professional service firms, and music entertainment centers have created a billion dollar–plus music-related economic cluster.[14] In fact, Nashville is no doubt responsible for Tennessee's over $2,000,000,000 in tourism revenue.[15] Nashville is more than music and health care. They are growing a technology-based economy as well. In fact, Dell Computers operates a manufacturing and technical support center that employs thousands, and the region is growing in the biotechnology field as well. The major goods produced in the Metro Nashville area center on printing and publishing, automotive products, trucks, automotive parts, clothing, shoes, lawnmowers, bicycles, telecommunications equipment, aerospace products, thermos bottles, kerosene lamps, and computers. Nashville formed Partnership 2010 to operate a regional economic development organization to better retain and attract companies to the region. It seems to be working.

Nashville's central location makes it a logistical hub for the south. The Cumberland River is a logistics center for Nashville, acting as a link to the Ohio River, Mississippi River, and ultimately global markets through the Gulf of Mexico. The distance to the Gulf of Mexico was cut by over 500 miles when the $1,800,000,000 Tennessee-Tombigbee waterway, connecting the Tennessee River in Northern Alabama with the Tombigbee River of Southern Alabama, connected Nashville to the Port of Mobile, saving in millions and transportation time.[16] A substantial highway system matched with a CSX Intermodal brings over 8000 containers a month through the region. Ninety trains pass through Nashville on a daily basis. Completing a compelling logistics initiative is the Nashville Air Cargo Link, which is a designated foreign trade zone and annually has shipped more than 65,000 tons of cargo.[17] Nashville is a part of the southern economic boom. The nearly 700,000 nonfarm workers come from a range of industries, and the average hourly earnings of production workers is $14.44.[18]

Major employers in Metro Nashville are led by Vanderbilt University Medical Center followed by Health Corporation of America, The Healthcare Company, St Thomas Health Services, Nissan Motor Manufacturing, Walmart, Kroger

Table 4.2 Metro comparison: Employment by industry

Industry	Metropolis Workers	Raleigh Workers	Nashville Workers
Total nonfarm workers	971,000	503,000	736,000
Construction and mining	31,600	29,400	32,400
Manufacturing	62,600	27,600	61,100
Trade, transportation, and utilities	178,800	87,000	147,200
Information	16,300	16,700	18,600
Financial activities	69,600	25,900	46,600
Professional and business services	154,100	90,500	102,400
Educational and health services	120,800	61,400	119,200
Leisure and hospitality	89,700	54,000	78,800
Government	150,100	86,000	99,100
Other services	36,400	24,500	30,600

Source: Economy at a Glance, Nashville-Davidson, Tennessee and Raleigh-Cary, North Carolina, Bureau of Labor Statistics, http://www.bls.gov/eag/eag.oh_columbus_msa.htm, http://www.bls.gov/eag/eag.nc_raleigh_msa.htm.

Company, Ingram Industries, Electrolux Home Products, Shoney's Restaurant, Dell Computers, Randstad Work Solutions, and Gaylord Entertainment.[19] Nashville promotes the region's low cost of doing business based on a state income tax limited to dividends and interest income, a 7 percent state sales tax with a small local sales tax but no local income tax, a property tax rate of $2.52 per $100 of assessed value, and residential property is assessed at 25 percent.[20] Table 4.2 provides a city by city comparison of employment by industry.

The Players

The players can be divided into three groups: the mayor and her council, the loyal opposition, and the interest group.

The Mayor and Her Council. The mayor is finishing her second term, preparing for reelection, a governor's race, and may be a desk on Pennsylvania Avenue. Metropolis has been the mayor's city, but, while the *Bugle*'s series brought the newspaper a Pulitzer Prize, it was causing the mayor nothing but problems. The overall economic performance of the city is good—not great like in the suburbs but good for a big city. The public is happy with her. Then the *Bugle* series ran. Now the city fathers, the corporate leaders of the community, were concerned. They demanded a response. The mayor felt like she needed a big juicy project to calm the nerves, but, in the back of her mind, she knew it would take more than a project. The mayor understands that urban redevelopment is about an overall initiative and not a series of disjointed development projects.

A number of Metropolis city council members are generally loyal to the mayor. However, a couple of the mayor's loyalists fancied themselves as New Urbanists— one in particular. He hates the freeways, supports preservation of historic structures, wants to redo all the development in the city, opposes most annexations, and has led the charge to ensure every new development meets the best of New Urbanist design standards. In addition, a couple of the mayor's council members are more loyal to organized labor than they are to the business community. Several other members of the mayor's council came directly from the ranks of community organizers. They ended up on city council because of their activity in the neighborhoods. They wanted the region to be economically successful but rarely agreed to do so at the cost of what the local neighbors want. Other members of the mayor's team are the city solicitor and the development director. The law director and the development director advise the mayor on the legal and development issues surrounding the redevelopment, growth, and expansion of the city. All members of the mayor's council are concerned about jobs and economic development and had a quiet fundraising alliance with developers and some business community leaders who helped them get reelected.

The Loyal Opposition. The loyal opposition knew one thing: they would rarely agree with the mayor and her council. The loyal opposition needed the public to see them as fighting for the taxpayers. Most of the public would not really pay attention to what the loyal opposition is fighting for, but they viewed the fighting as some form of action. The loyal opposition is led by the president of city council and they controlled the city council. That control is just by one, very shaky vote on most issues. The council president is young, aggressive, and an idea man. He liked the mayor personally but thought he would do a better job in that seat. The council president has strong ties with the business community but a very good ear for neighborhood concerns. The loyal opposition has several other members on city council, and many in that group are ambitious as well.

The Interest Groups. Various interest groups interact with the Metropolis city hall on a regular basis.

- City Fathers: The city fathers are civic-minded business executives focused on major city issues. They generally do not view economic development as an overall program but see it one development project at a time. When they get engaged, they are powerful as they put their money where their mouth is.
- Ohio Taxpayers League (OTL): OTL comprises conservative residents generally opposed to government spending and interference in the marketplace. They are not very popular with elected officials because they are rarely "for" anything, but they can often strike a chord with the public, and the news media loves them. OTL sees their role as keeping the city hall honest and the group is very focused on the development of charter schools as the solution to the urban school crisis.
- Developers: Metropolis has local and national developers in city hall on a regular basis. These developers are either for their own project or against someone else's. Developers do not really like government until it is time to build a "public-private partnership" (aka to get some government funds that make their project possible). Some developers do well working with neighbors, and other developers see the neighbors as a liability that must be overcome. Developers can also be "slum lords" and create a variety of residential products.

- Neighbors: Neighbors visiting Metropolis city hall are rarely happy. Happy neighbors near a proposed development in their community typically stay at home and remain happy. Angry neighbors are motivated to share their feelings directly with their elected officials. NIMBY is the general name for these folks. Everyone wants a nice restaurant to attend, but no one wants the other people going to the restaurant parking on their street. Some neighbors are reasonable and are looking for some small changes to a plan.
- Big Labor: Big labor is really not that big anymore, but they are still active politically. They encourage the city hall to use union construction companies and promote union-friendly projects whenever possible. Big labor includes not only industrial trade unions and building trades but also the powerful teachers and public sector worker unions. Big labor is focused on prevailing wage violations, developing a worker training center in the city, and supporting the public school system.
- New Urbanists Unite: New Urbanists Unite is a new group in Metropolis. Their mission is to improve the quality of development in the community. Until recently, Metropolis was just focused on growing period. However, rising gasoline prices and a weak mass transit system changed all of that. New Urbanist Unite includes architects, planners, and just plain rich people who like the look of this type of neighborhood design.
- Metropolis Preservation Society: Metropolis Preservation Society was born out of the urban renewal of the 1950s and 1960s. That timeframe in Metropolis saw many great buildings and landmarks torn down in the name of urban renewal. Surface parking lots were needed, public housing money had become available, and the almighty interstate highways needed to be built. The Metropolis Preservation Society's obvious focus is to prevent the tear-down of historically significant buildings.

The Facts

The city fathers are concerned. Metropolis is a younger city than its counterparts in the state, has a strong base of workers from local colleges and universities, and has grown through an aggressive annexation policy that helped the city to retain and attrac business. The concern started with the *Bugle* stories and led to a benchmark study done to compare Metropolis to its global counterparts. According to the benchmark study, the city is falling behind economically, with its schools and in its growth. The city fathers decided something must be done. They convinced their friend, the mayor, she should form a Metropolis Bicentennial Commission to adopt a vision for the city that will last another 200 years. Filled with city fathers, big labor, new urbanists, developers, and neighborhood leaders, the Metropolis Bicentennial Commission reviewed dozens of ideas. Some were quickly rejected, but some made it to the recommendation list. The city fathers kept a fairly tight level of control on what actually was adopted by this group. They were very open to everything being thrown on the table, but ultimately it would be their vision that helped the city through the next 200 years.

The main focus of the Metropolis Bicentennial Commission report is the development of a 2020 World Tech Expo in Metropolis. This global event will create an international image for the city and redevelop a struggling neighborhood. The 2020 World Tech Expo will be a high-tech version of a World's Fair. The World's Fair is a nineteenth-century invention. Cities put themselves on the map by building exhibit space that turned into small cities showing off the inventions and marvels of the Industrial Revolution. The twentieth-century version of the World's Fair created not just a tourist event but became a catalyst to develop an area.

The city fathers decided the location for the 2020 World Tech Expo should be the state fairgrounds located north of downtown and south of the university square in the middle of one of Metropolis' struggling neighborhoods. The fairgrounds used to be surrounded by factories that employed workers who lived close-by in working-class but stable housing. Move the clock forward. The factories are closed, unemployment rises, and the neighborhood becomes unsafe. However, the city fathers have always had their eyes on the neighborhood because the abandoned factories present a development opportunity—big blocks of land with infrastructure in place (water, sewer, rail, telecommunications, roads all linked to the interstate highway system). However, the state fairgrounds looked as bad off as the neighborhood it lives in. The state fair is another product of the nineteenth century. Governors throughout the twentieth and twenty-first centuries saw the political benefits to selling themselves to rural Ohio by promoting the fair and even sleeping in the barn with the animals and the families that brought them down for the competition. However, the state fair only provides a boost to Metropolis about 30 days out of the year.

Even more enticing is the large patches of ground south and north of the fairgrounds. The majority of the territory is covered by idle industrial factories. The roadway, rail, highway, water and sewer, and telecommunication infrastructure is in place. It is a major infill opportunity. The site has three property owners who are looking for anything to do with the land. They eagerly sold it to the city without anyone watching. Of course, the city also just bought all the environmental problems with the site as well. The site south of the fairgrounds does have one historically significant building. An 1856 school sits on the site at the corner of East Fifth Avenue and Fourth Street. This building is registered with the National Registration of Historic Places. Abraham Lincoln visited it in the 1860. It has been called Lincoln Elementary ever since. The Metropolis public schools have not had the building open for 30 years, but it has not been torn down.

The Metropolis Bicentennial Commission identified over $1,000,000,000 in costs needed to fund the redevelopment of the fairgrounds, improve the interstate highway system in Metropolis to handle the flow of visitors, and construct a light rail system for downtown with a link up to the university through the fairgrounds to ensure downtown benefited from the project and guests of the Tech Expo had a place to stay. In addition, millions in costs are involved in preparing a number of sites surrounding the fairgrounds for redevelopment, purchasing property for redevelopment, and spending millions on city water, sewer, rail, streetlights, and road improvements in the neighborhood.

The city fathers next looked for help from the state and federal government to fund the project. They got the help they needed. The governor, general assembly, and the State Fair Board agreed to a $400,000,000 update of the fairgrounds. The congress, through the reauthorization of the federal transportation bill, placed a $400,000,000 earmark for interstate highway improvements and funding for construction of a light rail system with a loop downtown connecting to the university through the fairgrounds. Both funding opportunities are contingent on two items: the city and the business community must come up with the rest of the $200,000,000 in funding, and the World Tech Expo Council must award Metropolis the 2020 Tech Expo. With these major victories in hand, the city fathers flew off to Paris and met with the officials from the Bureau International des Expositions that officially sanction Tech Expo event and thus determine which country and city will host a universal expo on a specific year. After much hard work, the city fathers received the official sanction from the Bureau International des Expositions for a 2020 slot.

According to the city fathers, Metropolis Expo 2020 will redevelop three major properties outside of the state fairgrounds, including the development of a major research and development park, a mixed-use retail, housing and office development, and a housing project.

- Expo Research Plus Technology Park: Partnering with the university, the city fathers plan for the city to develop a 200-acre research park on the site of the now-abandoned Chemicals R Us factory controlled by the city. The site is just south of the planned Centro development and just north of downtown Metropolis, bordered on the north by East Fifth Avenue, on the east by I-71, on the south by Second Avenue, and on the west by North Fourth Street. The university has committed $100,000,000 toward the development of the research park and surrounding area from its hefty endowment but is under pressure from its Board of Trustees to do so only if the project will be successful. The site is within the city of Metropolis but has major environmental contamination and needs at least $5,000,000 in Brownfield clean-up. A state of Ohio Brownfield clean-up grant application is competing with another site that is planned for the workforce training center in the Centro aspect of the project. None of these projects can move forward without the Brownfield grant. In addition, the expo research plus technology park needs a tax abatement and income tax refund program. City council must approve both the city's top priority for the Brownfield grant application and the blanket tax incentive for the university to agree to assist in the development of the park. Without the university, there is no expo research plus technology park, and the city fathers will lose half of the $200,000,000 needed to make the Expo a reality. Without the research park, few big companies will be locating in Metropolis after the Expo.
- Centro: Partnering with a private sector developer, the city fathers want to develop a mixed-use project called Centro with a shopping center, high-rent condos, and office buildings sprinkled throughout the site. The site is located just south of the state fairgrounds—bordered on the north by East Eleventh Avenue, on the east by I-71, on the south by East Fifth Avenue, and on the west by North Fourth Street. Giant Development (GD) is a national developer with an ability to potentially bring a major facility with 2,000 jobs right away

to the project. GD's vision is big and requires land outside the city boundaries. Metropolis needs to seize this property by eminent domain to make GD's vision a reality. The owner of the site, RB Slumlord, plans to actively oppose any efforts to sell the property or annex the property into the city. It is currently a nearly abandoned large apartment complex that is riddled with crime but still produces a healthy profit for RB Slumlord. GD also wants Lincoln Elementary torn down. They see the corner of East Fifth Avenue and Fourth Street as the grand entry into their development.

- Expo Village: Partnering with a private sector national developer, Land for Sale, LLC (LFS), the mayor wants to develop a market rate housing project on the land given to the city by the state just north of the state fairgrounds. The site in question is used for parking for the state fair and a major highway patrol station, but it still holds the state's historical society museum and an eighteenth-century pioneer's village. It is bordered on the north by Northwood Avenue, on the east by I-71, on the south by East Seventeenth Avenue, and on the west by North Fourth Street. LFS vision for the market rate housing initiative is New Urbanist in nature with a highly dense housing pattern and mixed-use sprinkled throughout the plan. The president of council instead supports the vision of Bigger is Better Development (B&B Development) to create a traditional market rate housing project. Several members of city council are also considering proposing federal government–subsidized housing at the site to ensure poor residents of the city benefit from this project. Housing for Everyone has proposed a government-subsidized housing project for the site.

All three sites need major infrastructure improvements totaling $100,000,000. A public finance vehicle is the route needed for funding these improvements.

Big Questions

Both the success of Metropolis in the new global economy and the prospects for redevelopment of the Big University neighborhood are impacted by the actions of the Metropolis government and its partners at the state government. Metropolis faces a series of decisions about all the issues related to economic development such as:

1. What will it take to make tough neighborhoods safe?

2. What zoning approach enables economic development?

3. Can the government's ultimate power of eminent domain find a use in this project?

4. Should annexation or smart growth tactics be used to grow the city into success?

5. What public finance tools are necessary for the development of essential public infrastructure?

6. Can the local and state government win the battle of tax incentives to lure companies to a complex site?

7. How can the urban schools be turned around to ensure long-term availability of a high-quality workforce?

8. Will good workforce housing be within reach of the average person in this community?

9. How can a public-private partnership be formed that ensures adequate funding to leverage the millions of private investment on the line?

10. Is technology-based economic development the model to follow?

11. Can a sustainable development model be created without killing the overall economic development project?

12. How can this community succeed in a global marketplace?

The mayor, city council, and state government leaders have to approach and answer these questions to make this development a reality.

Class Writing Assignment

Before any of those big decisions can be made, Metropolis needs an economic development strategy to guide policy makers and community leaders on where the city is going. Based upon the information presented above, write Metropolis's economic development strategic plan based upon the creation of an overall goal, a small number of objective measures of success, identified core strategies, and a limited list of action steps needed for the emerging city to succeed in a global age.

Additional Reading

Bert T. King and Irving L. "Janis, Comparison of the Effectiveness of Improvised versus Non-Improvised Role-playing in Producing Opinion Changes," *Human Relations*, 9, 2 (1956) 177–186.

Bruce S. Jannson, *Becoming an Effective Policy Advocate, From Policy Practice to Social Justice*, 6th ed. (Independence, KY: Brooks/Cole Cengage Learning, 2010).

Erwin de Leon and Elizabeth T. Boris, *The State of Society: Measuring Economic Success and Human Well-Being* (Washington, DC: The Urban Institute, 2010).

Eugene P. Trani and Robert D. Holsworth, *The Indispensable University* (Washington, DC: American Council on Higher Education Series, 2009).

John Pencavel, *The Role of Labor Unions in Fostering Economic Development* (New York, NY: The World Bank, 1999).

Keith Evans, *Common Sense Rules of Advocacy for Lawyers: A Practical Guide for Anyone Who Wants to Be a Better Advocate* (Washington, DC: The Capitol Net Inc, 2010).

Mike E. Miles, Richard L. Haney, Jr., and Gayle Berens, *Real Estate Development Principles and Process*, 2nd ed. (Washington, DC: Urban Land Institute, 1996).

Nancy A. Huelsberg and William F. Lincoln, *Successful Negotiating in Local Government* (Washington, DC: ICMA Press, 1985).

Niall Fitzgerald and Mandy Cormack, *The Role of Business in Society: An Action Agenda*, The Conference Board, Harvard University Kennedy School of Government and International Business Leaders Forum, November 2006, retrieved from http://www.hks.harvard.edu/m-rcbg/CSRI/publications/report_12_CGI percent20Role percent20of percent20Business percent20in percent20Society percent20Report percent20FINAL percent2010-03-06.pdf.

The Episcopal Network for Economic Justice, Economic Justice How-To-Manual, Chapter 4, Community Organizing and Community Economic Development, 2009, retrieved from http://www.enej.org/howtomanual.htm.

CHAPTER FIVE

ECONOMIC DEVELOPMENT BUILDING BLOCK: LAND USE REGULATION AND ZONING

Chapter Goals

1. Understand local zoning procedures and their legal basis with an emphasis on impact on development
2. See how zoning modifications and variances can modify, expedite, or hinder site selection and development
3. Examine how the differences in center city and suburban growth interact and impact overall regional development
4. Learn what "New Urbanism" is and its effect on existing and future metropolitan growth policies
5. Explore if zoning has a negative or positive impact on economic development

Land Use Regulation and Economic Development

The real estate development is a major aspect of economic development. Successful economic development is not possible without a stable and predictable legal process to purchase and develop real estate. The real estate proforma is a tool in the development process as it determines whether the project revenues exceed the expenses. Local government manages growth and development through a comprehensive plan that serves as a legally binding document setting overall goals, objectives, and policies to guide the local legislative body's real estate decision making. Economic development does not occur without land use regulation authorizing the type of use for the property in question. Land use regulation in most states starts with zoning. Specific sites have varying forms of zoning, but one major city, Houston, does not have traditional zoning.

Land use regulation protects property values, preserves public safety, and spurs economic development. The Port of Dubuque offers an example. The city of Dubuque (Iowa) is a small-town American success story in part due to a major riverfront development project. This town of nearly 60,000 people is on the far eastern side of Iowa on the Mississippi River almost connected more to Illinois and Minnesota than the rest of Iowa.[1] The Port of Dubuque had a challenging opportunity to redevelop a 133-acre riverfront Brownfield parcel. Dubuque created a Planned Commercial Development zoning scheme to invite development of this riverfront site. The Planned Commercial Development zoning scheme is based upon a land use master plan and specific design standards.[2] The zoning parameters are defined in the master plan and design standards such as uses, building placement, streets, blocks, and density requirements.[3] In addition, sustainability requirements are established and the city acts as a master developer.[4] The city manager holds administrative approval with applicants having the right to appeal decisions to city council.[5] Based upon in part to this zoning scheme, the Dubuque Riverfront is an impressive success.

The Port of Dubuque, branded as America's River, created a world-class $200,000,000 development that includes National Mississippi River Museum and Aquarium, River's Edge Plaza, Riverwalk, Alliant Amphitheater, Grand Harbor Resort and Waterpark, Grand River Conference and Education Center, and renovation of several historic structures.[6] Dubuque used its strategic location on the Mississippi River to create a predictable zoning process to facilitate and invite development in the small Iowa city. Based in part on the strong riverfront development, Dubuque is leader in the Iowa economy—ranking number one in job creation in the state.[7]

Land Use Regulation as an Economic Development Tool

Land use regulation includes traditional zoning, mixed-use, and Houston or no-zoning. All three approaches to land use regulation impact economic development. Traditional zoning is the regulation of land use based upon a separation of uses. It developed in the early twentieth century and is now widely utilized in communities throughout the United States. Local governments typically play a role in regulating the use of land as part of the real estate development process. Cities predominantly use the traditional "Euclidian Zoning" approach. Planned unit development is a form of traditional zoning that regulates the use of a larger parcel of land in urban, suburban, and rural communities. Mixed-use zoning is used selectively in targeted urban neighborhoods to revitalize a commercial strip often through the creation of an Urban overlay zoning strategy. Transit-oriented development is a form of mixed-use zoning that regulates land use and promotes development at prime transit stations. Houston is the only major city in the United States that does not have a zoning code, but the economic success of this city makes their zoning approach worthy of review.

Policy Arguments for Land Use Regulation

Land use regulation alleviates market failures, such as negative externalities or social costs, and provides a public good.[8] Land use regulation is the role of local government, and its goal is to protect the rights and property values of neighboring property owners in ways that private negotiations between property owners will not. Government plays the role of a neutral decision maker, balancing the interest of the property owners and the region as a whole with each economic development opportunity. An established system of land use regulation matched with a comprehensive land use master plan creates a predictable business climate under which public and private sector developers know where and what type of development can happen on particular parcels of land and what the process will be to accomplish this development.

Predictability is an important business issue that incentivizes financial commitments. Traditional land use regulation improves the welfare of landowners. It illuminates the negative externalities among different uses. Like uses are of greater value when grouped together.[9] Without land use regulation, landowner's property values decline.[10] Land use regulation improves landowner's property values due to the environmental amenities preserved by land use regulations. The mandated use of greenbelts through zoning regulations has a positive impact on landowner property values.[11] The creation of parkland and other green space in a neighborhood provides an economic benefit to the area in question.

Next-stage zoning, often through mixed-use zoning, has also proved of benefit to economic development. More compact developments create regional economic development benefits. Compact developments create a concentration of customers in a consumer-oriented service economy and develop stronger commercial strips to support surrounding residential centers.[12] Compact mixed-use developments reduce energy and infrastructure requirements and pollution as public transit becomes feasible.[13] They better connect residents in walkable communities.[14]

Finally, free market advocates promote land use regulation models used by Houston. Houston has land use controls. However, Houston does not have a mandatory, traditional Euclidian zoning or a mixed-use development process as does every other major US city. Houston's impressive economic development supports the argument that the marketplace, and not the government, provides the best incentives for the segregation of uses and even produces patterns of development similar to what is produced under zoning.[15] The Houston land use regulation model permits the marketplace to determine if it is a better location for a gas station or commercial strip center on a major roadway and not a residential center. The land use controls Houston has are less burdensome than most traditional zoning codes but cover the basic land use issues to provide a level of predictability for business.

Real Estate Development Process

The first step in the real estate development process is that a potential buyer gains control of the site and completes due diligence on the site such as confirming the zoning, determining if environmental contamination exists, if the title of the land is marketable, and if the project has tax incentives.[16] Prior to final land purchase, the potential buyer needs to gain all the necessary governmental approvals such as zoning, tax incentives, and Brownfield remediation protection.

Next, a corporate entity is formed to develop, own, and operate the property to address tax issues, limit personal liability for the developer, empower the developer to control the entity, provide a method for receiving outside equity if needed, and create an easy exit outcome for the developer. A purchase contract is then signed to memorialize the land purchase and addresses due diligence, marketability of the land title, and governmental approvals. The real estate purchase contract acts as a validation of all representations and warranties made in the contract by the seller/landowner. In the age of financial crisis, developers fund 60 percent of their development costs with construction debt obtained from a commercial bank or some other financial institution.

The developer works on a project design, which is attractive to the targeted customer, both aesthetically and functionally, that can be built "on budget" and "on time" by professional architecture and construction firms. Beyond design, the financial success of a project is directly tied to three lease negotiation objectives. The project is leased at rents consistent with or better than the project's initial financial projections, and the lease-up of the project should occur within the timeframe set forth in the business plan. Finally, the project is leased on business and legal terms consistent with the expectations of institutional investors who ultimately invest either debt or equity into the project. Once the project is fully leased and cash is flowing, the developer can sell the project or retain full or partial ownership to gain from lease rents.

Projects then are operated to maximize and stabilize the project's annual positive cash flow and enhance the long-term residual value of the project by keeping the project full of paying tenants and holding down project costs. A project's sale must be timed to maximize profit by picking the optimal time and is generally the last stage of a real estate development project.

Role of Real Estate Proforma in Job Creation

The real estate proforma not only determines whether the project makes or loses money but ultimately impacts whether the public-private partnership formed is substantial enough to warrant the project moving forward past the second stage of a real estate development. The proforma is based upon both expenses and revenues. The development cost budget addresses the expenses of the project and includes all of the costs directly related to a project. Hard costs are those expenses directly incurred in connection with the construction of the building, tenant space, and other site improvements. They include the contractor, legal, engineer, appraiser, insurer, and developer and commercial realtor fees, and the cost of all labor and materials provided to the project. Financing and utility charges, impact fees, marketing, and operating costs are also included. A contingency reserve is needed to cover any unexpected costs incurred during the development process.

Revenues come from a wide variety of sources, including tenant rents, resale of property associated with the project, government incentives, parking fees, and other sources. Ultimately, the real estate proforma is used by economic development practitioner as a tool by which a public-private partnership is built. The proforma tells the economic development practitioner where the project truly needs additional government resources.

Role of Planning and Design

The quality of project design impacts the value of property and the opportunities for economic development. However, not all projects follow the best design approach. Urban design theory identified eight core perceptual qualities of high-quality urban environment, including imaginability, enclosure, human scale, transparency, complexity, coherence, legibility, and linkage.[17] An imaginable city is well formed with distinct parts recognizable to visitors.[18] Enclosure is defined as the degree to which streets and public spaces are visually defined by buildings and other vertical elements, and human scale refers to a size, texture, and articulation of physical elements that match human proportions.[19] The degree to which people can see or perceive human activity that lies beyond the edge of a public space is its transparency, and the sense of visual order is known as coherence.[20] Finally, legibility is the ease a spatial structure can be navigated and understood, and linkages are the features that promote interconnections with different places.[21]

Local government manages design, growth, and development typically through a comprehensive plan that can serve as a legally binding document that sets the overall goals, objectives, and policies to guide the local legislative body's decision making regarding the development of a region or community. A comprehensive plan serves not only a resource for public policy makers but also as a guide for private sector developers looking to make strategic investments at specific locations for specific purposes. Also, comprehensive plans are optional or mandatory, use text and maps, and identify problems and issues. Comprehensive plans involve research to flesh out the details of problems and issues, formulate broad goals of the city for the land in question, and identify implementation methods to achieve those goals for the geography in question. Finally, comprehensive plans create a system of evaluation of the goals and methods to determine success and provide for the ability to amend the plan.[22]

The "rational process" for developing a comprehensive plan operates on five general principles. The planning should be future-oriented by focusing on the use of future land and the local government decisions regarding zoning and capital infrastructure investments.[23] The planning process is continuous in that it is a living and breathing document that serves as a guide but evolves over time so as to not become obsolete under changing public and private sector conditions.[24] The planning is based upon a determination of the present and projected conditions with the area being planned and does not constitute a list of "dreamed of" major civic projects.[25] Finally, the planning must be fair and involve an open process for community and private sector participation and must be comprehensive and not just cover individual issues such as sanitary conditions but take a broader view of the future of the city.[26]

One of the most famous comprehensive plans ever completed had its hundredth birthday in 2009. Daniel Burnham developed the 1909 Chicago Plan outlining a new vision for this city. A quick visit to Chicago illustrates the success of the plan. The 1909 Chicago Plan focused on six major physical elements: improving the lakefront, developing a highway system, improving the freight and passenger railway system, acquisition of an outer park system, arranging systematic streets, and creation of a civic center of cultural institutions and government.[27] Chicago is a city maximizing its use of the lakefront, developing complex transportation systems and park development, and has a center of major civic projects from Grant Park to Millennium Park and several of the leading museums in the world.[28]

Traditional Zoning

Zoning is a key component of the basic system of land use regulation. Cities without zoning regulations (e.g., Houston) stand out as exceptions. However, unincorporated land and rural communities operate with less zoning authority. Thus, these communities have few powers to regulate land use through the zoning process. Traditional zoning divides land within a jurisdiction into districts, or zones, with varying restrictions on uses that may be established and conducted in the different zones and standards (such as size and location of buildings, yard areas, and intensity) such uses must meet. Zoning regulations provide for orderly growth, generally in furtherance of comprehensive plans; limit the interaction of incompatible uses; and protect the public health, safety, and welfare. As an example, the 1922 Standard State Zoning Enabling Act empowers a local government legislative body to

> regulate and restrict the height, number of stories, and size of buildings and other structures, the percentage of a lot that may be occupied, the size of yards, courts, and other open spaces the density of population, and the location and use of buildings, structures and land for trade, industry, residences and other purposes...The local legislative body may divide the municipality into districts of such number, shape, and area as may be best and within such districts it may regulate and restrict the erection, construction, alteration, repair or use of buildings, structures or land.[29]

Impact of Euclidian Zoning

An economic development project typically cannot happen unless the land it is to be located on is properly zoned. Figure 5.1 illustrates a traditional zoning scheme outlined in map form. However, it is first important to understand the basis of power of the local government to exercise zoning authority.

Zoning regulation is an appropriate exercise of the police power, which is a basic governmental authority to protect the public health, safety, and welfare. The constitutionality of zoning regulation, as an exercise of the police power, is established by the Supreme Court in *Euclid v. Ambler Realty Corp.*[30] As a direct result of *Euclid*, most zoning in America creates housing subdivisions characterized by auto-dependent design and segregated land uses, resulting in massive suburban development. This conventional zoning creates neighborhoods with five key components:

- Housing subdivisions
- Shopping centers, composed of single-use retail buildings, usually a single story with exclusive parking areas
- Office/business parks, also single use and served by exclusive parking areas

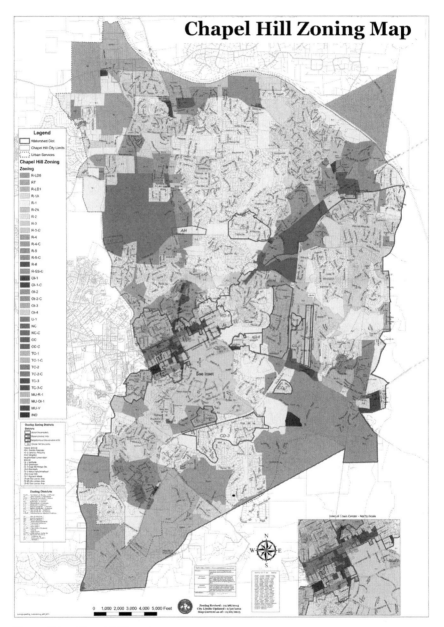

Figure 5.1   Chapel Hill zoning map.

Source: Chapel Hill, North Carolina Zoning Code.

- Civic institutions, such as churches, schools, and libraries, generally large and separated from other uses and served by exclusive parking areas
- Roadways connecting these separated land uses and designed exclusively for the use of automobiles[31]

These housing subdivisions have a hierarchical street pattern that channels local traffic onto collector roads in order to reach almost all destination points, increasing congestion and impeding nonauto access to typical daily destinations.[32] Ending "mixed use" is a major goal of the conventional American subdivision.

Traditional Zoning Process

The zoning process is an interaction with neighbors, local government staff and elected officials, and the developer, all with the hope of achieving agreement on what use is permitted on a specific piece of property. Many successful zoning applications start with an aggressive preapplication approach that begins with meeting the local government zoning staff and impacted community. Early completion of traffic and engineering studies pay big dividends later. Next, those seeking zoning changes obtain written service commitments for public sewer and water services, engineering approval of the legal description, and outline of the economic model and time constraint for the project.

The project may then be prepared to actually file a zoning application. The zoning application includes a statement of compliance to the comprehensive plan applicable to the area, detailed legal descriptions of all subareas, site plans, elevations, and construction materials palette. Project drawings illustrate how the proposed development "fits in." Also, the zoning applicants provide certification of financial capability to execute the project if approved and a vicinity map showing names of neighbors.

Notice is then provided to all persons mandated by the zoning ordinance/resolution, mailed to the tax mailing or street addresses, through publication in a newspaper of general circulation or posting a sign(s) on the property. Once the zoning application is received by the zoning official, the staff reviews for accuracy and completeness and hearing is held before a regional planning commission. A written recommendation to the jurisdictions planning commission is then created, and ultimately a vote is taken on the zoning by the city council. However, in many jurisdictions the citizens still retain the right to place a referendum on the ballot to overturn the zoning action by city council.

Dallas Zoning

Dallas (Texas) offers a typical urban zoning scheme based upon traditional Euclidian principles. Dallas offers seven zoning districts: central area, commercial service and industrial, mixed use, multiple commercial, office, residential, and retail.[33] Within Dallas' zoning districts, there is a wide range of standards established. Each district has multiple subcategories established with different setback (how far a structure must be from the property line), density, height, lot coverage, special standards, and primary use requirements.[34] As an example, the Dallas Zoning Districts establish:

- Minimum front yard of 15 feet
- 20-foot urban form setback for a building over 45 feet
- Minimum side yard of 20 feet
- Minimum rear yard of 20 feet
- Additional side and rear yard setback of 1 foot for each 2 feet of height for the portion of the structure over 45 feet
- Maximum height of 270 feet
- No maximum density requirement
- Maximum floor area ratio is 4.0
- 80 percent maximum lot coverage
- No minimum lot coverage
- Maximum 20 stories above grade, but parking garages are exempt but must comply with general height requirement
- No housing permitted
- Retail must be completely contained within the building and cannot exceed 10 percent of total floor area
- No balconies
- Off-street parking lots must be screened[35]

Dallas' zoning code offers economic developers the opportunity to predict where a specific development is permitted from a land use perspective and what the costs are associated with the project imposed from a land perspective.

Planned Unit Developments

A planned unit development (PUD) is a spin-off of traditional Euclidian zoning that identifies a specific type of development and a different regulatory process. The goal of PUD is to simplify the development process and enable a broader perspective for a particular piece of property.[36] PUDs are focused on unimproved land in suburban and rural communities and larger tracks of land in urban centers primed for redevelopment.[37] A major goal of PUDs is the preservation of some level of open space with clusters of recreational and protected natural areas.[38] From an economic development standpoint, the goal of a PUD is to provide economic development projects with an added degree of flexibility while protecting the public through the creation of high-quality developments. PUDs also improve economies of scale by increasing the density of development; however, PUDs may complicate the zoning process and create further development delays.[39] PUDs have failed legal tests if they are inconsistent with a community's overall comprehensive plan.[40]

PUDs do not guarantee successful economic development. Grand Rapids Township in Michigan illustrates one such example. It established a PUD for a life style center. Life style centers involve mixed-use developments that bring housing, retail, and office facilities all together in one location. Grand Rapids Township facilitated the development of a regional life style center through the creation of a PUD. The Grand Rapids Township permitted a range of specific retail, housing, and office establishments with specific permitted uses.[41] Eighty percent of the Grand Rapids Township is commercial and 20 percent is residential, and a minimum PUD size is 20 acres.[42] The Grand Rapids Township has not produced the mixed-use vision that was anticipated. After several fits and starts, the Village at Knapps Crossing was announced. However, the project has fallen into bankruptcy following the groundbreaking for the projects.[43] The Grand Rapids Township illustrates that PUDs cannot overcome larger economic struggles of a region. Sometimes the community vision hits hard economic reality.

Mixed-Use Zoning

Euclidian zoning succeeded and failed American economic development. The key characteristic of Euclidian zoning is separating the different types of uses in a neighborhood. Clearly, a success of this approach has been the removal of industrial factories as next-door neighbors to residential dwellings. However, Euclidian zoning creates challenges by developing dependence on cars and spurring sprawl–based development. New approaches to zoning are mixing uses to build more "up than out." Several land use development tools are used by local governments to manage growth and redefine zoning in a post–Euclidian zoning world.

New Urbanism

Traditional Euclidian zoning mandates a separation of uses. In a post–industrial society, this is proving unpopular in many urban centers searching for an economic renaissance. A new approach to land use and zoning is a mixed-use model known as New Urbanism. The New Urbanism movement promotes the creation and restoration of diverse, walkable, compact, vibrant, and mixed-use communities through land use planning and zoning. The New Urbanism development contains housing, workplaces, shops, entertainment, schools, parks, and civic facilities essential to the daily lives of the residents, all within easy walking distance. In addition, many New Urbanists support the increased use of trains and light rail, instead of more highways and roads. Many American cities look to Manhattan, the Loop in Chicago, and many other urban centers and wonder how they can transform their community into this New Urbanist vision. Table 5.1 lists the many principals that make up the New Urbanist model.

The goal of the New Urbanist is a neighborhood containing a clear center for commerce, culture, and civic activity; compact development within a five-minute walk of the center; a street network based on small, connected blocks, generally in a grid layout; narrow, versatile streets; mixed uses; and special sites for civic structures and buildings.[44] There is nothing new about this pattern. The oldest neighborhoods in most cities still illustrate this pattern unless "updates" have destroyed this approach. The New Urbanist neighborhood is limited in size with clear edges and a focused center. It mixes shops, workplaces, schools, and residences for all income groups with streets sized and detailed to equitably serve the needs of the automobile

Table 5.1 Ten principles of new urbanism

Principal	Description
Walkability	Neighborhoods where street design is pedestrian-friendly
Connectivity	A hierarchy of narrow streets laid out on an interconnected street grid network makes for a high-quality pedestrian network
Mixed use and diversity	A mix of shops, offices, apartments, and homes on–site with a diverse population
Mixed housing	A range of types, sizes, and prices in closer proximity
Quality architecture and urban design	Emphasis on beauty, aesthetics, human comfort, and creating a sense of place with a special placement of civic uses and sites within community
Transect plan	Discernible center and edge of the neighborhood with public space at center containing public art and a range of uses and densities within a 10–minute walk; transect planning creates the highest densities at the town center and progressively less density toward the edge by creating a series of specific natural habitats and/or urban lifestyle settings; transect plan integrates environmental methodology with zoning methodology for community design
Increased density	More buildings, residences, shops, and services closer together for ease of walking, to enable a more efficient use of services and resources, and to create a more convenient, enjoyable place to live
Smart transportation	A network of trains connecting cities, towns, and neighborhoods together and a pedestrian–friendly design that encourages a greater use of bicycles, rollerblades, scooters, and walking as daily transportation
Sustainability	Minimal environmental impact of development and its operations through ecofriendly technologies, respect for ecology and value of natural systems, energy efficiency through green technology, and more walking, less driving
Quality of life	All of these elements taken together add up to a high quality of life well worth living and create places that will last generations

Source: www.Newurbanism.org.

and the pedestrian. Its building size and character are regulated to spatially define streets with squares and parks distributed and designed as specialized places for social activity and recreation. Finally, the New Urbanist neighborhood has well-placed civic buildings acting as symbols of community identity and providing places for purposeful assembly.[45]

Urban Overlay District

New Urbanism also can focus on developing more commercial centers. One such example is an urban overlay district that brings businesses and residents up to the street level on commercial strips and puts the "dreaded" parking lot for the business behind the structure not in front. This would be the strip mall in reverse. While zoning is meant to apply to all areas of a community, certain areas are unique either in their environmental or their built characteristics.[46] These unique areas often require special regulations tailored to each place. The requirements of the overlay zone are in addition to the zoning requirements for the underlying district.[47] Often, the overlay zone modifies dimensional use requirements of the underlying zone, so new development can be consistent with the context of the additional standards.[48]

Within a city, an urban overlay district is a method of retaining and developing successful mixed-use developments. Nashville (Tennessee) offers an example of the successful use of an urban overlay district. Nashville's urban design overlay is a zoning tool that protects the character of a neighborhood or creates new development standards in line with New Urbanism goals.[49] Nashville's urban design overlay regulates building placement, size and height, architectural feathers, parking and loading, landscaping, and signage.[50] Nashville has 17 urban design overlays including its world-famous Music Row in downtown. Nashville's urban design overlay protects its billion-dollar music, entertainment, and tourism industry and assists develop neighborhoods all over the city.

Rather than just adjusting zoning for a street, many cities adopt zoning ordinances that permit larger mixed-use developments. Westmister (Colorado) is a 100,000-plus population city between Denver and Bolder.[51] Westmister is home to Bradburn Village, a $220,000,000, 125-acre mixed-use development.[52] Bradburn Village is planned around a pedestrian-friendly village core with shops, restaurants, offices, and residences. Bradburn Village is home to four neighborhoods ranging from near-urban to near-rural.[53] The over 800 homes, townhomes, lofts, and apartments provide a range of housing options.[54] The community has ample open space with nine community parks, schools, and is connected to parkland with 45 miles of trails.[55]

Transit-Oriented Development

One of the latest land use regulation strategies is transit-oriented development (TOD). A TOD creates communities with an average 2,000 feet walking distance to a transit stop and core commercial area. The ultimate goal is to increase density along transit corridors by locating residences, jobs, and retail destinations close to public transit facilities. TODs promote mixed-use developments within walking distance of residential areas and multimodal, interconnected transportation network through land use regulation. TOD follows urban design guidelines and encourages a more pedestrian and walkable community.

By establishing transportation corridors and concentrated urban centers, TODs encourage residents and workers to walk, ride bicycles, or utilize public transit rather than the automobile as a means of transportation. This land use strategy lowers congestion on surrounding roadways and reduces detrimental effects on air quality and balances the distribution of land uses to concentrate development around transportation nodes within developed areas, thus preserving rural, open space, agricultural, and environmental lands.[56]

Canton (Massachusetts) offers an example of a small community benefiting from a TOD. Canton, a community outside of Boston, implemented a TOD zoning scheme.[57] Canton's TOD concentrated around the transit station.[58] As a result of this zoning approach, over 200 residential units within five minutes of the train station have been built.[59] Three of these projects are adjacent to the train station, and some of these developments include street-level retail.[60] All these developments occurred on underutilized and Brownfield sites.[61]

No-Zoning Model

As zoning comes close to its hundredth birthday, a select number of communities are looking a step beyond mixed-use land use models and considering getting rid of zoning altogether. Houston is a global economic success story. Founded in the 1836, Houston moved from being a small oil town to the fourth largest city in the United States and a global energy and health-care hub. Houston is a winner in the global service economy. In fact, from 1990 to 2000, Houston had the third largest population in the country with above-average income levels and a lower cost of living.[62] Houston's economic success continued even in the face of global economic challenges that impacted all industries. How Houston finds itself on top is likely due to several factors, including its strategic location near large oil reserves in Texas connected to the Gulf of Mexico and some wise decisions by corporate leaders to develop a world-class medical and research center at Rice University.

In addition, there is a growing belief that Houston's land use policy is a major contributing factor to its economic success. Houston is also the only major city in America that lacks a traditional zoning code. Houston does have its own land use master plan. Its master plan goes back to the early 1900s and also regularly intervenes in local land use issues by assisting with land assembly and infrastructure as most cities do. Houston also makes some efforts to regulate land use without the adoption of a formal zoning code. The Houston City Code (Chapter 42) divides the city up into two zones, urban and suburban.[63] The urban zone within the Loop 610 corridor allows for higher-density developments with smaller lot sizes and narrower streets.[64] Houston also regulates minimum lot sizes, parking requirements, setbacks, street widths, block sizes, building lines, and prevailing size requirements of the surrounding neighborhood.[65] In addition, Houston has homeowners associations that use a range of deed restrictions that manage land use through private agreements.[66] Houston has over 80 "super neighborhoods" where residents, civic groups, and businesses work together to identify a land use plan and set neighborhood priorities.[67]

Big Questions

1. Why is it important to understand the real estate development process when studying economic development?

2. How does zoning impact economic development?

3. Is land use regulation essential in areas without industrial uses?

4. Does New Urbanism mean Euclidian zoning was a mistake?

5. Is Houston's the better land use approach?

Class Writing Assignment

The mayor is looking to build support for a more mixed-use zoning approach and asked you to write a 500-word op-ed piece advocating the economic benefits of a New Urbanist zoning approach. She expects you to define what New Urbanism means, how it differs from traditional zoning, and point out where it has produced economic development benefits in other cities.

Metropolis City Council Case Study Zoning Debate

Remember, LFS and the mayor proposed to develop market rate housing on city property just north of the state fairgrounds. LFS envisions a TOD called Expo Village, which incorporates an Ohio history theme linked with the existing Ohio Historical Society museum and takes advantage of the rail line that runs through the development. LFS and the mayor support a TOD ordinance that establishes strict density requirements by greatly limiting parking availability, lot sizes, setbacks, and other requirements. B&B Development and the president of city council have proposed a traditional neighborhood housing project that rejects the LFS New Urbanist approach. Instead, B&B Development proposes traditional neighborhood residential zoning with few limits on parking lot size and setbacks. Finally, several members of city council plan to propose an ordinance or amendment in support of the proposal by Housing for Everyone, which has an allocation for affordable senior and nonsenior housing that provides 800 homes for the poor of Metropolis. Housing for Everyone is open to either a New Urbanist TOD project or a traditional residential neighborhood model.

The president of city council plans to introduce an ordinance to zone the property as traditional residential. Other council members are likely to propose other ordinances or amendments to the president's ordinance. The class will divide into groups that include city council and advocates for the development and opponents of the development. The city council will conduct a debate on the matter after hearing from both sides of the issue. Negotiations may be involved among advocates and opponents, but ultimately city council must vote on the issue at hand.

Additional Readings

Charles Bohl, *New Urbanism in the City* (Washington, DC: Fannie Mae Foundation, Housing Policy Debate), 11, 4 (2000) 761–801.

E. M. Bassett, *The Masterplan with a Discussion of Community Land Planning* (New York, NY: Russell Sage Foundation, 1938).

Field Guide to the Transfer of Development Rights, National Association of Realtors, January 8, 2010, retrieved from www.nar.org.

Joel Garreau, *Edge City: Life on the New Frontier* (New York, NY: Anchor Books, 1992).

Jonathan Barnett, *Regional City: Planning for the End of Sprawl, the Regional Agenda* (Washington, DC: Island Press, 2001).

Kameshwari Pothkuucki, "Attracting Supermarkets to Inner City Neighborhoods: Economic Development outside the Box," *Economic Development Quarterly*, 19, 3 (November 2005) 232–244.

Kevin Nelson, *Essential Smart Growth Fixes for Planning, Zoning and development Codes* (Washington, DC: U.S. Environmental Protection Agency, February 2012), retrieved from www.usepa.gov.

Stephen Smith, "Urban(ism) Legends: Is Houston Really Planned?" *Market Urbanism*, December 20, 2008 retrieved from http://marketurbanism.com/2008/12/10/is-houston-really-unplanned/.

Stuart Meek and Kenneth Reardon, *Ohio Planning and Zoning Laws Handbook* (New York, NY: Banks Baldwin Publishing, 2013).

Susan Pigg, *Regionalism and Planned Based Strategies* (East Lansing, MI: Michigan State University Land Policy Institute, April 20, 2012).

Witold Rybczynski, "Suburban Despair," *Slate*, November 7, 2005.

Zhu Qian, "Without Zoning: Urban Development and Land Use Controls in Houston," *Cities*, 27, 1 (2010) 31–41.

Chapter Six

Economic Development Building Block: Eminent Domain

Chapter Goals

1. Understand the elements of eminent domain as a legal process
2. Recognize the role eminent domain played in economic development prior to the *Kelo* case
3. Comprehend what the *Kelo* case says and does not say
4. Recognize the strong reaction to *Kelo* from states across the nation
5. Distinguish between states that have been more hostile versus less hostile to the use of eminent domain for economic development projects

Eminent Domain and Economic Development

The availability of land for improvement and development is another essential building block for economic development. Government ensures land is available for development through a range of tactics, which include the use of eminent domain. Eminent domain is the power to take private property for a public purpose but to provide just compensation to the property owners. Eminent domain is a legal process used for a range of public policy reasons, including economic development. It is a long held government power guaranteed by the Fifth Amendment to the US Constitution. The US Supreme Court extended the power of eminent domain for economic development projects, but that approach was rejected by states across the nation. The Court extended the power of eminent domain for the acquisition of land for roads and highways, utility services, and housing. Public reaction to this decision was highly negative, and a number of state courts and legislatures limited *Kelo*'s application.

Lakewood (Colorado) offers an interesting case study in the use of eminent domain in the redevelopment of an aging and declining mall. Villa Italia Mall was a major regional shopping center built in the mid-1960s.[1] This 1,200,000-square-foot shopping mall at its peak generated $3,120,000 in sales tax, but by the 1990s, this "Greyfield Mall" was in total decline.[2] Lakewood, a suburb of Denver, knew something had to be done. In 1997, Lakewood voters authorized the use of urban renewal powers, and this massive 103-acre site provided the city with an opportunity to create a new town center.[3] In 1998, the city formed a public-private partnership with a private developer to redevelop the site into a modern "town center" based upon a grid-based street system, with a matrix of 22 streets scaled to the size of city blocks.[4] To assemble this site, the city was forced to use its eminent domain powers.[5]

The result is the creation of Belmar. Belmar is the new downtown for Lakewood. Belmar is $850,000,000 walkable town center containing 880,000-square-feet retail space, 250,000-square-feet office space, 5,000 public parking spaces, 800 residential units, two education institutions, public plazas, art, and green space.[6]

Eminent Domain as an Economic Development Tool

State and local governments utilize a small set of extraordinary government powers to foster infrastructure creation, housing, growth, and development. One such extraordinary power is eminent domain. State and local governments threaten to or actually use eminent domain to take private party from an individual, give them a compensation, and then award that property to another private party whose plan for use is highly regarded by the government. Local governments use eminent domain to encourage economic development. At one point, 10,000 eminent domain filings or condemnation were threatened against private parties.,[7] and eminent domain operated in 41 states for economic development purposes.[8]

Public Policy Argument for Eminent Domain's Use for Economic Development

The government uses eminent domain for economic development based upon the theory of public good. Eminent domain for economic development projects is a public purpose where the economic benefits of the taking would make the land in question available for use by all consumers.[9] Without the use of eminent domain for economic development, communities suffer from a highly inefficient use of land as the transaction cost of assembly parcels for higher and better uses exceed the actual value of the property in question.[10]

Eminent domain supports urban redevelopment projects. Urban center's smaller parcels require multiple land purchases. Eminent domain simplifies urban redevelopment by making the government and the court system the arbiter of land purchases. Eminent domain helps urban centers compete against suburban and rural communities. Rural communities with low cost, shovel-ready farm land connected to urban centers by the interstate highway system are cheap and easy to develop. Eminent domain reduces transaction costs for an economic development project and aligns eminent domain as an antisprawl tactic. Eminent domain's use for economic development purposes increases job opportunities and tax revenues in poorly performing urban centers.[11]

Eminent domain for an economic development project benefits communities by developing capital investment and job creation. A developer or company sees an opportunity for job creation at a site that can be a tremendous benefit for the community at large. Another major argument for the use of eminent domain for economic development projects is the lack of private property protections. For example, China has no private property rights. In China, land is taken for economic development projects without even the "public purpose" discussion more less the "just compensation" award hearings that take up critical months and years in an economic development project.

The argument against the use of eminent domain purely for economic development projects center around the American notion of the protection of private property as a pillar in the nation's economy and society. Advocates of this perspective argue that Jefferson, Madison, and the Founding Fathers may have never imagined that an American property owner would have his land taken by the government and given to another private person just because the government liked the new owner's planned use better. Regardless of whether policy makers side with the Founding Fathers or modern economic developers, the eminent domain process used for economic development purposes creates more emotion than most other economic development policy issues combined.

Process of Eminent Domain

Eminent domain follows a detailed legal process to comply with constitutional mandates. First, eminent domain is typically a state legal process guided by statutory and constitutional restrictions. The eminent domain process starts with a written notice to the property owner followed up by a good faith purchase price offer. The government, public utility, or other statutorily authorized party must provide the land owner with written notice of intent to acquire the property at least 30 days before filing an appropriation petition with a court.[12] The notice must be delivered personally or by certified mail and must include a written good faith offer to purchase.[13] If the parties are unable to agree on price, the appropriating entity must obtain an appraisal of the property before filing a petition and must provide a copy of the appraisal to the land owner.[14]

If the local government satisfies the notice requirements and yet is unable to obtain an agreement with the property owner, it then files a petition for appropriation. The petition must contain:

1. a verification
2. legal description of the property
3. statement that the appropriation is necessary for a public use
4. statement of purpose for the appropriation
5. statement of the interest sought to be appropriated
6. name/address of the property owner
7. statement showing that the utility has satisfied the notice requirements set forth above
8. prayer, or request, for relief[15]

The appropriation must be for a valid "public purpose."[16] A hearing on the right or necessity of an appropriation action when the property owner files an answer specifically denying either the right to make the appropriation or the necessity for the appropriation is a mandate.[17] Necessity has been variously defined. It may mean that which is indispensable or requisite, especially toward the attainment of some end. More generally, "necessity" is defined as that which is reasonably convenient or useful to the public.[18] It does not mean absolutely necessary or indispensable, but rather "reasonably necessary" to secure the end in view. [19]

In an appropriation case, the property owner is entitled to compensation for the property actually taken, as well as damages for injury to the property that remains after the taking, the residue.[20] Compensation and damages are two separate and distinct remedies. Compensation means the sum of money to pay the owner for the land actually taken, which is reflected in the fair market value of the land taken without deduction for benefits that may accrue to the remaining lands of the owner.[21]

By contrast, damage "means an allowance made for any injury that may result to the remaining lands by reason of the construction of the proposed improvement, after making all permissible allowances for special benefits, and the like, resulting thereto."[22]

The rule of valuation in a land appropriation proceeding is not what the property is worth for any particular use but what it is worth generally for any and all uses for which it might be suitable, including the most valuable uses to which it can reasonably and practically be adapted.[23] Accordingly, an expert appraiser is not required to confine his valuation testimony to the use permitted under, for example, existing zoning regulations, but is permitted to testify to the "highest and best" use that is not authorized by existing zoning regulations, even without evidence of a probable change in those regulations.[24]

All this is outlined to illustrate that eminent domain does not just happen. There is a lengthy process and much negotiations and give and take.

Lengths and Limits of Eminent Domain and E conomic Development

The US Supreme Court took its first big constitutional step in expanding the government's power beyond transferring private property into a public facility or transportation system when it established that eminent domain could be used to condemn blighted property as part of a "slum clearance" project. Eminent domain is used for a wide variety of "public purposes," ranging from public utility services to public housing to roads and infrastructure. In *Berman v. Parker*, the Supreme Court held it was a valid public purpose to use eminent domain to take blighted property and transfer its ownership to another private party due to the decaying nature of the property in question to use that property for housing.[25] Next, the Supreme Court determined it was a valid use of eminent domain to break up a land oligopoly in Hawaii in *Hawaii Housing Authority v. Midkiff*.[26]

The US Supreme Court, in *Kelo v. New London*, approved of the use of eminent domain for a nonblighted neighborhood and determined that economic development was enough of a public purpose to justify the taking of private property and transferring that property to another private land owner.[27] The US Supreme Court set off a firestorm when it decided that economic development is a valid public purpose.

In *Kelo*, the city of New London (Connecticut), once an economic success because of a nearby US navy submarine base, used eminent domain to seize the land of several property owners solely for the purpose of giving the land to a private developer to bring economic development to the site.[28] The development in question involved 1,000 jobs in the research and development field.[29] Following a long string of precedents from other public purpose areas, the US Supreme Court in this 2005 case held that economic development was in fact a valid public purpose for eminent domain and the citizens in this case could have their property taken.[30] However, the Court took the unusual step of permitting state courts to determine if this decision applied to states.[31]

Reaction to *Kelo*

Reaction to *Kelo* was swift and negative. Courts, legislatures, and even the people through state ballot issues spoke against *Kelo*. While *Kelo* was a major victory for local government's efforts to implement economic development, it has proven to be a classic case of winning the battle but losing the war. States have taken a wide-ranging approach to the use of eminent domain for economic development purposes after *Kelo*. Some states offer no legislative restrictions on the use of eminent domain, while others offer nominal or moderate legislative limitations, and many states provide major restrictions on the use of eminent domain for economic development purposes. In fact, 42 states have adopted eminent domain legislation and ballot measures in response to *Kelo*. These reactions fall into five categories: no economic development, clarifying what is a "public use," permitting its use in blighted areas, requiring greater public involvement, and addressing compensation issues.[32]

No Economic Development

The majority of states acting in response to *Kelo* prohibited the use of eminent domain for economic development purposes. This typically included prohibitions against eminent domain for purely tax revenue purposes or the transfer of someone's property to another private entity. Alabama passed legislation prohibiting the use of eminent domain for retail, commercial, residential, or apartment development, for generating tax revenue, or for the transfer of private property to another private party, but contains a blight exception.[33] California's voters approved an initiative prohibiting the use of eminent domain to acquire an owner-occupied residence to convey it to a private entity.[34] Idaho prohibits the use of eminent domain for economic development and defines economic development as the transfer of private property to another private entity for economic, tax revenue, or employment growth, or promoting the general economic health of the community.[35] Nebraska prohibits the use of eminent domain for economic development purposes, which means use by a commercial entity or to increase tax revenue, the tax base, employment, or general economic conditions.[36] In addition, Pennsylvania permits the use of eminent domain in economic development only where the private enterprise occupies an incidental area within a public project.[37]

Public Use

Many states' response to *Kelo* was to affirm what public uses would be permitted under their eminent domain laws and to list what would now not be permitted. Kentucky, Delaware, and several other states take the traditional definition of public use for eminent domain purposes, including the ownership, possession, occupation, or enjoyment of the property by a governmental entity, removal of blight, or for use by a public utility.[38] Arizona passed a statewide ballot issue that limits the use of eminent domain to public uses, which are defined to include use of the land by the general public or public agencies, public utilities; to eliminate a direct threat to public health or safety caused by the property's condition; or to acquire abandoned property, and public use does not include the public benefits of economic development.[39] New Hampshire defines public use to be not only the enjoyment of property by the public, public agencies, or public utilities, but also the removal of public health threats and private uses that occupy an incidental area within a public project.[40] Mississippi went so far to adopt a state constitutional provision to prohibit state and local government from taking private property by eminent domain, except for drainage and levee facilities, roads, bridges, ports, airports, common carriers, utilities, public nuisance, structures unfit for human habitation, or abandoned property, for a period of ten years after acquisition.[41] Finally, Maine defined permitted public uses to never include land used for agriculture, fishing, forestry, land improved with residential, commercial, or industrial buildings, or for private retail, office, commercial, industrial, or residential purposes.[42]

Blighted Property

Blight removal for the most part remains a permitted eminent domain. However, several states modified the definition of how blight is defined. The use of blight as eminent domain permits its use for economic development purposes only in targeted, mostly urban poor neighborhoods. Florida passed a highly restrictive eminent domain law that prohibits the transfer of private property through eminent domain to another private entity except for common carriers, public transportation, public utilities, public health, or where the private use is incidental to a public project.[43] However, Florida also prohibits the use of eminent domain to eliminate blight conditions or to generate additional tax revenue and requires a supermajority vote of the state legislature to permit the use of eminent domain to transfer private property to another private entity.[44]

Illinois prohibits the use of eminent domain to confer a benefit on a particular private entity but permits its use in a blighted area where the state and local government entered into a development agreement with a private entity.[45] Also, Iowa made many of the common restrictions on eminent domain's use for economic development purposes but permitted its use in blighted areas where at least 75 percent of the properties in the area are blighted and permits a buyback of the property where the original owner of property may purchase it if not put to a public use within five years.[46] New Mexico moved the other direction deciding to prohibit the use of eminent domain by cities for redevelopment projects under the Metropolitan Redevelopment Code.[47]

Public Involvement

Increased public involvement is also an approach many state policy makers took in reaction to *Kelo*. At times this public involvement appears to be a way to stop eminent domain, but it also appears to be used to create a vehicle to permit eminent domain's use for economic development projects. Connecticut requires a two-thirds vote of the legislative body of a municipality to approve the acquisition of real property through eminent domain by a development agency and prohibits the acquisition of real property through eminent domain if the primary purpose is to increase tax revenue.[48]

Georgia, like many other states, permits the use of eminent domain for the enjoyment of property by the public, public agencies, or public utilities, or for the removal of blight, but stops the use of eminent domain for economic development or tax revenue purposes and creates new local government mandates for public notice.[49] Finally, Missouri created the common restrictions on the use of eminent domain but also created an Office of Ombudsman for property rights in the Office of Public Counsel in the Department of Economic Development to assist property owners in obtaining information about eminent domain.[50]

Just Compensation

Payment reform for those losing their property through an eminent domain process is also a part of state policy makers' reaction to *Kelo*. Indiana limits the use of eminent domain to projects where the public enjoy the use of the property, public agencies, or public utilities, but prohibits its use for tax revenue or economic development purpose.[51] Indiana redefines "blighted areas" to emphasize properties that are detrimental to the public health and safety and requires payment of compensation where the property condemned is the person's primary residence at 150 percent of fair market value.[52]

Kansas takes a similar approach to prohibiting eminent domain's use for economic development, but does not apply these restrictions to a property in a redevelopment district created prior to the enactment of the law and increases the level of compensation to land owners whose property is condemned to 200 percent of the average appraised value of the property.[53] Michigan adopted a statewide ballot issue that mandates if a person's principal residence is taken for public use the amount of just compensation shall not be less than 125 percent of the property's fair market value.[54] Louisiana adopted a statewide ballot initiative that prohibits the sale or lease of property, with certain exceptions, that has been taken through eminent domain and held for less than 30 years unless the property is first offered to the original owner or his or her successor at fair market value and mandates that within a year after completion of a project any surplus property must be offered to the original owner or his or her successor at fair market value.[55] As Table 6.1 illustrates, states take different approaches to the use of eminent domain for economic development.

Table 6.1 State reaction to *Kelo*

Legislative Type	States
No legislative limitations	Arkansas, Connecticut, Hawaii, Kansas, Maryland, Massachusetts, Mississippi, Montana, Nevada, New Jersey, New York, Oklahoma, Rhode Island, South Carolina, and Virginia
Nominal legislative limitations	Alaska, California, Colorado, Delaware, Idaho, Illinois, Kentucky, Maine, Missouri, Nebraska, North Carolina, Tennessee, Texas, Vermont, West Virginia, and Wisconsin
Major legislative limitations	Alabama, Arizona, Florida, Louisiana, Michigan, Minnesota, New Hampshire, North Dakota, Ohio, Oregon, Pennsylvania, South Dakota, and Utah

Source: D. M. Carpenter and J. K. Ross, "Do Restrictions on Eminent Domain Harm Economic Development?" *Economic Development Quarterly*, 24, 4 (2010) 337–351.

Economic Development Policy Case 6.1: Ohio's New Approach to Eminent Domain

Ohio offers an example of a highly antieconomic development perspective in the eminent domain issue. It is also one of the early Supreme Court cases and legislative action in response to *Kelo*. Ohio's Supreme Court jumped into the fray by determining *Kelo* would not apply in the Buckeye state, and then the legislature for good measure made it even more difficult to use eminent domain in the state. The Ohio Supreme Court in *Norwood v. Horney* unanimously held that taking private homes for the purposes of creating an urban shopping and office center was unconstitutional. Based upon a developer-funded study, the city of Norwood declared a struggling middle-class neighborhood, once home to a major autoassembly factory, as "deteriorating" and thus triggered the use of eminent domain to address conditions of slum and blight.[56] A trial court found the neighborhood was not blighted, but agreed with the city that the neighborhood is "deteriorating."[57] The Ohio Supreme Court disagreed and held that *Kelo*'s rationale that takings for economic development are a "public use" did not apply in Ohio. They also found that courts should apply "heightened scrutiny" to uses of eminent domain, that statutes authorizing the taking of property cannot be vague, and that Norwood's definition of "deteriorating" failed that test, and an Ohio law allowing property to be taken and destroyed before an appeal is completed is unconstitutional.[58]

Not to be outdone, the Ohio general assembly got into the *Kelo* reaction with the passage of Senate Bill 7 (SB 7). SB 7 redefines Ohio's approach to eminent domain. First, SB 7 provides for a definition of blight for all purposes (other than for urban renewal tax increment financing bonds) and contains a requirement that at least 70 percent of parcels in a designated area qualify as blighted parcels for an area to be deemed a blighted area.[59] A property or area "blight" determination cannot take into account whether there is a better use for the property or area or whether the property could generate more tax revenues if put to another use.[60] Certain agricultural land may not be included in a blighted area, and no property may be appropriated based on a finding of blight made in an ordinance or resolution enacted as an emergency measure.[61]

SB 7 provides that no property may be taken by eminent domain for conveyance or lease to any private commercial enterprise unless (1) the entity, a public utility or common carrier, or a private entity that occupies a port authority transportation facility; (2) the private entity use is an incidental area within a publicly owned and occupied project; or (3) it is established by a preponderance of the evidence that the property or area is blighted.[62] The adoption of a comprehensive development plan describing the public need for the property, which must include a study documenting the public need, is required by SB 7 for a public entity to appropriate a property for a private use based on a finding that the area is blighted. The development of the plan must be publicly funded.[63]

SB 7 also creates a number of dramatic shifts in the law that favor property owners in eminent domain negotiations. SB 7 requires that a statutory form of notice at least 30 days before the filing of a petition for appropriation be sent to the property owner with a written good faith offer for the property, accompanied by an appraisal or summary of appraisal, and permits the property owner in most circumstances to repurchase the property within five years after the appropriation if the eminent domain project is abandoned before transfer of title from the governmental entity.[64]

The legislation, at the expense of the public agency, permits either party to request that the issue of the value of property be submitted to nonbinding mediation; changes the burden of proof to put more of a burden on the public entity to prove the necessity of the public purpose for the taking; and permits the property owner to appeal before the property may be taken by the public entity.[65] An appropriation by an unelected public agency, the elected officials of the public agency, or elected individual that appointed the "unelected agency" (or a majority thereof) may be vetoed.[66] If the public agency that is not elected is a state agency or instrumentality, such as a university, the governor has the "veto" authority.[67] SB 7 awards attorneys' fees and costs to property owners if the final compensation awarded is greater than 125 percent of the government's good faith offer, except for takings (other than of certain agricultural land) for public road or rail projects and for other exigencies or if the court determines in favor of the property owner as to the authority of the taking.[68] The legislation requires that property owners or tenants be compensated for their actual moving and relocation expenses, that businesses be compensated up to $10,000 for loss of goodwill, and that owners of businesses recover damages for actual economic loss resulting from an appropriation and relocation.[69.]

Ohio's reaction to *Kelo* came from both the Supreme Court and the general assembly and is not what economic development officials hoped *Kelo* would produce.

Economic Development Policy Case Study 6.2:
Tennessee Reaction to *Kelo*

Tennessee offers a counterbalance to Ohio when it comes to the state's reaction to the *Kelo* decision. In 2006, Tennessee Public Act 863 became law. The purpose of the law is to restrict the powers of local governments to condemn property for the transfer to another private party.[70] The focus of the law is to ensure a *Kelo*-like court decision could not happen in Tennessee. However, the Tennessee law did permit local government to delegate its eminent domain authority to housing authorities or development corporations.[71] Tennessee adopted the standard definition for "public use" that ensured a replay of *Kelo* would not happen in the state. Under the Tennessee statute, takings are permitted

- for "public uses" of roadways, public facilities, and transportation projects,
- common carrier or utility service,
- housing authorities or development corporations for the curing of blight in urban renewal based upon a statutory redevelopment plan,
- to an another private owner if they receive an incidental benefit from a public owner, and
- under the Tennessee Industrial Parks Act.[72]

Housing authorities' and community development agencies' use of eminent domain is long established in Tennessee. In Tennessee, land can be taken and sold to another private owner for redevelopment to achieve blight removal.[73] The private owner whose benefit is incidental to the larger public owner exception can best be thought of as a private vendor that operates within a public entity facility—a hot dog stand in an airport built through eminent domain. The definition of blight under the Tennessee law excludes all agricultural land and also excluded measuring the impact on the surrounding community.[74] The law does not set any special procedural advantages for the property owners in an eminent domain process, nor does it set payment for the property above the fair market value.

The Tennessee Industrial Park Act is a major proeconomic development exception to the eminent domain law that permits its use well outside of traditional blight exceptions. The Industrial Park Act permits cities to build industrial parks and related economic development facilities without passing a three-fourths majority referendum to approve bonds. Pledging the full faith and credit of the city requires a referendum. But with state approval, a city council may act on its own to issue bonds pledging fees, rents, tolls, and other charges connected with an industrial park.[75] The city may use eminent domain to acquire property for an industrial park but must gain a certificate of public purpose from the Tennessee Department of Economic and Community Development even if not borrowing money for the purchase. It may develop and operate an industrial park itself or turn the responsibility over to an organization, such as an industrial development corporation, and it may join with other local governments to develop and operate its industrial parks.[76] Locally managed industrial parks are all over the state of Tennessee, and their ability to use eminent domain is an economic development tool for many of these communities.

A recent battle in Nashville offers an example of how eminent domain is alive and well for economic development projects in a post-*Kelo* world. Music is big business in Nashville. A recent economic impact study indicates that the music industry in Nashville was a $6,380,000,000 business in the region creating 54,000 jobs paying an average salary of $40,000.[77]

In fact, the Nashville music business is larger than that of the states of Georgia, Austin, Seattle, and Memphis combined.[78] A pillar of the Nashville music scene is "Music Row," which serves as a center for performers and is a major tourist attraction with bars, restaurants, hotels, and convention business. Based upon a 1998 redevelopment plan, the Nashville Metropolitan Housing Authority launched eminent domain proceedings against a small story owner on music row in the hopes of supporting the development of a $70,000,000 office tower on the famed "Music Row."[79] The property owners doing battle over eminent domain had to eventually settle their claim, and a compromise was worked out that permitted these owners to keep their land and adjacent property was found for the office building.[80] Tennessee is operating in new world for eminent domain and economic development, but they found a way to make economic development happen.

Net Effect of *Kelo*

The net impact of the *Kelo* decision is the exact opposite of what the US Supreme Court intended. Instead of ratifying the use of eminent domain for economic development purposes, the public and political reaction to *Kelo* killed the use of eminent domain for economic development purposes. Grassroots opposition is strong against the decision. Many question whether the immediate reaction of public policy makers may harm the redevelopment efforts of many areas to use eminent domain not only for economic development purposes but also for housing and transportation projects. Eminent domain is a "dirty word" because of *Kelo* with the public. However, this "dirty word" is often the lynchpin to many essential public projects that serve a larger community good over the rights of one individual property owner. That is what the framers of the Constitution had in mind when they drafted the Takings Clause, but not really what the public is excited about right now. Time will tell how much the reaction to *Kelo* harms economic development and whether cooling temperatures on the topic will prevail in years to come.

Big Questions

1. Is the *Kelo* decision out of line with previous legal perspectives on eminent domain?

2. What policy decisions impact eminent domain's use for economic development?

3. Have the states overreacted to *Kelo*?

4. How can regions define themselves as being proeconomic development related to the use of eminent domain in the age of *Kelo*?

Class Writing Assignment

The mayor feels like taking a risk. The general assembly is debating additional restrictions on local governments' use of eminent domain and has asked you to develop one page of talking points advocating the state should permit eminent domain's use for economic development purposes.

Metropolis Case Study: Eminent Domain Debate

Remember, as part of the Centro mixed-use development, GD has proposed a project that could bring in a company (Project Alpha) with 2,000 highly paid employees. GD plans a $500,000,000 mixed-used project with a town center, high-rise band condos, and an urban-style office complex. Everyone on city council loves the design of Centro. However, while Centro does not face zoning issues, GD needs an additional parcel to accommodate its vision for Centro. Specifically, GD needs land currently owned by RB Slumlord. This property currently hosts a struggling apartment complex that is plagued with crime, abandoned apartments, and an overall ugly neighborhood.

Metropolis provided written notice to RB Slumlord of the plans to take his property through eminent domain. The notice was sent by certified mail and included a good faith offer to purchase. RB Slumlord was so upset that he refused to answer this letter or repeated phone calls from the Metropolis city solicitor. Metropolis moved forward by obtaining an appraisal. While the county auditor valued the property at $1,400,000, the appraiser valued the property at $1,000,000. Next, Metropolis conducted a blight study of RB Slumlord's property, which clearly indicated that 100 percent of the parcel in question was "blighted." GD actually funded the blight study to shorten the timeframe for processing the eminent domain application. Sixty days after the written notice with an offer to purchase the property for $1,000,000, Metropolis filed a petition for appropriation. RB Slumlord finally hired a counsel and decided to take the battle directly to city council. In general, city council is supportive of helping develop Centro, but eminent domain for economic development is a hot topic. Complicating the matter further is GD's plan to demolish Lincoln Elementary. This proposal has enraged the preservationists. Realizing they lack the support of a majority of the council, the preservationists approached several labor unions and developed a privately financed teaching center project to be housed in a remodeled Lincoln Elementary. All that is great, but not tearing down Lincoln Elementary will cost GD an additional $1,000,000 and completely disrupt its New Urbanist style for the project. The preservationists and labor unions are advocating a demolition moratorium on the Centro site. The city council president must decide what resolution to propose and get the votes to pass it.

The class will divide into groups that include city council and advocates for the development and opponents of the development. The city council will conduct a debate on the matter after hearing from both sides of the issue. Negotiations may be involved among city council members, advocates, and opponents, but ultimately the city council must vote on the issue at hand.

Questions for city council: As council debates proceeding with the eminent domain litigation, how do *Kelo* and *Norwood* impact the issue? Has Metropolis followed all the procedural steps for eminent domain? If not, do these statutory provisions provide another route for eminent domain?

Additional Readings

Aaron Olsen, "Eminent Domain: Its Uses and Abuses," *Expert Law Online*, July 2004.

Anthony Hargreaves, Gordon Mitchell, Aril Nerndeo, and Marcel Echenique, "Growing Cities Sustainably," *Journal of the American Planning Association*, 78, 2 (May 2012) 121–137.

Bruce Benson (ed.), *Property Right: Economic Development and Takings, Reexamined* (New York: Palgrave-Macmillan, 2012).

"Congress Works to Blunt Property Decision," *Associated Press*, June 30, 2005.

Dana Berliner, *Opening the Floodgates: Eminent Domain Abuse in the Post Kelo World* (Arlington, VA: Institute for Justice, June 2006).

Dick M. Carpenter II and John Ross, "Restriction on Eminent Domain Harm Economic Development?" *Economic Development Quarterly*, 24, 4 (November 2010) 337–351.

Eminent Domain Toolkit, International Economic Development Council, retrieved from www.iedc.org.

Monique Silverio, "The Use of Eminent Domain is a Contentious Issue for Corporate Site Selectors," *Area Development Online*, February–March 2010.

Steven Greenhut, *How Government Misuses Eminent Domain* (Santa Ana, CA: Seven Locks Press, 2004).

Thomas Merrill, *How to Reform Eminent Domain*, American Planning Association retrieved from www.planning.org/media/viewpoints.

Chapter Seven
Economic Development Building Block: Annexation

Chapter Goals

1. Understand the authority of local governments to annex property
2. Recognize the players in local annexation battles
3. Identify how annexation impacts economic development
4. Recognize how the provision of water, sewer, and other municipal services can impact the annexation battle
5. Understand the limits of annexation as an economic development tool

Annexation and Economic Development

A prime tool local governments use to prepare sites for economic development is annexation. Annexation encourages growth tied to economic development. It is a legal process by which a municipality brings land into its boundaries most often to ensure development occurs.[1] At its most basic level, annexation is a process for the adjustment of boundaries of municipal corporations by including adjacent, previously unincorporated territory within the municipality.[2] Annexation is a tool used in economic development to ensure potential areas have essential public services like in larger municipalities and Table 7.1 illustrates the importance of annexation to economic growth.

Case studies abound about how communities have fostered economic development and job creation through the use of annexation. Columbus offers just one example. It began relatively small. In 1965, the city of Columbus landed a $50,000,000 Anheuser-Busch brewery.[3] The site was in a township at the far northern boundary of the city of Columbus. However, water is an essential commodity. In Columbus, the only place to get water is from the city of Columbus itself. Thus, Columbus Mayor M. E. Sensenbrenner created a new annexation policy that gobbled up as much unincorporated or township land as possible for development. Any developer needing water and sewer service in a Central Ohio township needs to annex the property into Columbus. In addition, Columbus annexed surrounding township property to create "growth corridors" to ensure the city was not surrounded

Table 7.1 Columbus square mileage and population

Year	Approximate Square Mileage	Total Population
1950	42	375,901
1960	93	471,316
1970	146	540,025
1980	186	564,871
1990	201	632,910
2000	220	711,470
2010	217	787,073

Source: US Census Data.

Table 7.2 State methods of annexation

Method of Annexation	Description	Use
Popular determination	Annexation decisions are made by local residents through referendum or petition	20 states
Municipal determination	Municipal boundaries are expanded through the unilateral action of the local unit of government	8 states
Judicial determination	The state's judiciary decides whether or not an annexation should occur	5 states
Quasilegislative or administrative determination	An independent and nonjudicial commission decides whether or a not an annexation should occur	10 states
Legislative determination	The state legislature deliberates each annexation proposal	6 states

Source: Mary M. Edwards, "Municipal Annexation: Does State Policy Matter?" Land Use Policy, 28 (2011) 325–333.

by suburban communities. These two strategies helped Columbus gain from the sprawling development starting in the 1960s.

The city of Columbus' annexation process and other economic development strategies made this Central Ohio city a success story. While more established Ohio cities such as Cleveland, Akron, Canton, Toledo, and Youngstown suffer, Columbus is in strong fiscal health. Ohio's largest city is one of a handful of major cities with a AAA Bond rating and unemployment below the national average. To illustrate how Columbus used annexation to position itself as the leader in the region, the Columbus metropolitan statistical area is only the thirty-third largest in the United States with 1,700,000 people, but the city of Columbus is the fifteenth largest in the nation. Columbus has truly succeeded in large part due to the annexation policy built around the recruitment of the Anheuser Busch brewery in the 1960s. Table 7.2 illustrates how Columbus, Ohio has grown through annexation over the last several decades.

Columbus' growth also stands out because it occurred at a time when other Ohio cities saw a major decline in population and size. In fact, Columbus is larger than Cleveland and Cincinnati combined. The Anheuser Busch brewery is still running strong. Columbus is a success story in a challenged industrial Great Lakes region.[4] Instead of being landlocked with no outlet for suburban-style office parks, housing, and retail centers located on the outer belt like Cleveland, Cincinnati, Pittsburgh, and others, Columbus grew beyond the outer belt and prospered from that expansion. In fact, recently a major "big data" project bringing 500 jobs to Central Ohio was announced and located at a suburban-style office park located on the outer belt but within the city of Columbus.[5] Columbus uses annexation as a means for economic development.

Annexation as an Economic Development Tool

Annexation is a tool cities across America use to ensure potential areas have access to essential public services like in larger municipalities. Annexation has roots going back to the early 1800s as the most common approach to adjusting municipal boundaries.[6] From 1970 to 1979, municipalities undertook 61,000 annexations.[7] That number ballooned in the 1990s. Looking at the period from 1990 to 2005, annexations included over 1,000,000 people and about 4,600,000 acres.[8] Annexation is a local government tool to manage growth, spur economic development, coordinate land use, and consolidate cities to prevent numerous small local governments from being created.[9]

Annexation is a tool for economic growth for many cities. In fact, many older cities that were powers during the Industrial Revolution suffer because they are surrounded by other younger, more affluent suburban municipalities, leaving no room for annexation. Post–Industrial Revolution cities in the American south and west continue to grow through annexation. Major southern cities nearly doubled their average land areas through annexation in the 1960s and 1970s, but their northern counterparts saw stagnant geographic growth in the same timeframe.[10] Annexation is a tool used not only by small towns but also by major cities to capture growth and economic activity on its fringes. A heated debate exists about whether annexation is good for large cities. Annexation proponents point to the ability to grow the tax base through capturing economic growth in land often adjacent to the city. Failure to annex unincorporated territory surrounding a city could result in the growth happening in a suburban community and not in the major city.

Public Policy Arguments for Annexation

A predictable and simple annexation process enhances a community's overall economic development and job creation.[11] This long-established rationale for annexation is based upon the belief that business grows where a predictable market conditions are known. Where and how companies can locate on new municipal territory is a factor when companies are considering economic expansion. Annexation provides strong fiscal benefits for municipalities. Capturing the tax revenue created by sprawling development away from the central business district enables large cities to benefit from the post–World War II suburban development boom.

Citing proannexation examples of Kansas City and Columbus, many municipalities use annexation not just to spread geographic boundaries but to ensure growth corridors are established for a city's urban core.[12] These growth corridors capture increased population, jobs, and capital investment that would otherwise go to suburban communities but instead land in the major city in the community. Fiscal health for a city provides for additional city revenues for essential municipal services. Higher bond ratings for growing cities with strong fiscal performance permit local governments to borrow money at lower rates and provide "cheaper" money than cities without solid fiscal foundations. Annexation in Richmond (Virginia) include 23 square miles in addition to the municipal limits, which resulted in a 19 percent increase in the population of Richmond and an increase in the real property tax base of 23 percent.[13] Annexation in Richmond and other cities increased tax revenues. As cities start to expand using annexation, administrative and service efficiencies from serving a broader tax base would result in a decrease in the rate of growth in per capita spending and taxes.[14]

Opponents of annexation argue it encourages sprawl. Many critics point to Texas' aggressive annexation policy, which permits cities such as Houston to expand to its current boundary that is nearly 1300 square miles.[15] Houston's staggering growth is based not upon responding to a specific development need for city services. Houston reserves land for future growth through the state's annexation law and has even annexed another municipality. In fact, Houston's population density is far worse than Los Angeles, Chicago, and New York.[16] Houston's annexation policy creates a lack of population density and creates challenges to deliver essential city services, pay infrastructure costs, and deliver mass transit.

Opponents also argue annexation is a net fiscal loser for municipalities that overuse annexation to expand their boundaries. Many municipalities primarily annex housing developments that require city services but do not produce enough tax revenues to cover their infrastructure, public service, and public safety costs to a city. Nine city annexations in Georgia created a fiscal surplus for two cities; three cities experienced fiscal deficits; and four of the cities enjoyed at best mixed results.[17] However, there may in fact be an optimal level of annexation for a community.[18] Administrative and service inefficiencies prevail as the city uses its monopoly power over the larger land area. Capital spending and taxes actually increase over time.[19] Opponents argue that annexation simply spurs not just the geographic growth of government but also the size of spending. Communities face a case-by-case analysis to determine if annexation makes fiscal and economic sense. Older industrial-age cities landlocked into islands surrounded by more affluent suburbs are struggling in part because they cannot expand their geographic boundaries to include lower-cost real estate for development.

Annexation across the American Landscape

Annexation is a tool for municipalities across the nation, and the range of approaches vary dramatically. While municipalities may have some unique powers under their home rule authority, the process is typically a battle between different branches of local governments and potential private property owners. State laws heavily influence the actual annexation process followed. State annexation approaches can be broken down into several categories (Table 7.3).

Table 7.3 Legal restraints on annexation

Judicial review and oversight

Requirement for a vote of the people through a referendum

Requirement for a detailed public service plan

Approval required of county government officials

Creation of annexation impact reports on local governments

Review by a boundary agency body

Source: Rex L. Facer II, "Annexation Activity and State Law in the United States," *Urban Affairs Review*, 41, 5 (May 2006) 697–709, at 700.

Nearly all states generally require annexed land to be contiguous or connected physically to a city, but 14 states do make exceptions for noncontiguous property.[20] Twenty states require the annexing city to present a public service plan for the territory to be annexed, and seven states go a step further and require impact reports to be prepared that include an examination of fiscal impacts.[21] Typically, annexation is initiated through a local government ordinance, but two states, Alaska and Maine, do not permit cities to annex through local ordinance, and over half of the state laws require some form of election in the area to be annexed at some point in the process.[22]

Minnesota's independent commission determines annexations, while states such as Virginia put the annexation issue into the hands of the judiciary.[23] There is a clear trend against solely giving annexation authority to municipalities, and states are promoting more public involvement in the process. States such as Tennessee require a highly detailed service plan outlining the police and fire protection, sanitary sewer, solid waste disposal and water and electrical services, road and street construction and maintenance, recreational facilities, and zoning services of the land to be annexed.[24]

Annexation Process

As mentioned above, annexation is the primary legal mechanism for expanding municipal boundaries. Typically, the publicly stated reason for annexation is economic development, but the true rationale for most annexations is a city capturing unincorporated areas' tax revenue generated by private sector development. Almost all states in the United States have some form of annexation laws in effect. A number of legal restraints will typically be placed on annexations, and these include judicial review and oversight, requirement for a vote of the people through a referendum, requirement for a detailed public service plan, approval required of county government officials, creation of annexation impact reports on local governments, and review by a boundary agency body.[25]

In addition, many state laws have facilitators that ease the use of annexations. The facilitators promote efficient delivery of government service; protect public health, safety, and welfare; and ensure municipal control over municipal land. Facilitators include local municipal ordinances permitted to initiate annexation, property owners able to initiate annexation, expedited annexation procedures for unincorporated islands and municipally owned land outside a city's boundaries, permitting cross-county and noncontiguous annexation, using health and safety concerns as a basis for annexation, and state legislatively initiated annexation.[26]

Players in Annexation Wars

State constitutions often grant municipalities unique authority related to self-governance if the municipalities adopt a charter. Townships in many states do not have this authority. The annexation debate generally occurs when property in a township is being annexed into a municipality. Owners of property adjacent to or near a municipal corporation have a significant stake in whether their property is (or is not) annexed to the municipal corporation. The availability of low-cost municipal services is often a major driver for annexation. For example, a municipal corporation may be able to provide sewer service to support development of property that is unavailable without annexation. Regulatory requirements may also differ from one jurisdiction to another. Taxes and fees may also differ significantly. For example, an existing developed property that is able to secure adequate services from a township and/or county may resist annexation to avoid potentially higher tax obligations of an adjacent municipality. Under prior Ohio law, a key standard for determining whether annexation should occur was whether the "good of the territory sought to be annexed" would be served if annexation were to be approved, thus establishing property interests as a major focus.[27] Historically, however, annexation has been viewed more in terms of battles of "cities vs. townships" than owners choosing a particular political subdivision for their property.

Texas and Arizona as Progrowth Models for Annexation

Few states grew as much as Texas and Arizona in post–World War II America. Annexation is part of the reason how these warm-weather states built two of America's five largest cities, Houston and Phoenix.

Texas as a national leader in economic development is worthy of quick review related to their annexation policy. In Texas, a city's rights regarding property exists within its boundaries and area immediately surrounding it, known as extraterritorial jurisdiction (ETJ). Using Houston as an example, Texas' largest city has a five-mile band around the city's general-purpose boundaries that constitute its ETJ. Annexation is a key municipal power a city has within its ETJ. Texas cities such as Houston use different types of annexation: general-purpose annexation and limited-purpose annexation.[28] For general-purpose annexation, which is most commonly used, a city meets specific public notification requirements and all affected properties become part of the general-purpose boundaries.[29] This land is effectively subject to all municipal regulations, taxes, and services, and the residents have all the rights of citizenship.[30] Property considered for general-purpose annexation must be included in a municipality's annexation plan at least 3 years prior to annexation.[31] Limited-purpose annexation, authorized in 1999, may be conducted as part of a strategic partnership agreement (SPA) with a utility district.[32] It carries less stringent public notice requirements, is generally limited to commercial property only, does not apply to property taxes, but does include municipal sales tax on retail sales.[33] A SPA-annexed territory does not require a 3 year planning mandate, but does mandate which regulations and services apply to the territory.[34]

Annexation policy in Texas is clearly progrowth. In fact, annexation gained national attention when Houston annexed the upscale suburb of Kingwood and its 50,000 residents. Houston uses an aggressive annexation policy to reserve 1300 square miles of land for future growth and is currently nearly 600 square miles in size with its current population.[35] That is nearly three times the size of Columbus whose aggressive annexation policies made it an economic success story of the late twentieth and early twenty-first centuries. Houston is a twenty-first-century success story. When it comes to population growth, Houston is the fourth largest city in America and the fifth largest metro in the United States.[36] Houston is also a national leader in per capita income. Recent reports indicate that the Houston-Sugar Land-Baytown area's per capita income increased from $43,065 in 2009 to $47,612 in 2011, which constitutes nearly a 11 percent increase and a total well above the national average of just over $41,000.[37] Texas' aggressive and predictable annexation policy has positioned cities like Houston to have land available for development. Houston's unique approach to zoning and focus on the growing energy and health-care sectors fuel that growth, but the city itself prospers through the use of annexation.

Arizona offers another example of a state that enjoys economic growth. Arizona's largest city and America's fifth largest city, Phoenix, offers another model for how annexation impacts economic development. The state of Arizona's annexation law outlines a clear and predictable process for municipal annexation. The territory to be annexed must adjoin the boundary of the annexing city for at least 300 feet unless the territory in question is surrounded by the annexing city on three sides.[38] The size and the shape of the parcel must be a minimum of 200 feet in width at all points not including the rights-of-way and roadways, and each annexation must independently meet the length and width requirements.[39] However, unlike some other states, in Arizona a municipality may only annex unincorporated territory and it may not create an island of unincorporated territory.[40] As with many other states, Arizona's annexation process requires public notice provisions followed by the circulation of petitions to be signed in support for the annexation.[41] Arizona requires that fire districts be notified of the potential annexation and, following action by the annexing city council accepting the petitions and adopting the annexation ordinance, zoning of the land takes place.[42]

Phoenix offers a model for successful development of a city through annexation. In 1950, Phoenix was 17 square miles with a population of just over 100,000 and was America's ninety-ninth largest.[43] Today, Phoenix is over 500 square miles (see Figure 7.1) with over 1.4 million in population and is America's fifth largest city.

Phoenix not only grew through a population influx to the region, but the city expanded dramatically to take advantage of this population rush. Phoenix's aggressive annexation policy relies on the potential for the growth of tax revenues, but additional jobs, capital investment, and economic development are benefits as well.

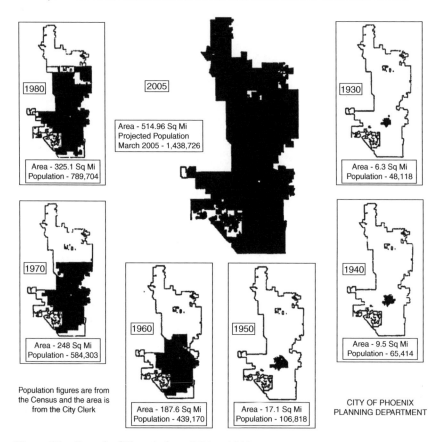

Figure 7.1   Growth of Phoenix from 1950 to 2005.

Source: Carol E. Heim, "Border Wars: Tax Revenues, Annexation, and Urban Growth in Phoenix," *International Journal of Urban and Regional Research*, 36, 4 (July 2012) 831–859.

The region benefits from economic growth through the use of annexation due to Phoenix's more relaxed zoning standards as compared to their suburban neighbors and the availability of Arizona's most scarce resource—water.[44] Arizona mandates new developments have a 100-year supply of water, and this requirement drove growth to Phoenix that could guarantee water supply due to the operation of a major municipal water system.[45]

Phoenix is an economic success story. Not only is the city enjoying skyrocketing population growth, but the median age of its residents is 31 years, significantly below the national median of 35 years.[46] This creates a large workforce pool, which made the region attractive to companies. The median household income is approximately $41,207, which is slightly above the national average.[47] Phoenix is noted for its highly diversified company base, ranging from financial services to health care to advanced energy. Annexation is part of the reason for that success.

Ohio as Model for Annexation Policy

Ohio has economic challenges. From 2000 to 2010, private nonfarm income in the Buckeye state dropped by 13 percent. While few argue a new state annexation policy was to blame, it is relevant for discussion. In the early 1990s, Ohio's annexation reform began to be introduced in the general assembly. Ultimately, SB 5 was enacted in 2001. Under the "new" Ohio's annexation statute, there are multiple annexation procedures: a "regular" (majority owner petition) annexation, a municipal petition process for property owned by the municipality, the county, or the state, and several "expedited" procedures on petition of all the owners of the property to be annexed.

The new Ohio "regular" annexation procedure is known as the majority owner procedure and is commenced by a petition signed by a majority of owners, including a map and legal description, filed with the county commissioners.[48] The petition must be accompanied by a list of all owners in and adjacent to or across the street from the proposed annexation area, and the agent must notify the municipality, township, and land owners in the area proposed for annexation of the filing of the petition and the hearing.[49] The notice must let the land owners know they can remove their signature within 21 days of date the notice was mailed, and notice must also be given to owners adjacent to and across the street from the proposed annexation area by mail and publication.[50] The municipality must adopt a service ordinance, and the county commissioners decide to approve or deny the annexation within 30 days after the hearing is concluded.[51]

The county commissioners must make specific findings of facts such as the petition satisfies the statute's technical requirements and that it was properly filed and signed by a majority of the owners of the property to be annexed.[52] Finally, the benefits to the territory proposed to be annexed and the surrounding area must outweigh the detriments to the territory proposed to be annexed and the surrounding area if the annexation petition is granted.[53] The surrounding area must include the unincorporated area within a half mile of the territory to be annexed; no street or highway will be divided or segmented so as to create a road maintenance problem; and the municipality must agree to assume road maintenance responsibility as a condition to annexation.[54] The county commissioners grant or deny the petition based on a preponderance of reliable and probative evidence on the whole record, and losers may appeal the decision to court.[55]

The Ohio "Municipal" petition process permits a city to petition for annexation of contiguous land owned by the municipality, the county, or the state.[56] The county commissioners must act on the petition within 30 days after filing, and no hearing is required.[57] If the annexation is of city-owned land, or if the land is owned by the state and the director of the Ohio Department of Administrative Services has consented in writing to the annexation, the commissioners are required to allow the annexation.[58] If the annexation is of county-owned land, the county commissioners use their discretion to grant or deny the petition.[59] The annexed territory remains a part of the township, and the land may not be excluded from the township.[60] No appeal is allowed from the grant of an annexation on the petition of a municipality, but an annexation will be void if the municipality purchases property below fair market value and sells or agrees to sell the property back to original owner.[61]

The Ohio "Expedited Type 1" annexation procedure requires an annexation petition to be signed by all of the property owners within the area to be annexed and may be accompanied by either an annexation agreement or a cooperative economic development agreement executed by the township and the municipality.[62] There is no hearing, no notice is required, and the county commissioners must approve the petition at the next regular board meeting with no appeal allowed.[63] The Ohio "Expedited Type 2" annexation procedure is permitted if all the property owners sign an annexation petition, the territory to be annexed does not exceed 500 acres, shares a common boundary with the municipality for a continuous length of at least 5 percent of the perimeter of the territory to be annexed, does not create an unincorporated area of the township that is completely surrounded by the territory to be annexed, and the municipality agrees to serve the annexed territory.[64] The township or city may object to the proposed annexation, and the county commissioners must grant or deny the petition within 30–45 days after the petition is filed.[65]

The Ohio "Expedited Type 3" annexation is only for significant economic development projects, which result in investment (private real and personal property, not including payments in lieu of taxes) of $10,000,000 or more and an annual payroll of $1,000,000 or more (excluding retail) as certified by the state director of development.[66] The petition must be signed by all of the property owners within the territory to be annexed, and the township and municipality may consent or object to the proposed annexation.[67] If both consent, the county commissioners must adopt a resolution granting the petition at their next regular session, and the county commissioners must conduct a hearing on the petition at their next regular session if an objection is filed.[68]

Ohio's new approach to annexation policy provides a more predictable framework for land use expansion in the state; however, it has shifted more powers to townships away from municipalities, and municipal annexation activity has slowed over the last decade. Proannexation cities such as Columbus are completing very few annexations under the new state annexation law.[69] Annexations that were used regularly have become rare. While some may argue this lack of annexation is a result of a depressed real estate market, it is interesting to note that the slowing of annexation happened as well after changes in state laws pushed by township advocates. Columbus still maintains strong fiscal performance but was forced to raise its income tax to meet its budget needs as revenues began to substantially decline for the first time in decades.

Limits of Municipal Powers with Annexation

Annexation is a battle between competing local governments, usually a township versus a city. A stick often used in the negotiations is the city's ability to provide water and sewer and other municipal services to a project or business in a community. Townships serve rural communities with a small population spread out over a large geographic area. A small customer base not closely clumped together generally means townships are not able to afford to offer water and sewer services like a city. A city typically has a larger number of residents more closely located together. The result is that cities offer water and sewer and other municipal services.

The existence of water, sewer, and other municipal services is what drives a project to a city over staying in a township. Courts support the use by cities of water and sewer services as leverage for a city to force annexation.[70] In fact, courts found that cities may or may not operate water and sewer services outside of the city boundaries or charge them an extra fee.[71] In addition, courts determined that cities choose not to serve residents outside of the city if those residents do not agree to be annexed into the city.[72] Few limits exist when it comes to a municipality's use of annexation other than not following the statutorily created process or complying with an existing contract.

Annexation and TIF

A public finance tool is a key enabler to growing through annexation. TIF is a central tool in funding roads, water and sewer lines, and other infrastructure that are essential for any economic development to occur. Annexing a farm field for building houses would be nothing but a plan for most developers and local governments unless a funding mechanism exists to build roads, water, sewer, and other services needed for development. In Wisconsin, TIF is responsible for as much as 119 square miles or 54 percent of all the areas annexed in the state.[73] Wisconsin illustrates that TIF and other public finance tools are an essential aspect to annexing property and creating economic and fiscal benefit for regions and cities.

Big Questions

1. Is annexation good or bad for economic development?

2. Does annexation cost local governments more than economic development produces in revenue?

3. What can states do to enhance economic development through annexation policy?

4. What lessons are learned from progrowth states such as Texas and Arizona?

5. What lessons are learned from states that have had declining growth such as Ohio related to its annexation policy?

Class Writing Assignment

A member of city council wishes to give a 3-minute speech supporting the use of annexation for economic development projects. He expects the speech to define what annexation is, how it has been used in the past, and why it is good for economic development.

Metropolis City Council Case Study: Annexation Debate

Remember, in partnership with a private sector developer, the city fathers wanted to develop a mixed-use project called Centro with a shopping center, high-rent condos, and office buildings sprinkled throughout the site. A local developer, FOM

Developer, is a friend of the mayor and has a New Urbanist vision for the project. GD is a national developer with an ability to potentially bring a major facility with 2,000 jobs right away, but its vision is broader and requires more land for development. GD's vision for the Centro site actually spills over onto land outside of control of the city. GD does not have New Urbanist projects.

The property in question includes land in the city of Metropolis, south of Fifth Avenue, west of I-71, east of North Fourth Street, and bounded on the south by Second Avenue. In addition, a parcel is needed in Franklin Township and involves seven long residential streets east of Cleveland Avenue, west of I-71, south of Fifth Avenue, and north of Second Avenue. The property in question constitutes 490 acres and shares a common boundary between Metropolis and Franklin Township for a continuous length of 25 percent of the perimeter of the territory to be annexed. This annexation will not create an unincorporated area of Franklin Township that is completely surrounded by the territory to be annexed, and Metropolis is proposing to agree to provide this area with required services such as road maintenance, water and sewer, and other services.

Most of the property in question is abandoned and crime-ridden. Ten residents are impacted and they oppose annexation. Unfortunately for the residents, they do not own the property, and the actual property owners have all signed an annexation petition prepared by GD's lawyers. The agreement and petition contain appeal waiver language in the form prescribed by state law, and proper notice has been provided to the township, the municipality, and adjacent property owners. The municipality created a service resolution setting forth the services to be provided and the approximate date by which they will be provided and agreed to require a buffer between uses if municipal zoning permits it. All of this was filed a month after the petition was filed.

GD's vision requires annexation of land from Franklin Township into the city of Metropolis or an alternative cooperative development arrangement between Franklin Township and Metropolis. The president of city council decided to move forward with a pure annexation approach and drafted and proposed an ordinance to that effect. The mayor and her supporters, in an effort to prevent passage of the council president's ordinance, argue the ordinance fails to meet the legal requirements of annexation and/or a better arrangement can be reached through cooperative development arrangement with Franklin Township.

Key points that need to be addressed by supporters and opponents of council president's resolution include:

- Why annexation is better for Metropolis?
- What type of annexation under Ohio law should be proposed?
- How the proposed annexation meets the technical requirements of Ohio law?
- If the proposed annexation resolution fails, what type of cooperative arrangement can be reached to make the agreement a reality?
- Should either annexation resolution or cooperative arrangement be opposed because GD's vision ignores the New Urbanist vision for the Metropolis Expo 2020 project?

Proponents of council president's resolution need to create a brief city council ordinance that will be the focus of debate, negotiation, and voting. Proponents, opponents, and interested parties must all prepare to testify, debate, and negotiate regarding passage of a final ordinance.

Additional Readings

A Guide for Annexation (Phoenix, AZ: League of Arizona Cities and Towns, November 2010).

Carol Hein, *Border Wars: Growth in Phoenix* (Boston, MA: University of Massachusetts Press, 2006).

D. Andrew Austin, "Politics vs Economics: Evidence from Municipal Annexations," *Journal of Urban Economics*, 45, 3 (May 1999) 501–532.

Mary M. Edwards, "Municipal Annexation: Does State Policy Matter?" *Land Use Policy*, 28, 1 (2011) 325–333.

Mary M. Edwards, "Understanding the Complexities of Annexation," *Journal of Planning Literature*, 23, 2 (November 2008) 119–135.

Mary M. Edwards and Yu Xiao, "Annexation, Local Government Spending, and the Complicating Role of Density," *Urban Affairs Review*, 45, 2 (November 2009) 147–165.

Michelle C. Kondo, "Immigrant Organizations in Pursuit of Inclusive Planning: Lessons from a Municipal Annexation Case," *Journal of Planning Education and Research*, 32, 3 (September 2012) 319–330.

Rex L. Facer, "Annexation Activity and State Law in the United States," *Urban Affairs Review*, 41, 5 (May 2006) 697–709.

Russell M. Smith and John T. Wise, "Influences on Municipal *Annexation* Methodology: An Intrastate Analysis of *Annexation* Activity in North Carolina, 2000–2010," *State and Local Government Review*, 44, 3 (December 2012) 185–195.

Zhu Qia, "Without Zoning: Urban Development and Land Use Controls in Houston," *Cities*, 27, 1 (2010) 31–41.

Chapter Eight

Economic Development Building Block: Infrastructure

Chapter Goals

1. Understand the basics of tax exempt securities use in financing economic development projects
2. Learn what defines a "public purpose" in an economic development venture
3. Understand the multiple public finance tools impacting infrastructure development
4. Become oriented to the basics of tax increment financing

Infrastructure and Economic Development

Provision of infrastructure is the most traditional public subsidy provided by local and state governments to incentivize economic development. Infrastructure is the roads, water, sewer, rail, power, and telecommunications services needed to operate any use of a property. It is an essential tool for enabling private sector economic development. Government uses its own resources to directly build the infrastructure tied to economic development projects. Local and state governments also use a range of public finance tools to provide infrastructure for economic development projects before they are announced or often after the project is promoted.

Case studies illustrate the link between infrastructure and economic development. Chicago's use of TIFs offers many examples of how one of America's largest cities revitalized its urban core. Figure 8.1 offers insight on the location and number of Chicago TIFs. TIF is an infrastructure financing tool Chicago uses to promote public and private investment. TIFs develop the infrastructure necessary to incentivize private investment by collecting the increased property tax value to fund infrastructure needs spurred by planned investment. TIF amounts are coordinated with area plans and the infrastructure needed in the proposed district.[1] Illinois permits TIFs to only be used in "blighted" areas, which are measured by a number of factors including age, obsolescence, code violations, excessive vacancies, overcrowding of facilities, lack of ventilation, light, sanitary facilities, excessive land coverage, inadequate utilities, deleterious land use or

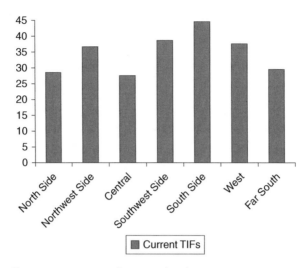

Figure 8.1   Chicago tax increment financing distribution.

layout, lack of physical maintenance, lack of community planning, or dilapidation or deterioration.[2]

Chicago is the "King" of TIFs in the United States. In 2011, the 171 TIF districts in Chicago took $454,000,000 in tax dollars to fund infrastructure projects all over the city.[3] Chicago's use of TIFs is controversial. In fact, the city announced a series of TIF reforms. Chicago increased transparency through the creation of a comprehensive online TIF database.[4] They mandated the use of an assessment report to address the number of jobs created and return on investment for the city to be posted online for every proposed private development TIF project before city council's vote on the project.[5]

TIFs in Chicago are a prime method for redeveloping this global city. Chicago is an early twenty-first-century economic success story and recovered from recent economic struggles faster than any other city in the United States.[6] While the use of TIFs is certainly not the only reason for the economic success of Chicago, this program is the city's prime economic development incentive to address higher-than-average infrastructure costs. Chicago is ranked one hundred seventy-fourth in cost of doing business nationally.[7] Chicago cites several TIF success stories such as the expansion of the Water Saver Faucet company. Water Saver Faucet is a family-owned company that manufactures brass and stainless steel faucet assemblies for use in industrial and laboratory applications.[8] Water Saver Facet utilized a $6,000,000 TIF to remain in Chicago but also to relocate a subsidiary, and the project retained the company's 200 jobs.[9]

Public Policy Arguments for Infrastructure

A range of public policy arguments exists to support the use of public subsidies to develop infrastructure for private development. First, infrastructure investment spurs productivity growth of employees and companies at a specific location. Public capital is seen as an input in the production in private firms.[10] Public infrastructure investment enhances not just individual growth of private firms but also the economic growth and vitality of a region.[11] Specific to the high-wage manufacturing industry, infrastructure investments support the expansion of manufacturing output and the employment growth in this industry.[12] Location theory supports public infrastructure investment as an essential economic development tool to reduce the cost of doing business for area businesses. Often known as the central place theory, economic success of a region is determined not just by how close the region is to major economic centers but how quickly customers and workers can be linked to those economic centers through infrastructure such as the interstate highway system, state highways, rail connections, and airports. This infrastructure investment benefits urban and suburban centers and eliminates the economic isolation of rural communities.[13]

Opponents of infrastructure investment point to the expenditure of public dollars for the economic benefit of just a few. Millions of dollars in infrastructure investment are geared toward real estate development rather than actually creating the high-wage jobs of economic development. The explosion of infrastructure tools such as TIFs creates hundreds of "big box" retail establishments at the expense of smaller, existing retail business, all paying traditionally low-wage salaries.[14]

Infrastructure as an Economic Development Tool

Infrastructure is defined as either point infrastructure or network infrastructure. Point infrastructure is the underlying core amenities in a community, such as water systems, local roads, and public buildings.[15] Network infrastructure consists of systems designed to facilitate linkages between units across space such as highways, railroads, and canals.[16] America and its state and local government infrastructure investments are not keeping up with demand:

- The average age of the 84,000 dams in the country is 52 years, and the number of high-hazard dams is 14,000, which cost $21,000,000,000 to repair.
- An estimated 240,000 water main breaks occur every year, illustrating the struggles of America's aging water infrastructure that could cost more than $1,000,000,000,000 to repair.
- An annual funding for superfund site clean-ups is estimated at $500,000,000 short of demand with 1,280 sites remaining on the National Priorities List and over 400,000 Brownfields sites in need of clean-up and redevelopment.
- An estimated 100,000 miles of levees are in all 50 states, and rehabilitation costs amount to $100,000,000,000.[17]

Public and private sector organizations focus on developing infrastructure funding for specific economic development projects. Government provides infrastructure for economic development projects either through their direct resources or through public finance tools that pay for infrastructure over a period of time.

Direct payment for the development of infrastructure uses state and local government funding from a state department of transportation and local government capital budgets. Public finance uses government guarantees and tax exempt financing to fund public infrastructure, primarily as an incentive for private sector development.

Public finance tools include the use of industrial revenue bonds (IRBs), special assessments, transportation improvement districts (TIDs), and TIFs. IRBs are local and state government financing tools that finance facilities and equipment for private sector organizations. Special assessments are a voted extra tax levied on property benefited by an improvement located in a municipality. TIFs are one of the most popular tools for local governments to finance public improvements within their districts or areas. TIF is where a local government pays for public improvements and infrastructure by capturing the future tax increments from the project's area.[18] The local government typically issues bonds to finance the project, and the bonds are paid for later through the increase in taxable property value the improved area receives.[19] TIDs are mechanisms to raise revenue for the repair of roads, highways, and bridges within a defined geographic area.[20] Each district is governed by a commission whose job is to oversee financing, construction, maintenance, and repair of highways and roads. To complete these tasks, districts must capture funding, which they do by imposing taxes, tolls, or other fees.[21]

State and Local Capital Improvement and Transportation Programming

State and local governments directly fund infrastructure through their own capital or operating budgets. Local government uses a capital improvement programming (CIP) budget to fund infrastructure improvements related to economic development. This tactic gets down to the simple use of city dollars to pay for essential infrastructure to facilitate public or private sector investment. A CIP provides public funds for acquiring, constructing, furnishing, or maintaining infrastructure such as airports, roads, water treatment plants and wastewater facilities, libraries, fire and police stations, and parks. Its purpose is to incentivize economic development by correcting deficiencies, maintaining sustainable levels of service for current capacities, and adding services or increasing service capacity to meet future demands. A CIP budget is typically created for multiple years, portioning out the percentage and dollar amount of the budget the city will spend on certain improvements (e.g., transportation, parks, utilities, and facilities).

Industrial Revenue Bonds

IRB is a public finance mechanism that promotes economic growth. Typically, IRBs are loans backed by state and local governments for private sector companies to finance facilities and equipment. State and local IRBs finance real and personal property in industry, commerce, distribution, or research for a project within that local government territory approved of by a community improvement corporation.[22] Prevailing wage applies to the project, but no cost limit applies.[23] State and local IRBs may finance projects in "blighted" areas. The revenues to finance the bonds include payments received by a municipality through leases or sale agreements and payments in lieu of taxes.[24] These bonds provide up to a 100 percent tax abatement of the increase in the value of the property, but anything higher than 75 percent requires school board approval.[25]

Special Assessments

Some states permit special assessments to be levied on property benefited by an improvement located in a municipality.[26] The process for levying a special assessment starts with the property owner filing a detailed petition, which identifies the cost for which the property owner is responsible.[27] City council then adopts a resolution regarding the necessity of the project and passes an ordinance that includes the assessment as outlined in the petition.[28] Local government offices may house the list of assessments, and the process continues until the total project costs are known.[29] Special assessment funding then can fund the development of targeted infrastructure.

Transportation Improvement Districts

TID is a mechanism to raise revenue for repair of roads, highways, and bridges within a defined geographic area.[30] Districts are governed by a commission whose job is to oversee financing, construction, maintenance, and repair of highways and roads. To complete these tasks, districts must capture funding, which they do by imposing taxes, tolls, or other fees.[31] Revenue raised from these taxes or fees is returned to the city or county's transportation improvement fund.[32] Although the US Department of Transportation has acknowledged these entities, no specific regulation or provision directly addresses them.[33] Therefore, the formation and regulation of TIDs occurs on the state and local government levels. In fact, at least two states (Ohio and Virginia) have legislation governing TIDs.

Ohio TID

In Ohio, TIDs are created by a board of county commissioners. The TID board consists of members appointed by the board of county commissioners, legislative authority of the most and second most populous municipal corporations in the district, the board of township trustees, the county engineer, and the legislative authority of any township or municipal corporation that cannot otherwise appoint a member and is within the geographic area covered by the district.[34] Each district is charged with financing, construction, maintenance, and repair of road and highway projects.[35] Ohio TIDs raise revenue for projects by levying special assessments and issuing bonds if it finds that the resulting improvement is beneficial to the general public.[36] If levying assessments, the district cannot exceed 10 percent of the assessable value of the lot or parcel of the land being assessed, and all proceeds raised by the TIDs shall be applied to road or highway projects.[37]

Southwestern Ohio is managing economic growth through the aggressive use of TIDs. This growing Ohio region's TIDs used $480,000,000 in funding to address multiple transportation projects.[38] The Warren county Ohio TID took over a $4,400,000 project for Springboro to build a new northbound ramp from Ohio State Route 73 onto I-75.[39] The Warren county Ohio TID is also funding of $25,500,000 in improvements near the Fields-Ertel Interchange off I-71.[40] This growing suburban community is connected to both the Cincinnati and Dayton regions and is bursting with population and industry. Without this TID funding, Warren county's economy would stall due to traffic congestion.

Virginia TID

In Virginia, TIDs are created by a board of county commissioners and have the power to construct and operate transportation improvements in the district.[41] They can acquire property by gift, purchase, lease, and in-kind contribution to construction costs.[42] Virginia TIDs negotiate and contract with any person with regard to any matter necessary to transportation improvements and enter into contracts.[43] They prepare an annual audit of the district's financial obligations and revenues.[44] To carry out these duties, each local governing body levies and collects an annual special improvements tax on taxable real estate zoned for commercial or industrial use (or used for such purposes).[45] The tax is levied on the assessed fair market value of the taxable real property, and all revenues received shall be paid to the commission for that particular TID.[46]

The development of Northern Virginia is an economic development success story tied to the growth of Washington, DC. However, as this region has boomed in population and industry, Northern Virginia struggled to keep up with infrastructure demands. Jammed highways and long commute times threaten the development of Northern Virginia. To address these infrastructure demands and increase the economic impact of the Dulles Airport, Northern Virginia is expanding the Washington DC metro network to connect it to Dulles. The funding for this billion-dollar project is in part coming from multiple Virginia TIDs. Phase 1 Dulles rail TID is a special tax district that operates on a levy of $0.21 per $100 assessed value on commercial and industrial zoned property or property used for commercial or industrial purposes within the district.[47] This tax levy does not apply to residential property. Phase 2 Dulles rail TID is a second special tax district that applies a tax rate of $0.20 per $100 assessed value on commercial and industrial zoned property within the district.[48]

Tax Increment Financing

TIF is the most popular tool for local governments to finance public improvements within their districts or areas. TIFs started in California in the 1950s, and today, the

District of Columbia and all of the states, other than Arizona, have adopted some form of TIF program.[49] Local government pays for public improvements and infrastructure by capturing the future tax increments from the project's area under a TIF.[50] The local government issues bonds to finance the project, and the bonds are paid for later through the increase in taxable property value the improved area receives.[51] This increase in taxable property value is the "tax increment," and it goes directly toward repaying the debt incurred by the local government on the issued bonds.[52] TIF does not require an increase in taxes or a new tax levy; thus, it is a politically favorable option. However, TIF is criticized for being a tool that pushes low-income residents out of neighborhoods or for financing questionable "public infrastructure," particularly when private businesses receive the direct benefits of the infrastructure.[53] Despite this criticism, the use of TIFs by local governments and states is increasing, and the infrastructure it is being used to finance is broadening in range.

As Figure 8.2 illustrates, TIFs must provide an assured level of tax gains to provide the funding needed for the infrastructure planned. The crux of a TIF is the actual financing mechanism itself. Once a TIF project or district is approved, the local government can start collecting certain taxes from the project area. Generally, property taxes are the type collected, but a few states allow for other taxes, like sales taxes, to be included in the collection.[54] The taxes are then placed in a special fund, which reimburses the principal and the interest of the issued bonds.[55] Once the value of the property increases, the gain in the taxable value goes to the local government to repay the debt incurred by the issued bonds. Thus, if the process works as planned, the project is self-sustaining and provides a benefit to the community without any new or increased taxes.

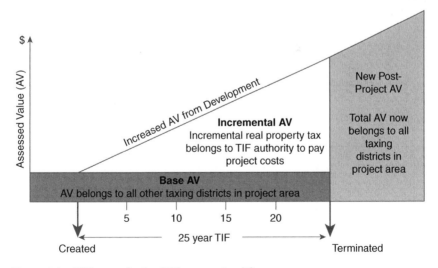

Figure 8.2 TIF assessed value (AV) over project life.
Source: National Board of Realtors.

The method of issuing bonds varies from state to state. Most jurisdictions issue bonds from the outset, in anticipation that the project will increase the property value as planned. A few jurisdictions, though, do a "pay-as-you-go" system to limit a municipality's financial risk.[56] In a non-pay-as-you-go system, if improvements or infrastructure do not improve the property value as expected, the local community will be liable for the debt incurred on its behalf.[57] The "pay-as-you-go" system makes a developer finance the project, with the local government promising to pay the developer back to the extent the tax increments from the project are collected.[58] This allows a local government to incur no debt or risk on its part and gives incentives to developers to increase the property's value as much as possible. This method of TIF, though, is used in a minority of states. Most states create debt from the outset of the projects.[59] Because of the risk, though, many states have debt limits or do not issue bonds that are backed "by the full faith and credit" of the municipality.

A TIF is enacted by ordinance or declaration of the local governing body, but only after certain procedural requirements have been met.[60] Some states do not allow TIF for projects until the local government completes a lengthy and involved process.[61] Other states have minimal "hurdles," leaving the local government discretion and flexibility in using TIF for projects. Key elements of TIF statutes are establishment of authority, needs assessment, redevelopment planning, plan adoption, project finance, monitoring, and termination.[62] TIFs are used in primarily two different ways: to finance development projects or to finance development of an entire area.[63] Typically, the municipality or a committee creates a plan outlining the district or project that will use a TIF. The TIF plan explains the infrastructure and improvements planned, purposes for the infrastructure, and improvements and how other statutory requirements will be met.[64]

Most states require the local government to show that the proposed development area is "blighted" or somehow economically depressed.[65] The definition of blight varies between states, but typically a blighted area involves structures, land, and businesses that are in such a damaged or poor state that they damage or threaten the entire municipality or county.[66] Some states allow areas that are commercially or residentially deficient to benefit from TIF projects as well.[67] A few states allow almost any TIF projects that the local government deems beneficial to the public or to economic development.[68] Besides having to work toward certain purposes, a project plan must be financially and economically sound. For a project to be worth a government's efforts and costs, the local government must ensure a tax increment will result from the plan. Also, a project plan must show that the planned infrastructure and improvements are economically feasible and cost-effective. Many states require the local government to prove that the proposed development area will not naturally regenerate itself or that private development cannot improve the area alone without the government's aid.[69] All of these additional requirements restrict a local government's freedom in funding projects, but they are necessary defenses against abuse of TIF.

States require public input or review from other interested parties before TIF legislation may be enacted.[70] A local government notifies the public and holds a public hearing about proposed TIF projects.[71] At these hearings, any individual can state reasons for or against the project. While this ensures public involvement, very rarely is public approval needed for TIF. Instead, the hearings merely serve as a way for a community to express itself. Sometimes, the relevant school board or tax authority is also given a role in the TIF approval process. School districts can make recommendations to the municipality, and a small number of states do not allow a TIF ordinance to go forward without school board or tax authority permission.[72] Because a significant amount of taxes could be taken from these entities, some states give the entities a legitimate mechanism to approve or object to the plan.[73] As previously mentioned, TIFs are being used with greater frequency and for more purposes than it was originally established.

TIF bonds are permitted to fund project costs and "public infrastructure." What constitutes a public infrastructure varies greatly from state to state. Public infrastructures is defined as improvements to land, streets, water lines, sewer facilities, buildings, bridges, highways, pedestrian walkways, storm drainage, traffic-related instruments, landscaping, schools, and parking structures.[74] More expansive jurisdictions allow for the funding of commercial, industrial, and residential structures.[75] Further, the use of eminent domain to acquire land is permitted in most TIF projects. As to project costs, they typically encompass all necessary and incidental costs of a development project such as the costs of issuing obligations, relocating displaced persons, organizational costs, and professional services fees.[76]

TIF Tax-Exempt Benefits

A major benefit of TIF is the ability of a municipality to issue tax-exempt bonds. Interest on the bond is excludable from gross income. This leads to a lower interest rate for a municipality and any involved developers. There are two types of tax-exempt bonds: governmental bonds or qualified private activity bonds.[77] Governmental bonds are used for public purposes. For a governmental bond, 90 percent or more of the proceeds from the bond have to be used for governmental purposes, and 90 percent or more of the repayment cannot come from private sources.[78] All bonds that do not fit these requirements are "private activity" bonds, which do not receive tax-exempt status, unless they are "qualified" private activity bonds.[79] Qualified private activities include the financing of airport construction, acquisition of student loans, borrowing by 501(c)(3) exempt organizations, and the removal of blight.[80] Governmental bonds are preferred over qualified private activity bonds. Qualified activity bonds are subject to many more restrictions, which decrease their advantages. These restrictions include many specific directives on where proceeds can go and where they cannot go. A volume cap is placed on qualified private activity bonds, and property transfers under those bonds are regulated as well. For these reasons, most developers and municipalities try to gain tax-exempt status by meeting the standards of governmental bonds and avoiding the standards for qualified private activity bonds.

TIF Project Oversight and Termination

Either local governments or designated committees or agencies are put in charge of each individual TIF project or district. Many times, the committees or agencies have a statutorily defined composition including residents from the project area, representatives from the relevant school board and local tax authorities.[81] The committees or agencies are given the power to regulate the entire TIF project, provide reports on the project's progress, and ensure the project is complying with the ordinance.[82] TIF districts or projects last between 20 and 30 years, but some jurisdictions have much stricter project windows. Other states put no time limitations at all on TIF legislation.[83] Local governments either explicitly place an end date in the project plan, or they issue an ordinance terminating the project once all obligations are paid or the project's improvements have all been completed.

TIFs and Urban Centers

While many state TIF programs apply to nonurban areas, some states apply TIF programs to urban areas. For example, Oregon's Urban Renewal TIF program applies only to those "blighted" areas where rehabilitation and development are "necessary to protect the public health, safety or welfare of the municipality."[84] To qualify, the municipality creates an urban renewal agency to oversee the preparation of an urban renewal plan.[85] A valid plan contains an explanation of its objectives regarding appropriate land uses and improved traffic, public transportation, public utilities, telecommunications utilities, recreational and community facilities, and other public improvements, and make provisions for accommodating any displaced persons.[86] It also contains an economic feasibility, financial analysis, and fiscal impact reports estimating the impact of the tax increment financing.[87] After a public hearing, the municipality adopts the plan by an ordinance.[88] The ordinance allows the urban renewal agency to use public funding for the acquisition, conservation, rehabilitation, redevelopment, clearance, replanning, rebuilding, and prevention of blight for public purposes. Oregon TIFs redevelop urban centers by stimulating residential construction, appropriating land uses, improving traffic, public transportation, public utilities, recreational, and community facilities.[89] The infrastructure improvements may be for residential, commercial, or industrial purposes.[90] To obtain the funds necessary to make the improvements, the agency may "borrow money and accept advances, loans, grants and any other form of financial assistance."[91] The municipality then recuperates its costs through a TIF, which dedicates the increased (ad valorem) tax revenue attributable to the increased property values from the improvement toward the cost of the improvement.[92] Oregon even allows the municipality to assess a special levy if the ad valorem tax revenues are not sufficient to pay for the debt incurred.[93]

TIFs and Schools

States have statutory models for TIFs. As cities generally bear the prime responsibility for economic development among local governments, the state statuary model makes municipalities the referee for how TIFs are structured. Municipalities take the gains in local tax dollars a development generates away from schools and other forms of local governments funded by these tax dollars. Some states "protect" schools from a total loss of tax gains through a TIF. Some TIFs are limited to 75 percent of the cost of improvements for no more than 10 years and cannot reach the full 100 percent unless the school district agrees.[94] School boards are empowered to approve, reject, or do a combination of both with regard to specific provisions of the TIF proposal.[95] Even with board approval, often 100 percent of the improvements can be exempted and the exemption can last up to 30 years.[96] School board approval for a TIF proposal that exceeds the statutory default is not necessary where the taxpayer at issue directs the service payments it would have paid if it had not received an exemption directly to the school board.[97] All service payments in lieu of taxes are then put into a separate fund that specifically is used to finance the public infrastructure improvements designated in the ordinance.[98] If an exempted project generates annual payroll for "new employees" of $1,000,000 or more, a municipality and the relevant school board must try to create a revenue-sharing agreement.[99] "New employees" are persons employed in construction on the exempted real property and persons who are first employed at the exempted property and who were not subject, prior to being employed at the site, to income taxation by the municipality within the two previous years.[100] If they do not reach an acceptable compensation agreement within six months following the passage of the TIF legislation, the municipal income tax revenues generated from the new employees are divided on a 50/50 basis between the two parties for a term of up to 30 years.[101]

TIF Explosion

The 1980s and 1990s saw the explosion of the use of TIFs to encourage development. States such as Iowa and Minnesota now have more than 2,000 TIF districts in both urban centers and Greenfield locations.[102] Thirty-six TIF districts in Chicago diverted $1,300,000,000 in tax revenues from schools and other local government agencies.[103] Greenfields are highly attractive locations for TIFs. Even a small improvement to a "cornfield" enhances the tax value of the land. This tax value enhancement provides the areas infrastructure at no cost to the government through a TIF. Minnesota TIFs since 2000 created 8,200 jobs and three-fourth of these deals were in suburban areas.[104] Many have challenged whether TIFs really enhance economic development or is merely a tool to fund private sector infrastructure that will happen anyway at the expense of the public. The use of TIFs for industrial development creates jobs and wealth for a city and a region.[105] However, TIFs used for retail-oriented developments in all likelihood merely shift more development toward larger, "big box" retailers away from smaller retail establishments and shift retail development among neighboring communities rather than create new, high-wage jobs for the region as a whole.[106] Challenged or not, TIFs are a popular tool to develop infrastructure for all types of real estate development projects.

Economic Development Case Study 8.1: Information Age Infrastructure—Broadband

Broadband is today a critical infrastructure and impacts economic development as much as roads, water, and sewer service. Broadband refers to high-speed telecommunications services providing multiple channels of data over a single communication medium, typically using some form of frequency or wave division multiplexing.[107] Broadband access allows the delivery of an entirely new breed of media services and communications-oriented applications than traditional telephone service. Broadband networks utilize a new generation of telecommunications networks built on fiber optic line and wireless networks that move telecommunications data in packets at speeds not thought possible a decade ago.

Economic development is impacted in a positive way by the availability of broadband, but it is not a complete panacea for economic success. The availability of broadband does have a major impact in retaining and recruiting companies that rely more on information technology and in areas with lower population densities.[108] Broadband expansion is associated with population growth, but the average wage and the employment rate are unaffected by broadband expansion.[109] Also, expanding broadband availability does not change the prevalence of telecommuting or other home-based work.[110]

Broadband and Rural Economic Development

Broadband has a positive impact on a rural community's economic development.[111] High-speed data networks serving rural communities reduce the effective cost of distance by linking these isolated communities to larger urban and global markets through electronic means and act as a magnet for attracting new businesses.[112] A key obstacle to developing the broadband network in rural areas is cost. Investment per subscriber in rural systems averaged $2,921 compared with $1,920 in urban locations.[113] The lack of population density and great distances from other major telecommunications facilities creates cost disparity and results in the private sector not wanting to make the upfront costs of building a broadband network.[114] The US Department of Agriculture's Broadband Loan Program positively impacts employment, annual payroll, and number of business establishments in a recipient community; however, these grants are more successful because they were given to areas closer to urban areas.[115]

Broadband Debate: Public versus Private Sector Development

Debate is on whether the public or private sector should provide broadband service. A Florida community's investment in a regional, public broadband network illustrates its impact on the economic well-being of the area. Lake County (Florida), a small county in Central Florida, has a municipal broadband network resulting in economic benefit for the region.[116] Lake County's municipal fiber network in 2001 began offering private businesses and municipal institutions access to one of Florida's most extensive, municipally owned broadband networks, with fiber optic connections to hospitals, doctor offices, private businesses, and 44 schools.[117] Lake County experienced approximately 100 percent greater growth in economic activity—a doubling —relative to comparable Florida counties since making its municipal broadband network available to businesses and municipal institutions in the county.[118] This municipal broadband network creates lower prices for area customers by aggregating their services into a larger offering that created an economic justification for the use of fiber optic lines that typically are too costly for individual users.[119] Bigger became better for this controversial model for broadband development.

Opponents of municipal broadband projects point to projects like in North Carolina that stirred public controversy. The towns of Mooresville and Davidson jointly created MI-Connections Communications Systems from the bankrupt Adelphia Communications cable system.[120] This municipal fiber network operates a telephone and cable company owned by local governments that required a start-up investment of $80,000,000 plus an additional $12,500,000 to upgrade the system a year later by these two North Carolina communities.[121] MI-Connections caused a financial drain on taxpayers due to millions of dollars in subsidies provided by Mooresville and Davidson to its operation and meeting financial shortfalls.[122] Time will tell whether this initial investment will pay off for these communities, but in tough financial times these investments clearly cause controversy.

Big Questions

1. Can economic development happen without infrastructure?

2. Who should pay for this infrastructure?

3. How can TIDs be held accountable by the public?

4. Why are TIFs so popular?

5. Who may be harmed by the use of a TIF?

Class Writing Assignment

The Metropolis Zoo is a national entertainment center. It is funded by a local tax levy that loses money every time a TIF agreement is reached. The director of the Metropolis Zoo asked you to draft a letter to the president of city council demanding a moratorium on all future TIFs unless the local governmental units impacted by the TIF are made whole. The letter should explain what a TIF is and how it impacts local governments and does not really support economic development.

Metropolis City Council Case Study Debate: TIF Ordinance

Remember, LFS and the mayor proposed to develop market rate housing on city property just north of the state fairgrounds. LFS envisions a TOD called Expo

Village, which incorporates an Ohio history theme linked with the existing Ohio Historical Society museum and takes advantage of the rail line that runs through the development. LFS and the mayor support a TOD ordinance that establishes strict density requirements by greatly limiting parking availability, lot sizes, setbacks, and other requirements. B&B Development and the president of city council have proposed a traditional neighborhood housing project that rejects the LFS New Urbanist approach. Instead, B&B Development proposes traditional neighborhood residential zoning with few limits on parking lot size and setbacks. Finally, several members of city council plan to propose an ordinance or amendment in support of the proposal by Housing for Everyone, which has an allocation for affordable senior and nonsenior housing that provide 800 homes for the poor of Metropolis. Housing for Everyone is open to either a New Urbanist TOD project or a traditional residential neighborhood model.

The president of city council introduced and passed a zoning ordinance supporting one of these developments. Now the developer approached the council with a new issue: $25,000,000 infrastructure bill. City council has three options:

1. reject the use of any public infrastructure funding in Expo Village and require the developer to provide the infrastructure funding
2. fund the infrastructure with city capital improvement dollars but this will nearly empty the capital improvement budget for the year
3. agree to provide a TIF for the development that provides the $25,000,000 in needed infrastructure but takes tax dollars away from social service agencies relying on the increased tax value of the land and potentially requires the developer to guarantee the TIF should the estimated property tax revenues not appear.

The president of council proposes a public finance ordinance from the options above. Other council members are likely to propose ordinances or amendments to the president's ordinance. The class will divide into groups that include city council, advocates for the development, and opponents of the development. The city council will conduct a debate on the matter after hearing from both sides of the issue. Negotiations may be involved among city council members and advocates and opponents, but ultimately city council must vote on the issue at hand.

Additional Readings

Charles Long, *Finance for Real Estate Development* (Washington, DC: Urban Land Institute, April 25, 2011).

Economic Development Finance Programs, Georgia Department of Community Affairs, August 2010.

Emerging Trends in Real Estate, 2012, Price Waterhouse and Coopers, Urban Land Institute, Washington, D.C.).

Greg LeRoy, "TIF, Greenfields and Sprawl: How an Incentive Created to Alleviate Slums has Come to Subsidize Upscale Malls and New Urbanist Developments," *Planning & Environmental Law*, 60, 2 (February 2008) 3–12.

James Laughlin and Vincent Digirolamo, "A Market Based Approach to Economic Development Finance," *Economic Development Quarterly*, 8, 4 (December 1994) 316–324.

Janet M. Rives and Michael T. Heaney, "Infrastructure and Local Economic Development," *Regional Science Perspectives*, 25, 1 (1995) 58–74.

Karl Seidman, *Economic Development Finance* (Thousand Oaks, CA: Sage Publications, 2004).

Lars-Hendrik Roller & Leonard Waverman, "Telecommunications Infrastructure and Economic Development: A Simultaneous Approach," *American Economic Review*, 91, 4, (September, 2001) 909–923.

Special Assessments, Research Department, Minnesota House of Representatives, September 8, 2008.

Tax Exempt Financing: A Primer, Government Finance Officers Association, retrieved from www.gfoa.org.

CHAPTER NINE

ECONOMIC DEVELOPMENT BUILDING BLOCK: WORKFORCE READINESS

Chapter Goals

1. Discuss the role of a state or region's general education policies and practices in growing a successful economy
2. Understand the critical nature of a trained workforce in successful economic growth
3. Learn how private business can partner with public and private educational institutions to provide workforce training and employment opportunities
4. Recognize what role socioeconomic factors play in an area's economic growth

Workforce Development and Economic Development

No business can succeed without the availability of a quality workforce. In the past, the availability of a reliable, high-quality workforce was a given for many companies when deciding whether to grow and where to expand. Those days are gone.

- 600,000—that is the total number of jobs in the manufacturing sector waiting for skilled workers. Manufacturing jobs are coming back to the United States, but the world's global manufacturing leader is not ready to fill all the positions.[1]
- 50 percent—that is the number of the energy industry's 5,000,000 pool of skilled workers who will retire within a decade. At the same time, a shale energy job explosion is expanding well beyond the Texas-Oklahoma-Louisiana energy triangle into North Dakota, Ohio, Pennsylvania, and West Virginia, and this boom creates thousands of energy jobs over the next decade, right when half the current workers are retiring.[2]
- 56 percent—that is the percentage of information technology executives who said their largest barrier to success is a lack of staff to implement the mission of the company.[3] Much like energy, information technology is a growing aspect of the American economy and provides the basis for global success in many US

regional markets. Regions without a strong base of skilled information technology workers simply will not be able to compete with global tech regions.

- 500,000 nurses and 125,000 doctors—that is the shortage expected by 2020 in what is the largest sector of most regional economies—health care. Health care is a major employer everywhere.[4] Regions without a skilled workforce for the health-care industry struggle to grow this sector, and many employers find it hard to retain employees who need quality health care.

The retirement of the Baby Boom generation, low performance of America's schools, a welfare system not creating workers, and a lack of alignment between industry and higher education all create widespread shortages in qualified workforce even in times of high unemployment. Regions that are successful with the retention of a high-quality workforce start with a strategy of targeting good jobs using initial upfront training and job-matching services and create support for workers such as childcare and transportation networks plus financial incentives for companies that take such an approach.[5]

Hampton-Newport News (Virginia) offers a case study for how a state's workforce development policy can transform an economy. Hampton-Newport News is an American port city. The region's population is nearly 500,000, and the opportunities in the logistics marketplace seem almost endless.[6] As Americans make fewer consumer goods, they still have a desire for the end product that is coming from overseas. That end product arrives by large container ships, lands at a major US port, and is then shipped by rail or truck to regional markets. For regions such as Hampton-Newport News, this global economic shift is a major economic development opportunity.

The availability of a high-quality workforce is an attribute all successful regions possess to win in this competitive logistics marketplace. Hampton-Newport News answered this challenge with the creation of the Peninsula Workforce Development Center based upon funding from the state of Virginia and six local municipalities.[7] Housed in Old Dominion University's Peninsula Higher Education Center, the Peninsula Workforce Development Center works with area workers to ensure they have the skills to succeed.[8] They discovered a major skill gap when local employers reported that eight out of ten new hires lacked applied math, literacy, workplace, and other technical skills needed.[9] This skill gap analysis identified eleven top occupations with job openings and linked those occupations with the jobs and potential workers.[10] The center creates alignment with the needs of industry by listening to area businesses through the Peninsula Council for Workforce Development and is linked to the local Workforce Investment Board and its one-stop center to link those looking for work with potential employers.[11]

Policy Arguments for Workforce Development

Workforce development is a core building block economic development strategy. Investments in human capital are good for workers but also a necessary condition for a region to thrive.[12] Investments in a person's ability to do more advanced levels of work produce higher wages and a better quality of life. Individuals with higher levels of education earn more and are more likely to be employed. Individuals with a bachelor's degree working full time earned on average $55,700. That amount is $21,900 more than high school graduates.[13] Those with a college degree are also more likely to be employed. For those in the age group of 20–24, the unemployment rate for high school graduates was 2.6 times as high as that for college graduates.[14]

In addition, globalism as an economic trend is forcing Americans to address workforce development. The low-skill jobs requiring little to no formal education are in other countries that now produce the apparel, consumer device, and other products. Many successful regions are based upon the availability of a knowledge workforce.[15] Building high-tech or service-based economies dependent upon college and university graduates is not the only aspect of how workforce development impacts economic development. Today's modern business needs workers who are learners and have the ability to master educational material and evolve and grow in the workplace.[16]

Investments in human capital provide both direct and indirect economic impact. Investing in human capital has internal and external productivity effect.[17] An individual's human capital increases their own productivity and that of their coworkers'. Investments in human capital increase the overall stock of knowledge of a region and lead to technology breakthroughs that trigger wage-increasing innovation, new companies, new products and services, and new applications of existing products and services.[18] These direct and indirect channels create innovation and economic growth for the workers and regions making investments in the training and education of their workforce.

Opponents of workforce development as a central economic development tactic do not attack the value of investment in human capital but question whether there is a reasonable return on the investment for individuals to truly gain on the money spent on a university degree in particular. They claim higher education costs are producing a mountain of debt young people cannot afford to repay.[19] Others claim workforce development programs train workers for jobs that may never appear and waste the time of the worker and the money of the government.

Workforce Development as an Economic Development Tool

Companies looking to grow and expand have no choice but to create a workforce strategy. Regions and states recognizing this fact position their communities by creating workforce development programs. These workforce development programs start with locating in markets with a base of workers, develop an industry cluster analysis aligned with the regional priorities, develop strong connections between regional educational institutions, encourage friendliness to immigrant workers, and fund local and state programs geared toward creating a strong workforce.

This workforce development strategy involves the company and regions and states creating a comprehensive economic development strategy. First, demographic data need to be identified defining the base of workers available for specific industries. Second, companies are more likely to find the long-term pool of workers they need by locating in a region with their industry cluster. Quality primary and secondary institutions are also an essential element in preparing today's workers. Another long-term workforce approach is the alignment of higher education, community college, and universities with industry to produce the workers needed. In addition, for many companies in the tech sector, regions and states that are friendly to immigrant workers are more likely to have a strong base of highly educated global workers available. Finally, even in "worker rich" regions, these companies need to negotiate tax incentives that include grants for workforce training. Preparation of a region's population for working in targeted industries is just one piece of developing a workforce, which is a tool to recruit industry to remain, locate, or expand operations.

Regional Workforce Pool

Companies locate in regions with a large pool of workers ready to work. The workforce in America is in a state of natural decline. The United States has a population of 308,000,000, and this is anticipated to grow to 341,000,000 by 2020.[20] The American labor force is getting older and more racially diverse with more women than ever entering the workforce. Of the total population, 164,000,000 Americans will be in the workforce by 2020, constituting 64 percent of the American population.[21] Youth labor, defined as workers in the age group of 16–24, will decline from 20,900,000 to 18,300,000, bringing a 1,600,000 reduction.[22] Those workers in the age group of 25–55 years constitute 102,000,000, nearly 67 percent of the American workforce.[23] This group will decline as well by 2020.

In short, the American workforce is losing the "Baby Boom" generation to retirement or death while there is a distinctly smaller generation moving into the workforce. As demography is a driving force in the American economy, the nation as a whole faces a workforce shortage in the aggregate. Thus, regions and states developing a qualified pool of workers are well positioned for economic growth.

The nation as a whole is struggling to grow its workforce, but not all regions and states are born alike. There are clear winners and losers when it comes to population and workforce growth. Major states such as Texas, California, and Florida still have the largest population growth in the aggregate, but Georgia and Arizona round out the top five in population growth from 2000 to 2009.[24] In the Information Age, many service and high-tech companies are not just interested in which states have a large pool of potential workers, but they are searching for highly educated workers. These companies focus growth on states with higher-than-average attainment of college degrees among their population. Roughly 27 percent of Americans have a college degree, while Canada has a degree attainment rating of 55 percent. However, again not all states are created equal and several states are standouts when it comes to attracting college educated workers. States such as Massachusetts, Maryland, Colorado, Connecticut, and New Jersey top the list of states for college graduates.[25]

The raw number of workers is not the only consideration for the growth of a company. Traditional issues of cost of doing business matter to all companies; thus, the cost of labor matters in workforce development.

Not all regions are born alike when it comes to wage rates (Figure 9.1). The south's lower wage rates in part offer evidence of how they have successfully gained major global manufacturing projects that once were the domain of the industrial

Figure 9.1 Cost of doing business and workforce.
Source: US Department of Labor.

midwest. The high wage rates of the west and northeast also illustrate why many manufacturers abandoned these regions for global markets or the southern part of the United States. Employees are the largest expense of a business, and regions offering a lower average wage rate are on the top of the list when it comes to competing for corporate site location projects.

Industry Cluster's Workforce Impact

A large pool of workers willing to work for a competitive wage is not the only way to attract companies to a region or state. Companies are attracted to a region that is home to a large pool of competitors or like companies. Industry clusters are a central economic development strategy with a workforce component. An industry cluster has a geographic boundary of concentrated similar, related, or complementary businesses and active channels for communications and transactions between those businesses.[26] They also share infrastructure such as transportation, labor markets, services, and common strategic threats and opportunities.[27]

Industry clusters are firms with significant horizontal and/or vertical linkages, or firms with similar resource and/or labor needs. Firms in an industry cluster interact through purchase-sale relationships, interfirm collaboration in product development, marketing or research, or a shared reliance on specialized services and labor markets.[28] The targeting of economic development programs at specific industry clusters provides several advantages. It illustrates which industries are succeeding in a region. Cluster analysis provides scientific analysis behind policy decisions to pick "winners" and "losers" through economic development incentives. The multiplier effect connected with attracting new firms to a cluster is greater than from non-cluster companies. Also, members of a industry cluster have stronger employment growth over time than noncluster firms, and industry clusters have greater potential for new firm start-ups than groupings of unrelated companies.[29]

One of the largest benefits of a company locating near like or similar companies is the availability of a high-quality workforce. Competing companies know they can regularly recruit workers from like businesses and work in common with like companies to develop workers they all need. Much like how the natural resources and minerals of a region are the reason to locate a steel factory in a specific geographic region, people are now natural resource a region offers that provides an attraction for businesses to locate in a region.

Occupational Marketing Campaign

Through the use of industry cluster analysis, communities are able to launch occupational marketing campaigns that use their strong base of workers in targeted industries as a retention and recruitment tool. Occupational marketing campaigns identify existing industry strengths through review of company and regional demographic information, define existing occupations in the region, connect regional industries with common workforce needs, and target marketing strategies to connected industries around a workforce message.

As an example, a region with a large number of college-educated and experienced engineers creates an opportunity for retention and recruitment of companies in need of that skilled workforce. Southern California used this approach to recruit a new generation of companies looking for skilled engineers that were available due to the downsizing in the defense industry in this region.

Companies do not have to be in the same industry to benefit from a common workforce base in a region. Lander county (Nevada) is a small community with a population of just under 6,000 and major employers in the gold mining industry.[30] This dominance of a single industry creates challenges for Lander county as the ups and downs of this industry create employment challenges. Lander county's response to this economic development challenge is to understand the skills of the mining industry's workforce and identify other industries that may need workers with similar skills.[31] Using federal labor data, Lander county determined that the top gold mining occupations were operating engineers, mobile heavy-equipment operators, continuing mining machine operators, and truck drivers.[32] Occupation skills in other industries were examined to see who matched up with the top gold-mining occupation skills. It was determined that the two industrial sectors employing the next largest pool of operating engineers and other construction equipment operators are the nonmetallic mineral mining and the sand, gravel, clay, ceramic, and refractory minerals mining and quarrying sector.[33] Even small communities such as Lander county use occupation data to determine which industry cluster they should prioritize for economic development marketing purposes. Once they know the occupations they possess, economic development leaders prioritize strategies targeting industries in which they are able to promise a good pool of skilled workers in that industry. Lander county is part of a national trend toward economic development strategies targeting occupations rather than just industries alone.

Advancement Support

All regions have a workforce pool. The more challenging question is do they have a pool of qualified workers for the industry in need of employees. All regions have a percentage of their population unemployed and undereducated. Those students dropping out of high school have few low-skill jobs to go to that pay a living wage. This portion of the workforce is in need of advancement support to move from low-skill, low-wage jobs into high-skill, high-wage jobs. Leaving welfare is a process, not an event. Typically, this process does not happen overnight and does not occur with a single job move.[34] Successful welfare-to-work initiatives offer reemployment services for jobseekers. Not every American needs a college degree. Prior to the Information Age, Americans could simply graduate from a quality high school and get a job in a factory. That is not the case anymore even for most manufacturing jobs.

Efforts to move workers up the career ladder in traditional ways through company advancement are being hampered by a range of factors, including the growing emphasis on skill acquisition for labor market advancement, lack of unions in the workplace, and the low literacy and basic math skills of most low-wage workers.[35] There is a struggle to connect social workers operating the national welfare system and business partners lacking the patience or motivation to solve potential workers' social challenges.

The federal government offers a wide range of training programs to address these challenges. The Departments of Labor, Education, and Health and Human Services largely administer these programs. In fiscal year 2009, nine federal agencies spent approximately $18,000,000,000 to administer 47 programs—an increase of three programs and roughly $5,000,000,000 since 2003 based primarily upon federal stimulus program.[36] Congress created the Workforce Investment Act (WIA) in 1998.[37] WIA centers operate in all states and require that numerous programs provide their services through the centers.[38] WIA imposes no income eligibility requirements for adult applicants receiving job search assistance and employment fcounseling and assessment.[39] One-stop centers are a place to look for a job, receive career counseling, and gain access to a range of vocational education programs.[40]

While WIA consolidated prior workforce programs through the Jobs Training Partnership Act youth programs and strengthened the service delivery of key workforce development programs, most employment and training programs are separately funded and are operated by multiple agencies.[41] WIA also provides "supportive services," such as transportation, childcare, dependent care, housing, and needs-related payments under certain circumstances to allow an individual to participate in the program, as well as rapid response services at the employment site for employers and workers who are expected to lose jobs as a result of company closings and mass layoffs.[42] International trade programs may provide services to workers whose layoff was created or affected by international trade, and states are responsible for program management and operations including enrollment, service delivery, and certification of training providers under WIA.[43]

Table 9.1 Targeted industries for high-growth job training

Advanced manufacturing	Geospatial technology
Aerospace	Health care
Automotive	Hospitality
Biotechnology	Information technology
Construction	Retail
Energy	Transportation
Financial services	

Source: US Department of Labor.

Federal employment and training programs are criticized for overlapping with each other.[44] Stronger requirements for WIA to focus training dollars only on occupations in areas of demand help, but workforce intermediaries are needed to create this critical link between the unemployed and underqualified potential worker and a good-quality job.[45] Federal administrative agency officials acknowledge that greater administrative efficiencies could be achieved in delivering these services, but claim the fact that the number of clients any one-stop center can serve and its proximity to clients, particularly in rural areas, warrants multiple entities provide the same services.[46] Federal government training efforts struggle in the minds of many employers because they are not company-focused but instead center on the welfare recipient. "Employer-driven" welfare systems more strongly engage employers in the process to identify the skills needed in the workplace and among key industry groups and then require those on welfare to gain the training. The welfare recipient must be ready for work, and the employer must be engaged in the process to bring that special worker into the company.[47]

The federal government is also trying to help identify which industries workers should focus. The high-growth job training initiative is an effort to prepare workers to take advantage of job opportunities in high-demand markets.[48] Core targeted industries have been prioritized (Table 9.1).

Workforce Intermediaries

Workforce intermediaries create qualified workers for a region and serve disadvantaged populations. Workforce intermediaries prepare job seekers for labor market entry through targeted training programs but also establish close connections with regional employers to determine workforce skill needs and demands. Community colleges are leading workforce intermediaries. Community colleges serve a wide array of labor needs, have access to a diverse population, and have a track record of listening to and working well with businesses to create flexible training programs to fit the needs of area companies.[49]

Community colleges take a "dual customer" approach.[50] They manage the relationship between specific regional employers and job seekers to create employment opportunities for a workforce that lacks the basic skills. In addition, these workforce intermediaries actually shape the demand for particular workforce skills by creating a pool of qualified workers prior to a company even locating in a region or training workers for an existing regional industry.[51] Several successful examples of workforce intermediary projects through regional community colleges illustrate the strength of this approach as an economic development tool.

BioWork North Carolina

RTP is a global model for technology-based economic development. However, the Raleigh-Durham region of North Carolina's economic success is based upon more than the pool of highly educated researchers at Duke University, University of North Carolina, and North Carolina State University. The RTP region has transformed itself from a sleepy state capital into a leading pharmaceutical and bioprocessing manufacturer. It may seem like a long time ago, but North Carolina needed to undergo an economic transformation. Its old-line industries of tobacco processing, textiles, and furniture lost 200,000 jobs since the 1990s.[52] North Carolina's large pool of low-skilled workers was looking for jobs after the closure of their manufacturing facilities due to global competition.

North Carolina's answer to this global competition is drugs. Not the kind that leads to a life of crime, but the manufacture of pharmaceutical and bio-products. North Carolina starts with a large research and development base in the pharmaceutical and bioindustry with three national research universities in the RTP. They next recruited for this industry high-school graduates, not just professors.

BioWork North Carolina is the prime method used to lure biocompanies to the RTP. BioWork is a 128-hour certificate program training workers for entry-level jobs in the pharmaceutical and bioprocessing manufacturing (PBM) industry.[53] Applicants must have a high-school degree and is coordinated by 13 out of North Carolina's 55 community colleges training 1,000 applicants annually.[54] The PBM industry designed the program curriculum with community college faculty to ensure complete alignment with industry workplace needs. This program is not just about classroom learning but also vocational education based upon a strong working relationship with the 40 PBMs in the region. BioWork even negotiates employment opportunities for their students to create a strong job placement link.[55] This job placement link is both an asset for the students and the employers. Students enrolled in BioWork are more likely to secure jobs in the PBM sector. [56]

BioWork pays big dividends. Biotechnology is now a $64,000,000,000 business in North Carolina. The 250,000 jobs constitute a global economic driver for the RTP and all of North Carolina.[57] Even during struggling national economic times, bioscience and biotechnology industry in North Carolina grew by more than 200 additional individual businesses from 2008 to 2010 for a total of 1,339.[58] The growth rate of North Carolina's biotechnology sector continues to exceed that for the nation and all other industries in this booming state. The best economic development news of the bioindustry in North Carolina is the wage rates. Average earnings for the bio-sector workers in North Carolina reached $74,829 and are $35,000 greater than the average earnings for North Carolina private sector workers.[59] The bioresearch and development efforts in North Carolina are a part of the attraction for biocompanies to the RTP, but biomanufacturers are also attracted by the large pool of qualified factory workers.

Immigrant Worker Pool

Immigrants have a positive impact on economic development. While the topic of illegal immigration is highly controversial, the role of immigrants in the American economy is and has been substantial since the founding of the republic. In the 1990s alone, skilled immigrants boosted GDP by between 1.4 percent and 2.4 percent.[60] The immigrant workforce consists of both high- and low-skilled workers and are more likely to be employed compared to nonimmigrants. Since 1980, the share of working-age immigrants with a bachelor's degree rose from 19 percent to 30 percent.[61] These high-skilled immigrants locate throughout the United States. Forty-four of the America's 100 largest metropolitan areas are destinations of high-skilled immigrants.[62] Immigrants with advanced degrees boost employment for US natives, and temporary foreign workers, both skilled and less skilled, boost US employment.[63] Little evidence exists that foreign-born workers, taken in the aggregate, hurt US employment. Highly educated immigrants pay far more in taxes than they receive in benefits.[64]

A rising demand exists for skilled workers in the United States. Matched with an aging workforce, immigrants are an increasingly important source of labor. The share of the immigrant workforce more than tripled, from nearly 5 percent in 1970 to over 16 percent in 2010.[65] The percentage goes to 25 percent if the children of immigrants are included. The growth in the US labor force over the next 40 years will come from immigrants and their children.[66] A growing US economy needs this base of immigrant workers. Increasing the number of immigrants into the United States for economic development purposes would grow the economy. Giving priority to foreign workers who earn advanced degrees from US universities, especially those who work in STEM fields, adds substantial economic benefits.[67] The United States making available more temporary visas for both skilled and less-skilled workers drives additional growth.[68]

Some communities get the need for skilled, immigrant workers. Once-mighty industrial cities that benefited from immigrant labor are recruiting a new generation of immigrants to their shores to lead an economic revival. Baltimore is one such example. Baltimore's mayor plans to recruit 10,000 immigrants to the city to address workforce issues.[69] Dayton and Cleveland are undertaking similar immigrant recruitment programs to address staggering population losses.[70] Dayton is a struggling midwest industrial city hard-hit by the loss of many traditional manufacturing facilities. Its population dipped to its lowest level—142,000—since 1920.[71] Dayton launched a "Welcome Dayton Plan" to bring new workers and entrepreneurs to this southwest Ohio city. The Welcome Dayton Plan focuses on four key areas: business and economic development, government and justice system, social and health services, and community, culture, arts, and education.[72] The goal of the Welcome Dayton Plan is to implement policies that help newly arrived immigrants get settled, reduce barriers for immigrants to create companies, participate in government and community organizations, reduce their risk of being exploited by employers, and ease access to social services. Dayton is working on developing an international marketplace, fostering immigrant business growth linked to Wright Patterson Air Force base, facilitate an immigrant entrepreneur ambassador program, and create an inclusive community-wide campaign around immigrant entrepreneurship that facilitates start-ups to promote immigrant business development.[73] From a local government and social service standpoint, Dayton is working to improve language interpreter capabilities, offer incentives to encourage government employees to learn a foreign language, implement a diversity hiring plan aimed at hiring immigrants, push law enforcement policies that are "immigrant friendly" that center on stopping violent crime, and training officers in cross-cultural competencies.[74] Dayton is also getting immigrants more involved in community groups through the promotion of citizenship classes and the creation of an immigrant advisory group for City Hall.[75]

Dayton is not alone. Global Michigan is a project targeting international students and skilled immigrants to come to Michigan.[76] Iowa's effort at immigrant recruitment pre-dates both Michigan and Dayton, launched in response to the family farm crisis of the 1980s and focused on recruiting immigrants from Bosnia, Sudan, and Mexico who were the source of Iowa's net growth for many years.[77]

Not all state and regions see immigrants as an asset. States such as Arizona, South Carolina, Georgia, and Alabama adopted aggressive laws to keep illegal immigrants out of their states. While some leaders insist those laws have little influence if any on their economic development efforts with international companies, others acknowledge the negative impact.

Alabama offers an example of a state making major economic development advances with the recruitment of global auto and aerospace companies, but taking a step backward with the passage of immigration reform legislation. Alabama enacted aggressive enforcing immigration laws to stem illegal immigration. Alabama's version of immigration reform halts public benefits to illegal immigrants and increases safety.[78] Alabama's immigration reform law prohibits any employer from employing undocumented immigrants and requires employers and state government to use the E-Verify program in order to verify an employee's eligibility.[79] It also creates criminal sanctions for employers failing to follow this law and requires law enforcement to make a "reasonable attempt" to determine the immigration status of any person when reasonable suspicion exists that the person is an undocumented immigrant.[80] Finally, the law creates criminal penalties for concealing or harboring an undocumented immigrant.[81]

While the goal of the Alabama law is to address illegal immigrants, the law's annual economic and fiscal impact of going after the 40,000 to 80,000 illegal immigrants who earn between $15,000 and $30,000 a year will cost the state up to $5,800,000,000 in earnings, $10,800,000,000 in economic output, $264,000,000 in state income and sales tax, and $93,100,000 in local sales tax.[82] The Alabama law is anticipated to cost the state at least 70,000 jobs.[83]

Workforce Incentives

Many regions and states and their companies access state and federal government incentives and grant programs to address workforce development issues. A wide array of federal government programs geared toward larger institutions and federal tax credits is available to companies that hire workers in a designated class. State workforce programs are grants or tax incentives geared toward individual companies making a commitment to retain or create jobs as part of a larger tax incentive deal.

The federal government offers a number of grant programs and tax credits for workforce development purposes. The Make it in America Challenge program provides competitive grants to encourage reshoring of productive activity by US firms and funds a targeted number of workforce development projects.[84] In addition, the Work Opportunity Tax Credit is a federal tax credit ranging from $1,200 to $9,600 available to employers for hiring certain veterans, welfare recipients, residents in targeted neighborhoods, disabled workers, ex-felons, summer youth, and vocational rehab program graduates who have consistently faced significant barriers to employment.[85] Federal agencies have also made contributions to workforce development programs geared toward health care and education. The federal government recently awarded 39 grants totaling over $157,000,000 to deliver training in a range of health-care fields and $14,700,000 in health-care–focused grants to develop and launch the Healthcare Virtual Career Platform capacity-building grants.[86]

The Trade Adjustment Assistance Community College and Career Training initiative promotes skill development and employment opportunities in fields such as advanced manufacturing, transportation and health care, and science, technology, engineering, and math careers through partnerships between training providers and local employers.[87] Till now, 297 schools received grants, and educational institutions use these funds to create training programs that meet industry needs, invest in staff and educational resources, and provide access to free digital learning materials.[88] Each grantee is required to collect student outcome data annually and conduct final evaluations at the end of the grant period to build knowledge about which strategies are most effective in placing graduates in jobs.[89]

The community-based job training grants support workforce training for high-growth/high-demand industries through community and technical colleges and an array of allied health-care professions. These projects expand the pipeline of youth entering the health-care profession, identify alternative labor pools, develop alternative training strategies for educating and training health-care professionals, and enhance the capacity of educational institutions through increased numbers of qualified faculty and new models for clinical training.[90] It also funds strategy development to help current health-care workers move into higher-level positions in shortage areas and those workers in declining industries to build on existing skills for health-care professions.[91] Successful applicants focus on the skill and competency needs of high-growth/high-demand industries that are locally defined in a regional economy where strategic partnerships are formed around industry-driven capacity-building and training efforts that leverage resources for projects that can be successfully replicated.[92]

State governments are also very active with workforce incentive programs. Again, many are tied to some form of economic performance and are only paid if the "jobs" are created. State programs are targeted to prime industry targets for individual states that pay high wages in successful industry clusters. States offer "employer-driven" programs that either direct funds to companies or to community colleges that create a training program for a specific employer based upon the specific state grant.

Examples of state government grant and tax credits for workforce development exist. Delaware offers Blue Collar Training funds to businesses for customized training programs to upgrade and/or retrain their employees and provide financial assistance to full-time employees.[93] In addition, Delaware offer the Governor's Workforce Development Grant for up to $2,000 to qualified individuals in a part-time employment to participate in a part-time undergraduate study.[94] Workers can qualify for this grant program if they are employed full-time for a Delaware small business with 100 or fewer employees.[95]

The Montana Department of Commerce manages a state workforce training program that offers a state government match of three to one of private workforce development spending up to $5,000.[96] Jobs must pay $12.60 an hour with benefits, and the program spends $1,300,000 annually.[97] Alabama's Incumbent Worker Training Program helps employers cover expenses for workers to upgrade and acquire new skills, helping companies to meet foreign competition, avoid layoffs, and stay open.[98] This program is specifically designed for businesses to apply for skill-training upgrades for existing employees.[99]

Texas's skills development fund provides training dollars for businesses and workers up to $500,000 for high-quality, customized job training projects across the state.[100] Once a Texas business, consortium of businesses, or trade union identifies a training need, a public community or technical college is found to fill its specific needs.[101] The business-community college partnership is a mandatory collaboration to gain Texas funding for the training in which the community college administers the grant tied to job creation.[102] During fiscal year 2012, this program awarded 50 skills development fund grants, totaling $22,441,693, serving 111 Texas businesses to create 5,108 new jobs and upgrading the skills of 14,732 workers in existing jobs.[103]

Ohio's Incumbent Workforce Training Voucher Program fills a gap in current workforce development programs by providing training dollars to Ohio's incumbent workforce.[104] The ultimate goal of this program is to allow employers to retain and grow their existing Ohio workforce to meet the demands of an ever-changing economy. Not all employers are eligible. Targeted industries of the Ohio program include advanced manufacturing, aerospace and aviation, automotive, biohealth, corporate headquarters, energy, financial services, food processing, information technology and services, and polymers and chemicals.[105] The program is employer-driven and covers specific training costs for employees to upgrade their skills in targeted industries. Up to a $4,000 per employee reimbursement is provided for up to 50 percent of the training costs.[106] A $500,000 cap was established for any Ohio company eligible to apply.[107]

Big Questions

1. Why does workforce matter to economic development?

2. How should regions and states handle the paradox that low wage rates make them attractive to companies but run counter to the overall goal of economic development?

3. What role does higher education play in economic development?

4. How can workforce training be improved to better serve employers?

5. Are training grants and tax credits really just a "give away" to employers?

Class Writing Assignment

The Metropolis city council president needs a plan to address a workforce short-age for high-tech workers. Metropolis has plenty of workers, and many of them are recent college graduates. The challenge is that the high-tech industry is really not a big player in the city, but the city council president wants it to be. To recruit these high-tech companies, the city council president has asked you to draft a workforce development plan (2–3 pages) built around gaining more high-tech workers to the city. The policy brief must define the problem, outline potential solutions tried by other regions, and recommend an approach for Metropolis.

Metropolis City Council Case Study: Workforce Debate

Metropolis needs more STEM-educated workers to recruit in the high-tech compa-nies. The city council president decided an immigration recruitment program, but the mayor in an unusual play to the "Tea Party" advocates in Metropolis opposes this plan and is crafting a high-tech worker plan of her own. Advocates for the council president will present her plan to city council, and opponents, including the mayor, will argue against the council president's plan and for a plan of their own. Each plan must be presented to city council, which will then decide how to vote on the ordinance.

Additional Readings

Christine Nolan, Ed Morrison, Indraneel Kumar, Hamilton Galloway, and Sam Cordes, "Linking Industry and Occupation Clusters in Regional Economic Development," *Economic Development Quarterly*, 25, 1 (February 2011) 26–35.

Darrell M. West, *Creating a "Brain Gain" for U.S. Employers: The Role of Immigration* (Washington, DC: Brookings Institution, January 2011).

Elsie Harper Anderson, "Measuring the Connection between Workforce Development and Economic Development: Examining the Role of Sectors for Local Outcomes," *Economic Development Quarterly*, 22, 2 (May 2008) 119–135.

Emily Evans, Stacy Pancratz, and Annalisa Martinez, *Employment Research in Brief, an Annotated Bibliography*, U.S. Department of Labor, 2002.

Henry T. Kasper, "The Changing Role of Community College," *Occupational Outlook Quarterly*, 46, 4 (Winter 2002–2003) 14–22. *The 2012 Brown Report on American Education*, Brookings Institution Press, April 2012.

Joe L. Kincheloe, *How Do We Talk to the Workers? The Socio-Economic Foundation of Work and Vocational Education* (New York: Peter Lang Publishing, 1996).

Kathleen McConnell, *State of America's Cities, Special Section on Workforce Development*, National League of Cities, 2011.

Robert P. Giloth, "Learning From the Field: Economic Growth and Workforce Development in the 1990's," *Economic Development Quarterly*, 14, 4 (November 2000) 340–359.

Shari Garmise, *People and the Competitive Advantage of Place, Building a Workforce for the Twenty First Century* (Armonk, NY: M.E. Sharpe, 2006).

Vijay K. Mathur, "Human Capital-Based Strategy for Regional Economic Development," *Economic Development Quarterly*, 13, 3 (August 1999) 203–216.

CHAPTER TEN
ECONOMIC DEVELOPMENT BUILDING BLOCK: TAX POLICY

Chapter Goals

1. Understand how federal, state, and local tax policy can hinder or help economic growth
2. Discuss the corporate site selection process.
3. Learn the differences between different types of development finance subsides and the role of each in site procurement and improvement
4. Understand the legal impediments involved in structuring the financing of a project

Economic Development and Tax Policy

Tax policy is a prime building block economic development strategy. How much and what type of local, state, and federal taxes companies and their employees are charged is the highest-profile economic development policy issue. The local, state, and federal governments use a range of tax credits, abatements, and programs to incentivize economic development. The federal government operates with a high corporate tax rate but has a deep list of "tax expenditures" to support targeted areas and industries. Regions and states use economic development incentives as a central tool for business retention and attraction efforts to address perceived shortfalls in local, state, and federal tax policy. Every state and region of the country has economic development incentives, and the process by which those incentives are awarded is known as the corporate site location.

Regions and states use tax policy to retain and attract companies. The state of Georgia is the site of the "deal of the year." The Peach state landed a $172,000,000 Starbucks manufacturing facility in Augusta. Starbucks, the global coffee magnet, is locating its fifth manufacturing facility in the United States in the 1,500-acre Augusta Corporate Park.[1] Augusta is now home to more than the world-famous Augusta National Golf Club that hosts The Master's. Tax incentives were a major factor in Starbucks decision to build a manufacturing facility in Georgia. The company received $600,000 in local infrastructure improvements such as grading, water, and sewer lines to prepare the site for development. Starbucks also gained employee training, job credits, and tax credits for using the Port of Savannah to import its supplies and to export to England its finished product.[2] The 180,000-square-foot plant produces 4,000 metric tons of products currently manufactured abroad and creates 140 jobs.[3] Georgia's aggressive tax incentive package led Starbucks to bring back manufacturing to the United States.

Policy Arguments for Business-Friendly Tax Policy

Taxes fund the operation of government and raise the cost of doing business for companies. Businesses benefit from the services of public safety forces, infrastructure investments, and investments in the education of the population geared toward creating an educated citizenry for future workforce needs. The United States has the highest corporate tax rate in the industrialized world and charges the 31,000,000 small businesses, which make up nearly 90 percent of all organizations, a 39.6 percent tax rate.[4] Higher marginal tax rates impact economic growth.[5] Local, state, and federal tax policy is crafted to appeal to targeted companies or select industries of interest to address the negative impact of business taxes.

States get into the act as well. Seven states, Alaska, Florida, Nevada, South Dakota, Texas, Washington, and Wyoming, recruit companies by not having an income tax. States without an income tax experience higher state domestic product growth as compared to states with a state income tax.[6] However, reducing or eliminating the state income tax likely results in increasing other taxes. Sales or property tax fund local and state governments in no-income-tax states.

Whether a state has an income tax or not, all states use local and state economic development tax incentives to retain and attract companies. Local and state governments spend $80,000,000,000 annually in tax incentives.[7] This is a drop in the bucket of the total $2,000,000,000,000 in state and local government spending.[8] Tax incentives are meant to incentivize job creation and capital investment in a state and locality and address high taxes and other issues such as cost of doing business. Tax incentives support successful job training, manufacturing, and urban redevelopment initiatives. Tax incentives have a positive economic impact, in particular, if they are focused on economically distressed regions. The federal Empowerment Zone Program produces positive economic development results through improved labor market conditions and moderate rent increases.[9] Challenges to economic development tax incentives are based upon the lack of a causal link between the tax incentive given and the jobs being created. In particular, challenges to tax incentives, such as state enterprise zone programs that provide a location-based tax abatement, question whether they are merely rewarding economic behavior that will otherwise happen.[10] Local and state tax incentives can be an outgrowth of effective lobbying rather than having an impact on economic development.[11]

Tax Policy as an Economic Development Tool

Tax policy is a major building block economic development strategy. Tax policy strategies include tax incentives and state and federal tax structures. Effective economic development incentives are performance-based. A company only receives the tax credit, tax abatement, grant, or loan if it meets the jobs and capital investment numbers promised. Effective economic development programs target high-wage industries such as manufacturing by offering a sales tax credit for the purchase of machinery. Some tax incentives are targeted toward distressed areas to encourage investment in struggling communities. Effective economic development programs prioritize incentives in areas with high unemployment and poverty struggling to retain and attract jobs. Finally, tax incentives address the issues of high cost of doing business created by other policy and market conditions. The struggles of the industrial midwest to hold on to its manufacturing jobs offer a prime example of how a region is forced into the use of economic development incentives to play defense against not just global competitors but the southern region of the United States.

State and federal tax structure is also used to create economic development opportunities. Tax credits, tax exemptions, and federal "tax expenditures" support specific industries and company types deemed essential for economic growth. In addition, tax rates and activities taxed by government have an impact on economic growth.

Federal Government and Economic Development: Tax Policy, Credits, and Programs

The federal government is rarely a player in company recruitment. However, the federal government's tax policy, credits, and programs all impact local and regional efforts to retain and attract companies in a global economy.

Federal Tax Policy

Federal corporate taxes impact economic development. As taxes add to the cost of doing business, they impact the decision of companies as to where and when to make investments. The federal government has the highest corporate tax rate in the industrialized world at 35 percent, and the rates are even higher for the majority of companies that operate as "pass-through entities," in which most of these businesses owners are taxed at nearly 40 percent of their income.[12] However, the federal government spends what equates to nearly 8 percent of the national GDP on an array of "tax expenditures" that reduce individuals' and companies' tax burden.[13] These tax expenditures include anything from home mortgage deduction to research and development (R&D) and a long list of other business-oriented tax credits.

Federal Economic Development Tax Credits and Programs

On the federal level, tax credits are used to enhance economic growth. Six major federal tax credits impact economic development. The total cost for these tax credits is $45,000,000,000 from 2008 to 2012.[14] Compared to the mortgage interest deduction cost of $444,000,000,000 in the same timeframe, the price tag for federal economic development tax credits is a drop in the bucket. The Work Opportunity Tax Credit permits employers to claim a tax credit on their federal taxes for each qualifying new hire based upon the amount of wages paid to each eligible worker.[15] Relatives, former employees, or undocumented workers are not eligible, and each eligible worker must be employed for at least 120 hours in order for the employer to claim the tax credit.[16] If the new hire has another job at the time they are hired by the requesting employer, but otherwise meets the eligibility criteria, then the new employer can claim the tax credit.[17]

Federal Empowerment Zones concentrate an array of federal funding initiatives and tax credits into concentrated geographic areas in economic distress. Companies in one of the federally designated Empowerment Zones are eligible for a $3,000 annual tax credit for each employee who lives and works in the zone.[18] These companies are eligible for a deduction up to $35,000 of the cost of eligible equipment purchases and exclusions from taxable income for the sale of stock for qualified small business.[19] State or local governments are able to issue bonds in Empowerment Zones at lower interest rates to finance private or school construction.[20] Empowerment Zones were created in 1994 with the designation of the first 105 distressed communities as either Empowerment Zones or Department of Agriculture enterprise communities.[21] The program evolved into the Renewal Communities Program, permitting business to take an annual tax credit of up to $1,500 for each employee who lives and works for the business in a renewal community.[22] These programs illustrate a strong track record of encouraging job growth[23] (Figure 10.1). The urban Empowerment Zones use federal funding to create partnerships that have leveraged more than $12,000,000,000 in public and private investment.[24]

The federal government also offers the Low Income Housing Tax Credit (LIHTC) and the Treasury Department's New Market Tax Credit (NMTC) to spur economic investment. Both programs encourage private equity actors and private developers to invest into economically depressed and underprivileged communities either by generating new business, and thus new jobs, or improving the quality of life within these communities.[25] The LIHTC allocates federal tax credits to private developers for costs they incur as a result of developing low-income housing units, while the NMTC allocates tax credits to private equity investments into new market businesses.[26] Within the last decade, the federal

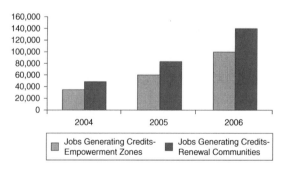

Figure 10.1   Federal empowerment zone performance.

Source: U.S. Department of Housing and Urban Development, retrieved from http://portal.hud.gov/hudportal/ HUD?src=/program_offices/comm_planning/economicdevelopment/programs/rc/hudirs.

government nearly doubled the amount of affordable housing in major US cities and has encouraged the start-up of new business enterprises by awarding these credits. The LIHTC funded 36,364 projects and almost 2,235,000 housing units placed in service between 1987 and 2010, allocating nearly $8,000,000,000 for local and state governments.[27]

The Treasury Department made several large, and noteworthy, awards of NMTCs in recent years. Chicago offers an array of success stories for the use of NMTCs to enhance economic development. In 2010, Chicago Development Fund provided a $4,900,000 allocation of NMTCs to Charter Steel Trading Company, a national distributor of premium steel products.[28] The financing provided the acquisition and renovation of an approximately 100,000-square-foot building on the west side of Chicago and is a successful economic retention project adding 30 jobs.[29] In 2009, the Chicago Development Fund provided $9,300,000 in NMTCs to the Community Career Training and Economic Development Center, creating a job training and placement center targeting high-growth industry sectors of manufacturing and transportation, distribution, and logistics.[30] The project was also made possible by a $3,100,000 TIF negotiated with the city of Chicago.[31]

Federal Economic Development Grant Programs

The federal government awards grants impacting economic development through several departments and agencies, including the EDA, the National Institute of Standards and Technology, the Small Business Administration (SBA), and the Environmental Protection Agency. Most grants awarded by these agencies have common drivers: increasing the competitiveness of US firms and manufacturers against foreign imports and encouraging immediate growth and developing strategies for long-term economic development in poor communities. Although many grants have the same underlying purpose, geographic requirements for grants can vary depending upon the program.

Still, other programs are directed at benefiting specific industries rather than specific regions of the country. Both the Manufacturing Tech Extension grant and the Trade Adjustment Assistance programs are aimed at improving targeted industries.[32] The Manufacturing Tech Extension program improves smaller manufacturing firms' use of appropriate manufacturing technology. The Trade Adjustment Assistance program aids firms and industries adversely affected by an increase in imports of directly competitive articles.[33]

Federal Public Works and Economic Development Investments

EDA public works grants fund infrastructure related to company attraction and expansion. The program supports locally developed projects that encourage long-term economic self-sufficiency and global competitiveness.[34] These investments support redevelopment of Brownfield and business/industrial development. Public works and economic development program supports infrastructure for industrial park, port, and Brownfield development.[35]

Federal Loans

The federal government has a goal to ensure small businesses have access to capital. The SBA 7(a) Loan Program is a small business lending program. It includes an array of specific types of loans. These loans help companies to purchase land or buildings, cover new construction, and expansion or conversion of existing facilities.[36] They fund equipment, machinery, furniture, fixtures, supplies, or materials purchases for long- or short-term working capital and to finance existing inventory.[37] SBA 7(a) loans cannot be used to refinance existing debt where the lender is in a position to sustain a loss or where the SBA would take over that loss through refinancing.[38] Reimbursement of funds owed to any owner or the repayment of delinquent state or federal withholding taxes is not a proper use for 7(a) loans.[39]

The 504 Program is a long-term financing tool for economic development within a community. The 504 Program provides growing businesses with long-term, fixed-rate financing for major fixed assets such as land and buildings.[40] To be eligible, a for-profit business must fall within the size standards set by the SBA.[41] Companies with a tangible net worth in excess of $7,500,000 or an average net income in excess of $2,500,000 are not eligible for the 504 Program.[42]

The use of federal government funds to loan small companies is controversial. Many question whether these companies would get loans from private banks without government subsidy or whether the companies are a bad investment for the government to make. However, the SBA loan program is a substantial pool of funding for groups such as early-stage start-ups and women- and minority-owned firms that historically faced capital funding challenges.[43]

State and Local Tax Incentives

State and local governments offer a wide array of economic development programs. State economic development programs are implemented and negotiated at the local level, but nearly companies creating jobs and making capital investments have the opportunity to gain from both local and state government economic development incentives.

State Tax Credits

Tax credits are tools private developers, investors, and companies use to reduce tax burden in exchange for economic growth. States offer a variety of tax credits to businesses in different sectors to encourage job creation and capital investment. Corporate tax credits are direct subsidies paid to businesses as a recognition of partial payment already made toward taxes due. The incentives retain and attract major businesses to a state. Tax credits are awarded competitively in exchange for job creation and capital investment, and tax credits get larger as the jobs and capital total increase. The award of credits involves negotiation and value decisions by the state.

Most US states offer some tax credits to businesses. Those states that do not (such as Alaska, Minnesota, Nevada, South Dakota, and Wyoming) have other tax incentives that are attractive to businesses, such as no tax on income or available tax exemptions.[44] States offer "long-term care insurance credits" for insurance premiums to businesses employing persons responsible for long-term care of relatives.[45] Similarly, the majority of states offer some form of "enterprise zone tax credits" to stimulate economic growth and create job opportunities in economically depressed areas.[46]

States vary in the number of tax credits they offer. Some states, like Hawaii, Maryland, and Massachusetts, offer less than five credits, while others, like Kansas, Kentucky, and Oklahoma, offer more than 20 different credits.[47] Common tax credits include R&D, using renewable energy, employing people below the poverty line, subsidizing employee continuing education, training employees, building daycare facilities, establishing a business headquarters in the state, starting a new business, investing in small businesses, and infrastructure and technology purchases in targeted industries. Some credits also act as a supplement to already existing federal tax credits.[48] States offer credits beyond the federally offered credits for things like historic building preservation, solar energy use, child and dependent care funding, and emerging market investment.

Each state tax credit specifies what tax the credit applies to, and the applicable tax varies. Credits are provided to offset income, franchise, sales, property, or commercial activity taxes. The most common tax that credits are offered against is the income tax because that allows businesses to pay less tax overall upon following certain initiatives like increasing R&D or funding employee education. Otherwise, tax credits are linked to the taxes that are increased as a result of the business earning the credit. For example, tax credits on storing inventory at in-state warehouses are applied to property taxes because property taxes increase as a result of the need for more warehouses. Credits to building headquarters in a state often apply to franchise or corporate income taxes. Similarly, credits for infrastructure improvement or machine purchases come as a sales tax credit. Generally, states specify approved uses of tax credit money in the law creating the credit.

States delegate to certain agencies the task of setting approved standards for credit-worthy expenditures. For example, only buildings that are listed in the National Historic Building Registry are considered for this competitively awarded historic preservation tax credit.

Tax credits may be either refundable or nonrefundable. A refundable tax credit, a moderate form of negative income tax, can reduce the tax owed below zero and result in a net payment to the taxpayer beyond its own payment into the tax system. A nonrefundable tax credit cannot reduce the tax owed below 0; thus, taxpayers do not receive a refund exceeding their payments into the tax system. Some tax credits are only refundable over a timeframe in which they must be spent on the specified tax credit expenditure. Nonrenewable tax credits, therefore, only last within the taxable year when they are awarded. For tax credits that are renewable, the average duration of the credit is 5 to 15 years. Tax credits are invaluable tools that allow states to incentivize economic development and spur growth.

Good tax credits create a win-win situation where states can effectuate their economic and social initiatives, and companies can save money. Companies looking to start or expand their businesses should closely examine the tax credits offered by each state and their competitive edge in potentially receiving those credits.

State and Local Tax Abatements

To attract new businesses and encourage the expansion of existing businesses, state and local governments offer tax abatements as an economic development incentive. Tax abatements temporarily decrease the amount of taxes a business owes. While this tax incentive has a general effect on property taxes, the means employed by state and local governments to achieve this effect vary from program to program. In 1936, Mississippi and Louisiana became the first states to employ tax abatement programs, with both offering tax abatements to industrial businesses.[49] By 1941, 13 other states followed suit.[50] The number of states offering this tax incentive has risen dramatically over the last half-century, with 40 states currently offering some form of tax abatement to new or expanding businesses.

In some programs, such as Minnesota's Economic Development Tax Abatement program, the state or local government rebates property taxes to the property owner.[51] Alternatively, some governments grant businesses full tax exemptions for a defined period. For example, the Ohio Community Reinvestment Area Program permits counties and municipalities to grant a 100 percent exemption to qualifying businesses for up to 15 years.[52] The most prevalent approach, however, is where the state or local government permits the business owner to exclude the property's increased value from the property tax valuation. Illinois' Enterprise Zone Program and Indiana's Economic Revitalization Area Program are examples of this latter approach.[53]

State and local governments offer these abatements through standalone programs, where the only offered incentive is the property tax abatement. Other governments offer tax abatements as part of a larger development incentive package that includes income tax credits, property tax credits, sales tax credits, or tax increment financing. Iowa's High-Quality Job Creation Program is an example of one of these more comprehensive incentive packages.[54] Eligible Iowa businesses receive a local property tax abatement of up to 100 percent of the value added to new, expanded, or modified property.[55] In addition, this program offers qualifying businesses a refund of state sales, service, or use taxes paid to contractors or subcontractors during construction, a refund of sales and use taxes paid on specified equipment, and an amortized investment tax credit equal to a percentage of the qualifying investment.[56]

The number of tax abatement programs differs from state to state. Michigan leads the way with four separate tax abatement programs, but Arkansas, Colorado, Nebraska, New Mexico, North Carolina, and Utah offer no tax abatements.[57] On a regional scale, midwestern states offer tax abatements more liberally than states in other US regions. Iowa, Indiana, Illinois, Michigan, and Ohio all offer at least two programs. States such as Arkansas, Kansas, and South Carolina declared their entire state an enterprise zone providing expansive tax abatements to business.[58] Western states, on the other hand, offer fewer tax abatements. With state and local governments offering these incentives primarily to manufacturing and industrial businesses, the midwestern trend may be attributable to the greater location of these types of businesses in those states. The recent economic decline in many midwestern states may also contribute to this trend.

When offered, abatement programs involve a state and local partnership, with both governing bodies playing a role. The state determines the basic parameters of the abatement by defining the types of properties that qualify, the maximum duration of the benefit, and the basic requirements that businesses must meet to qualify for abatement. Because the taxes abated through the programs are municipal or county property taxes, the local government implements the programs. These county or municipal governments normally integrate additional requirements, determine the duration of abatement, handle the application process, and oversee the projects to ensure that the businesses comply with the abatement requirements.

Because these abatements generally apply to real or personal property taxes, state or local governments identify classes or specific types of property that are eligible for the incentive. Very few programs permit abatement of taxes on land. Most programs apply only to new machinery or equipment and to new or improved buildings; however, the specific type of property that the abatement applies to is determined according to the economic goals of the individual program. For example, Louisiana's Restoration Tax Abatement Program only abates taxes on certain qualified historic buildings.[59] To encourage the preservation of these buildings, this program allows owners who renovate historic buildings to freeze the assessed value of the property at preimprovement levels.[60]

Other programs encourage industrial, commercial, or residential expansion in economically underdeveloped areas by allowing tax abatement of new machinery, improved machinery, or real property. State and local governments offer abatements for new or improved retail, warehousing and distribution, processing, telecommunications, tourism, R&D, and rehabilitation facilities and finance, insurance, real estate, and daycare service projects. In addition to property type restrictions, state and local abatement programs usually require applicants to meet other common eligibility criteria. First, most programs require that businesses locate or expand in certain designated areas. These tax abatement programs have minimum investment requirements and tie the duration and extent of abatement to the amount invested. Other requirements include minimum job creation, advance notice prior to initiating the project, and yearly reporting.

Enterprise Zones is the most common tax abatement program. Currently, over 40 states offer some variation of this program.[61] These programs offer real and personal tax incentives to businesses that expand or locate within designated Enterprise Zones. First, the locality must designate an area as an Enterprise Zone, which is based upon the poverty and unemployment rate of the are. However, state law may not limit which municipality may use the Enterprise Zone program; thus, Enterprise Zones are as prevalent in wealthy suburban communities as they are in the poor, inner city neighborhoods. This goes against the original intent of the Enterprise Zone program. Once designated, businesses that wish to build or expand in Enterprise Zones can apply for the program's abatement. Generally, the tax incentive permits the local government to offer a full or partial exemption of the real or personal property values attributable to the new development.

The duration of abatement varies from program to program. The common maximum abatement periods are 5–10 years. Some states, however, prefer longer abatement periods. For example, Iowa and Rhode Island permit local governments to abate property taxes for 20 years, and Missouri's Urban Redevelopment Corporation Law permits property tax abatement for up to 25 years.[62] At the other end of the spectrum, Nevada's program only abates taxes for 2 years, while the abatement offered in Oregon's Renewable Energy Development Zone Program may only last 3 years.[63] Regardless of the maximum permissible duration, most programs permit the local governing body to specify the actual duration of the property tax abatement.

State Economic Development Grants

States offer outright grants for companies in exchange for the retention and creation of an agreed upon number of jobs and capital investment. A recent trend is the use of "closing funds" as the dominant form of economic development incentives. States moved to streamline their economic development incentives and focus on the creation of a large fund that makes cash awards to companies through major corporate site location projects.

The Texas Enterprise Fund (TEF) is a "deal closing fund" used for a variety of infrastructure and community development, job training programs, and business incentives.[64] Before funds can be awarded, the governor, lieutenant governor, and speaker must unanimously agree to support the use of the TEF for each specific project.[65] The TEF attracts new business to the state or assists with the expansion of an existing business as part of competitive recruitment, but it can also be used to leverage other resources for an economic development project.[66] To be eligible for TEF support, a project must demonstrate a significant return on the state's investment and strong local support.[67] The review process considers job creation and wages, capital investment, financial strength of the applicant, applicant's business history, analysis of the relevant business sector, and public and private sector financial support.[68] As with all tax incentives, the TEF is controversial, but the $300,000,000 granted to companies over the last 7 years helped Texas become the leading job-producing state in the nation.[69]

State Low-Interest Government Loans

Low- or no-interest, government-sponsored loans are an attractive alternative to bank or other private sector financing for a planned economic development. The collapse of the financial services industry changed the way companies gain financing. Enhanced federal government regulations create challenges for banks to play their traditional economic development. Companies with growth potential face new challenges to gain the financing needed to move to the next level.

Government at the state and federal levels offers an option for financing growing companies, but gaining a loan from the government is different than the private sector. What type of government loan a company can gain depends on the stage and industry of the company. Looking at the state of Ohio as an example, early-stage companies nearing market entry and larger R&D organizations in targeted tech sectors have a wide range of loans and grants through the Ohio Third Frontier program, which include:

- Commercial Acceleration Loan Program—$500,000 to $2,000,000 loans to Ohio for-profit companies addressing technical and cost barriers to commercialization of high-tech products and processes for companies that have gained venture capital or angel funding
- Industrial R&D Center Program—$5,000,000 to recruit major corporate, nonprofit or federal R&D centers
- Open Innovation Incentive—$2,000,000 grants to Ohio middle-market companies for accelerating time to market of Ohio technology products, processes, or services
- Technology Asset Grant—$5,000,000 to purchase specialized technical equipment or unique technical facilities for Ohio for-profit companies for near-term commercial usage of products or services[70]

Nonretail Ohio companies creating at least 25 jobs in a traditional industry or ten jobs in a high-tech industry paying 150 percent minimum wage and making a fixed asset investment also have a range of other government loan programs available to them, including:

- Innovation Ohio Loan Fund—$500,000 to $1,000,000 loan for 75 percent of project cost for a wide range of needs of high-tech company
- 166 Direct and Regional Loan Fund—$500,000 to $1,500,000 loan for 50 percent of fixed asset costs
- JobsOhio Growth Fund—capital for expansion projects to companies that have limited access to capital and funding from conventional, private sources of financing
- R&D Investment Loan—$500,000 to $5,000,000 loans for R&D activity and a dollar-for-dollar, nonrefundable Ohio commercial activity tax credit for loan payments made during the year up to $150,000[71]

Politics also matters when it comes to gaining government financing, but not the Red-versus-Blue kind. The politics in questions might be what region a company is from, what industry is hot, and, at times, connections to help position a client's project in a highly competitive process. States may place requirements to only loan funds to companies in select industries based upon an economic development cluster analysis of the state.

The process different for gaining government loans as compared to negotiating a traditional bank loan. Companies requesting a government loan first need to prepare a long list of documents the government will request. They need a make a business plan outlining their sustainable competitive advantage based upon an analysis of the market, competitors, profit model, and management team. Elements of a business plan also include a company and product and service line description, marketing and sales plan, financial projections, contracts, resumes, permits, and leases. Next, the company needs a complete financial statement outlining the available working capital and planned use for the government loan. A collateral list is also required as most government loans demand some form of collateral. The government may want to gain a personal guarantee from the company leadership and review the company and executive's credit ratings. Finally, the government reviews the list of investors in the company to ensure they are not alone. Not only does the government ask all the same questions as a bank and negotiate through a term sheet to a contract, but government also must gain the approval of the executive agency director and at times legislative bodies.

Many of the terms associated with these loan programs are similar to the requirements to gain a loan from a private lending institution, but the government loans generally have a reduced interest rate. However, the basis of the low-interest government loans is job creation and capital expenditures; they provide a percentage of financing for the total project cost and not the entire cost (often up to 40%), carry the burden of prevailing wage if that is law of that state, and need some interest in capital assets associated with the project.

Finally, the players matter. Companies need to work the maze of local economic development officials, leaders in state government, and private sector economic development organizations at the regional and state levels. Government offers a vehicle for financing company growth for operating and capital needs. However, the programs, politics, process, and players all impact how much money a company can gain and what the terms of the loan and/or grant are.

The Good, Bad, and Ugly of State and Local Tax Incentives

Policy makers struggle with the application of state and local tax incentives. How they are used, where they are used, and how much they cost taxpayers stir great debate. Stories abound of abuse of state and local tax incentives. New Mexico's Film Tax Credit ran up a $60,000,000 bill on this small state and generated just 14 cents per dollar in new revenue.[72] A Minnesota tax credit program cost taxpayers $26,900 and $30,800 per job.[73] Nevada's tax incentive programs cost taxpayers $30,000 per job.[74] Enterprise Zone programs created for poor inner city neighborhoods may be available everywhere.

Abuses or not, state and local tax incentives are a fifty-state game and are not going away. Best practices from around the nation preventing abuses are clear. First, state and local tax incentives are targeted and selective. If every company can get one, the value of the incentive decreases, and state governments would be better off with a remake of their tax code rather than redoing the tax code one company at a time. Targeting incentives means using them only in neighborhoods struggling economically, focusing only on high-wage jobs in targeted industry clusters a state and region is connected to and the industry is growing. State and local governments do a return on investment (ROI) analysis to determine if the company incentive provides more in taxes than they cost if the incentive is awarded. State and local governments regularly evaluate the operation of tax incentives and determine whether the tax incentives are achieving the state's economic goals. Economic development incentives in a vacuum cannot turn a state's economy around. Michigan spends billions of dollars on tax incentives in a highly aggressive fashion, but the state still lags behind in economic success.

Many best practices exist with state and local tax incentives. Oregon tax incentives expire every 6 years unless lawmakers extend them and a spending cap on expiring incentives exists.[75] Oregon lawmakers make tough choices and use real analysis to determine what incentives are working and which ones are not. The state of Washington began a 10-year process in 2007, reviewing all the state's tax incentives working with a citizen's commission to make recommendations to lawmakers.[76] Louisiana analyzes its economic development incentives by taking into account the in-state jobs displaced by a new company coming to town through the use of tax incentives.[77] The state of Ohio now not only uses a complex ROI formula to ensure a company receiving incentives pays more in taxes than they receive in economic development incentives but the state changed its Job Creation Tax Credit program to create an annual payroll requirement of $660,000 that mandates high-wage jobs for the incentive to be awarded.[78]

The Corporate Site Location Process

Companies looking to consolidate, relocate, or expand operations follow a structured process to negotiate a corporate site location package involving some form of economic development incentives. The most important phase of a corporate site location project is the initial project definition phase. It is during this initial phase the company decides if the business case exists to move forward with a relocation, consolidation, or expansion that gives rise to a corporate site location process. The company examines its current business situation to identify current facility locations, employee count, capital investment, commitment to the community, and taxes paid to all sources.

In addition, the company decides if the business case exists for relocation, consolidation, or expansion of a facility(s). If the business case exists, the company identifies the planned job growth and capital/equipment investment and potential geographic locations or sites for planned expansion or relocation based upon client needs and legal issues. The company gathers all additional information to promote a positive message about the brand and the economic impact the company would have on any region, state, or nation it chooses to location. This message centers on an economic impact study. An economic impact study determines the increase in total jobs and total income caused by the operation of the facility, allocates the increase in total income to the local retail activity, and estimates the effect of the increased employment on the demand for housing. Economic impact studies also analyze the direct employment of the facility, estimate the magnitude of the local economic multiplier, calculate the total change in local employment and income, and determine the percentage of the household budget spent on various categories of retail goods and services. The economic impact study is used for both incentive negotiations purposes and public relations–related efforts if and when the project goes public.

During this phase it proves useful to perform a fiscal impact study as to the costs and benefits a company facility would provide to any community. A fiscal impact study quantifies the property, income, sales, and other taxes generated by the company's project and compares that to any potential public service costs that would be needed for the project. The fiscal impact study defines the benefit to local and state government of the company's project.

Finally, the actual plans are developed for the new or remodel facility. These plans outline the facility size and design, force agreement on corporate and operational requirements, prepare operational and capital cost budget, create plans for the project site including engineering and architectural drawings and a detailed cost analysis of all construction and facility cost. Next, the company identifies several potential regions, states, or nations that they wish to consider for a potential facility location that meets the needs of their business case. A location analysis explores demographic, business costs, cost of living, and quality-of-life issues around each of those locations. This location analysis identifies regional and state growth rates, major corporate and institutional assets, taxes used, tax rates, tax exemptions, average population age, wage rate, housing price, unionization rates, school ratings, health-care availability, major airport locations, and other data relevant to the company's interests.

In addition, research is conducted as to tax incentive programs available in each of those regions and states from all sources of potential incentives from local, state, and federal governments for tax abatements, tax credits, infrastructure grants, Brownfield redevelopment grants, low-interest government loans, worker training grants, and R&D grants. Next, a letter, not identifying the company, announcing the project is sent to multiple states and local economic development leaders. The letter names, announces, and defines the project in terms of the positive economic impact the corporate site location could have on a region. The centerpiece of the economic impact is the number of jobs, capital investment, and taxes produced for the region should the company choose to locate in that region.

Very specific demographic, cost-of-living, and quality-of-life information is requested to confirm the location analysis report. The letter defines the space and location needs of the project and any other site-specific needs the company may have. Finally, the letter asks for an economic development incentive offer tied to specific geographic sites for the company's review. The state and local economic development officials are given a short timeframe, usually two weeks, to respond to the project introduction letter. Informal discussions are initiated with the state and local economic development leaders to illustrate the seriousness of the project. Following a review of the proposals from state and local governments, the company narrows the list of potential locations to two or three in an effort to prepare more detailed discussions and negotiations. Briefings are held with relevant public officials on the importance of the project in each of the regions and states where the company chooses to negotiate. During these project-positioning sessions, the company does a site visit as well to personally sees the proposed sites in each region and state and to meet with corporate leaders in the community privately to gain an impression of the business climate. These business briefings are a good marketing opportunity for the company.

Internal positioning of the project also matters. If and when a relocation, expansion, or consolidation goes public, company leadership needs a communications plan in place and ready to directly tell employees about the decision and plan from a human resources and legal standpoint as to how the decision impacts existing and new employees. Negotiation sessions are then held with each one of the two or three regions and states to gain a final incentive offer from the local and state governments or economic development organizations designated to negotiate the deal. The company then reviews the incentive offers and the location analysis and specific benefits and costs of the proposed sites to determine which location suits their needs best. The choice and availability of specific incentives vary based upon the location and the state chosen. Each local and state government has a slightly different menu of incentive choices, and some incentives are more attractive to a company based upon the location chosen and industry of the business. As an example, a company interested in an urban infill site with environmental contamination is interested in local and state programs to provide liability protection and clean-up money for the site. Those company needs are completely different than an office park project looking for a suburban greenfield location.

Once that location is chosen, a formal economic development incentive agreement is negotiated and signed contingent upon the final land purchase or lease of the property for the site. Upon completion of the incentive agreement, the company then proceeds to finalize a purchase or lease of the site in question. The company cannot buy or lease the property first without making receipt of economic development incentives a contingency of the final purchase. Receipt of the incentives does not happen unless the local and state government agencies provide final approval to the incentive deal.

Finally, the company participates in a public announcement with local and state government leaders announcing the deal. However, prior to that public announcement, companies utilize an aggressive and confidential communications strategy with their employees to communicate plans for the expansion, relocation, or consolidation. Briefings and other advocacy efforts with local and state government officials are needed to communicate the economic benefits of the proposed tax incentive deal. Once the deal is approved, the local and state governments monitor the progress of the project and require the creation of annual reports to verify the legal basis for the tax incentive in question.

Big Questions

1. Why does tax policy impact economic development?

2. Would you agree economic development incentives are unneeded corporate welfare?

3. How can communities ensure companies do not leave after receiving economic development incentives?

4. What are performance-based economic development incentives?

5. Do economic development incentives truly impact job location decisions?

Class Writing Assignment

Metropolis has an opportunity to gain 2,000 jobs from an economic development project identified as Project Alpha. Project Alpha involves a company in the information technology industry that is a global software developer. The average annual wage is $65,000, and the planned capital investment is $50,000,000 to build a state-of-the-art campus of four buildings. Three sites are under consideration with one each in Metropolis, Nashville, and Raleigh-Durham. The site of Project Alpha is a brownfield in Metropolis that costs $5,000,000 to clean up and a green field site with no environmental contamination in Nashville or Raleigh-Durham. Infrastructure costs are $15,000,000 to clear the site and build an internal road and provide water and sewer systems in Metropolis.

Metropolis, Nashville, and Raleigh-Durham offer different tax structures, but the annual property tax liability is $1,000,000 in all three sites. Taxable income from the site is $200,000,000. Metropolis has a 2 percent municipal income tax, but Nashville and Raleigh-Durham do not have a local government income tax.

The Project Alpha expects free parking for its employees and has a major customer in Metropolis. The company has an interest in gaining all possible local, state, and federal government tax credits, tax abatements, grants, and low-interest government loans.

Research the local and state incentives available in Metropolis, Ohio, Nashville, Tennessee, and Raleigh and the other costs of doing business and the business market conditions to prepare the following four documents:

1. a confidential letter from a corporate site selector defining the project and requesting incentive offers from Ohio, Tennessee, and North Carolina with specific sites identified and tax incentive offers
2. a response from the state of Ohio with a specific tax incentive offer
3. a response from the state of Tennessee with a specific tax incentive offer
4. a response from the state of North Carolina with a specific tax incentive offer

Metropolis City Council Case Study: Tax Incentives Debate

The mayor of Metropolis decided the city council must approve of the local and state tax incentive offer to be made for Project Alpha. The mayor and proponents of the tax incentive offer will argue the long-term economic benefits of the offer. The mayor's opponents on city council will no doubt see this offer as an example of corporate welfare.

Additional Readings

Alan Peters and Peter Fisher, "The Failures of Economic Development Incentives," *Journal of the American Planning Association*, 70, 1 (Winter 2004) 27–39.

Economic Development Programs, the U.S. Economic Development Administration, retrieved from www.usdoc.gov.

James Buchanan and Richard Musgrave, *Public Finance and Public Choice: Two Contesting of Visions of the State* (Cambridge, MA: MIT Press, 1999).

Katie Maurer, *Effectiveness of Tax Abatements*, April 20, 2002, retrieved from http://www.umich.edu/~econdev/taxabatemts/.

Louise Story, "As Companies Seek Tax Deals, Governments Pay High Price," *The New York Times*, December 1, 2012.Matias Busso and Patrick Kline, "Do Local Economic Development Programs Work? Evidence from the Federal Empowerment Zone Program," *Cowles Foundation Discussion Paper, No. 1638,* February 2008.

M. E. Warner and L. Zheng, "Business Incentive Adoption in the Recession," *Economic Development Quarterly*, 27, 2 (2013) 90–101.

Ohio Department of Development website, Economic Development Incentives, 2012, available at www.developmentohio.gov.

Peter Phillips, *Kentucky's Prevailing Wage Law*, September 1999 retrieved from http://www.faircontracting.org/PDFs/prevailing_wages/kentucky_prevailing_wage.pdf.

Robert T. Greenbaum and Jim Landers, "Why Are State Policy Makers Still Proponents of Enterprise Zones? What Explains Their Action in the Face of the Preponderance of the Research?" *International Regional Science Review*, 32, 4 (October 2009) 466–470.

Steven McBride, *Site Planning and Design* (Morgantown, WV: Web Book of Regional Science, West Virginia University, 2006).

Terry F. Buss, "The Effect of State Tax Incentives on Economic Growth and Firm Location Decisions: An Overview of the Literature," *Economic Development Quarterly*, 15 (February 2001) 90–105.

Timothy Bortik, "Solving the Problem of Economic Development Incentives," *Growth and Change*, 36, 2 (Spring 2005) 139–166.

CHAPTER ELEVEN

ECONOMIC DEVELOPMENT BUILDING BLOCK: QUALITY OF LIFE

Chapter Goals

1. Understand how quality-of-life factors impact economic development
2. Discuss the roles public safety and quality of schools play in neighborhood and regional economic development
3. Understand the ways in which health care impacts the quality of life in a region
4. Recognize the role of workforce housing and how its regulation and subsidization impacts the retention and creation of jobs
5. Identify the roles cultural and recreational amenities can play in economic development particularly in rural regions

Quality of Life and Economic Development

The quality of life of a community impacts its regional and statewide efforts to create wealth. Surveys of corporate site location consultants indicate quality of life is a factor for a company in deciding where to locate, but quality of life rarely makes the top ten of overall corporate site location factors.[1] Quality of life does not make up for poor infrastructure, low-quality workers, high taxes, and a lack of available sites. However, quality of a life in a region or state impacts a company's decision to stay or go. Core quality-of-life issues center around the safety of the community, availability of workforce housing, quality of schools, access to quality health care, and the growing role for cultural and recreational amenities.

Large global manufacturing projects are impacted by a region's quality of life. When states were competing for the location of a major Nissan facility in the United States, Nashville with its high-quality workforce, entertainment venues, and relatively low cost of life emerged the winner.[2] The reality for these major global site location projects is they are of such a size and scale that they receive multimillion dollar tax incentives from multiple states with the infrastructure in place from day one. Tennessee had the sustainable competitive advantage of its entertainment district matched with a major, high-quality university and a market where factory workers can actually purchase a home. Nashville promotes a cost of living composite score of less than half of New York City and lower than San Francisco, Boston, Seattle, Chicago, Cleveland, Orlando, Atlanta, and Austin.[3] Quality-of-life factors can be a tipping point for economic development decisions that bring thousands of high-wage jobs.

Policy Arguments for Linking Quality of Life and Economic Development

The quality of life a region is a major factor in the residents' economic success. First, natural amenities impact population migration in a positive way.[4] Amenities create economic opportunities. They are part of every economic development pitch, and investments in quality of life–related services have the added benefit of improving the life of its residents, not just potential companies coming to town. The development of a better quality of life as an economic development strategy works not just in urban centers but is also effective in smaller, rural markets.[5] Improving the quality of life with a focus on health care also improves the life expectancy of a region. Regions where residents live longer and healthier are more productive.[6] Finally, quality of life as a factor in economic development decisions varies in relevancy among industries but is important to workers in the high-wage, high-tech sector.[7]

Opponents of the focus on quality of life in the economic development context believe spending on quality of life cannot create an adequate return on investment. They believe the increased costs on area businesses caused by quality of life investments go against the traditional location theory of economic development. Higher costs associated with a location create a disincentive for companies to remain or move into the community.

Quality of Life as an Economic Development Tool

Quality of life matters for economic development purposes.[8] Sites plagued by crime struggle to develop. Regions with poor public schools and a lack of high-quality colleges and universities are not attractive to a highly mobile workplace. Communities

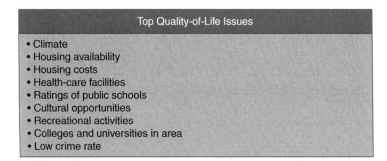

Figure 11.1 Role of quality of life in economic development.
Source: Area Development Magazine, Winter 2013.

in which workforce housing is out of reach for the average worker lose out compared to regions with more affordable, high-quality housing options. Communities with cultural and recreational activities serve as a magnet for younger workers and executives looking for start-up companies. A fundamental question when looking to improve a region's quality of life is how is "quality of life" defined. Economic development strategies addressing quality of life are education, safety, housing, health care, and recreational opportunities (Figure 11.1).

Education and Economic Development

The availability of quality primary and secondary schools impacts economic development. Good schools are where all good workers start. Good schools recruit workers and their families to stay or remain in a region. The performance of American schools compared globally is a hot policy debate. In fact, US economy could be $1,000,000,000,000 a year stronger if Americans only performed at Canada's level in math.[9] The United States ranked fourteenth out of 34 industrialized nations in reading skills, seventeenth in science, and a below-average twenty-fifth in math.[10] Boosting US scores for reading, math, and science by 25 points over the next 20 years would result in a $41,000,000,000,000 gain for the economy over the lifetime of the generation born after 2010.[11]

To address this workforce challenge, the start of the twenty-first century is an age of American education reform. Public policy efforts to develop world-class education systems range from creating systems of accountability to paying teachers based upon performance, to creating competition among public school systems.

Accountability Measures

The age of reform for America's education system is centered on creating a system of strong accountability for public schools. Accountability takes many forms. States test students on core subjects and publish the results. These "report cards" inform the public whether a school district's students are succeeding or not. Many school districts are discussing linking compensation of staff with the performance of their students. Sometimes known as "merit pay," this approach creates an incentive for schools to effectively educate their students. Efforts in Nashville and other communities offer promising results for the pay-for-performance model in public education, but recent budget challenges and questions about the effectiveness of the program have led to major cuts in the funding for merit-pay initiatives in Texas and New York City.[12]

Management of Schools: Mayoral Leadership

States and their large cities are addressing challenges with urban schools by moving to mayoral control of the schools. Boston, Chicago, New York, Cleveland, Detroit, Baltimore, Philadelphia, Washington, DC, and others have city schools controlled in one way or the other by the mayor's office. It is hoped that this approach to public school management can accomplish better results than the traditional public school board. Whether the management of a public school system is through a mayor or elected Board of Education, high expectations for student achievements and quality instruction and a shared belief about students' ability to learn and schools' ability to teach at high levels are top factors impacting student success. Less time spent on operations and more time on policies to improve student achievement and collaborative relationships with district staff and community members for setting up district goals and school districts that are able to address weaknesses are also factors for school success. Professional development and other resources aligned with district goals of academic achievement, and a school board united as a team with strong collaboration and trust matched by joint training and team development with the superintendent all impact whether a school district succeeds or not.[13]

Choice and Competition

Competition and choice is another approach to improve the performance of the public school system. School choice means public funding of either private non-religious charter schools or faith-based religious schools. The use of vouchers to fund students' attendance at religiously affiliated schools involves both legal and public policy issues debated over the last 50 years. The First Amendment to the US Constitution creates a separation between church and state. It reads thus: "Congress shall make no law respecting an establishment of religion, or prohibiting the free exercise thereof; or abridging the freedom of speech, or of the press; or the right of the people peaceably to assemble, and to petition the government for a redress of grievances." Decades of opinions of the US Supreme Court determined the limits of a prohibition of an establishment of a national religion related to public aid to religious institutions such as parochial primary and secondary schools.

In 2002, the Supreme Court handed proponents of school choice a major victory when it expanded the concept of aid to religiously affiliated schools to include the ability of a state to provide vouchers or direct payments for students to attend a private, religiously affiliated school.[14] The state of Ohio, out of concern that the Cleveland Public Schools were simply not serving students well in this struggling urban center, enacted a program that permitted the state to pay a limited number of vouchers for students who chose to attend private schools in the city of Cleveland.[15] The majority of these students chose to attend parochial and, for the most part, Catholic schools in inner city Cleveland, but the Cleveland Voucher Program was not specifically limited to students wishing to attend religious primary and secondary schools.[16] Vouchers are a hotly debated policy issue, and the Court answered the big question policy makers were facing for decades.[17] The key to the Court's analysis in this case was the fact that the Ohio program was neutral toward religion; any monies flowing to religious schools flowed through the decisions of individuals rather than as direct payments from the state; and the program offered parents genuine secular options for their children's schooling.[18]

Crime and Economic Development

No region or state develops jobs and companies without safe streets. Crime discourages domestic investment and FDI, reduces the competitiveness of firms, and

Table 11.1 Growth from 1960 to 2000 in the number of murders per 100,000 residents

City	1960	2000
Cleveland	5.3	14.8
Detroit	5.1	41.6
Milwaukee	1.4	20.4
Philadelphia	4.8	21.0
Washington, DC	10.6	41.8

Source: Federal Bureau of Investigation.

reallocates resources and encourages unemployment in youths—all creating economic uncertainty and inefficiency.[19] As Table 11.1 shows, American urban centers struggle with crime. Concerns about crime near a potential job site kill a deal faster than almost any other issue. Again, just ask the corporate site selectors who negotiate job-creating deals and the corporate executives who ultimately decide where jobs are created. A low crime rate is the number one quality-of-life issue from the most recent surveys of both groups of these business leaders.[20] Crime counts when it comes to creating jobs. From the 1960s to the 1990s, the amounts of crime, particularly in America's urban centers, dramatically increased.

The explosion of violent crime in our central cities is a contributing factor in the decline of many urban areas.

Gun Control

Crime is a public policy challenge very much addressed by America's court system and other legal approaches. Much focus is given to the public policy debate between gun control advocates and gun rights supporters. The US Supreme Court recently struck down Washington's and Chicago's gun control ordinances. State courts reviewing state constitutional mandates also jumped into the gun control debate. The majority of states enacted "conceal carry" legislation permitting those participating in hand gun safety programs to carry a gun concealed on their person. The goal of conceal carry legislation is to fight crime by arming the law-abiding citizens. Armed citizens are supposed to provide a deterrent to criminals attacking the average person on the street. Needless to say, gun control advocates and most municipal leaders oppose conceal carry legislation. Courts agree conceal carry legislation in fact passes constitutional muster. However, whether a community encourages or discourages its residents to be armed, aggressive new police tactics have the largest impact in stopping crime.

Economic Development Policy Case Study 11.1: Crime in Times Square

New York City has a story to tell when it comes to addressing crime and the success of this strategy to make America's largest city a safer place to live. It uses a new approach to policing known as CompStat. CompStat stands for "Computer

Comparison Statistics," a system for managing police operations. CompStat combines modern management and accountability tools with the Information Age to identify where specific crimes are happening and what is being done to address that. The goal of CompStat is to collect, analyze, map, and review crime data on a regular basis; develop and implement strategies in a short period of time; and hold police accountable for their performance as measured by the data.[21]

The link between a reduction in New York City's crime rate and its economic renaissance is a well-established story. The economic turnaround of Times Square provides a case study of how crime and grime removal can turn a neighborhood into a global economic engine. Times Square was a crime-ridden neighborhood. In 1984, Times Square was the scene of over 2,000 crimes, and the area employed only 3,000 people in legitimate businesses and produced only $6,000,000 in property taxes.[22] CompStat saved Times Square. Even before it had a name, the Midtown South New York City Police Precinct was applying the early stages of arresting low-level offenders and tracking crime by geographic location.[23] It did not have a name yet, but innovative police tactics were beginning to take shape in Times Square. By the end of 1991, Times Square's crime rate was 12 percent lower than in 1984.[24]

New York City next attacked the sex trade. Starting in the mid-1980s, New York City began to condemn Times Square's sex shops for economic blight.[25] By 1990, New York City had taken down two-thirds of the sex shops and, in essence, driven the industry out of Times Square.[26]

Finally, New York City used a range of tax incentives to recruit major companies to Times Square. George Klein received a $240,000,000 tax abatement, Morgan Stanley received a $40,000,000 abatement, Disney received a $25,000,000 low-interest loan, and Ernst & Young gained a $20,000,000 incentive package, and there were many others.[27]

Business is no longer avoiding Times Square. The economic development strategy to save Times Square is an impressive American success story. Times Square represents only 0.1 percent of New York City's land area, but 5 percent of New York City's jobs are located there, and the district generates 10 percent of the city's economic output.[28] Times Square hosts 200,000 jobs, with approximately 70 percent of them in finance and creative industries.[29] As an indirect economic impact, Times Square adds an additional 190,000 jobs throughout New York City and the neighborhood contributes $1,100,000,000 in annual taxes to New York City and $1,300,000,000 in annual taxes to the state of New York.[30] Times Square turned the corner in large part because the policy has restored order to this American icon.

Economic Development and Housing

Quality housing to rich and poor is another essential economic development pillar. In partnership with the federal government, regions and states develop a readily available supply of workforce housing. An affordable and stable housing market makes a region attractive for companies looking to grow or locate in a region and contributes to the stability of a region's neighborhoods. If workers cannot afford housing, it drives up wage costs or forces companies to move to lower cost markets.

Housing costs are impacted by the overall cost of living of the region. Regions with high wage rates and a high concentration of wealth often have average home prices far above that of a more struggling economy. Housing costs is one area where it may not completely pay to have an otherwise successful economy. Of course, many of these regions with lower housing costs also have higher poverty rates and more struggling neighborhoods that may impact a company's decision to expand or locate in a region.[31]

Government Subsidization of the Housing Marketplace

The government wants Americans to own their homes. The government provides substantial "carrots" to encourage the growth and development not just of cities and suburbs but to create incentives for Americans to work harder to pay for a home. The federal government provides tax benefits to Americans who purchase homes. Most of these tax benefits are not triggered by income levels—everyone gets them, and they can apply to purchase a second home of value up to $1,000,000.[32]

The tax code subsidizes housing in several ways. The first involves not taxing the flow of housing services received by owner-occupants—known as imputed rent. Under this approach, a home is an asset that delivers services such as shelter to a homeowner.[33] These services could be rented to another. Those living in their own home have to pay no income taxes on this imputed rent.[34] Secondly, taxpayers deduct the mortgage interest and property tax and receive a special benefit by avoiding capital gain tax on the sale of certain homes.[35] The federal government permits home buyers to deduct interest in the year that it is paid and loan discount points and origination fees regardless of who pays them.[36]

In addition, the home buyer deducts interest charged on a loan used to acquire or improve a principal residence in the year it is paid.[37] Most home mortgages pay interest first. The ability to deduct mortgage interest is still the greatest tax loophole in American history. The cost of mortgage interest deduction to the treasury is substantial, an estimated $80,000,000,000.[38] This dollar total is more than the budget expenditure for the Department of Housing and Urban Development (HUD). Property taxes deducted from this purchase cost an estimated $25,000,000,000, and the tax subsidy related to imputed rent for homeowners is estimated at $198,000,000,000 for 2010.[39] The US total housing subsidy has been estimated at $304,000,000,000 when all the credits and exemptions are combined.[40]

Economic Development Policy Case Study 11.2:
Role of Fannie and Freddie

The federal government's subsidization of the housing industry is much larger than just billions of dollars in tax credits and exemptions. The government is in the mortgage guarantee business. It started as a New Deal program of the Roosevelt administration.[41] In 1933, half the mortgages in the United States were in default, and home building was nonexistent because of the Great Depression.[42] The federal government created the Federal Housing Administration (FHA) to put the workers back to building homes.[43] FHA created a new financing tool for the purchase of homes. Prior to the FHA, private banks would make home loans but require 30–50 percent of the home cost as a down payment and demand settlement by 10 years.[44]

The FHA created a new mortgage model familiar to most Americans—the 30-year mortgage. Under the FHA 30-year mortgage, the banks provide home loans, but the loans are guaranteed by the federal government and require only 10 percent as a down payment.[45] As the focus of this program centered on construction jobs, it should not be surprising that FHA homes are newly built and largely located outside of the central city.

The Federal National Mortgage Association, aka Fannie Mae, was another New Deal creation established to provide local banks with federal money to finance home mortgages.[46] Fannie Mae operates home loans and greatly reduces the interest rates charged to home owners, and it created the secondary mortgage market.[47] Fannie Mae is permitted to borrow money at low interest rates, provide fixed-rate mortgages, and make a profit between the rate borrowed and the rate loaned.[48] For the first 30 years, Fannie Mae had monopoly in the American secondary mortgage market.[49]

In 1970, the Federal Home Mortgage Corporation, nicknamed Freddie Mac, was created as a competitor to Fannie Mae.[50] Fannie Mae was privatized in the 1960s, and both organizations operated as government-sponsored enterprises.[51] These companies are supported by the federal government.[52] Government support still included access to a line of credit through the US Treasury, exemption from state and local income taxes, and exemption from Securities and Exchange Commission oversight.[53]

Direct Federal Government Spending on Housing

The tax code and subsidies for the housing industry are not the only means by which the federal government supports the development of workforce housing. The HUD operates an array of programs geared toward single-family and multifamily housing. HUD's proposed 2010 budget was $46,000,000,000. The single-family housing programs assist with mortgage insurance on loans to purchase new or existing homes, condominiums, manufactured housing, and houses needing rehabilitation, and for reverse-equity mortgages for elderly homeowners. The multifamily housing programs provide mortgage insurance to HUD-approved lenders to facilitate the construction, rehabilitation, purchase, and refinancing of multifamily housing projects and health-care facilities.

Health Care and Economic Development

Health care plays a major role in the retention and recruitment of companies to an area. Ten of the 20 fastest growing occupations are in the health-care industry.[54] From 2008 to 2018, the health-care industry is hoped to generate 3,200,000 new jobs—more than in any other industry.[55] In addition, the health-care industry is more likely recession-proof, and the companies pay high wages to workers from a range of backgrounds. Also, healthy populations serve as an engine for the region's economic growth.[56] Healthy workers are more productive, and as life expectancy touches nearly 80 across the United States, workers would be productive for longer periods. Health care is essential in community infrastructure and for regional workers and residents. Companies operating in a global economy expect access to both high-quality and affordable health care for their workers. A world-class health-care system no one can afford does not help the average worker. The counter is true as well. An affordable but low-quality regional health-care system is equally unattractive to the typically company searching for suitable sites.

Health-care quality matters from an economic development standpoint. Regions with a population that lives longer and healthier are more productive.[57] Even more interesting is that warm climates are not the key to a longer life. Of the top five states for average American life expectancy, only Hawaii and California are in the warm climate world.[58] Minnesota, New York, and Connecticut make the top five as well[59] (Figure 11.2).

Many states have launched aggressive efforts to address health-care quality. Top states for health-care quality are Connecticut, District of Columbia, Wisconsin, Minnesota, Massachusetts, Vermont, and Hawaii.[60] The Massachusetts health-care plan is the most high-profile, state-based plan in place. Wisconsin has been operating statewide affordable care organizations (ACOs) to create innovative partnerships with employers and health-care providers. Bellin Health–ThedaCare was selected by the federal government to operate as an ACO. ACOs are health-care teams using technology and knowledge around patient needs to improve health-care quality in coordination with private insurance companies and employers.[61] This Wisconsin ACO saved a Marinette manufacturer $2,000,000 in its first year of operation, and a Green Bay manufacturer has kept health care cost to less than 2 percent over the last 4 years.[62] Bellin Health insures more than 2,500 employers, with 75 located at on-site primary care clinics.[63]

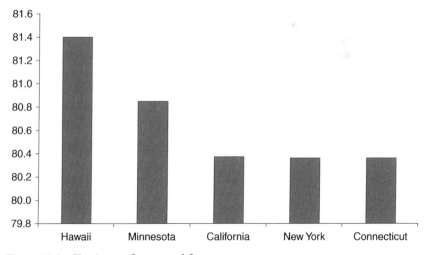

Figure 11.2   Top 5 states for average life expectancy.
Source: http://www.worldlifeexpectancy.com/usa/life-expectancy.

Regional health-care costs is the other major driver for companies considering a location decision. Many states are digging into "payment reform" and other initiatives to address the cost of health care. Wisconsin launched a collaboration between hospitals, health insurance, and private employers, which has resulted in health-care cost reductions estimated at nearly 50 percent.[64] This can result in millions of dollars of savings for companies that often have health insurance as a major cost.

Recreational Amenities and Economic Development

When quality of life is mentioned, most think about parks, sports team, and other activities that residents can enjoy. Quality of life is defined in economic development terms as a region's recreational and cultural amenities, climate, and local environmental quality.[65] Many regions excuse their lack of economic performance on the fact that they have no "mountains or ocean in their backyard." This excuse ignores the fact that many successful regions have no mountains or oceans, but they all pay attention to other recreational and cultural amenities that make their community a better place to live and raise a family.

Using a region's amenities as an economic growth tool is an established method for promoting economic development.[66] It is unclear whether people follow jobs or jobs simply follow people. Quality of life is of greater importance for economic development purposes as many companies may be drawn to these regions in the long term rather than by an array of tax incentives.[67]

The prime policy argument in favor of the use of recreational amenities as an economic development tool is its ability to shift population. America is a mobile society. Transportation and telecommunications networks create connections across a geographic location. Households and firms maximize the utility of goods and services through their decisions as to where to locate. This mobility implies regions with a high quality of life, and a strong set of recreational amenities would be appealing to both households and firms as they have the ability to work anywhere. This expansion of technology and transportation networks illustrates why natural resources and other recreational amenities are major contributors to the theory that the quality of life is a long-term economic development strategy.[68] Quality of life directly impacts population migration and solves challenges with customer and workforce density many rural regions face.[69]

Utah offers a model for how recreational activities impact economic development. Not every region has mountains or the ocean, but some do. Unique geographic features give communities an opportunity to create a successful economic development model around tourism and recreational activities. Utah has one of these examples at Park City. Park City built a global tourism model for regional economic development on the back of some impressive mountains and even better skiing and other recreational activity. Park City also created a downtown experience that made the region a true destination point. Park City was founded as a silver-mining town in 1869 and did not discover the benefits of skiing until 1963.[70] Park City is home to three of the nation's leading ski resorts, namely Park City Mountain Resort, The Canyons, and Deer Valley Resort, and a revitalized downtown that is host to restaurants and other entertainment venues.

Utah's skiing industry is 50 years old and has an economic impact of well over $1,600,000,000.[71] How did this sleepy village just outside of Salt Lake City turn into a global tourism powerhouse? The Olympics is the answer. Park City was the center of the 2002 Winter Olympics, and it put this region on the map for tourism in a way no other event could. The economic impact of the 2002 Winter Olympics included $4,800,000,000 in sales during the Olympics and a 25 percent hotel room usage increase from 2002 to 2009.[72] The statewide hotel occupancy increased from 58.8 percent in 2003 to 59.7 percent in 2010, and skiing in the region enjoyed a 42 percent increase since the Olympics.[73] Direct expenditures from skiers and snowboarders increased 67 percent from $704,000,000 in 2002–2003 to $1,200,000,000 in 2010–2011.[74] The Park City/Salt Lake City region is proof that tourism- and amenity-based economic development can create wealth, and the launch of major events such as the Olympics is such an initiative.

Using recreational amenities as an economic development tool also holds special appeal for rural communities.[75] Rural communities in many parts of the United States have been as badly hit as many urban centers. Manufacturing and agriculture are not the economic base for rural America that once were. The productivity and efficiency of both industries left more goods produced with far fewer workers. The challenge rural communities have is a lack of population density. Without a core of residents, companies are unlikely to locate either for retail centers or manufacturing facilities. Rural communities use their natural amenities to attract economic growth.[76] These amenities act not only as a tool to attract industry but to create a tourism industry itself. Natural amenities such as parks can create major "export" opportunities in rural communities. State parks in rural Georgia produced nearly $65,000,000 in gross economic output and were a driving force in the regional economy through the attraction of tourists the region never enjoyed otherwise.[77]

Workers in the high-tech field are attracted to regions with a strong base of recreational and cultural amenities.[78] Mobile, high-tech workers have proven to have a strong interest into not just the job they want but the region in which they wish to live. New-economy firms are less tied to the raw materials of a region and the transportation infrastructure. They are mobile and regions are forced to compete for these firms on a completely new level. These have been described as "footloose" firms that rely more on the quality of a highly skilled workforce and less on traditional "location theory" of cost of doing business.[79] This younger, highly educated, and mobile workforce is more connected to recreational and cultural amenities than their parents ever were. Whether tourism or attraction of high-tech workers is the goal, quality of life is an economic development strategy central to a region's economic success.

Big Questions

1. Is quality of life too "fuzzy" of a notion to be used in economic development strategy?

2. Is weather and topography the most important quality-of-life measure?

3. If cost of living is kept low, does that mean wages are low as well?

4. If wages are low, is economic development successful?

5. If cost of living is high, does that mean the quality of schools, public safety, and neighborhoods is high as well?

Class Writing Assignment

The mayor is concerned about the impact of declining housing market on Metropolis. She has asked you to write a policy brief on suggested steps the city can take to address the issues of rising foreclosure rates, vacant homes, and the lack of affordable housing in the city. The mayor expects your two-page policy paper to outline the scope of the issue, define what other local governments are doing to address the issue, and make three concrete policy recommendations for her consideration.

Metropolis City Council Case Study: Housing Debate

Expo Village partnering with a private sector national developer LFS, the mayor wants to develop a market-rate housing project on the land given to the city by the state just north of the state fairgrounds. It is bordered on the north by Northwood Avenue, on the east by I-71, on the south by East Seventeenth Avenue, and on the west by North Fourth Street. The president of council supports the vision of B&B Development to create a traditional, market-rate housing project. Several members of city council are also considering to propose federal government–subsidized housing at the site to ensure poor residents of the city benefit from this project. Housing for Everyone has proposed a government-subsidized housing project for the site. City council must vote upon which development will happen in Expo Village.

Additional Readings

"America's Animal Health Corridor," *Area Development Magazine*, October/November 2009, retrieved from http://www.areadevelopment.com/stateResources/kansas/Americas-animal-health-corridor-KansasCity008.shtml?Page=1.

Clyde Wilcox and John Bruce (ed.), *The Changing Politics of Gun Control* (Lanham, MD: Rowman and Littlefield, 1998).

David R. Boews, "A Two Stage Model of the Simultaneous Relationship between Economic Development and Crime," *Economic Development Quarterly*, 21, 1 (February 2007) 79–90.

David Salvesen and Henry Renski, *The Importance of Quality of Life in the Location Decision of New Economy Firms*, Center for Urban and Regional Studies, University of North Carolina at Chapel Hill, January 2003, retrieved from https://curs.unc.edu/files/2013/04/neweconomyreport.pdf.

George A. O. Alleyne and Daniel Cohen, *Health, Economic Growth and Poverty Reduction*, World Health Organization, April 2002, retrieved from http://whqlibdoc.who.int/publications/9241590092.pdf.

James Q. Wilson and George Kelling, "Broken Windows: The Police and Neighborhood Safety," *Atlantic Monthly*, 249, 3 (March 1982) 29–38.

Kate Bristol and Roger Montgomery, *Pruitt-Igoe* (Monteciello, IL: Council of Planning Libraries, 1987).

Lou Cannon, *Official Negligence, How Rodney King and the Riot Changed Los Angeles and the Los Angeles Police Department* (New York: Basic Books, 1999).

Marla Nelson and Laura Wolf-Powers, "Chains and Ladders: Exploring the Opportunities for Workforce Development and Poverty Reduction in the Hospital Sector," *Economic Development Quarterly,* 24, 1 (February 2010) 33–44.

Michael D. Usdan, "Mayors and Public Education: The Case for Greater Involvement," *Harvard Educational Review,* 76, 2 (Summer 2006) 147–152.

Richard Bither, *Confessions of a Subprime Lender* (New York: Wiley and Sons, 2008).

Sethard Fisher, "Economic Development and Crime," *American Journal of Economics and Sociology,* 46, 1 (January 1987) 17–34.

Steven C. Deller, Tsung-Hsui Tsai, David W. Marcouiller, and Donald B. K. English, "The Role of Amenities and Quality of Life in Rural Economic Growth," *American Journal of Agricultural Economics,* 83, 2 (May 2001) 352–365.

Steve Gibbons, "The Cost of Urban Property Crime," *The Economic Journal,* 114 (2004) 441–463.

CHAPTER TWELVE

ECONOMIC DRIVER: ENERGY-LED ECONOMIC DEVELOPMENT

Chapter Goals

1. Know how environment policy plays a key role in hindering or helping an economic development opportunity
2. Discuss the laws and regulations, such as historic preservation, that play a direct role in an economic development project
3. Understand what constitutes sustainable development in relation to economic development
4. Discuss specific examples of successful economic development projects with their focus on sustainable development

Energy-Led Economic Development

Energy-led economic development capitalizes on existing regional natural resources and creates wealth through long-term sustainable development strategies. This new economic development model delivers high-wage jobs through traditional building block economic development tactics and innovative regulations. Successful energy-led economic development promotes the exploration of the region for traditional and alternative energy sources. This approach promotes an environmentally friendly land use strategy. Energy development, such as shale exploration, biomass facilities, and wind or solar farms, creates wealth in many parts of the United States. Redeveloping existing brownfield sites and historic structures also takes advantage of existing infrastructure and creates jobs where pollution once stagnated. Workforce strategies develop energy workers a region or a state needs. In an energy-led economic development model, tax policy promotes the adoption of energy-efficient "green buildings" to retain or recruit energy companies. Quality-of-life strategies matter as well for the energy crowd, and finally, a regulatory approach that demands environmentally friendly sources such as wind, solar, biomass, and other renewable sources is a prime strategy to recruit energy companies to a region or state.

North Dakota is one of the several states benefiting from shale oil boom and natural gas exploration. In 2001, North Dakota ranked thirty-eighth in real GDP among the 50 states. However, the quintupling of crude oil and tripling of natural gas production in North Dakota since 2007 made it a leader in GDP growth. North Dakota leads the nation in per capita income growth. The economic success of North Dakota is directly related to the exploration of shale oil and natural gas in the Bakken region. North Dakota is building a new economy based upon high-tech oil and natural gas exploration strategies.

Oregon is a leader among states in developing an energy-led economic development model. Oregon's model builds around the attraction of the alternative energy industry matched with the use of smart land use tactics to manage development in an environmentally sensitive fashion. Oregon is a leader in renewable energy standards, and Oregon's Green Jobs Growth Plan lays out a roadmap for adopting economic development incentives, workforce programs, and market efforts toward the development of jobs in the environmental industry sector. Oregon has over 43,000 green jobs spread across 4,339 employers, making up 3 percent of the state's employment.[1] Oregon's green jobs are from every major industry and occupational group. Oregon's green jobs pay $23.07 an hour compared to $19.83 for all nonfederal jobs in the state and the $16.31 statewide median wage.[2] Oregon is winning economically through a green jobs platform.

Policy Arguments for Energy-Led Economic Development

Many policy arguments exist as to why an energy-led economic development model works. First, energy is big business. The global energy market is $6,000,000,000,000,000. Whether your region is winning in the Industrial Age or the Information Age, the products and services are more dependent on power. Many of US's leaders in wealth creation, such as North Dakota, South Dakota, and Texas, are building economic success chasing the growing demand for energy.

Shale gas development, in particular, is spurring wealth creation. Advanced drilling technology, known as hydraulic fracturing, is pulling out massive deposits of oil and natural gas from deep shale rock formations. The boom in shale natural gas constituted 27 percent of the overall US natural gas production in 2010.[3] Shale gas is also a job producer. It supported more than 600,000 direct, indirect, and induced jobs.[4] Shale gas has not only created new wealth for once-poor landowners, but it is moving the United States toward energy self-sufficiency. The United States will be the top producer of oil globally within 5 years, an exporter of natural gas by 2020, and an oil exporter by 2030, all because of shale gas development.[5] The United States imports one-fifth of its present energy needs, but looks like it will be energy self-sufficient by 2025.[6] This has been a geopolitical and economic development goal since the Arab oil embargo of the 1970s.

From a land use perspective, the cost of urban sprawl is substantial. Urban sprawl creates costs for local governments as the demand for services added by newly developed land outpaces the revenue it creates.[7] These costs include additional infrastructure, water and sewer, police, fire, solid waste, and other local government services needed to expand developments. Urban sprawl has also created a negative environmental impact, affecting the health of area residents and dramatically increasing the demand for fossil fuels.[8]

The "Green Economy" is an established and successful high-wage job creator.[9] The explosion of green technology matched with public concerns over America's reliance on foreign lands for energy is encouraging the energy-led economic development movement. The green jobs sector is small but a powerful group with 2,700,000 workers—this constitutes more workers than the fossil fuel industry.[10] Green jobs include manufacturing and public services such as wastewater and mass transit. A smaller percentage of these green jobs are in energy-related industries such as solar photovoltaic cell, wind, fuel cell, smart grid, biofuel, and battery industries.[11] Twenty-six percent of all green jobs are in manufacturing compared to 9 percent of the national economy, and green companies export roughly twice the value of the typical American job.[12] Heavy green manufacturing sectors include electric vehicles, green chemical products, and lighting segments, which are highly export-intensive.[13] Green jobs pay high wages for low- and middle-skilled workers. The average wage of green jobs is 13 percent higher than the US wage average.[14] Yet a disproportionate percentage of jobs in the clean economy is staffed by workers with relatively little formal education in moderately well-paying "green collar" occupations.[15] Opponents of the green jobs movement point to the high cost of regulation that spurs much of this job creation, which only happens through state-based regulation mandating the use of expensive alternative energy sources.

Energy as an Economic Development Tool

Energy-led economic development tools are dominated by land use tactics to address urban sprawl, and tax and regulatory policy to recruit energy industry jobs. Urban sprawl of residential, commercial, and industrial development expands public infrastructure spending beyond the means of many state and local governments. The challenges of sprawl encourage the redevelopment of evacuated urban centers for residential, commercial, and industrial growth that was once too costly. Rising gas and transportation costs matched with hour-long commuting push Americans to rely less on automobiles and more on mass transit. The urban core offers strong public infrastructure and a large base of customers. Land use is not the only aspect to an energy-led economic development model. Regulatory policies and infrastructure encouraging shale gas drilling and renewable energy development are leading an economic renaissance in many regions of the United States. Regions leading America's economic recovery are doing so on the backs of the energy industry. Regions are putting an energy-led economic development model to work by addressing urban sprawl through land use regulation, funding brownfield site redevelopment, and promoting the adoption of sustainable building standards, renewable energy mandates, and energy exploration.

Sustainable Development Land Use Model

Developing unimproved land is simpler and cheaper. Whereas, a higher transaction cost is imposed on remodeling existing structures and local government zoning is in place.[16] Zoning discourages development in an already developed area. Many rural regions either lack zoning or have few neighbors around to complain about a development. In addition, these rural communities are typically governed by townships that are given fewer land use powers under state law. Zoning in urban areas is a contributing factor toward growth and development moving out.

The result is a sprawl. Sprawl is the real estate development process in which the spread of property improvement far outpaces population growth. It is a phase when population is dispersed in low-density areas with rigidly separated homes, shops, and workplaces. These areas are served by a network of roads marked by huge blocks and poor access and a lack of well-defined, thriving activity centers.[17] A lack of development patterns provides a negative fiscal impact on government. In fact, local governments spent nearly $140,000,000,000 to create new infrastructure such as schools, roads, and sewer and utility systems, and over $200,000,000,000 was spent on recurring costs such as infrastructure maintenance, police and fire services, and garbage collection.[18]

Measuring the success of antisprawl activities typically considers residential density, neighborhood mix of homes, jobs, and services, strength of activity centers and downtowns, and accessibility of the street network.[19] Density examines the proportion of residents living in very spread-out suburban areas compared to the portion of residents living very close together in town centers.[20] Sprawl losers include regions such as Riverside (California).[21] This community received low marks because more than 66 percent of the population lives over ten miles from a central business district, and just 28 percent of residents live within one-half block of any business. Also, less than 1 percent of the residents live in communities with enough density to be served by transit, and over 70 percent of its blocks are larger than traditional urban size.[22]

Smart growth winners include traditional high-density areas such as New York City, Jersey City, San Francisco, Boston, and Miami and, surprisingly, cities such as Omaha, Providence, Honolulu, and Portland[23] (Table 12.1).

Table 12.1 Smart growth America's sprawl index losers

Metro Region	Sprawl Index	Rank
Riverside-San Bernardino, CA	14.2	First
Greensboro-Winston-Salem-High Point, NC	46.8	Second
Raleigh-Durham, NC	54.2	Third
Atlanta, GA	57.7	Fourth
Greenville-Spartanburg, SC	58.6	Fifth
West Palm Beach-Boca Raton-Delray Beach, FL	67.7	Sixth
Bridgeport-Stamford-Norwalk-Danbury, CT	68.4	Seventh
Knoxville, TN	68.7	Eighth
Oxnard-Ventura, CA	75.1	Ninth
Fort Worth-Arlington, TX	77.2	Tenth

Source: Mark Muro and Robert Puentes, *Investing in a Better Future: A Review of the Fiscal and Competitive Advantages of Smarter Growth Development Patters* (Washington, DC: Brookings Institution, 2004).

Antisprawl opponents point to a long list of negative impacts of sprawl. Regions with higher rates of sprawl drive cars for longer distances—on average 180 cars per 100 households compared to lower-sprawl regions that average 162 cars per 100 households.[24] Sprawling regions have more air pollution, greater risk of fatal accidents, and high traffic congestion.[25] Another major negative impact of sprawl relates to the infrastructure spending and resulting gap in infrastructure that sprawl creates. Many regions such as Atlanta and Raleigh have seen huge job growth during the post–World War II era. That job growth led to booming development in these regions. Unfortunately, for many of these high-growth regions, development patterns spread out into urban sprawl rather than concentrated development. Infrastructure simply did not keep up with the supply of growth that brought people and cars to the region.

The real downside of America's sprawling development model is that it happens everywhere—in high-growth and low-growth regions. Detroit, Cleveland, and other struggling industrial cities have seen regional growth spread far outside of the central city. This sprawl in struggling areas happens for a variety of reasons such as crime and the educational system, but also because the real estate outside of the center city is typically unimproved—farmland or forest. It is cheap, flat, and connected to the region by the interstate highway system.

Growth through sprawl expands existing highways to address the increased car traffic. The nation's surface transportation infrastructure alone needs $1,700,000,000,000 before 2020 in highway and transit projects.[26] The United States is on track to spend $877,000,000,000 during this timeframe, creating an infrastructure spending gap of $846,000,000,000 over 9 years.[27]

Smart growth is a planning concept that entails considering the environment and economic growth as a means for creating energy-led economic development. It means using comprehensive planning to guide, design, develop, revitalize, and build communities in a way that preserves and enhances natural and cultural resources. It distributes development costs and benefits, expands transportation, employment, and housing options in a fiscally responsible manner. Smart growth values long-range regional considerations for sustainability and promotes public health.[28] The stereotypical smart growth development is mixed-use, compact, transit-accessible, and pedestrian-oriented.[29]

One method to promote greater economic redevelopment is to incentivize the "smart growth" of communities within the existing urban footprint rather than extending it out farther away from the center of the city. Local government smart growth tactics include regional planning, development moratoria, capital improvement programming, infrastructure finance, developer funding of infrastructure (property dedication, impact fees, and linkage and mitigation fees), transferred development rights, and green space protection.

A transferable development right (TDR) is an emerging land use regulation strategy in which the development potential of a specified land is traded on the open market for other specified land.[166] The land being protected from development may be environmentally sensitive or just a boundary line where sprawl is being stopped. A TDR provides a means to economically benefit owners of land by a means other than development while stopping sprawl. Local governments use TDRs to preserve historic structures and protect agricultural lands, forest lands, and open space. TDRs shift development from the protected area to a designated growth zone, which is typically close to public services.

For example, Montgomery county (Maryland) enacted a TDR ordinance to preserve agricultural land in the face of expanding residential subdivisions and commercial development.[31] Under the ordinance, rural areas of the county were downzoned from one dwelling unit for every five acres to one dwelling unit for every 25 acres.[32] The TDR creates a permanent easement to regulate residential density. Owners were given five transferable rights, allowing them to build one additional dwelling unit per each 25 acres.[33] The development rights can be purchased if the purchaser receives a permit to do so, and such a permit may be issued concurrently with the subdivision plat approval.[34] In 2000, the market value for a single TDR right was approximately $10,000, and more than 38,000 acres of the approximately 91,000 rural acres had been preserved.[35] The county also has a Purchase of Development Rights Program allowing the county to use public funds to purchase TDRs so that the county can then place a perpetual deed restriction on the property that limits it to only agricultural uses.[36]

The use of land as green space preserves wildlife, maintains water quality, provides for recreation areas, provides space for alternative corridors, and provides another wall against suburban sprawl. Parklands, preserves, and green space enhance the value of existing residential and commercial property. Green space is protected through city purchases of land, adoption of a conservations easement that restricts future development, private donation of land to a local land preservation trust, and local impact fees or special tax on future development. Land banking is a preservation tool where the government purchases land to preserve it as green space. In some instances, the government can resell the land with restrictions (i.e., a conservation easement) prohibiting any development. A conservation easement is a legally binding contract between a land owner and an agency or government in which the land owner agrees to permanently refrain from certain land uses that would conflict with conservation goals.[37]

Starting in 1990, San Juan county (Washington) began a large Land Bank Program.[38] The Program is funded by a voter-approved 1 percent real estate transfer tax on any property purchased in the county.[39] Since its inception, the Program protected over 4,800 acres from development.[40] The land targeted includes marine shorelines, woodlands, farmland, wetlands, and historic homesteads that meet the Program's specified criteria.[41] The Program's selection criteria must be met before a project can be pursued. The property must provide a conservation resource, which must be vulnerable to adverse change and which can be adequately protected through the Program.[42] There must also be adequate public support for the project, and the acquisition must make effective use of the Land Bank's funds and resources.[43] Just recently, the Land Bank spent $2,100,000 on a 120-acre historic farm, which was targeted by developers.[44] Through a conservation easement, the Land Bank eliminated any potential residential development on the land, and the property remained a working farm.[45]

Oregon is an example of a state with a fully integrated planning system encompassing all levels of government that works to manage smart growth.[46] The state government and all local governments must adopt a comprehensive land use plan that is consistent with statewide planning goals.[47] To ensure the plans are consistent, Oregon created the Land Conservation and Development Commission.[48] The Commission's duties include reviewing state, county, city, and other local agency comprehensive plans for consistency and compliance with statewide goals and laws. The Commission is responsible for preparing, adopting, amending, and revising statewide land planning goals.[49] The Commission has the power to issue orders requiring a government or state agency to comply with state planning laws and goals.[50] The Commission may remedy noncompliance by requiring oversight by the Department of Land Conservation and Development for any land use action or decision made by the noncomplying body, withholding grant money or certain revenues from the noncomplying body or enjoining some of the noncomplying body's actions.[51]

Oregon also allows regions to coordinate their planning efforts by developing a Metropolitan Service District. The Metropolitan Service District must complete a comprehensive plan for the region, which includes a provision for building and housing sustainability within urban growth boundaries for at least 20 years.[52] The Portland metro has its own governing body. Portland metro performs functions such as operating regional services and has a binding authority to review local plans.[53] Under its charter, the regional framework plan details goals and policies on land use, transportation, parks and open space, water management, and natural hazards, and implements measures for an urban growth boundary.[54] It includes a provision outlining the population levels and settlement patterns the region can accommodate in the future. This planning takes into consideration the carrying capacity of the land, water, air, educational, and economic resources.[55] The Portland metro also works to coordinate local comprehensive plans, implementing regulations, and a regional transportation plan. Overall, the Portland metro framework seeks to manage growth in the multicounty region for 50 years.[56]

Green Workforce

Regions and states use workforce development strategies to recruit green jobs. Green jobs offer opportunities for college graduates and non–college graduates to transition from the struggling traditional manufacturing industry to new, high-tech companies. Green workforce initiatives exist across the United States and tend to work hand-in-hand with broader sustainability initiatives such as renewable energy standards, weatherization funding, and alternative energy recruitment efforts.

Green jobs require a slightly different set of workforce skills. While not every green job requires a specific certification, many sustainable industries would prefer workers certified in their specific industry. As an example, the solar industry finds it attractive if their installers obtain a nationally recognized certification from the North American Board of Certified Energy Practitioners.[57] Other important green job certifications include the Association of Energy Engineers for energy efficiency–related certifications for facility managers and heating, ventilation, and air conditioning installers.[58] The Building Performance Institute offers certifications for building analysts and heating and air-conditioning professionals, and Energy

Star provides online training to contractors on energy-efficient building design.[59] Solar Energy International is a private training provider that offers course in renewable energy, and The Green Building Certification Institute runs the high-profile Leadership in Environmental and Energy Design (LEED) Accredited Professionals program, which is utilized by a range of professionals from lawyers to engineers to architects for green building certification.[60]

Green jobs are not just in Oregon, Washington, and other havens of smart growth. Traditional larger states are also havens for green jobs. Figure 12.1 outlines which states are succeeding in attracting green jobs.

Pennsylvania positioned itself as a leader in the development of green jobs. Working in tandem with alternative energy regulatory policy and economic incentives, Pennsylvania developed its green workforce. Pennsylvania shifted its workforce development strategy to an industry-based approach geared toward targeted industry clusters in high-priority occupations and then developed industry partnerships to address workforce needs. This approach works well with the alternative energy industry in the state. Lancaster county (Pennsylvania) plays a leadership role by coordinating all alternative energy workforce training in the region, creating a Building Energy Technology Program in collaboration with Thaddeus Stevens College of Technology in partnership with local companies, and advertising green job opportunities to area workers.[61]

Chicago, the prime driver of the Illinois economy, offers a model for developing a green job workforce as well. Chicago's regional workforce development strategy targets eight industry clusters and works in partnership with the region's 20 community colleges.[62] In addition, they create a green curriculum for targeted skills in weatherization and other areas.[63]

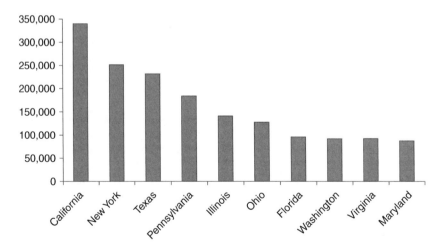

Figure 12.1 States with the most green jobs.
Source: Economic Policy Institute.

Capitalizing on Existing Infrastructure:
Brownfield Redevelopment

Brownfield is real property, the expansion, redevelopment, or reuse of which may be complicated by the presence of hazardous substances. Brownfield sites are those contaminated by petroleum or petroleum products and controlled substances, as well as mine-scarred lands.[64] However, brownfield programs exclude facilities listed on the National Priorities List (US Environmental Protection Agency [EPA] Superfund List), facilities subject to unilateral administrative orders, and facilities subject to the jurisdiction, custody, or control of the US government.[65]

Federal and state environmental laws create liability for contamination at sites that freeze development. Federal law creates liability for the environmental contamination of a site. Under federal law, a property owner can establish a "bona fide prospective purchaser defense" before purchasing the property if a property owner can establish that a release or threatened release was caused by the act or omission of a contractually unrelated third party.[66] The prospective property owner cannot be contractually related to prior owners or know about hazardous substances.[67] To obtain protection, the prospective owner must undertake all appropriate inquiry into the previous ownership and uses of the property consistent with good commercial and customary practice.[68] For liability purposes and potential grant and other government funding opportunities, the prospective owner will hire an environmental consultant to perform phase I and phase II reviews of the site.

In the United States, 500,000 to 1,000,000 brownfields exist.[69] The redevelopment of brownfield sites creates economic development opportunities and promotes the concept of building within the existing regional footprint without sprawling further out. The majority of brownfields are waiting for redevelopment, and many are in highly sought-after locations surrounded by infrastructure and customers. Addressing environmental contamination is often the major issue associated with the redevelopment of an urban infill site.

Federal Brownfield Program

The US EPA offers incentives to prospective developers undertaking brownfield assessment, clean-up, revolving loans, and environmental job training. Assessment grants provide funding to inventory, characterize, assess, and conduct planning and community involvement related to brownfield sites.[70] An eligible entity may apply for $200,000 up to $700,000 to assess a site contaminated by hazardous substances, pollutants, or petroleum.[71] Clean-up grants provide funding to carry out clean-up activities at brownfield sites. Applicants are limited to funding for five sites and must have a 20 percent cost share.[72] An eligible entity may apply for up to $200,000 per site.[73] The relatively low dollar amount of the federal grant rarely serves as enough funding to clean up most remediation projects.

Brownfield job training grants bring together community groups, job training organizations, educators, labor, and private sector leaders to provide environmental employment and training for residents in communities impacted by brownfields.[74] Grant awards go to nonprofit organizations, colleges and universities, and regional, state, and local government agencies. For-profit organizations are not eligible for this type of funding, and the maximum annual funding award is $300,000 for up to 5 years (for a total of $1,500,000).[75] These grants may be used to address sites contaminated by petroleum, hazardous substances, or pollutants.[76]

Brownfield Revolving Loan Fund provides up to $1,000,000 in loans over 5 years. For-profit organizations are ineligible for this type of funding.[77] Eligible recipients for Revolving Loan Funds include state, local, and tribal governments and political subdivisions of states.[78] The federal government's brownfield program claims many victories.

For instance, $17.39 is leveraged for every EPA dollar expended, and 71,833 jobs nationwide are created by this EPA program.[79] Reduced storm water run-off from brownfield redevelopment is 43 percent to 60 percent lower than alternative green-field scenarios and can increase residential property values 2 percent to 3 percent when nearby brownfields are addressed.[80]

State Brownfield Programs

State governments also operate brownfield redevelopment programs. In 2010, 12,864 brownfields were remediated by states, municipalities, and tribal agencies constituting a 10 percent increase over the previous year.[81] Brownfields program leveraged more than $14,000,000,000 in brownfields clean-up and redevelopment funding from the private and public sectors and created over 60,000 jobs.[82]

Ohio's program redevelops brownfield sites. It addresses both environmental liability and funding needs for brownfield sites through two distinct but connected programs. Ohio's Voluntary Action Program (VAP) is administered by the Ohio EPA and addresses liability issues. The VAP allows a developer or property owner to hire a certified professional to assess a site and direct clean-up activities to achieve state-set standards. Improving this process substantially in Ohio was the memorandum of understanding established between the Ohio EPA and US EPA on the VAP.[83] If an applicant follows the requirements of the memorandum of understanding, US EPA agrees not to use its legal authority unless a serious threat to health arises.[84] However, there is no funding available through the VAP to help with the cost of property acquisition, assessment, environmental remediation, or redevelopment.

The Clean Ohio Fund was operated by the Ohio Department of Development and addresses funding of brownfield remediation for redevelopment purposes.[85] The Clean Ohio Fund has brought $627,000,000 to support brownfield remediation and passive parkland, bike trail, and farmland preservation initiatives. Eligible applicants are local government agencies not associated with contaminating the site.[86] However, grants were not awarded to a site that does not have a public or private sector developer ready and willing to redevelop the site and a 25 percent minimum match.[87] Eligible projects included brownfield sites where a clean-up is required to redevelop the site.[88] Eligible activities for grant funding are assessments, acquisition, clearance/demolition, remediation/clean-up, and infrastructure neces-sary to serve the brownfield site.[89] The Clean Ohio Fund provided $40,000,000 in brownfield remediation funding each year for 4 years, and the program was extended beyond its original planned life.[90] The program's grants do not just reach urban neighborhoods. The Clean Ohio Fund's main brownfield program looked to the recommendation of local government leaders first through the recommendations of local communities.[91] This local ranking process was then carried forward to a statewide Clean Ohio Council that makes the final determination as to which projects were awarded up to $3,000,000 grants for brownfield remediation from the Clean Ohio Fund's Clean Ohio Revitalization Fund.[92] The Clean Ohio Fund program has been transferred to the private sector–led JobsOhio organization, who is implemented by a $40,000,000 urban redevelopment fund.

The Clean Ohio Fund and the VAP were connected. Only projects undergoing Ohio EPA's VAP process are eligible for grants. Clean Ohio Fund applications were enhanced based upon its economic impact of a project, use of an active remedy for environmental damage, and proximity of the site to a sensitive area.[93] The use of green building standards and sustainable redevelopment tactics, such as the reuse of existing structures or on-site materials, also enhances the project's chances of gaining grants from Clean Ohio Funds.[94] Major drawbacks in an application include a contaminant exceeding applicable standards remain at site, a combination of active and nonactive remedies, or asbestos is the only contaminant. "Orphan property" (no existing owner) or a lack of financial support from the party responsible for the contamination can harm the application as well.[95]

Ohio developed many successful projects through Clean Ohio Fund. One in particular is the clean-up of the Akron Airdock facility. This 22-story facility could hold two Washington Monuments end to end and was a home to the famous Goodyear Blimp.[96] It was purchased in 2003 by Lockheed Martin with the goal of using it for a new space age version of the blimp.[97] The use of $3,000,000 in Clean Ohio Funds was matched by funds by Lockheed Martin and the local government to clean up contaminants at the site. The result was the retention of over 500 jobs and creation of nearly 100 more.[98]

Tax Policy: Green Building Codes

Many regions and states are pursuing alternative energy companies. Tactics to attract these companies include the use of tax policy, but are evolving into the use of green building codes. Green building codes are a statement about the environmental sensitivity of a region and help to develop a "green" company supply chain. The economic development goal behind green building initiatives is to be a global leader in developing, designing, and constructing the buildings of the future. Communities that create incentives for new "green" building approaches are where these product and service businesses choose to locate and grow. Many cities, and at least one state, have begun instituting green policies, codes, or incentives for land and building redevelopment.

US Green Building Council's LEED Certification

The LEED program is a facility certification based upon the number of points accumulated for fulfilling different "green" requirements throughout the design and building process.[99] There are four achievement levels: Certified, Silver, Gold, and

Platinum.[100] Each certification level indicates a higher point total for portions of the project.[101] With regard to New Construction/Renovation certification, there are points available to accumulate over six major building components: Sustainable Sites, Water Efficiency, Energy and Atmosphere, Materials and Resources, Indoor Environmental Quality, and Innovation in Design.[102]

Each component provides a list of green activities, materials, methods, or other considerations that accumulate points based on the level of participation.[103] The project owner is free to "pick and choose" which activities fit best in the project.[104] The components are detailed as to what is required to accumulate individual points.[105] The type of site developed for new construction, the amount of public/alternative transportation available, roof coverings, and water use reduction all move a building up the LEED process.[106] Renewable energy use, refrigerant elimination, power measurement verification, recycling collection, and building material recycling and reuse also help increase a building's green certification.[107] Finally, waste management, use of regionally produced material, indoor air quality considerations, low-emission paints and solvents, daylight visibility, climate control, and lighting controls give a project added weight.[108] Each requirement, or "credit," provides the performance level needed for earning points and the reasons behind the requirement. Finally, a US Green Building Council Board evaluates the two submissions, one at the design phase and one at the construction phase, to determine the final certification level.[19]

Green Building Incentives

Regions use incentives to encourage the development of "green buildings." Again, Portland (Oregon) is a leader in green building incentives. Oregon looks to the carbon footprint of new and renovated buildings not through a green building code but rather through the creation of financial incentives. Portland's financial incentives include the Green Investment Fund.[110] This Fund was established in 2005 as a 5-year, $2,500,000 competitive grant to support Portland-based green building projects.[111] From 2005 through 2009, $425,000 was awarded annually for 36 public and private industrial, multifamily, residential, commercial, mixed-use and nonprofit projects.[112]

Growing-up through Historic Preservation

Saving historic structures can be a key element to an energy-led economic development model. Promoting the use of historic preservation increases land values and enhances the regional economy.[113] Historic preservation has a 30-year-plus track record of creating more than 2,000,000 jobs and generating more than $90,000,000,000 in investment.[114] Rehabilitative construction has been found to create 50 percent more jobs than new-build construction.[115] Historic preservation is a tool local governments use to revive neighborhoods. It enhances the environmental quality and reduces overall community infrastructure costs by promoting development in existing areas rather than sprawling away from the center city.[116]

Historic preservation is a government process to provide aesthetic regulation through land use regulation and state and federal tax credits, which incentivize investment in properties with a historic designation. Aesthetic regulation, often implemented through architectural control, is a process driven by local governments through the zoning process. It is coordinated through the creation of a "historic district" in a city. Once the historic district boundaries are established by the local government, any alteration or new building that might affect the integrity of the historic district may require an "independent analysis by an architectural historian" to evaluate the project's impact on historic resources.[117] Any exterior modifications that are approved must conform to federal guidelines for historic structures.[118] Most historic preservation codes have a strict policy on demolition of historic buildings. No building identified as "historic" can be demolished unless health and safety requirements are in play.[119]

State and federal governments promote historic preservation through the use of tax credits to incentivize investments in properties designated as historic. Kentucky is one of nearly 30 states that uses historic preservation tax credits to promote economic development. Created in 2005, the Kentucky Historic Tax Credit offers a state tax credit for rehabilitation of commercial and residential projects listed on the National Register of Historic Places.[120] Kentucky offers a 30 percent tax credit for qualified owner-occupied residents and a 20 percent tax credit for commercial and rental units with a total credit of $60,000 and $400,000, respectively.[121] For every $1,000,000 invested in the rehabilitation of a property, Kentucky state and local governments have a combined increase of $184,000 in new revenue.[122]

The federal government also makes an investment in historic preservation through the use of the Federal Historic Tax Credit. Created in 1976, the Federal Historic Tax Credit finances approximately 1,000 projects nationally annually, with $4,000,000 in tax credits.[123] Three different Federal Historic Tax Credits exist: a 20 percent credit for historic properties, a 10 percent credit for nonhistoric properties built prior to 1936, and tax benefits linked to the use of historic preservation easements.[124] The Federal Historic Tax Credit produces a positive economic development outcome but also creates a net revenue gain for the federal government, producing $22,300,000,000 in federal tax revenue while costing the federal government $17,500,000,000 in tax expenditures.[125] Historic preservation leads to job creation, increases in property values, creation of the heritage tourism industry, enhancement of environmental and social impacts through a reduction of urban sprawl, and revitalization of downtown cores.[126] The listing of a building on the National Register of Historic Places stabilizes, if not increases, its value and that of its surrounding property.[127] In addition, neighborhood historic preservation districts are a component of creating a tourism industry, one that did not exist.[128] Historic preservation projects save 50 percent to 80 percent in infrastructure costs compared to new suburban development.[129]

Renewable Energy Incentives and Mandates

States use renewable energy incentives and mandates to recruit alternative energy companies. Nearly all 50 states offer financial incentives for the development of renewable energy production facilities and programs to reward consumers for using them. Oregon offers a Business Energy Tax Credit to companies investing in renewable energy. Companies manufacturing renewable energy equipment may be eligible for a 50 percent tax credit up to $40,000,000.[130] The Iowa Power Fund finances renewable energy projects, and Montana's Clean and Green program offers property tax incentives to energy facilities.[131] State regulators and policy makers in nearly 30 states decided that utilities must gain a set percentage of power from renewable or alternative sources. Solar, wind, biomass, agriculture waste, municipal solid waste, and even nuclear have been identified as alternative or renewable sources. Many of these states have adopted energy efficiency mandates and incentives for companies and utilities.

States adopting renewable energy mandates are diversifying power sources but also recruiting advanced energy companies. A state must have a renewable energy mandate to recruit global wind mill manufacturers. The renewable energy standards are a government regulation meant to create a market for alternative energy products. Opponents of renewable energy mandates focus on the increased power costs that residential and business consumers face with renewable energy. However, unique coalitions including farmers are becoming stronger advocates for renewable energy mandates as it creates new markets for biomass or agriculture waste.

Traditional Energy Recruitment

The shale explosion creates wealth in places that rarely benefited from energy production. States such as North Dakota, South Dakota, Ohio, and Pennsylvania are dramatically increasing the level of oil and natural gas production through advanced horizontal drilling techniques, known as "fracking." Ohio's Utica shale production illustrates the growth potential in job and wealth. In 2012, 215 horizontal wells were drilled in Ohio, but only 87 were in production.[132] These wells produced 636,000 barrels of oil and more than 12,800,000,000 cubic feet of gas.[133] The Utica shale development creates economic opportunity on several fronts. Regions of eastern Ohio are selling land for imaginable prices. The Utica shale region covers an Appalachian region of Ohio. Shale is transitioning land owners from poor to rich. The real benefit of shale is in the opportunity for "midstream development" and access to a low-cost power source. Blue Racer Midstream is a $1,500,000,000 facility that processes the natural gas collected in eastern Ohio.[134] NiSource Midstream Services is planning a billion-dollar natural gas processing facility as well.[135] The Utica shale development also created a form of cheap energy for eastern Ohio, which has attracted manufacturing companies. Economic impact studies of the Utica shale play estimate nearly $10,000,000,000 in economic output and almost $4,500,000,000 in state and local taxes in 2014.[136]

Opponents of shale development question the validity of economic impact studies but have stronger objections to the environmental impacts of "fracking." Environmentalists believe "fracking" can have an impact on air and drinking water for decades to come.

Ohio has also been an object of public policy debates regarding how to best develop shale gas and oil. Ohio's governor proposed an increase in the state's severance tax to capitalize on the Utica shale exploration, but the general assembly rejected this proposal. The rejection is a sign the general assembly wants to encourage further investment by the oil industry. Also, shale development created public policy debates about the cost to local governments for resources needed for heavy drilling equipment. Again, Ohio is debating new impact fees local governments could use to fund the infrastructure needed for shale development.

Big Questions

1. Do smart growth strategies help or harm economic development?

2. Do "green regulations" harm traditional development?

3. Is it a smart economic development plan to replace a former contaminated factory site with an apartment complex?

4. Do "green" building standards really have to be part of a regional economic development strategy?

5. Is the shale boom temporary? Will it prove more harm than help as time goes on?

Class Writing Assignment

The mayor received a nasty letter from a constituent, Sally Davidson. The letter is a pretty strong rebuke regarding any effort to promote "green jobs" as a waste of taxpayer dollars, an unfair picking of winners and losers among the private sector, and a jump into a market Metropolis has no experience in. The mayor likes "green jobs" and is planning on making them the centerpiece of some future economic development efforts. She has asked you to draft a constituent response letter, no more than one page, politely disagreeing with Ms Davidson and stating why "green jobs" are a worthy investment for Metropolis.

Metropolis Sustainability Debate

Remember, the Expo Research and Development Park is a planned 200-acre research park that comes with an essential $100,000,000 in university foundation funding, but it sits on an environmentally contaminated site. The $100,000,000 in university funding is the movement the university or other private sector entity can provide. The Expo Research and Development Park will not happen if Metropolis cannot secure funding for environmental remediation. Budgets are tight. Metropolis needs to gain this $5,000,000 in brownfield clean-up funding from another governmental source.

Internal competition for brownfield clean-up funds in Metropolis and across Ohio is fierce through the Clean Ohio Fund and various federal programs. Metropolis will likely get only one project funded from state and federal government sources, and city council must select the project that will win.

The Expo Research and Development Park will reportedly create up to 20,000 jobs when the build-out is complete. However, the only confirmed tenant is a university-based technology start-up that is ready to move from the region's tech incubator. Z Spot has $100,000,000 in financial backing to create a proton therapy machine that is reportedly the next big thing in cure for cancer. Z Spot plans to open a global proton therapy facility, and the Expo Research and Development Park is a great location primarily because it is near the university. Z Spot is very capital-intensive and only employs 100 workers who make an average of $85,000 annually. The Expo Research and Development Park pays $250,000 in property taxes, and its workers when the park is built out will pay $400,000 annually in city income taxes with the current 2 percent rate. Z Spot will pay $50,000 in property taxes and $170,000 in city income taxes.

The property in question for the Expo Research and Development Park, and specifically Z Spot, is vacant except for environmental contaminants at the site. The environmental consultant for the Expo Research and Development Park has recommended an active remedy, and after remedy, the area may still be below acceptable environmental standards. The site is nowhere near a home, school, daycare, or water source. All of the Expo Research and Development Park will be LEED-certified at the highest level.

The former chemical company that polluted the site is long gone, but the university is providing $100,000,000 for other aspects of site redevelopment. The project is centered on redeveloping a poor area but will not likely employ many area residents. Proton therapy is regarded a risky investment, but it is part of a major regional economic development plan.

The university has an option to purchase the property from Chemical R Us. The brownfield funding request centers solely on removal of contaminants from the site. Infrastructure and demolition will be funded by the university. The university held several briefings with the neighborhood and gathered multiple letters of support for its grant application. However, several neighbors did raise questions regarding the safety of the first-of-its-kind proton technology.

The Lincoln Workforce Center is a proposal supported by preservationists and labor leaders. The centerpiece of this project will be the revitalization of a historically significant nineteenth-century school house into a twenty-first-century training center to create a high-tech workforce. The Lincoln Workforce Center will train 2,000 workers annually and will employ 50 instructors paid $50,000 annually. The American Federation of Labor-Congress of Industrial Organizations – (AFL-CIO) has an option to purchase the building from the Metropolis schools. The prime contaminant at the site is asbestos from a previous remodeling effort, and an active environmental remedy is planned. The site is within 100 feet of a residential neighborhood, but not near a school, daycare facility, or water source.

The cost for remediation is $500,000, and the AFL–CIO has committed $2,000,000 to further remodeling and operation of the center. Metropolis schools will transfer title to Lincoln Elementary at no cost. This would constitute a $500,000 value. The project is specifically geared to train the neighborhood's lower-income workers for high-tech companies that may attend the Metropolis Tech Expo. The Lincoln Workforce Center will be LEED-certified, but only at the lowest level to manage cost.

The class will divide into groups that include city council, advocates for the development, and opponents of the development. The city council will conduct a debate on the matter after hearing from both sides of the issue. Negotiations may be involved among city council members, advocates, and opponents, but ultimately city council must vote on the issue at hand. City council must vote on a brownfield funding recommendation for each project. Only one project can be recommended for the Clean Ohio Revitalization Fund.

Additional Readings

Adam Rose and Dan Wei, "Macroeconomic impacts of the Florida Energy and Climate Change Action Plan," *Climate Policy*, University of Southern California, 12, 1 (2012) 50–69.

Brownfields and Land Revitalization, U.S. Environmental Protection Agency, available at usepa.gov.

Economic Impact Study of Ohio's Utica Shale, sponsored by the Ohio Chamber of Commerce, retrieved from http://urban.csuohio.edu/publications/center/center_for_economic_development/Ec_Impact_Ohio_Utica_Shale_2012.pdf.

Edward McMahon, "The Greening of the Real Estate Industry," *Urban Land Management*, The Urban Land Institute, January 20, 2012.

Environmental, Socioeconomic and Governance Report, 2011, Goldman Sachs, retrieved from www.goldmansachs.com.

Juita-Elana (Wie) Yusuf and Katharine A. Neill, "State Energy-Based Economic Development Policies and Examples," *Economic Development Quarterly*, 27, 3 (2013) 240–249.

"North Dakota sees Increase in Real GDP per capita Following Bakken Production," *Today in Energy*, U.S. Energy Information Administration, July 12, 2013.

Richard Hula and Rebecca Bromley-Trujillo, *Cleaning Up the Mess: The Redevelopment of Urban Brownfield's*, *Economic Development Quarterly*, 23, 3 (August 2010) 276–287.

Sanya Carley, Sara Lawrence, Adrienne Brown, Andrew Nourafshan, and Elinor Benami, "Energy-based Economic Development," *Renewable and Sustainable Energy Reviews*, 15, 1 (2011) 282–295.

Scott Campbell, "Green Cities, Just Cities? Urban Planning and the Contradictions of Sustainable Development," *Journal of the American Planning Association*, 62, 3 (Summer 2006) 296–313.

Stephan Vachon and Fredric Menz, "The Role of Social, Political and Economic Interests in Promoting State Green Energy Policies," *Environmental Science & Policy*, 9, 7–8 (2006) 652–662.

Tatyana Soubbotuna, *Beyond Economic Growth, An Introduction to Sustainable Development*, 2nd ed., World Bank Group (Washington, DC), 2004.

Ulrich Bayerlin, *Sustainable Development*, Max Planck of Institute of Comparative and International Law, April 2009.

Urban Brownfields: Why Toxic Brownfields are Tough to Redevelop, State Impact NPR, Texas, retrieved from www.npr.org/texas.

Chapter Thirteen
Economic Driver: Technology-Based Economic Development

Chapter Goals

1. Understand the role technology plays in modern economic development
2. Learn the relationship between technology, entrepreneurialism, and regional growth
3. Understand the importance of tax policies in developing a successful high-technology effort
4. Appreciate the role of higher education institutions in high-technology initiatives
5. Identify some sources of venture capital for high-tech economic development

Technology-Based Economic Development

The birth of the computer launched the Information Age and the creation of technology-based economic development. Similar as the Industrial Revolution positioned Michigan, Pennsylvania, Ohio, and the industrial midwest to be global economic leaders, the Information Age offers these regions, and several others, a chance to lead. Today, a regional technology-based economy creates jobs and companies in the STEM fields. It is a strong marriage between global research institutions and entrepreneurs willing to risk it all to start up and grow a high-tech company. Developing a technology-based economic development strategy is a prime tool many regions and states are using to create high-wage jobs and growing companies.

Tech-heavy North Carolina's RTP produces thousands of jobs, paying 45 percent higher wages than the national average.[1] Boston is another global technology-based economic development center primarily because of the role of their research universities. Active companies founded by MIT graduates would be the seventeenth largest economy in the world, and an estimated 6,900 MIT alumni companies based in Massachusetts alone have global sales of approximately $164,000,000,000, representing 26 percent of the sales of all Massachusetts companies.[2] MIT's influence extends beyond Massachusetts, as 4,100 MIT alumni-founded firms are based in California and generate an estimated $134,000,000,000 in worldwide sales. The

Silicon Valley story is well known. Half of the nation's tech-based venture capital, which drives the location of most early-stage tech stars, comes from Northern California. Regions and states aspire to be Silicon Valley, Route 128 in Boston, and the RTP. However, achieving that goal requires the implementation of a technology-based economic development strategy.

Policy Arguments for Technology-Based Economic Development

Technology-based economic development initiatives are attractive because they create high-wage "multiplier" jobs with companies in the growth mode for the Information Age economy. Half of the jobs created in the United States have been in firms that did not exist a decade ago.[3] Many of these jobs were born in the high-tech revolution that boomed in the 1990s and continues even today.

The Information Age industry is run by workers and executives skilled in STEM occupations. STEM occupations consist of nearly 100 specific occupations, making up 6 percent of US employment counting nearly 8,000,000 jobs.[4] STEM jobs are high-wage positions paying on average $77,880, and only four of the 97 STEM occupations had mean wages below the US average of $43,460.[5] Biological technicians employed in pharmaceutical manufacturing earned an average of $42,950 per year, just below the national average, but most health-care occupations pay a wage far above the national average.[6]

Regions with high concentrations of high-tech companies and STEM jobs define who is leading the development of high-tech jobs. The top metropolitan areas for STEM jobs are:

1. St Mary's county, MD (207 per 1,000 jobs)
2. San Jose-Sunnyvale-Santa Clara, CA (193 per 1,000 jobs)
3. Boulder, CO (173 per 1,000 jobs)
4. Huntsville, AL (167 per 1,000 jobs)
5. Framingham, MA (162 per 1,000 jobs)
6. Lowell-Billerica-Chelmsford, MA-NH (158 per 1,000 jobs)
7. Durham, NC (157 per 1,000 jobs)[7]

Idaho Falls (Idaho) had the highest annual average wages for STEM occupations at $110,660, followed by San Jose-Sunnyvale-Santa Clara, CA ($109,930), San Francisco-San Mateo-Redwood City, CA ($97,970), Washington-Arlington-Alexandria, DC-VA-MD-WV ($94,610), and Lowell-Billerica-Chelmsford, MA-NH ($94,190).[8]

A technology-based economic development model creates jobs for researchers and manufacturers. R&D in total generates trillions of dollars for the US economy. Turning R&D into products is good not just for companies but also their regions and states. These high-tech jobs serve as "multipliers" for enhanced economic growth due to their wage rates.

Many growing global industries are central to technology-based economic development initiatives, including information technology, advanced materials, biomedical, nanotechnology, and energy.

Technology-based regional economies are also attractive because they create a new generation of successful companies. Entrepreneurs are business owners who seek to generate value through the creation or expansion of economic activity and by identifying and exploiting new products, processes, or markets.[9] States and regions embracing entrepreneurism are in far better economic shape than regions that do not. From 1990 to 2001, entrepreneurial regions, both small and large, had 125 percent higher employment growth and 58 percent higher wage growth.[10] These regions benefit from 109 percent higher productivity, expended nearly 54 percent more R&D, and recorded 67 percent more patents per labor force participant.[11] They had a 63 percent higher percentage of high-tech establishments and a 42 percent higher portion of college-educated population than the least entrepreneurial regions.[12]

Techology-Based Economic Development as an Economic Development Tool

A successful technology-based economic development strategy builds company and workforce capacity in the STEM fields, leverages the research and educational assets of local universities and research institutions, and creates pools of venture capital. These regions also address workforce, land use, broadband, and tax policy issues for high-tech companies to compete. Land use policies built around research parks offer a new twist on retaining and attracting high-tech companies. World-class research institutions are the basis for global technology-based economic development initiatives. Research universities not only provide a workforce for high-tech companies that demand STEM occupations but also serve as economic engine by transferring research from the university to the marketplace. This process of technology transfer is also known as commercializing research and is outlined in Figure 13.1.

Promoting entrepreneurism is another technology-based economic development tactic. State and regions embrace entrepreneurs by encouraging small business start-ups in a range of industries. Facilitating entrepreneurship focuses primarily on educating and stimulating productive activity. The process is not a simple task. Everyone wants to be Silicon Valley, and very few places are even close. Entrepreneurship programs develop a network to entice and support business leaders and create capital access and business management tools that are often critical to early-stage companies. Cultivating entrepreneurship creates tech-based economic development

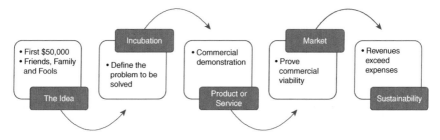

Figure 13.1 Technology commercialization framework.

organizations to offer services, programs, and delivery mechanisms to business leaders interested in leaving the comfortable world of academia or Fortune 500 companies and launching their own venture. These tech-based economic development organizations identify technology that can be turned into products and services, provide a suite of business development services, and create capital access funds. There organizations develop social networks and operate facilities for a group of start-up companies. The presence of, and access to, technology generators is the lynchpin for developing an innovation-based economy. Universities, nonprofit research institutions, and large corporations are recognized sources of new technologies.[13]

The provision of business development services for start-up companies is a critical role in developing an entrepreneurial environment. General entrepreneurial training for capital access, marketing, accounting, and legal services is provided to tech start-ups. Small start-up companies need the same services as mid- to large-sized companies, but they cannot afford the talent that provides these professional services. The Ewing Marion Kauffman Foundation's FastTrac provides a comprehensive entrepreneurship educational program that teaches business insights, leadership skills, and professional networking.[14] This program prepares business leaders to create a new business or expand an existing enterprise.[15] First started as part of USC's California Entrepreneurship Program in 1986, the Kauffman Foundation took this program national since 1993 and provided by 270 partners to nearly 100,000 participants.[16]

Economic Development Policy Case Study 13.1: Ohio's Technology-Based Economic Transformation

Ohio offers a leading state-based technology economic development program. In 2002, in response to the state's struggling manufacturing industry, Ohio created a $1,600,000,000, 10-year Third Frontier Program. It targets company growth of a select number of technology-based industry clusters by supporting world-class research, encouraging collaborative research, and commercialization activities with a mix of grants and loan programs with substantial match requirements and partnership mandates. The ultimate goal of Third Frontier is spurring new technology company formation all in these targeted industry clusters.[17] The $681,000,000 Third Frontier expenditures generated $6,600,000,000 of economic activity, 41,300 total jobs, and $2,400,000,000 in employee wages and benefits.[18] Ohio has gained nearly a $10 return on every dollar of the state's investment in the period from 2003 to 2008.[19] Ohio's Third Frontier Program increases the availability of early-stage capital and improves the entrepreneurial environment for technology and research collaboration. It drives employment growth in Ohio's technology sector and makes strides to diversify Ohio's manufacturers.[20]

Leveraging University Assets

A successful technology-based economic development strategy leverages local university assets to build new companies and a STEM workforce. Universities are a vital player in developing high-tech company start-ups. High-tech companies pay higher wages and provide an entrepreneurial culture that pays big dividends for a

Figure 13.2   Steps in university technology commercialization.
Source: University of Texas Tech Transfer Office.

region. The university technology commercialization process follows some important steps and is outlined in Figure 13.2.

Starting with the invention, university technology commercialization follows legal and business marketing steps in a precise order to ensure the intellectual capital of the product or service is protected. Capital investors quickly ask if the technology a company is founded on is protected to determine if the project is "safe" for investment. University technology commercialization also takes the faculty member through the important business plan development steps that prepare an idea or invention for the marketplace.

University research leaders are measured by whether they do academic research, industry-based research, and ultimately whether their research is commercialized. A university performing academic or even industry-based research is not guaranteed to produce high-tech companies and jobs. A more important measure of university success related to technology-based economic development is the licensing income that is created for the university. University licensing technology is successful at commercializing research and moving it from the lab into the marketplace. In 2012, American universities filed 22,150 patent applications. This constitutes a 11 percent increase.[21] University licensing income was $6,200,000,000, and the universities formed over 700 start-up companies employing 15,000 people, but that constitutes just under a 2 percent increase.[22] These companies generated over $16,000,000,000 in revenue.[23] In 2011, Northwestern University led the nation with nearly $200,000,000 in licensing income, but they only developed eight start-up companies.[24] The University of California System led the pack with 58 start-up companies, followed by MIT, University of Texas, University of Illinois, and University of Utah.[25]

Regional technology-based economic development has at its core a research university. Boston's concentration of world-class research universities, including Harvard University and MIT, develops economic success. In Massachusetts alone, 6,900 MIT alumni companies with worldwide sales of approximately $164,000,000,000 are located and represent 26 percent of the sales of all Massachusetts companies.[26] Austin is positioned for tech success as home of the University of Texas.

The region that host a university should then gain economic benefits from new high-tech company creation. The University of Utah's success in technology commercialization is a contributing factor to that state's economic success. The success of Silicon Valley, Boston, and Austin is well known due to their region's link to local world-class research universities. University commercialization of research produces economic development for the host region.

Universities are also economic assets for the graduates they produce. In the case of technology-based economic development, STEM graduates are the key to economic success. National rankings of colleges that produce STEM graduates for the most part differ little from than the list of leading research universities. It follows that tthe states with high rankings for STEM jobs are also home to leading research universities. Massachusetts has two of the leading research universitiesand the California Institute for Technology tops on the list.[27]

Workforce in the Digital Age

A regional technology-based economic development initiative should develop a STEM workforce. STEM workers constitute about 5 percent of the US workforce but accounts for more than 50 percent of the nation's sustained economic growth.[28] Sixty-one percent of opinion leaders and 40 percent of the general public identify math, science, and technology skills as the most important ingredients to compete in the global economy.[29] If current trends continue, more than 90 percent of all scientists and engineers in the world will live in Asia.[30] The growth in STEM-related jobs is expected to exceed the demand for non–STEM-related occupations.[31] The United States leads all industrial nations in the number of STEM graduates, but is losing ground when it comes to young workers.[32] STEM workforce strategies focus on the number, rate, and diversity of undergraduates in STEM disciplines and align undergraduate education with STEM industry workforce in targeted areas. A national STEM initiative should increase student interest and success in mathematics and science and produce more graduates in the STEM disciplines. The initiative works to improve student achievement in mathematics, science, engineering, and technology and fosters new methods of recruiting and training K-12 teachers in mathematics and science. It also builds STEM alliances among business, education, and government.[33]

Many national leaders in STEM workforce development are also the ones that emerged winners of technology-based economic development, including Northern California, Washington, DC, and Boston.[34] However, Houston, Baltimore, and San Diego are also on the list.

Many other states are working to develop a STEM workforce. Colorado's STEM strategy is a national model. STEM-EC is a Colorado-based coalition of business and education leaders connecting industry and the K-16 academic community to produce more STEM students.[35] Industry partners include Qwest, Lockheed Martin Space Systems, BB2e.com, Sun Microsystems, Hewlett Packard, and CH2M HILL.[36] Colorado's STEM effort starts with the leadership of both business and education sectors. The industry link is an essential element as the academic community needs assistance to identify specific STEM fields in which jobs are available and to absorb specific training and curriculum to prepare students for STEM jobs.

Washington STEM offers another statewide model. It not only links industry and the academic community but has created a statewide network and provides a series of grants to local STEM programs.[37] An example of a Washington STEM grant is a $10,000 award to Ellensburg School District for the Robotics Meets Biotech program to ignite Advanced Placement Biology students' interest in exploring how robotics can enhance biotechnology research.[38]

Technology Infrastructure: Operating in the Wireless Revolution

Regions and states must understand how the telecommunications industries impact economic development to achieve success in technology-based economic development. Global companies and community residents more and more rely on wireless communications networks to do business and to live.

Figure 13.3 illustrates the global dominance of the wireless telecommunications industry, but a more interesting fact is that telephone service just 11 years before was the dominant telecommunication service most people used.[39] Rates for telephone service have remained stable, but customers of wireless telecommunication service boomed. America lives in a world of wireless communications. Regions and states without a world-class wireless telecommunication infrastructure have little chance in competing for high-tech companies.

Land Use and Technology-Based Economic Development: Research Parks

Research parks, business incubators, and business accelerators are land use tools to develop a technology-based economy. Technology-based economic development provides start-up companies with facilities to operate their business. These facilities

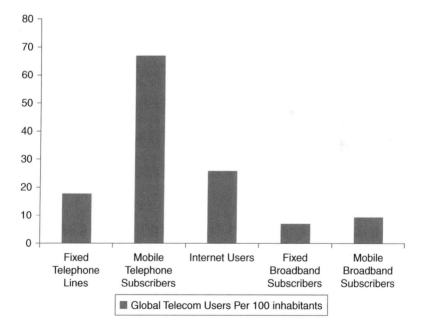

Figure 13.3 Global telecommunication users, 2009.

Source: Maryam Farhadi, Rahmah Ismail, and Masood Fooladi, "Information and Communication Technology Use and Economic Growth," *PLoS ONE*, 7, 11 (2012).

initially take the form of a business incubator where similar start-up companies are housed in their own offices all within the same building. These multitenant spaces facilitate the provision of professional business development services. All the companies in the business incubator have access to a suite of professional services essential for their success. Limited resources create struggles for start-up companies in accessing affordable facility space that suits the needs of the business. As an example, companies in the biotech field are in need of wet lab space for the development of biomedical products. Incubators are available to start-up companies who agree to "graduate" within a defined period of time and who, in most cases, pay a low rent subsidized by the tech-based economic development organization. These business incubators also provide an additional networking opportunity for companies located in the facility.

A technology accelerator facility takes equity in high-tech company start-ups in return for small amounts of capital and mentorship. Accelerators are more of a program than a long-term real estate solution. Accelerators operate three- to four-month programs and are built around industry clusters. The start-up company graduates at the end of the program. Idealab started in 1996 builds and operates high-tech companies.[40] Idealab prototypes and tests products.[41] They have successfully created over 125 companies and over 40 initial public offerings.[42]

Research parks are developments in which land and buildings house public and private research-oriented organizations and technology companies. Universities operate research parks. University-based research parks add a real estate and business support services angle to their technology transfer development facilities. By linking high-tech and science-based companies with support services in close proximity to faculty, staff, and students, university research parks hope to foster

Table 13.1 University-based research park benchmarks

Park Aspect	National Benchmark
Capital access	Substantial program to provide capital access to companies
Employment	Typical park employs 750 people
Financing	Under $1,000,000 budget with revenues from park operations and local, state and federal sources
Governance	Operated by university or university-affiliated nonprofit
Infrastructure	Roads, water, sewer, and fiber optics readily available
Land use planning	Overall master plan developed for average 114-acre site
Major voice	Region benefits from senior leadership promoting parks
Mission	Incubating technology start–ups and attracting major technology tenants
Research university	Direct link to a research university
Services	Business commercialization services—access to state programs, business planning, marketing/sales advice, and technology/market assessment
Tax incentives	Utilization of tax incentives to recruit companies
Tech transfer	Major effort to bring ideas from classroom to marketplace
Workforce	Free training grants for companies and other workforce initiatives are typical

Source: Battelle Technology Partnership Practice, *Characteristics and Trends in North American Research Parks: Twenty First Century Directions*, available at http://www.aurp.net/more/FinalBattelle.pdf.

commercialization and recruit larger technology companies. Table 13.1 illustrates the characteristics of successful university based research parks.

There is no shortage of efforts to build university-based research parks. According to the Association of University Research Parks, over 400 university-based research parks exist—at least in name. Research parks can house business incubators and accelerators but are really an opportunity to recruit larger technology-oriented companies and institutions.

Tax Policy: Developing Capital Access

Gaining access to capital is a major issue for entrepreneurs. Capital access approaches begin with a solid business plan. That business plan is not just the foundation for the operation of the company but can serve as a tool to use funding to operate and grow the company. Once a business plan is complete, a company turns to federal and state governments for venture capital funds. Most entrepreneurs do not have access to traditional financial services firms. A lack of assets and customers creates a struggle for the entrepreneur in attracting traditional bank loan. They are forced into venture capital market in many cases. Venture capital may be invested in all stages of a start-up firm's development, including preseed, seed stage, start-up stage, and expansion stage as illustrated by Table 13.2.

Venture capital tends to concentrate in select industry groups. Software, biotechnology, medical devices and equipment, and information technology services constitute well over half of all recent venture capital deals.[43] Later stage, expansion stage, and early stage dominate most venture capital investments. Start-up seed funding barely reached 5 percent of the total recent deals.[44] States and regions trailing in the battle to gain access to venture capital encourage private investment, direct funding to companies, and local funds. Private investments are encouraged through arranging social interaction between entrepreneurs and funding sources and using state tax credits to incentivize investment.

Table 13.2   Stages of venture capital

Stage	Description
Preseed stage	Earliest stage in the development of a business, when a business plan may be under development, but no formal or concrete steps have been taken to set up the business
Seed stage	Development phase prior to start-up when founders conduct research, develop products, and explore market potential; the future business entity is beginning to take shape, but founders have not yet established commercial operations
Start-up stage	Stage at which a firm has established operations and has launched or is about to bring products or services to the market; this stage typically requires a lot of capital since revenues are not yet able to cover operational and development costs
Expansion stage	Stage at which capital is required by a more established firm to finance growth; investments are made in activities such as R&D or production capacity

Source: *Measuring Entrepreneurship, A Collection of Indicators*, 2009 edition, OECD-Eurostat Entrepreneurship Indicators Programme.

States develop special tax credits to incentivize investment in early-stage ventures. Indiana's Venture Capital Investment Tax Credit program improves access to early-stage capital. Qualified investors who provide debt or equity capital to Indiana companies receive a credit against their tax liability.[45] The maximum amount of tax credits available in a year is $12,500,000.[46] The maximum amount of tax credits available to investors is the total amount of the investment multiplied by 20 percent to a maximum of $1,000,000.[47] The taxpayer may carry over the excess state tax liability to the following year.[48]

Networking and business education programs are also a big part of encouraging private investment in start-up companies. The Washington Technology Center Angel Network provides entrepreneurs with access to a statewide network of angel groups.[49] Entrepreneurs gain coaching and business plan reviews.[50] The Washington Technology Angel Network provides funding support and access to capital and facilitates research collaboration. They provide access to laboratory facilities.[51] They create $14 for every dollar invested.[52] Even the home of Bill Gates needs a program to promote access to early-stage capital.

Another high-tech capital access development approach is state and local tax credits. Certified capital companies (CAPCOs) originated in Louisiana where insurance companies receive premium tax credits equal to 100 percent to 120 percent of the amount they loan to or invest in a CAPCO.[53] Following Louisiana, which started it CAPCO in 1988, Missouri, New York, Wisconsin, Florida, Colorado, Alabama, Texas, and Washington, DC, all have some form of a CAPCO program.[54] Opponents of CAPCOs argue that regulations are needed to ensure the money invested remains in the state, and they also question the use of tax dollars to support a risk-free venture. The public sector may provide direct funding into technology-based companies for grants, contingent loans, convertible debentures, equity funding, or tax credits.

The federal Small Business Innovation Research (SBIR) and Small Business Technology Transfer (STTR) programs are a source of billions of dollars in proof-of-concept and very early-stage funding for fledgling technology companies. Eleven federal agencies are required to provide the funds by setting aside 2.5 percent of their annual extramural R&D budgets for use exclusively by US small businesses' new product R&D.[55] The program consists of multiple phases and requires no repayment, no equity sacrifice, and the small business retains most intellectual property rights.[56] These federal government programs are meant to address the challenges of funding for R&D at the proof-of-concept stage.[57] A SBIR/STTR award grants a business not just capital but a high-profile award for gaining more capital and ultimately customers.

Some states manage SBIR/STTR programs to promote research among small business. The University of Wyoming SBIR/STTR initiative is a statewide outreach program to encourage participation of Wyoming individuals and small businesses.[58] The Wyoming Business Council offers a major advantage to Wyoming SBIR/STTR participants by providing up to 24 awards annually of $5,000 each to assist small businesses in the preparation of competitive phase I SBIR/STTR proposals.[59]

A regional program in Pennsylvania offers an approach beyond the traditional SBIR/STTR. The Ben Franklin Technology Partners of Northeastern Pennsylvania invests in early-stage companies without assuming an equity position but instead provides financial support in the form of subordinated debt to qualified client start-ups.[60] The payments range from $30,000 to $150,000, and the program is credited with creating 408 new technology companies.[61] The debt is paid back over an eight-year term.[62] The principal and any accrued, nonpaid interest are due by the end of the eighth year in the form of a balloon payment.[63]

Many states have followed the lead of Oklahoma and used tax credits and direct funding to local, regional-based venture capital funds. The state of Oklahoma created the Oklahoma Capital Investment Board in 1993 to promote equity investment in state-based companies by building up the regional venture capital network throughout the state.[64] Oklahoma achieves this goal by borrowing from institutional lenders with the assignment of the Board's guarantee and then invests this capital in partnerships.[65] The Oklahoma program is backed by Oklahoma income tax and premium tax credits.[66] The Oklahoma effort has reportedly supported 19 venture capital funds, attracting over $130,000,000 in Oklahoma investments and generating in excess of $1,300,000,000 in economic activity for Oklahoma.[67]

The Utah Fund of Funds, with an initial charter of $100,000,000 in 2003 and $200,000,000 added in 2008, invests in a select number of venture capital/private equity firms agreeing to explore investments in promising Utah early-stage companies.[68] As of July 2008, more than 200 funds applied to the program.[69] Utah invested in 20 high-quality venture capital/private equity firms.[70] Seven of them are from Utah.[71] The Utah Fund of Funds portfolio firms have completed 359 in-depth reviews of Utah companies and selected 25 to receive funding over $127,000,000.[72] These companies raised an additional $365,000,000 and created over 1,000 jobs with an annual average salary of approximately $60,000.[73] The early focus of investments has centered on information technology and biosciences sectors.[74]

High-Tech Quality of Life: The Smart City

Quality of life is a major factor in developing a technology-based economy. Smart city strategies develop quality of life for technology firms. The smart city initiative has a strong link to high-tech industries in identified business parks with a highly educated population and local government connected via Information Age techniques of "egovernance" and smart transportation systems.[75] Future trends for smart cities include a continued focus on renewable energy, transportation and public safety, and city services such as water and information technology for greater citizen participation in government.[76] North America's top smart cities are Boston, San Francisco, Seattle, Vancouver, New York City, Toronto, Chicago, Los Angeles, and Montreal.[77] A smart city's objectives are to improve social, environmental, and economic pillars around infrastructure and transportation. City assets such as utilities, transportation, real estate, and services are outlined.[78]

Dubuque (Iowa) offers an example of a smart city. This 60,000-person city made a decision of reducing its impact on the environment while continuing to provide essential public services.[79] To meet this objective, Dubuque recognized it had limited insight into its water consumption and management, which resulted in higher water consumption and costs.[80] To address this challenge, Dubuque built a prototype platform for monitoring water consumption every 15 minutes, and water utilization decreased by 89,090 gallons among 151 households over a nine-week pilot project.[81]

Big Questions

1. Can every region build a successful technology-based economic development initiative?

2. What is the most important element of a technology-based economic development initiative?

3. Does a university at the center of a technology-based economic development need to be a world-class research center?

4. How can a culture of entrepreneurism be created?

5. How can regions compete with Silicon Valley for venture capital access?

Class Writing Assignment: Technology Commercialization

The president of Big University needs to give a speech regarding how they plan to succeed in commercializing their research. The three-minute speech needs to cover how they commercialize research and what best practices they plan to adopt.

Metropolis City Council Debate: Venture Capital Fund

The city council president thinks the mayor's proposal to redevelop the Big University neighborhood falls short of being a true globally successful technology-based economic development model. The president believes the development needs a venture capital fund to be created to support high-tech start-ups. The mayor does not necessarily disagree from a policy standpoint but is concerned with the $50,000,000 price tag and is never really that excited about making his main opponent in City Hall look good. However, the Tea Party thinks the idea of a local government loaning private sector companies is crazy. They plan to oppose the effort with all their might. Traditional advocacy groups such as the region's business leaders and organized labor could care less. They are too far removed from the early-stage start-up world. The city council president must prepare a detailed outline of what exactly this Metropolis Venture Capital Fund is, who it would serve, how it would hand out money, who would be the partners, and other key details city council will need to know. The class will divide into groups that include city council, advocates for the venture capital, and opponents of the fund. The city council will conduct a debate on the matter after hearing from both sides of the issue. Negotiations may be involved among city council members, advocates, and opponents, but ultimately city council must vote on the issue at hand.

Additional Readings

Albert Link, *From Seed to Harvest: The Growth of the Research Triangle* (Durham, NC: The Research Triangle Foundation, 2002).

Albert Link, *Generosity of Spirit: An Early History of The Research Triangle* (Durham, NC: Research Triangle Foundation of North Carolina, 1995).

Diane Palminterra, *Technology Transfer and Community Partnerships* (Berkley, CA: University of California Press, 2007).

Gregory Cromov, *Legal Bridge Spanning One Hundred Years: From the Gold Mines of El Dorado to the "Golden" Startups of Silicon Valley*, January 20, 2012, retrieved from www.netvalley.com.

Harvey Goldstein and Joshua Drucker, "The Economic Development impact of Universities on Regions; Do Size and Distance Matter," *Economic Development Quarterly*, 20, 1 (February 2006) 22–43.

Irving Lendel, "The Impact of Research Universities on Regional Economies," *Economic Development Quarterly*, 24, 3 (August 2010) 210–230.

Joonghae Suh and Derek H. C. Chen (ed.), *Korea as a Knowledge Economy* (Washington, DC: The World Bank, 2006).

Maryam Farhadi, Rahmah Ismail, and Masood Fooladi, "Information and Communication Technology Use and Economic Growth," *PLoS ONE*, 7, 11 (2012).

Mayor's Task Force on Technology, City of Columbus, Ohio, available at montrosegoupp.llc.com.

The Center for Science, Technology and Economic Development, SRI International, retrieved from www.sri.com.

CHAPTER FOURTEEN
ECONOMIC DEVELOPMENT DRIVER: GLOBALISM

Chapter Goals

1. Understand how the world is "shrinking" and how intrastate regional markets now face global competition
2. Discover ways in which competing in these global markets can give an edge to a region's economy
3. Discuss how to create and develop relationships with foreign-owned enterprises to help develop a regional economy
4. Identify the key role export promotion plays in successful economic development

Globalism and Economic Development

The global economy impacts all local American economies. Regions embracing globalism are growing their economies. Companies exporting goods and services pay higher wages than firms that do not. Global firms pay higher wages and support more research and development than other American companies. Regions and states launch export and FDI campaigns to gain these high-wage jobs. Quality of life, workforce, tax, land use policies, and economic gardening strategies increase the benefits from the global marketplace. Major cities connected to global ports and inland locations are successful at developing FDI and encouraging their companies to export goods and services.

Globalism success stories exist all across the United States. South Carolina and BMW are just one. BMW opened an autoassembly facility in Spartanburg in 1994.[1] The economic impact as measured in 2007 was $1,900,000,000 on a statewide basis.[2] The BMW's South Carolina complex supports 23,050 jobs and generates $1,200,000,000 in wages and salaries annually in the state with a 4.3 multiplier effect for each job created.[3] The share of total South Carolina employment attributed to BMW is 1.2 percent, and direct employment at the plant accounts for 2.2 percent of the state's manufacturing employment.[4] The total economic output of goods and services to BMW and its employees' annual economic activities is more than $8,800,000,000 in South Carolina.[5] The BMW facility creates a supplier network of 187 additional companies to serve its North American autoassembly plant.[6] The BMW facility makes South Carolina an export success. In 2007, BMW produced 157,530 units, of which approximately 60 percent were exported.[7] Finally, the BMW spurred innovation in South Carolina as its investments encouraged the creation of Clemson University's International Center for Automotive Research.

Policy Arguments for Globalism

Globalism represents access to growing markets. Seventy percent of the world's customers are outside of the United States.[8] In 2010, US exports of goods and services totaled $1,830,000,000,000 and accounted for 12.5 percent of the nation's GDP.[9] In 2008, 6,800,000 US jobs were supported by US manufacturingexporting firms, and US companies that export grow faster and are less likely to go out of business as compared to nonexporters.[10] Globalism represents higher wages for American workers employed by global firms in the United States. The average annual compensation at foreign-owned firms typically exceeds $73,000.[11] US affiliates of foreign companies in 2009 invested $40,000,000,000 on research and development and $183,000,000,000 on plants and equipment.[12] Americans working for export firms earn 15 percent more than similar workers at firms that do not export, and exports already support over a third of America's manufacturing jobs.[13] In addition, more than 1,000,000,000 new customers will enter the middle-class ranks in the next 15 years; global middle-class consumption is expected to grow from $21,000,000,000,000 to $35,000,000,000,000 by 2020, and 80 percent of this growth will be outside of the United States.[14] As manufacturing moves from the United States to global locations, American companies have no choice but to sell to these global markets. That is where customers, and money, are. A region's manufacturing sector cannot succeed unless it develops an aggressive export strategy. Exports are an economic driver in the American economy. American exports support 11,800,000 jobs nationally and 7,700,000 jobs in the top 100 metro areas.[15] These jobs amount to 8.3 percent of the nation's employment and 8.1 percent of all employment in the largest 100 metros.[16]

Regions attracting FDI reap economic benefits. FDI is measured by the investment of majority-owned US affiliates of foreign-domiciled companies. These firms produce $670,000,000,000 in goods and services.[17] They account for nearly 6 percent of total US private output—over 42 percent of which is concentrated in the US manufacturing sector. The 5,700,000 workers employed by these firms account for 5 percent of the US private workforce.[18] These same firms invest $188,000,000,000 in capital expenditures and account for over 11 percent of total US private capital investment.[19] Firms linked to FDI also lead in research and development. They produce $40,500,000,000 and account for over 14 percent of total US private investment in research and development.[20] These firms also export more than 18 percent of total US merchandise.[21]

FDI firms pay 30 percent more wages than other US jobs. [22] These firms paid out wages and other forms of compensation averaging more than $71,000 per US employee.[23] All other American full-time workers average $54,000 annually in compensation.[24] During the last 10 years, majority-owned US affiliates of foreign companies have employed between 5,000,000 and 6,000,000 workers, supported 2,000,000 manufacturing jobs, and totaled $194,000,000,000 in revenues.[25]

Opponents to globalism as an economic development strategy look at Youngstown, Detroit, and other industrial midwest cities that are losers in the global trade battle. They argue globalism does not promote high-wage jobs but drives jobs to overseas markets that pay workers low wages, such as China. Opponents of globalism point to a weak history of enforcing "fair trade" among nations and a lack of training dollars to prepare workers for their next profession.

Globalism as an Economic Development Tool

To address opportunities in global markets, regions and states work with their existing businesses to enhance their exports opportunities and launch attraction campaigns to promote FDI. Export strategies improve advocacy and trade promotion efforts on behalf of US exporters through trade missions and direct linkage between small and medium-sized US companies and global trade partners. These strategies increase access to export financing through the import-export bank and remove trade barriers to closed markets. Launching an FDI campaign should first define what constitutes FDI and the core regional industry clusters. FDI benefits are defined, and marketing to the core regional industry clusters to promote the community as a prime site for a corporate site location is undertaken. Regions also market to global firms not connected via ownership or by supply chain with existing local companies. In addition, regions and states build "mega sites" and adopt labor and tax policies friendly to global manufacturers.

Regional Export Campaign

Exporting goods and services globally enhances the economic vitality of a region. The same small and medium-sized companies that states target for growth make up the majority of successful exporters. Successful regions use a proactive approach to support local companies' exporting of goods and services. Export initiatives provide counseling, data, and marketing services for these small and medium-sized companies. Regions provide the scale and scope to promote a global export strategy. An export strategy targets local companies with global locations for corporate headquarters, customers, and supply chain. The strategy takes into account regulatory and trade policies of countries to ensure they are friendly to US products and services.

Benchmarking success in an export campaign requires understanding which American industries do best at exporting and which countries are most likely to accept American exports. Traditional manufacturing centers are the big export winners. Sixty-five percent of Wichita's (Kansas) exports are transportation equipment, mainly airplanes and airplane parts.[26] Portland (San Jose) and Palm Bay (Florida) rely on computer exports in a similar fashion, and Oxnard's (California) chemical and computer companies constitute 42 percent of all the metro's exports.[27] Export-oriented metropolitan areas are more innovative.[28] The manufacturing portion of

US exported goods is the overwhelming percentage of total US exports. However, the growth of exports is impacted by the fact thatAmerican manufacturing is not the manufacturing giant it once was. In 1948, the United States produced 21 percent of the world's goods exports.[29] By 2008, that share dropped to below 10 percent, and the emerging economies of China, India, Brazil, and the Middle East gained dramatically in the share of global exports.[30]

As America transitions to a service-based economy, the service sector grows in export potential. The United States exports $525,000,000,000 in commercial service exports.[31] This total constitutes nearly 14 percent of all global commercial service exports and tops the global list.[32] Export campaigns need a service sector aspect.

Regional Export Leaders

Success in exporting American goods and services is not an equal-opportunity game. Major regional differences exist as to who is winning and losing. Interestingly, this list of winners and losers is different from many other economic measures of success. Twenty-one metro areas are national leaders when it comes to succeeding at exporting goods and services.[33] These regions include Albany, New York; Augusta, Georgia; Austin, Texas; Baton Rouge, Louisiana; Buffalo, New York; Columbia, South Carolina; Dallas, Texas; Des Moines, Iowa; El Paso, Texas; Honolulu, Hawaii; Houston, Texas, Jackson, Mississippi; Little Rock, Arkansas; Madison, Wisconsin; McAllen, Texas; Oklahoma City, Oklahoma; Omaha, Nebraska; Rochester, New York; San Antonio, Texas, Tulsa, Oklahoma; and Washington, DC.[34] The geographic measure of export success is different than many other economic measures. The south is not the total export winner, but the west and midwest make up many success stories. This illustrates the importance of manufacturing in export success but also that a successful export strategy alone does not guarantee economic success. Western and midwestern states' economic struggles have not been erased by export victories. Exports need to be tied with innovation and a strong job retention and attraction program built upon a low cost of doing business for a region to succeed. Four US regions doubled the real value of their exports, namely Houston, Wichita, Portland, and New Orleans.

Economic Development Case Study 14.1: Wichita and Aviation

Wichita is the largest city in Kansas with 350,000 and a metropolitan service area of nearly 600,000.[35] Wichita promotes a safe city, with good schools and strong transportation infrastructure with lower-than-average cost of living.[36] Manufacturing makes up nearly 20 percent of the region's economy, over double the national percentage.[37] Wichita has a strong cluster of aviation-based manufacturing centers with Spirit AeroSystems, Cessna Aircraft, and Hawker Beechcraft, Boeing, Bombardier, and American Airlines.[38] Wichita has the highest concentration of aircraft and aircraft parts manufacturing employment and related skilled workforce.[39] Wichita's impressive aerospace workforce helps several area manufacturers to utilize these skills to produce high value-added products such as industrial commercial machinery, computer equipment, fabricated metal products, instrumentation and controls, photographic equipment, plastic and composite products, chemicals, petroleum refining equipment, and electronic equipment.[40]

Wichita's success in developing an export-based economy is driven by the aviation industry's focus on global markets. The US general aviation industry is growing its global sales with 2009 being the first year when exports accounted for more than half of the industry sales.[41] Cessna and Hawker Beechcraft are bringing the benefits of the global economy to Wichita. Cessna's exports grew by 165.5 percent between 2005 and 2008, driven by strong sales into developing regions such as Latin America, Asia, and the Middle East. [42] Exports reached 44.1 percent of the company's sales in 2008.[43]

Government-backed financing from the export-import bank plays a role in the Wichita success story. A $500,000,000 direct loan from the export-import bank assisted Cessna's growth plans.[44] Cessna's growth is multiplied by the large number of suppliers located around the Wichita facility that service the operation of the manufacturing center.[45] Even in the current economic down cycle, Wichita generated $4,900,000,000 in exports during 2010.[46]

Did Wichita become the general aviation capital of America by accident? No. A cluster of aviation companies began locating in this region, and Wichita found ways to support the industry through innovation and workforce. On the innovation side, Wichita State University operates the National Institute for Aviation Research (NIAR) to improve aircraft safety and performance.[47] NIAR operates on a nonprofit budget that has steadily increased to more than $45,000,000 and claims the status of the largest university aviation R&D institution in the United States.[48] NIAR operates more than 250,000 square feet of laboratory and office space, employs 350, and serves a range of private sector clients, including Boeing, Bombardier Learjet, Cessna, Hawker Beechcraft, and Spirit Aerosystems.[49] NIAR studies aerodynamics, aging aircraft, crash dynamics, composites and advanced materials, aircraft icing, structural components, virtual reality, computational mechanics, among others.[50]

NIAR sought and received federal government recognition and funding for general aviation research through several centers of excellence. NIAR uses a formal structure for sharing ideas among government, industry, and academia. NIAR hosts two Federal Aviation Administration Center of Excellence designations and is home to the National Center for Advanced Materials Performance.[51] This program is sponsored by NASA, the US Air Force, and a National Science Foundation Center for Friction Stir Processing.[52] NIAR funding traditionally is split among federal government, state government, and private industry.[53] NIAR makes Wichita the intellectual center for general aviation.

Wichita also does not take the availability of an aviation industry–ready workforce for granted. The National Center for Aviation Training (NCAT) develops Wichita's aviation workforce.[54] NCAT trains aviation maintenance workers in composite materials, robotics technology, and aircraft completion.[55] NCAT awards technical certificates and associate of applied science degrees for a wide range of aviation specialties.[56] Finally, NCAT partners with the Wichita Area Technical College as well as with the NIAR to develop a R&D-oriented workforce.[57]

Wichita knows it has a good thing going as one of only a handful of global avia-tion business clusters in the world. The state cannot rest on its laurels. Oklahoma, Kansas' neighbor to the south, reinstituted a tax credit designed to recruit aerospace companies to the Sooner state.[58] Other existing global general aviation clusters can be found in Seattle, Washington, Dallas/Fort Worth, Texas, Montreal, Canada, and Toulouse in France. Any of these regions could compete with Wichita for the strong base of general aviation jobs.

Seattle and Exports

It is surprising but Seattle is not on the list of top 21 major exporting metros. Its sheer size creates 196,000 jobs from export activity in 2008, and Seattle ranks tenth largest in total jobs related to exports. However, the same year Wichita led the nation with 27 percent of its regional economy tied to exports. Seattle did not even make this list. This does not mean Seattle is an economic weakling. Seattle, as compared to Wichita, is much bigger—with a metro region population of over 3,700,000 and a strategic location directly connected to the Pacific Ocean and the exploding Asian marketplace.[59] Seattle has a highly successful regional economy with Boeing, Microsoft, Amazon, and Real Networks. Seattle is working to move up the list of top exports. Washington's Trade Development Alliance of Greater Seattle (TDA) promotes the brand identity of the region in targeted world markets and hosts an annual Seattle trade mission in a global city.[60] TDA works with the US export-import bank and the regional federal export assistance center to assist local companies with international business interests, and it measures the success of their export effort by benchmarking against other global cities.[61]

Quality-of-Life Debate: Wichita versus Seattle

Quality-of-life factors are an element of both Wichita's and Seattle's argument as to why the aerospace industry should grow in their respective hometown. How can Wichita compete against a city with a Space Needle with residents like Bill Gates and corporate headquarters for Microsoflt and Starbucks with ocean access? They do. The Wichitas of the world compete by focusing on export-oriented companies that produce quality jobs with higher-than-average wages, but they also succeed because of lower cost of doing business.

As Table 14.1 indicates, Wichita compares well both against the national average and Seattle when it comes to a measure of the cost of living. Wichita is competing

Table 14.1   Cost of living: Wichita versus Seattle

Cost of Living Indicators	Wichita, Kansas	Seattle, Washington	American Average
Median household income	$44,405	$60,843	$50,221
Median home value	$115,800	$452,000	$185,400
Average gross rent	$628	$992	$817
Cost of living index	93	120	100

Source: Census Data, City Data.com, and Kiplinger Cost of Living Index

successfully against Seattle and other global regions in the battle for export-related companies through an affordable quality of life and strong research and workforce development support of the aerospace industry.

FDI and Economic Development

Gaining FDI provides high-wage jobs and produces regional economic development winners. All states of the nation succeed at FDI. (Figure 14.1)

A number of nations are leaders in US FDI. In 2010, 84 percent of FDI in the United States came from Switzerland, United Kingdom, Japan, France, Germany, Luxembourg, Netherlands, and Canada.[62] Since 2000, employment by majority-owned US affiliates of foreign companies has held steady with these companies employing more than 5,000,000 American workers, and 2,000,000 of these jobs are in manufacturing.

The FDI Campaign

FDI is divided into greenfield investment (creation of new businesses through the development or expansion of production facilities) and mergers and acquisitions of existing businesses. The Internet grows FDI.[63] Internet-based research and data collection methods provide information for even the smallest region on global markets. FDI is also stimulated by local firms with global connections. Local company's corporate headquarters, customer base, and supply chain are a source of global prospects. Specific nations prove strong prospects for FDI. FDI among China and OPEC countries proves opportunities for luring investments and potential facility locations.[64]

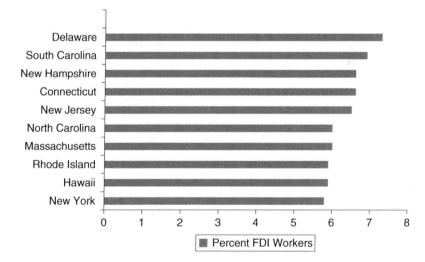

Figure 14.1   Top 10 states by percentage of FDI workers.
Source: 2010 Census Data.

Key steps in an FDI campaign include:

1. First, a definition of FDI is established.[65] A broad definition encompasses any assets that are acquired using foreign capital, ranging from real estate to factories to bank deposits and the foreign acquisition or construction of productive capital, such as factories, hotels, or stores, and the associated brands and technologies.[66]
2. Regions then focus on planned industries they wish to recruit through FDI through a standard industry cluster analysis.[67] Global company targets focus on regional economic strengths matched with growing industries and markets.
3. Prior to marketing, regions define the benefits, as compared to other regions, their area possesses that would attract global companies. Defining the region's strategic market location, available workforce, and quality of life are tops on the global firm's wish list.[68] Of course, available sites, wage rates, and tax and labor policies all impact the global firm's cost of doing business.[69]
4. Marketing for FDI first promotes the economic benefits of a region to existing companies in that area and then to companies across the globe. The best sales person for a region is existing companies, and successful FDI programs are implemented by existing companies communicating with their suppliers and fellow global companies.[70] Brand awareness matters, but it ultimately comes down to direct sales.
5. The final stage of an FDI campaign is pure hunting. Landing a global company in the United States is at the opposite end of economic gardening. It is a pure sales job to global companies searching for a US location and working with area companies to identify global corporate partners, competitors, and the supply chain of companies that have a reason to locate a facility in a specific region or state.[71]

A key FDI strategy is to find friends who can help save time and money. These friends can be universities, state governments, regional state government organizations, and the federal government that all can help promote a region to a particular industry around the globe. Few regional development organizations have a budget to launch their own global campaigns. Sharing costs and intelligence not only promotes greater regional cooperation but it saves time and resources. In addition, regions need to be attractive to the target country and its culture. It is easier to target Japanese companies if a region has successfully operated a Honda car factory for decades. This region has proved that it can operate a business from a global perspective and is open to global citizens to live and raise a family.

Globalism and Tax Policy: Foreign Trade Zones

As with all five drivers of economic development, local, state, and federal tax policy impacts global investment. Foreign Trade Zones (FTZs) are a tax incentive program designed to promote global trade and investment. FTZs were born in 1934, and sites are designated as FTZs by the US Department of Commerce. FTZs blossomed as an economic development tool since the 1970s. In 1970, ten general-purpose FTZs existed, tied to 1,401 jobs and $104,000,000 in volume of global goods received.[72] Today, 256 general-purpose FTZs exist, and 174 are active producing 370,000 jobs and $732,000,000,000 in volume of global goods received.[73] In 2011, 12 percent of all foreign goods entered the United States through an FTZ, and oil dominated the list of goods.[74]

FTZs are a magnet for manufacturers interested in exports and incoming global investments. Qualifying goods received by an FTZ from abroad are subject to inspection, but are not subject to duties, taxes, or import quotas unless they are to be sold in the United States.[75] Goods that are imported into an FTZ and reexported without entering US commerce are not subject to US duties, taxes, or import quotas.[76] FTZs grant federal income tax and excise tax deferral.[77] The seller retains the title to goods held in an FTZ regardless of whether they have been sold.[78] They also provide quota avoidance as goods are held in an FTZ until quotas expire.[79] Companies in FTZs repackage or reassemble goods into other products to take advantage of lower tariffs.[80] They enjoy insurance cost reduction as assessed value in an FTZ includes only goods and freight, not duties and taxes.[81]

FTZs are all over the United States and have an impact on economic development. Exports totaled $34,000,000 from FTZs in 2010 and housed 300,000 employees and 2,400 firms.[82] Many state and regions benefit from FTZs. Texas is one of many states using FTZs. The Alliance FTZ #196 ranked the top general-purpose FTZ in terms of the value of foreign goods admitted in 2010.[83] The Alliance FTZ admitted over $4,000,000,000 in foreign products, constituting a 36 percent increase over 2009.[84] This is the fourth time in 5 years the Alliance FTZ has received the top US ranking.[85] Cinram, Hyundai, LEGO, Motorola, GENCO ATC, and Callaway Golf utilize the Alliance FTZ.[86] Eighty percent of foreign goods receivd by Alliance FTZ arrived from China.[87] South Korea was a distant second at 12 percent.[88]

Globalism and Land Use Strategies: The Mega Site

The global autoassembly plant is every state's goal. Ohio, Indiana, South Carolina, Alabama, and Tennessee have achieved success in this front. The economic upside for these facilities is huge. The "build it and they will come model" takes the form of creating mega sites. A "mega site" is unimproved land—large in size, connected to critical road, water, power, broadband, sewer, and rail infrastructure—prepared for development.[89] These sites are strategically located near required workforce, are zoned ready for development, and marketed to major manufacturers.[90]

Many regions and states have a list of mega sites prepared and awaiting global facilities. The Tennessee Valley Authority (TVA) in partnership with its regional partners established mega sites throughout its service territory.[91] Not only do these sites offer reduced power rates from the TVA, but they offer large tracts of land ready for development after environmental and geotechnical testing.[92] These sites offer proximity to interstate highways, railways, and suppliers, a large labor supply, and an infrastructure development plan.[93] The TVA's mega site strategy began with a 1980 meeting with the then governor Lamar Alexander and an elderly widow over iced tea that led to a swap of her farm for one elsewhere so that Nissan could build an auto plant in Smyrna.[94] Five years later, a similar trade was arranged for General Motors to gain a site to build the Saturn.[95] The TVA formalized its land use strategy in 2004 by streamlining the giant industrial site selection process into the Mega Site Program.[96] TVA's Mega Site Program provides large prepurchased, "shovel-ready" sites for large-scale industrial developments.[97] Since 2004, five mega sites have been sold to major corporations: Dow Corning /Hemlock Semiconductor, VW, Paccar, and Toyota.[98] The pay-off has been that Chattanooga gained a new $1,000,000,000 Volkswagen plant and Clarksville won a $1,200,000,000 Hemlock semiconductor solar equipment plant on TVA mega sites.[99]

Tennessee made a policy decision to devote public dollars to the development of their mega sites. The state allocated in the case of Hemlock $40,000,000 for the land purchase and a $170,000,000 bond issue to develop the Volkswagen site that includes equipment purchases, site grading, utility lines, road and rail extensions, and construction.[100] The TVA promotes two remaining mega sites. The first is the I-24 mega site in Hopkinsville (Kentucky). This mega site is located on 2,100 acres adjacent to I-24 and only one hour from the Nashville airport with CSX Railroad connected to site.[101] The Memphis Regional Mega Site is located on 1,720 acres, plus 3,000 under option adjacent to I-40 and only 30 minutes east of Memphis with CSX Railroad next to site.[102]

Building a Global Workforce: Southern Labor Policies

The cost and availability of a regional workface pool impacts recruitment of local companies. The southern region of the United States has a strong record of recent success in recruiting global manufacturing companies. A recent report illustrated durable goods manufacturing was the fastest growing industry in eight southern states.[103] A major asset in this new FDI-based southern economy is the strong cluster of foreign automakers located in states such as Alabama with Honda, Hyundai, Toyota, and Mercedes-Benz facilities. Tennessee has Nissan and Volkswagen assembly plants, and Mississippi hosts Nissan and Toyota facilities.[104] Steel is also being made in the south, thanks to an investment by a German company, ThyssenKrupp, in Mobile (Alabama).[105] This facility and its over 2,000 employees is a byproduct of the region's success in the autoassembly plant market.[106] Assembly plants sprout hundreds of suppliers, including steel processing and manufacturers. Not to be outdone, Louisiana was the winner of steel facility location of Nucor Corp, which should produce over 1,000 jobs.[107]

The south is not just relying on traditional industries but is going after alternative energy businesses. Arkansas gained over 2,000 jobs in a growing cluster of wind energy companies, including global companies such as Mitsubishi.[108] It creates 275 new jobs to produce extra-high-voltage shell-type power transformers and serves as Mitsubishi's national headquarters for the production of heavy electrical equipment.[109]

The south is making a strong showing in the manufacturing sector even though the global economy is struggling.[110] Much of that impressive growth is due to FDI wins around the autoindustry. Tax incentives lured these projects away from the traditional manufacturing powerhouses of the midwest. The midwest's labor-friendly policies did not help them either with these projects. The south's antilabor union perspective built around the adoption of Right to Work laws and comparable low costs of living and doing business make this region attractive to global manufacturers. The southern states are gaining global jobs as the midwest and northeast lose existing manufacturers in the global corporate site location battle.

Southern labor policies are growing global manufacturing. The south's status as Right to Work states permitting employees to decide if or not they will join a union at the workplace impacts the region's economic success. However, several southern states are putting this global attraction strategy at risk by launching state-based immigration reform policy initiatives. Alabama offers an example. Legislators enacted a state immigration reform law. Alabama state leaders are concerned about the influx of illegal immigrants and the costs for local and state social welfare and criminal justice systems. HB 56 was enacted by the state of Alabama, and the bill allows local law enforcement to demand papers or detain those suspected to be in the country illegally.[111] HN 56 makes it a crime for undocumented immigrants to hold a job in Alabama, for any immigrant in the state to be caught without documentation proving status and for a company to sign a contract with undocumented immigrants.[112] It is a crime to rent property to illegal immigrants or to hire them for jobs. Alabama companies must use E-Verify to document the status of workers. Alabama parents must report the immigration status of their children to public schools, and the schools need to maintain legal status records on all their students and document the costs of educating undocumented children.[113]

This law is modeled after Arizona and other state immigration reforms. HB 56 is subject to legal challenge, but the economic impact could be larger than the civil rights fight. Opponents of the law claim that it unfairly harms the state's agricultural industry, actually costs the state and local tax dollars, and results in a $40,000,000 reduction in the Alabama economy.[114] Maybe a larger impact is that it sends a signal to global companies that Alabama might not be as open to foreign workers and businesses as they claim. The Alabama immigration debate illustrates the struggles policy makers face when trying to address social and criminal justice issues that run in the face of global business community.

Infrastructure: Growing Globalism through Gardening

Small to mid-sized companies are targets for export-related activity. Locally owned and operated companies are more likely to remain and grow in a region. These emerging "second-stage companies" produce a large number of jobs. The Denver Regional Council of Governments reported that from 2002 to 2005, 81 percent of net new jobs in the Denver region were attributable to 21 percent of all firms.[115] However, growing global opportunities for mid-sized companies require the development of infrastructure for these emerging businesses. This infrastructure is more than the roads, water, sewer, and telecommunications services all businesses need. Instead, to succeed in the global marketplace, emerging mid-sized companies need a core set of business support services for their expansion into new, foreign markets. The economic development strategy known as economic gardening creates the infrastructure support needed to promote export activity for small to mid-sized companies. The goal of an economic gardening program is to cultivate these companies and organizations and to create supportive environments so they can thrive.

Economic Gardening and Littleton

Economic gardening grows jobs through entrepreneurial activity instead of recruiting. Recruiting new companies always makes headlines but often only entails a single-digit percentage of local job creation.[116] However, not all local companies were made equal. In fact, only 3 percent to 5 percent of all were high-growth companies, and these were creating a great majority of new jobs.[117] These companies are known as "gazelles" due to their fast-growth horizon. True economic gardening demands the program be geared toward only a targeted portion of the small business community. In addition, these gazelles are tied not just to growth but to innovation.[118] Littleton (Colorado) points to the success of its economic gardening program. From 1989 to 2005, the number of jobs in Littleton more than doubled from approximately 15,000 to over 35,000, while sales taxes almost tripled to 20,000,000, and the city's population grew by only 30 percent.[119] These statistics far outpaced those of any other centers in the United States, and this period saw two recessions.[120]

Economic gardening spread to a number of communities across the United States, including Lake Elsinore, San Bernardino, Chico, and San Luis Obispo in California; Santa Fe, New Mexico; Lancaster county, Pennsylvania; Steamboat Springs, Colorado; and the North Down Borough of Northern Ireland. Today, states like Michigan, Wyoming, Georgia, Florida, and Wyoming have also taken an economic gardening approach.[121]

Economic Gardening and Export Success

Business counseling services related to export-based sales and development of global markets for small to medium-sized companies are an essential part of developing connections through an economic gardening strategy. Developing an export-focused strategy for second-stage entrepreneurs utilizes federal government sources at the Commerce Department, the International Trade Administration, state government, and private sector sources. Companies and regions starting an export strategy pick the best market possible to export. Variables impacting which overseas market should be targeted range from cultural preferences to foreign exchange rates to availability of raw materials, all of which impact a company's sales price.[122] Creating an export team is essential for the small to mid-sized companies. The team includes legal, financial, and distribution assistance.[123] A lawyer is needed to draft and review distributor agreements and exclusivity agreements, interpret global regulations, and advise the company on intellectual property protection issues.[124] A banker is needed to structure financing, assess payment methods, and advise the company of financial risks and how to offset them.[125] Finally, a freight forwarder handles shipping, insurance, and any licensing hurdles involved in reaching the company's products to its international destination.[126]

Many regions of the country are succeeding by linking gazelles with growing global markets. GrowFL is a University of Central Florida program that operates an economic gardening institute and helped create more than 400 jobs throughout the state in 2010, the program's first year of operation.[127] GrowFL is funded by the state of Florida and provides a suite of business counseling and advisory services to a select number of companies in second stage of growth (known as "Companies to Watch") that are most likely to create jobs.[128] GrowFL's inaugural class of "Companies to Watch" to support the development of privately held companies that employ up to 99 employees have between $750,000 and $50,000,000 in annual revenue or capital and are notable for "positively impacting Florida's future."[129] According to reports, these small but growing companies generated $423,000,000 in annual revenue and 510 net new jobs in 2010.[130]

Big Questions

1. How can American manufacturers succeed in exporting goods to low-cost markets such as China?

2. What does the example of Wichita tell other mid-sized cities about the export market opportunities?

3. Is the mega site political risk worth the potential reward?

4. How does the immigration issue impact efforts to recruit global companies?

5. How can economic gardening enhance a region's globalism strategy?

Class Writing Assignment: Metropolis and FDI

The mayor has a meeting coming up with the business community regarding the city's economic development strategy. She wants to focus on growing FDI. Outline an economic development plan no exceeding two pages for Metropolis to succeed in recruiting global companies as part of an overall FDI strategy, which includes how the Metropolis 2020 project can help in this process.

Metropolis City Council Debate: Globalism

The Tea Party is alive and well in Metropolis. The leadership of the Tea Party is highly unhappy with the package of government incentives being used to promote the mayor's project near Big University. They are searching for a hot social issue to impact the development. Out of the blue, a relatively low key member of city council, who is known to be looking for a way to quickly climb up the political ladder, announces plans for a resolution identifying English as the official language of Metropolis. The Tea Party activists jump up in support of the resolution and threaten a city charter amendment if city council does not act.

Needless to say, the mayor and business leaders are unexcited about the debate. The issue is popular with the public of Metropolis but may very well impact that ability of the region to promote its companies with global companies in Brazil, India, China, and other countries. Organized labor is torn. Their membership probably supports the ordinance, but global exporting is a major driver for union-based manufacturing jobs in Metropolis.

The class will divide into groups that include city council, advocates for English as the official language of Metropolis, and opponents of the resolution. The city council will conduct a debate on the matter after hearing from both sides of the issue. Negotiations may be involved among city council members, advocates, and opponents, but ultimately city council must vote on the issue at hand.

Additional Readings

A. J. Jacobs, "Collaborative Regionalism and Foreign Direct Investment: The Case of the Southeast Automotive Core and the 'New Domestics'," *Economic Development Quarterly*, 26, 3 (August 2012) 199–219.

Ann Breling, *A Road Map to Globalization* (Washington, DC: International Economic Development Council, 2009).

Daniel Griswold, *Mad About Trade; Why Main Street America Should Embrace Globalization* (Washington, DC: Cato Institute, 2009).

Eli Miloslavsky and Howard J. Shatz, "Services Exports and the States: Measuring the Potential," *Economic Development Quarterly*, 20, 1 (February 2006) 3–21.

How Honda succeeded in the United States, Adam Richardson, Design Mind, August 15, 2011, retrieved from http://designmind.frogdesign.com/category/blog/10/term/culture.

How Nations Thrive in the Information Age, Leveraging Information and Communications for Economic Development, IBM Institute for Business Values, 2009.

Jurgen Osterhannel and Neils Peterson, *Globalization: A short History* (Princeton, NJ: Princeton University Press, 2005).

Michael Porter, "Location, Competition and Economic Development; Local Clusters in a Global Economy," *Economic Development Quarterly*, 14, 1 (February, 2000) 15–34.

Mustafa Dinc and Kingsley E. Haynes, "International Trade and Shift-Share Analysis: A Specification Note," *Economic Development Quarterly*, 12, 4 (November 1998) 337–343.

Powering Export Growth: 2012, U.S. Department of Commerce, Commercial Service Annual report.

Rosabeth Moss-Kanter, *World Class; Thinking Locally in the Global Economy* (New York, NY: Basic Books, 1997).

Thomas Friedman, *The World is Flat, A Brief History of the Twenty First Century* (New York, NY: Farrar, Strauss, Giroux, 2005).

CHAPTER FIFTEEN

ECONOMIC DEVELOPMENT DRIVER: ADVANCED MANUFACTURING STRATEGY

Chapter Goals

1. Recognize the "wealth creation" value of the manufacturing sector
2. Identify the challenges regions and states face in retaining their manufacturing base
3. Describe the regions' and states' "offensive" efforts to attract the manufacturing industry
4. Recognize the role of unions in retaining and attracting manufacturing companies

Advanced Manufacturing and Economic Development

Manufacturing dominated the American economy for the past 100 years. The term manufacturing may refer to a range of activities, but is most commonly applied to industrial production when raw materials are transformed into finished goods on a large scale. These finished goods may be either used for manufacturing other products like aircraft, household appliances, or automobiles, or sold to wholesalers and ultimately to consumers through retail outlets.

By 1950, nearly one-third of American workers were engaged in the manufacturing industry.[1] That dominance is over. Manufacturing jobs bled from the United States due to globalization and productivity gains. From 2000 to 2009, America lost over 30 percent of its manufacturing jobs, and the percentage of the US economy based on manufacturing dropped from just over 13 percent to around 9 percent.[2] However, manufacturing is still important to many regional economies. Existing manufacturers, while not providing the total number of jobs they once did, still are large employers paying above-average wages.

Today, America is home to advanced manufacturing. Advanced manufacturing operates high-tech facilities that are more reliant on technology than on people. Consider the American steel industry. US Steel, Andrew Carnegie's invention, once dominated the global steel industry and employed hundreds of thousands. Today, US Steel continues to operate but is shifting to a new advanced manufacturing model. US Steel's Pro-Tec factory in rural Leipsic (Ohio) offers a glimpse at modern American manufacturing. Three hundred twelve workers operate this $400,000,000, seven-story plant.[3] Employees earn $20 an hour.[4] This compares with the thousands of employees traditionally required to operate a steel factory. They still make steel in Ohio and throughout the industrial midwest, but this industry is not the major employer they once were.

Policy Arguments for Advanced Manufacturing

Manufacturing jobs are not just high-wage jobs but jobs that do not require an advanced professional or college degree. Manufacturing jobs are a pathway to a middle-class life for millions of American families as Figure 15.1 illustrates.

Manufacturing workers earn more than those in other industries as measured on a weekly earnings basis.[5] They provide not just higher wages but also increased level of benefits. Opponents of advanced manufacturing as an economic development strategy cite not the high wages paid but the startling decline in the total number of jobs in this industry.

The obituary of the American manufacturing industry has been written. However, this sector of the economy is still important because its productivity is rarely matched by global competitors and the wages it pays is above the national average. Manufacturing is also a major driver for export growth and an essential FDI tool. The American manufacturing industry is actually growing jobs in the midst of current economic struggles. Manufacturing employment expanded by 489,000 jobs or four percent, and the number of job openings surged by over 200 percent, to 253,000.[6] Manufacturing contributes more than 25 percent of the overall growth in GDP between 2009 and 2011 and adding roughly 500,000 new jobs between the beginning of 2010 and the end of 2012.[7]

Advanced Manufacturing as an Economic Development Tool

Manufacturing facilities in the United States survive through not just reasonable labor agreements and tax incentive offers from local governments, but they adopt

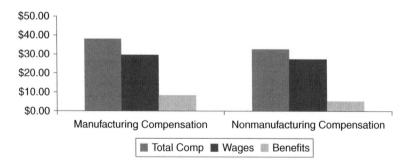

Figure 15.1   Employee compensation per house by major industry 2010.
Source: Federal Reserve Bank of Chicago.

technological innovations that change the face of manufacturing and manage logistics costs. The term that best identifies existing American manufacturing facilities is advanced manufacturing. Low-cost, low-tech products are not made in the United States anymore. China and other low-cost markets have taken those jobs. The American manufacturing industry transformed into a technological wonder. High-tech entered the American manufacturing industry, and productivity levels prove this point.

Technological advancements control costs, improve product quality, and increase productivity. The pathway to advanced manufacturing is similar to the agriculture sector's transformation. American advanced manufacturing permitted this industry to outpace productivity gains for the larger American economy.[8] Advanced manufacturing companies can do more with less. Manufacturing employment fell 1.5 percent per year since 1980, while manufacturing output rose 3.1 percent per year.[9]

Productivity of the American worker is not the only factor way advanced manufacturing initiatives succeed in the United States. Regions for decades developed industrial parks as a land use strategy to prepare land for a manufacturing facility through zoning and providing infrastructure suited to manufacturing firms. The availability of reliable and affordable power, either electricity or natural gas, is essential for any region to attract advanced manufacturing facilities. Manufacturing facilities are large consumers of power, and often their electricity bill is the second largest expense following wages and salaries. Employees, being the largest cost of doing business for manufacturers, impact the success of advanced manufacturing initiatives. Right to Work states adopting legislation that weakens organized labor are more successful at recruiting advanced manufacturing facilities. Tax incentives are a tool regions and states use to attract manufacturing, and finally quality of life for the manufacturing executives and workers impacts both the cost of doing business and the ability to recruit talents.

Benchmarking Successful American Manufacturing

Regions and states are working to retain and attract advanced manufacturing facilities. These high-wage jobs and a supply chain a mile long are simply too attractive for any region to ignore. Not all regions of the United States are succeeding when it comes to winning advanced manufacturing jobs. Twenty percent (169) of all US counties had earnings paid to manufacturing employees that accounted for at least 20 percent of total earnings of all employees.[10] The industrial midwest still leads the nation with the highest concentration of manufacturing jobs, but the southern states are working to capture the manufacturing job crown. These manufacturing jobs are likely to be located outside of metropolitan areas. About 68 percent of counties with at least 20 percent of total earnings derived from manufacturing were located in rural or metropolitan areas.[11]

Big states with big markets dominate American manufacturing in an absolute sense. California is the state with the largest manufacturing economy, accounting for 13.4 percent of all manufacturing worker compensation and 11 percent of all US manufacturing jobs.[12] However, absolute market size is not the only way to measure the role manufacturing plays in regional and state economies. In the

Table 15.1 Manufacturing earnings and employment share, top ten states 2010

Earnings		Employment	
Indiana	22.3%	Indiana	13.1%
Wisconsin	20.2%	Wisconsin	12.9%
Iowa	17.6%	Iowa	10.6%
Michigan	16.8%	Arkansas	10.6%
Ohio	16.0%	Ohio	10.0%
Kansas	14.9%	Michigan	9.9%
Alabama	14.8%	Alabama	9.8%
Arkansas	14.6%	Mississippi	9.4%
South Carolina	14.6%	Kansas	9.2%
New Hampshire	14.5%	Kentucky	9.2%
National Average	9.9%	National Average	7.0%

Source: Brittany M. Bond, "The Geographic Concentration of Manufacturing Across the United States," *ESA Issue Brief #01–13* (January 2013).

industrial midwest states of Indiana, Wisconsin, Michigan, Iowa, and Ohio, manufacturing accounted for over 15 percent of each state's total earnings as Table 15.1 illustrates.[13]

Again, no matter the measure, the industrial midwest is the national leader in manufacturing; however, the south has risen and is making a strong play to capture the manufacturing base from the midwest.

Advanced Manufacturing and Land Use Policies

Land use policies impact the retention and expansion of advanced manufacturing facilities. Euclidian zoning was founded on the notion of separating dirty factories from workers' residents. This separation of uses is the foundation of modern American land use policies. Industrial parks are segregated real estate developments that primarily target manufacturing businesses. The creation and growth of industrial parks in urban centers are the result of land use and the interstate highway transportation system. Industrial parks, connected to the road, water, sewer, broadband, power, and rail network, separate manufacturing from commercial, retail, and resident developments. It moves "dirty" manufacturing centers away from populated areas while keeping the jobs somewhat close for workers.[14]

Trafford Park was the first industrial park established by a company named Shipcanal and Docks near Manchester, England, in 1896.[15] The American version of an industrial park began in the 1970s. Industrial parks first included not just a structure for locating manufacturers but also administrative office buildings, which would constitute 10–15 percent of the park space.[16] Second-generation industrial parks focused on more technology-related companies from 1975 to 1985.[17] The third generation of industrial parks focuses on elastic use of the area, a wide portfolio of services, and more space devoted to administrative office uses.[18] Today's office parks began in the 1990s and focus on companies using high-end technologies with storage houses located outside the park and the development of connected recreational areas.[19]

A more recent outgrowth of traditional industrial parks is the "eco-industrial park." The Kalundborg industrial symbiosis is a success among early eco-industrial park developments.[20] Industrial symbiosis is a collaborative business process whereby waste of one industry becomes a valuable resource for other businesses.[21] Kalundborg is a Dutch city home to 16,500 residents.

Kalundborg's industrial symbiosis is a "green industrial park" that houses eight companies: DONG Energy Asnæs Power Station, Statoil-Hydro Refinery, Gyproc A/S, Novo Nordisk, Novozymes, recycling company RGS 90 A/S, waste company Kara Noveren I/S, and Kalundborg municipality.[22] Each company is connected to the other via an intricate network of flows of steam, gas, water, gypsum, fly ash, and sludge.[23] These companies generate "raw materials" needed for each other's manufacturing.

Research and Development Link to Advanced Manufacturing

Serving as the intellectual capital for the manufacturing industry is a tactic many states utilize to retain and recruit advanced manufacturing companies. These state-based initiatives recognize low-cost manufacturing is unlikely to remain in the United States. Instead, state research and development efforts use the brain power located at universities and private research institutes to develop advanced manufacturing techniques and even products to grow local companies. Government and private research groups are the research and development wing for regional manufacturing companies. They also operate research and development initiatives to recruit industries of interest. States launch research and development strategies to help manufacturers innovate and improve their performance.

State manufacturing research and development programs target industries and are operated by government-based development groups or university-oriented research groups. They are funded through a combination of state and federal governments and industry funding. They also operate in partnership with company researchers.

Manufacturing may not be the economic powerhouse it was in the 1950s, but it still matters across the nation—even in service economy–intensive Connecticut. Connecticut is home to over 4000 manufacturers employing nearly 200,000 workers paying $12,400,000,000 in wages.[24] These Connecticut companies pay nearly $90,000 in annual average wages, and manufacturing constitutes ten percent of the state's economy.[25] Connecticut is not a low-cost state, but instead retains and attracts manufacturers through research and development initiatives. The Connecticut Center for Advanced Technology is one example of a research and development initiative to support the state's manufacturers. It partners with regional aerospace/defense suppliers to address technology capacity and organizational efficiency.[26] It works with military and civilian industrial manufacturing companies to stimulate innovation; they research and field-test lasers, nanotechnology, computational modeling, and next-generation manufacturing.[27] Its Advanced Manufacturing Center consists of the laser applications laboratory, the machining applications laboratory, and the modeling and simulation metrology laboratory.[28] The laser applications laboratory increases technical capabilities in laser materials processing in the areas of ablation, cladding, cutting, drilling, welding, and additive manufacturing.[29] The machining applications laboratory addresses process improvement of a regional manufacturer by researching runtime optimization for milling and turning, solving production problems, fixture design and fabrication, and hands-on training.[30] Finally, the modeling and simulation metrology laboratory develops software tools for machining process optimization and noncontact inspection system development.[31]

Other states combine research and development strategies with workforce development strategies. Manufacturing is not the first word one would think of when the state of Florida is discussed. However, the sunshine state hosts 18,107 manufacturers, employing 314,800 workers paying an average annual salary of $52,378.[32] While this wage is lower than that of Connecticut and other states, it is $10,000 more than the average annual wage in Florida.[33] Florida is business-friendly as it does not have a state income tax. Florida is second among states for aviation, aerospace, and space companies with more than 2,000 firms employing 87,000 workers.[34] Florida's aerospace leadership is supported by the presence of virtually every major defense contractor, NASA's Kennedy Space Center and the Cape Canaveral Spaceport, and multiple military installations.[35] Florida is not resting on its past success in aerospace, but is building on it with a research and development initiative. The Florida Center for Advanced Aero-Propulsion, funded by state government and the aerospace industry, is operated by Florida universities to train aerospace workforce, develop new technologies, and help aerospace firms adopt new technologies.[36] The Florida Center for Advanced Aero-Propulsion researches active flow and noise control with design of sensors and actuators, low-order modeling, and systems and controls design.[37] They also research advanced propulsion with alternative aviation power and advanced gas turbines and next-generation air vehicles and systems technology and air traffic management.[38] Finally, the organization coordinates aerospace workforce development programs. It also works with an impressive list of federal, government, and industry partners such as NASA, the Air Force Research Lab, Lockheed Martin, Defense Advanced Research Project Agency, Boeing, Pratt & Whitney, Seimens, GE Energy, and Gulfstream.[39]

Environmental Regulation and Advanced Manufacturing

The year 1970 saw the development of federal environmental laws with the goal of protecting the quality of America's air, water, and land. No longer can companies "pollute" without gaining approval from the US EPA. Ultimately, the federal government permitted state governments to operate and implement federal environmental laws. Federal environmental laws act as a floor and not as a ceiling. State governments are permitted to enact environmental regulations beyond the federal laws and regulations.

State and federal environmental laws and regulations impact the retention and expansion of the manufacturing industry. The manufacturing process can be dirty. Pollutants result from making goods. CEOs who make corporate site location decisions place a high priority on the state's regulatory climate.[40] Environmental regulations are tops of the list of concerns for manufacturing leaders. Traditionally, state and federal environmental regulations are a major factor for cost of doing business, which force manufacturing firms to leave regulated areas for regions and nations that provide little environmental regulation. Manufacturing firms seek "pollution havens" such as China, which has weak environmental laws. In fact, the regulation of certain pollutants slowed productivity growth by 43 percent in the United States since the 1970s.[41] Advocates of the traditional location theory of economic development note that states with higher environmental regulations than the federal minimum put themselves at a competitive disadvantage compared to states meeting only the minimum of regulation.[42]

Proponents of environment regulation point to the public health and quality-of-life benefits on life expectancy since the 1970s. Also, they note the significant research and development success and productivity gains spurred by environmental regulations.[43]

Distribution Strategies and Advanced Manufacturing

As global trade, both exports and imports, dominates the American marketplace, regions and states are looking to capitalize on this economic trend by creating logistics and distribution initiatives. Logistics strategies reduce manufacturers' cost of doing business by developing a local supply chain network and incentivizing the location of distribution centers close to their facilities. These also serve to attract global investment by serving as the landing point for global goods in the United States.

Logistics involves a set of activities dedicated to the transformation and distribution of goods, from raw material sourcing to final product distribution and the related information flows enabling greater transportation efficiencies through modes, terminals, routes, and scheduling.[44] Logistics adds value to the goods through impacting the location, time, and control of elements of the supply chain.[45] Logistics addresses a complex set of decisions around the location of suppliers, required transportation modes, and the timing and sequencing of deliveries.[46] Most importantly, logistics centers create jobs and important links to regional manufacturers and retail companies looking for low-cost and efficient logistics near existing or potential facilities.

Regional logistics initiatives develop supply chain networks and build a strong infrastructure system for distribution centers. Indianapolis offers a model for logistics initiative designed to create jobs and build strong links with its region and state's manufacturing supply chain. Indianapolis is home to a growing logistics industry at Indianapolis International Airport. Seventy-five percent of all US businesses are within a day-and-a-half truck connection, and 1,500 logistics-oriented companies employ over 100,000.[47] Central Indiana has more interstate highway connections than any other metropolitan service area in the United States and is connected by four railroads.[48] Central Indiana moves more than 5,000,000,000 in air cargo, including the second largest Fed Ex hub in the nation.[49] The region also benefits from an active FTZ and low cost of doing business for taxes and workers' compensation.[50] This results in a lower monthly average wage in the transportation sector than its midwest regional competitors and a lower net industrial rental than its national competitors.[51]

Infrastructure Needed for Manufacturing

The manufacturing industry, more than most other industries, is highly dependent upon the cost and reliability of the power to operate an advanced manufacturing facility. The policy debate about the best approach for the provision of energy, by electricity and natural gas in particular, is intense. In addition, how electric and natural gas utility companies are regulated also impacts the role these companies play in the economic development of a region or state.

Power Costs and Retaining and Attracting Manufacturing Sector

Utility companies provide power to residential and business customers and play a pivotal role in economic development. The cost of power is the second largest expense of advanced manufacturing facilities. The cost of power varies among regions and states and serves as a competitive advantage. How utilities are regulated impacts a region's or state's strategies to retain and attract advanced manufacturing facilities.

Regulation impacts the cost of power but also establishes whether the cost of power is dictated by the market or regulatory fiat. Utilities regulated as a monopoly have rates set by public utility commissioners. Regulated utilities operate under a traditional rate-of-return monopoly framework. They are guaranteed a set price and revenues based upon a commitment to make a specific capital investment and to provide service to anyone in their service territory. Power companies build relationships with manufacturers looking to expand operations in the former's service territory. By helping manufacturers with such expansions, power companies sell more power.

Most regulated states permit the utilities to offer an economic development incentive or "Rider Program." Rider programs reduce power rates for industrial customers based upon power purchase commitments or economic development commitments to the territory of the utility. Rider programs are regulated utility states' version of an economic development program. Duke Energy Carolinas offers an economic development rider that grants a four-year billing credit that can max out at 20 percent and decline to zero after 48 months.[52] The Duke Economic Development Rider is available for customers who add a minimum of 1,000 kilowatts (KW) new load at one delivery point, a capital business investment of $400,000 per 1,000 KW of load added, plus a net increase of at least 75 full-time employees per 1,000 KW per new load in Duke Energy's service area.[53] These customers agree to a minimum contract term with Duke Energy for ten years and maintain a monthly average electric demand of 250 hours.[54] Retail or government institutions are not eligible for this program.[55] Customers have to apply for the Economic Development Rider, and its availability must be a factor in their decision to locate the new load on the Duke Energy system.[56] The 500 KW must be at one delivery point, at one voltage, and must not result in additional investment in distribution facilities.[57] Rider programs make utilities a partner in a region's or state's economic development effort.

A competitively deregulated power market, on the other hand, dampens incentives for utility involvement in economic development. However, moving from a regulated market to a competitive market should drive down cost and increase innovation in the power industry. In a competitive market, customers are free to choose retail power from whomever they wish. Their choice is not dictated solely by the geography of their business. However, it is the role of the market to drive down power rates as electric and natural gas companies compete for retail customers. States such as Texas and Ohio are looking more and more to the marketplace to provide best rates and services for electric service. While models vary, all encounter a complex web of regulatory decisions as to how to move from a regulated monopoly to a market that provides retail energy competition. Most competitive markets recognize that a limited number of companies, often the traditional monopoly electric companies, generate most power in a region—as electricity can only travel certain distances. Much of the transmission business in the electric industry is done on a multistate regional level to build the most efficient system possible. Competition in the power business is limited to the retail sale.

State policy makers decide whether the market or monopoly regulation best serves economic development. Under either scenario, those companies using the most power gain the best rate. The market and the regulator understand the economic necessity of that approach.

Workforce Policies Impacting Manufacturing

One of the great benefits of the manufacturing industry is not just its high-wage jobs but the disproportionately high number of jobs for less-educated workers. Forty-eight percent of manufacturing workers, compared to only 37 percent of non-manufacturing workers, have only a high school education.[58] This larger share of jobs for the less-educated workers matched with the above-average wage and benefit rates built the American dream for generations of Americans. The profile of the American manufacturing worker is changing in the age of advanced manufacturing. The educational attainment of the manufacturing workforce increased substantially over the last decade. In 2011, 53 percent of all manufacturing workers had at least some college education, up from 43 percent in 1994.[59] The advanced manufacturing sector relies on workers with STEM education. In 2011, nearly one-third of college-educated manufacturing workers had a STEM job, compared to ten percent in nonmanufacturing sectors. Higher educational attainment for manufacturing workers brings higher wages and benefits. Regions and states looking to enhance opportunities in the advanced manufacturing sector focus on the development of STEM workers.

Role of Unions in Retaining and Attracting the Manufacturing Sector

Organized labor is a factor impacting the economic development of a region or state. Labor unions were born in the manufacturing industry. The danger of the industrial workplace made the nineteenth- and twentieth-century manufacturing centers prime locations for organized labor for collectively bargaining health, safety, wage, and benefit issues.

Labor unions gained policy support with the rise of Franklin Roosevelt's New Deal. However, recently, union membership declined in the United States. The union membership rate fell to 11.3 percent of all workers, and total membership fell by about 400,000 to 14,400,000.[60] The union membership rate is lowest since the 1930s.[61] The drop in union membership is blamed on a wave of state policy decisions to enact collective bargaining reform for government workers and the adoption of Right to Work laws that empower employees to decide whether to join a union or not. More than half the loss—about 234,000—came from government workers, including teachers, firefighters, and public administrators.[62] However, unions also saw losses in the private sector, even as the economy expanded. Private sector union membership fell from 6.9 percent to 6.6 percent.[63] Another bad sign for unions is an aging membership that is not being replaced by younger, 16- to-24-year-olds. New York has the highest union density, and North Carolina had the lowest.[64] This reflects the union presence in the northeast and midwest and lack of it in the southern region of the United States.

Right to Work's Impact on Manufacturing Growth

Right to Work is a hotly debated public policy issue. Right to Work laws permit workers to decide whether or not to join a union even if a majority of the workers agree to form a union in a company. Just over half the states count themselves under Right to Work. The manufacturing growth of the southern United States is due in part to Right to Work. The south is a manufacturing powerhouse. Over the past 50 years, southern population doubled and its average growth rate has been about 30 percent faster than the nation as a whole. [65] A major manufacturing driver for the south has been the automanufacturing industry.[66] Ford, General Motors, Toyota, Nissan, Mercedes, BMW, Hyundai, and Volkswagen are just a few of the companies expanding their automobile facilities in the south over the last decade. This economic growth is created by low-cost labor as compared to high-cost regions such as the northeast and midwest.[67]

Opponents of Right to Work argue that the economic success of many southern states is unrelated to labor union rules:

- North Carolina's investment in higher education creates a global advanced manufacturing and bio jobs at the RTP.
- Virginia's location near the Pentagon enables a global services and technology–based economy around the defense industry.
- Georgia grew on the backs of its mega city, Atlanta, as the "corporate capital" of the south.
- Alabama is expanding into the manufacturing center through the use of $100,000,000 plus economic development tax incentive packages.

- Texas, Florida, Tennessee, and other southern states have grown due to particular industry success and a lack of an income tax policy appealing to many small business leaders.

States with Right to Work laws have lower wages for the manufacturing industry. Recent US Department of Labor statistics illustrate that the southern states paid a wage rate nearly $2 an hour lower than the midwest, $4 less than the west, and $7 less than the northeast.[68] The midwest was once the low-cost alternative to the northeast and the west. While that fact is still true, the south has now proved it can attract and keep manufacturing companies, but it also pays a lower, standard wage rate. This lower wage rate matched with a lower cost of living makes the south attractive to global manufacturers.

Union membership is very low in the southern part of the United States. The southern states are all below the national average, and the states with the lowest union membership are all from the south and include North Carolina (2.9%), Arkansas (3.2%), and South Carolina (3.3%).[69] A low union membership in the south is part of the reason for this overall low wage rate. The south is in a strong position to attract manufacturers concerned with labor unions and looking for competitive wage rage.

Manufacturers and Tax Policies

The tax law and policies impacting manufacturers offer lessons for regions and states looking to retain and attract manufacturing jobs. Tax policy supports the growth of manufacturing jobs.

Economic development incentives are a tax policy used to recruit and retain advanced manufacturing facilities. The decline of the industrial midwest creates an opportunity for southern states to establish a manufacturing industry from scratch.

Alabama is a global manufacturing powerhouse, and economic development incentives helped that happen. Alabama attracted three autoassembly plants and landed an Airbus facility, producing thousands of jobs. While Alabama has half the population of Ohio, the two states have the same number of autoassembly plants. Just consider the factors that shaped Airbus' decision when comparing Alabama to Ohio. Ohio is home to GE Jet Aviation, the US Air Force Research Lab, NASA Glenn Research Center, and NetJets. Yet Alabama landed a high-profile global aviation project. How? The Alabama Airbus deal did not happen because of the weather. State and local incentives totaling nearly $158,500,000 helped secure the $600,000,000 Airbus SAS final assembly plant in Mobile. Local incentives total $33,600,000 between the city, county, and airport for a project that will create 1,000 direct jobs, but have an overall economic impact estimated at $162,000,000 over three years. The state and local governments have their return on investment within three years, and the region benefits for decades from this opening to the global aviation marketplace. In addition, Alabama proved a success for three global automakers as a manufacturing success story. If the Crimson Tide can build cars, they can surely build airplanes.

Big Questions

1. With the decline in American manufacturing jobs, is it really worth the effort to retain and attract these jobs?

2. What infrastructure matters for manufacturers?

3. Does Right to Work really impact the retention and recruitment of manufacturers?

4. Will Alabama's immigration policy prove a setback for its recent success in attracting global manufacturers?

Class Writing Assignment: Workforce as the Key to Manufacturing Success

The city council president is preparing for a fight over Right to Work. She does not support it. She asked you, her Chief of Staff, to draft a one-page policy brief outlining how workforce training is actually the key to succeeding in the retention and expansion of manufacturing companies. She encouraged you to research examples of best practices proving this point and to make a specific policy recommendation.

Metropolis City Council Debate: Right to Work

Metropolis is focused on gaining new manufacturing facilities with the planned success of the Tech Expo. As part of that effort, the mayor is planning to ask city council to petition state government to adopt a Right to Work law. The debate will be so intense. The city council president opposes the measure, and it should be a good show with supporters and opponents lining up to advocate for and against Right to Work as well as outlining what they believe the state should do to retain and attract manufacturing facilities.

Additional Reading

Brent D. Ryan and Daniel Campo, "Autopia's End: The Decline and Fall of Detroit's Automotive Manufacturing Landscape," *Journal of Planning History*, 12, 2 (May 2013) 95–132.

Enang B. Udah, "Industrial Development, Electricity Crisis and Economic Performance in Nigeria," *European Journal of Economics, Finance and Administrative Sciences*, 18, 34 (2010) 151–121.

Fabio Iraldo, Francesco Testa, Michela Melis, and Marco Frey, "A Literature Review on the Links between Environmental Regulation and Competitiveness," *Environmental Policy and Governance*, 21, 3 (2011) 210–222.

James M Tien, "Manufacturing and Services: From Mass Production to Mass Customization," *Journal of Systems Science and Systems Engineering*, 20, 2 (2011) 129–154.

Jason Hackworth and Kirsten Stein, "The Collision of Faith and Economic Development in Toronto's Inner Suburban Industrial Districts," *Urban Affairs Review*, 48, 1 (2012) 37–63.

Josh Cable, "Advanced Manufacturing on a Roll in Virginia: Economic Development Officials see 'Game-changing Research Facility' as a Magnet for More Growth." *Industry Week*, 260, 9 (September 2011) 56, 1.

Nichola J. Lowe, "Beyond the Deal: Using Industrial Recruitment as a Strategic Tool for Manufacturing Development," *Economic Development Quarterly*, 27, 2 (May 2013) 90–101.

R. Wilkinson Ferguson and W. Hill, "Electricity use and economic development," *Energy Policy*, 28, 13 (November 2000) 923–934(12).

Shanthini, Rajaratnam, "Could Sri Lanka Afford Sustainable Electricity Consumption Practices without Harming her Economic Growth?" *MPRA Paper* 29582, University Library of Munich, Germany, 2010.

Stuart A. Rosenfeld, *Competitive Manufacturing: New Strategies for Regional Development* (New Brunswick, NJ: Center for Urban Policy Research, 1992).

W. Robert Reed, "How Right-To-Work Laws Affect Wages," *Journal of Labor Research*, 24, 4 (2003) 713–730.

Chapter Sixteen

Economic Development Driver:
The Regional Service Economy

Chapter Goals

1. Recognize the role of the service industry in the American economy
2. Identify the high-wage service jobs that can be built around successful regional economies
3. Understand the strategies needed to develop a successful regional service-based economy
4. Recognize the roles land use and workforce policy play in developing a successful regional service-based economy

Regional Service Economy and Economic Development

America transitioned from a manufacturing-based to a service-based economy. The service sector of the American economy produces intangible goods. By any measure, the US service sector is the largest and accounts for 80 percent of GDP.[1] The service sector revenues in the United States account for about one-third of service sector revenues worldwide.[2] Exports of services totaled $502,000,000,000, creating a $132,000,000,000 surplus.[3] This surplus is the largest in the world and accounts for 32 percent of total US exports.[4] Service-related jobs also dominate the ten largest occupations of Americans and account for 20 percent of total American employment.[5]

As American manufacturing facilities declined, the service sector is where Americans went to work. Health care, retail, and hospitality are leading the growth curve to replace the typical manufacturing job. Any successful regional economy has the service industry as part of its strategy. Successful regional service economies focus on health care, corporate headquarters, and professional services firms to develop high-wage service jobs. To retain and attract these high-wage service jobs, regions and states use the economic development building block strategies such as developing critical connections through airport infrastructure, creating a university-educated workforce, addressing critical quality-of-life issues such as traffic congestion, land use policies to build attractive office locations, and tax incentives.

Houston is a global economic success story. It is the fourth largest city in the United States. Its metro region has a 6,100,000 population and actually gained 313,800 new residents recently, while mega city counterparts such as New York, Los Angeles, and Chicago have lost population.[6] Houston's GDP is $399,700,000,000.[7] In the midst of fiscal and economic crisis, Houston is still growing. Its employment recently increased 3.3 percent, and Houston is ranked the fortieth largest economy in the world.[8] Why is Houston booming beyond any other American city? The city's base of energy industry corporate headquarters explains its growth. Houston has 68 publicly trading company headquarters, with more than $1,000,000,000 in sales, second only to New York. Chevron U.S.A. announced plans to construct a new 50-story, 1,700,000-square-foot tower in downtown Houston, creating 1,752 jobs.[9] The city of Houston's $3,000,000 tax abatement and the state of Texas' $12,000,000 Texas Enterprise Zone enticed Chevron to make this massive investment. Direct Energy chose to move to Houston, hire 200 people, and create an estimated $59,000,000 in annual local economic impact.[10] Exxon Mobil is building a 385-acre Houston corporate campus for 10,000 employees. In addition, BP and Anadarko Petroleum are consolidating US operations in Houston as well.[11]

Houston has also been diversifying its economy. Energy is responsible for 50 percent of Houston's jobs related to the export of goods and services, but that total is down from 87 percent in the 1980s.[12] This statistic is not a bad sign for Houston. Economic diversification is a key to any successful regional economy. Houston's economic diversification is built around logistics and health care. The Port of Houston generates $179,000,000,000 in annual statewide economic impact and ranks first in the United States in foreign cargo and imports.[13] Houston's health-care industry is booming as well. The Texas Medical Center in Houston employs nearly 100,000 people and serves as a global research and development center with an annual budget of $14,000,000,000.[14] Houston is booming based in large part on high-wage service jobs.

Policy Arguments for a Regional Service Economy

The American economy is now service-based. The question all regions face is whether they will be at the low or high end of the wage scale in this industry. Unfortunately, the largest service industry occupations are low-paying. The annual mean salary of American occupations is $45,230, or $21.74 per hour.[15] The wages for the balance of the ten largest service occupations range from $18,790 for combined food preparation and serving workers to $33,120 for customer service representatives.[16] Of concern for efforts to grow a vibrant private sector economy, five of the ten largest occupations in the service industry were public sector jobs.[17]

Successful regional service economies focus on high-paying "white collar" jobs in management, legal, health care, computer and mathematical, and architecture and engineering occupations.[18] As an example, only one of the 35 architecture and engineering occupations had an average wage below the US all-occupations mean.[19] Looking at the ten largest service industry occupations, only registered nurses, with an annual mean wage of $69,110, had an average wage above the US average.[20] However, registered nurses are the largest occupation in this sector, with nearly

2,400,000 jobs, almost 70 percent of which were in hospitals.[21] Those opposed to a focus on service industry jobs point to the low-wage nature of the majority of service jobs and the mobile nature of all the service positions. They argue that high-wage service jobs require higher levels of education than the average American has; thus, service jobs are a weak low-wage replacement for high-wage manufacturing positions.

Regional Service Economy as an Economic Development Tool

A successful regional service economy focuses on health care, corporate headquarters, and professional services firms to create high-wage jobs. First, they focus on the retention and attraction of corporate headquarters for big and small companies alike. Regions with a strong base of corporate headquarters not only bring high-wage jobs within those companies but also become a magnet for high-wage professional services firms in the legal, information technology, financial, public relations, and accounting fields.[22] Successful regional service economies also address infrastructure issues. The infrastructure in demand for the service industry is regional airports. Airports provide links for the workforce and leadership of high-wage service jobs. A prime land use development tool to build a successful regional service economy is a thriving central business district. Quality-of-life factors are also an essential element of building a high-wage regional service economy. While many quality-of-life factors are relevant, traffic congestion is a major issue for service workers leading to longer commute times. Last but certainly not least, a college-educated workforce ready to fill the jobs of a regional service economy is absolutely vital. High-wage service jobs require some level of advanced degrees beyond a high school education. Many regional service economies are built on the top of a strong higher education system.

The White-Collar Office Campaign

Successful service-based regional economies are rarely built on one industry but succeed by having a strong base of white-collar office jobs. Landing as many corporate headquarters is the best method to land as many white-collar jobs, but also the high-paying professional services firms, health care, and arts centers build strong regional service economies. In addition, corporate headquarters are more engaged with the community and bring larger budgets to address economic and societal challenges. Corporate headquarters cluster in a small number of metropolitan areas. Mega cities such as New York City, Chicago, Dallas, Washington, DC, and San Francisco traditionally led the pack with major corporate headquarter locations. Of course, many other major metropolitan cities are strong bases for high-wage service industry facilities in targeted industries such as manufacturing (Detroit, Cleveland, and Pittsburgh), financial services (Columbus and Charlotte), and defense (Northern Virginia).

The leading states for corporate headquarters are dominated by larger states from a population basis and states with a historical base in the Industrial Age and manufacturing. The top states for the location of Fortune 500 companies are the nation's

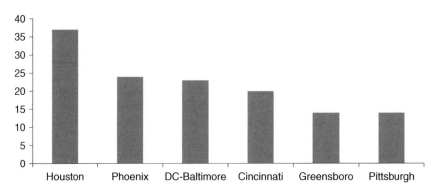

Figure 16.1   Net corporate headquarters gain.

Source: Vanessa Strauss-Kahn and Xavier Vives, *Why and Where Do Headquarters Move?* Working Paper, IESE Business School, University of Navarra, September 2006.

largest states from a population and economic standpoint. California just edges out Texas, which barely edged out New York in rank for the number of Fortune 500 companies they call home.[23] Illinois, with the mega city of Chicago, ranks four and Ohio, with its industrial base in northeast Ohio and a strong service industry presence in central and southwestern Ohio, finishes at number five.[24] However, the rise of the south is awaiting with Virginia now at number six.[25] Corporate headquarters move to different locations on a regular basis. Among the largest 500 headquarters, 36 moved between 1996 and 2001.[26] However, while previous state leaders in corporate America remained somewhat in place, southern and western cities have seen a growth in net new corporate headquarters recently as Figure 16.1 illustrates.

Many factors impact the location of a corporate headquarters. First, company headquarters, particularly globally oriented firms, locate in large metropolitan centers with airport facilities. Corporate tax rates, connection to business services, common industry specialization, and a core cluster of common commons matter as well. In addition, tax policy through specially created tax incentive programs retains and attracts corporate headquarters facilities.

Tax Policy and Headquarters Incentives

States use tax incentives to lure corporate headquarters.[27] Indiana offers the Headquarters Relocation Tax Credit. Eligible corporate headquarters must have annual worldwide revenue of at least $100,000,000 with at least 75 employees in state.[28] The Headquarters Relocation Tax Credit equals 50 percent of a corporation's costs of relocating its headquarters to Indiana and offsets the corporation's Indiana personal and corporate-adjusted gross income tax and financial institutions tax.[29] South Carolina offers a 20 percent tax credit based on the cost of the actual portion of the facility dedicated to the headquarters operation or direct lease costs for the first 5 years of operation.[30] The South Carolina headquarters tax credit can be applied against either the state's corporate income tax or the license fee, and the credits are not limited in their ability to eliminate corporate income taxes.[31] It potentially eliminates corporate income taxes for as long as 10 years from the year earned.[32] Tennessee offers a headquarters tax credit for companies that locate its headquarters facility in a central business district or economic recovery zone.[33] Tennessee's headquarters tax credit requires a $50,000,000 facility investment or a $10,000,000 investment and the creation of 100 new full-time jobs paying at least 150 percent of Tennessee's average occupational wage.[34]

Infrastructure and Corporate Headquarters Jobs: Airports

Infrastructure is a prime consideration when a company decides where to locate its corporate headquarters or major high-wage service industry facility. Beyond the traditional roads, water, sewer, and telecommunications infrastructure, corporate headquarters focus on slightly different infrastructure needs such as airports. Airports have a major economic impact on a community. Long-term corporate headquarters and emerging regions are growing high-wage jobs in part because of the global connections provided by their airports. Most are publicly owned and are organized as a port authority. Airports support the travel and tourism business of a community. Airports employ thousands of workers directly through airlines, airline suppliers, and airport officials. Finally, as port authorities, airports can be a public finance resource for a company searching for tax-exempt financing.

All states have airports. In a global economy, airports act as a link for high-wage service jobs to the world. Ease of travel matters to corporate executives.

As Table 16.1 indicates, commercial airports link the movement of people, goods, and services across the world. Four hundred ninety commercial airports in the United States support 10,500,000 jobs, create an annual payroll of $365,000,000,000, and produce an annual output of $1,200,000,000,000.[35]

O'Hare Airport is one of the reasons Chicago remains a global economic player. Unlike New York, Los Angeles, and Houston, Chicago does not have a direct access

Table 16.1 Total economic impacts of commercial airports in the United States

State	Airports	Jobs	Payroll	Output
California	29	1,380,230	$47,096,901,000	$157,996,816,000
Florida	21	1,209,580	$39,870,632,000	$125,850,286,000
Texas	26	970,310	$34,471,506,000	$116,622,794,000
New York	16	974,110	$28,343,957,000	$85,968,063,000
Georgia	9	637,360	$27,129,525,000	$80,534,186,000
Illinois	10	454,280	$18,282,773,000	$50,673,207,000
Virginia	9	437,180	$15,277,939,000	$49,628,495,000
Arizona	11	362,210	$12,506,488,000	$44,070,762,000
Nevada	5	313,640	$11,766,736,000	$40,533,175,000
Colorado	14	325,060	$11,278,290,000	$34,646,508,000

Source: Economic Impact of Commercial Airports, 2010, Airports Council International, North America.

to global markets through a major harbor directly linked to the ocean. O'Hare Airport plays that role for the high-wage service industry in Chicago. O'Hare, the fourth busiest airport in the world, serves over 66,000,000 passengers annually and is the only dual-hub airport in the nation with over 40 airlines providing nonstop service to New York, Los Angeles, London, San Francisco, Frankfurt, Shanghai, and other global and domestic destinations.[36] In addition, O'Hare transports over 1,500,000 tons of cargo annually.[37] Chicago's status as a global economic leader is supported by O'Hare Airport.

Land Use and Corporate Headquarters Jobs

Land use policies impact the location of service industry facilities. The high-wage service industry is located in a central business district (aka downtown) and suburban office parks. America's euclidian zoning model separates uses into industrial, commercial, retail, and residential. Urban centers began with development downtown and spread out over the decades. With the birth of the interstate highway system and a post–World War II industrial boom, much of America's growth in the second half of the twentieth century was in the suburbs. This growth was not just limited to residential housing but also included office projects.

As Table 16.2 indicates, even successful American cities are struggling to retain downtown office tenants. The loss of tenants in central business districts is even occurring during an urban renaissance in which downtown became full of housing, retail rebirths, sports stadiums, and other major civic projects. Downtown with its confined spaces, expensive parking, and existing owners of small parcels is a challenging place to develop as compared to the greenfield site with its new interstate off ramp, location close the suburban homes of its executives, and much of free parking.

Urban thinkers are looking at new and better ways to redevelop downtowns and sprawling suburban office parks to attract white-collar jobs. New suburban office parks embrace mixed use, break up massive superblocks built only for the automobile, and embrace transit to address transportation but also to raise the level of the suburban office product.[38] Downtown development is a hot topic. Miami offers an interesting example. Miami offers the Solid Shutter Removal and Facade

Table 16.2 Vacancy rate in downtown versus suburban development offices

City	Downtown	Suburban
Boston	47.9%	34.9%
Chicago	53.7%	53.4%
Dallas	18.4%	14.9%
Houston	29.2%	27.3%
Atlanta	13.6%	11.9%

Source: *Urban Land*, July 2008, p. 144.

Improvement Grant Program. The Program provides grant funding for qualified exterior improvements.[39] Similar to facade improvement programs across the country, Miami provides 100 percent grant funding for the removal of solid metal shutters in the target area, and its facade program requires a dollar-for-dollar match from the business owner on qualified exterior improvements to commercial buildings and properties.[40]

Urban centers are also offering tax credits and abatements for companies to locate downtown. Columbus provides for a 50 percent tax credit on the income tax a company's employees pay to the city if they located in downtown.[41] Columbus also created a TIF district in downtown to fund the building of three public parking garages to reduce the overall price of parking in the central business district and operates a Special Improvement District to charge a fee from downtown property owners for special services in the area. With all these efforts, only a handful of Columbus' Fortune 500 companies have their headquarters in downtown. Nearly two-thirds of these highly successful companies are located on the outerbelt/suburban office market. The case of Columbus illustrates how even successful cities face challenges to locate corporate headquarters downtown compared to lush, suburban sites.

Professional Service Firm Campaigns

Professional service firms are an expanding sector of the US economy, paying a higher-than-average wage. Professional service firms offer a supporting role as well for the remaining manufacturers, major service companies, and corporate headquarters locations in a region.[42] These professional service firms receive much of the "outsourced" work from larger companies in a wide range of industries. Both the professional service firm and the larger company grow together in a region. Professional service firms generate exports and increase productivity and innovation. Professional service firms employ knowledge-based workers, who have grown as manufacturers declined.

From 1970 to 2005, services employment jumped from 69 percent to 83 percent of total employment, and education and health sectors were the fastest growing service sectors over this timeframe.[43] In 1970, there were 17,800,000 manufacturing jobs compared to 5,300,000 professional service jobs, but by 2005, manufacturing jobs totaled 14,200,000 and professional service firms totaled 16,800,000.[44] The growth rate of professional service jobs has outpaced services and total employment growth. Between 1990 and 2005, professional service firms accounted for 25 percent of total US job growth.[45]

Workers in professional service firms are highly educated. Forty-one percent of workers in professional service firms hold at least a bachelor's degree, more than double the percentage of workers in manufacturing and other service sectors.[46] The professional service firms are reliant upon the ability to attract and retain college-educated workers. Workforce is a major issue for professional service firms and regions wishing to attract these high-wage employers. Not many regions have succeeded in developing professional service firms. First, most professional service

Table 16.3   Tampa Bay industry composition

	Establishments	Employment
Retail trade	24,631	270,658
Finance, insurance, real estate	30,429	171,904
Services	109,613	1,039,357
Agriculture and natural resources	753	9,108
Resource extraction	70	603
Construction	15,357	104,401
Manufacturing	5,479	101,610
Transportation/communications, utilities	3,468	41,514
Wholesale trade	7,205	93,948
Government	3,237	90,288
Total	200,242	1,923,391

Source: http://www.tampabay.us/demographics.aspx.

firms are concentrated in large urban areas to create proximity with major customers. Regions in the successful recruitment of professional service firms include Tampa, Washington, DC, San Jose, Miami, and Orlando.

Tampa is a leader in attracting professional service firms and in the service economy in general. It is a port city on Florida's west coast. As Table 16.3 illustrates, the Tampa region has over 4,300,000 residents, and its prime business is the service industry.

Historically, the Tampa Bay is the cigar capital of the United States, and today, the cigar industry is part of the region's tourism trade. Instead of just being a major vacation spot, Tampa turned into Florida's leading regional service industry headquarters location. This is not an accident. Tampa Bay's leaders adopted an economic development plan to retain and attract high-wage service companies. They identified four clusters in the business and services industry category:

- Business process outsourcing (BPO) and shared services—outsourcing or internalized shared centers for a broad range of back office and non–revenue-generating processes, such as human resources, sales, marketing and customer service, payment services, finance/accounting, and administration.
- Financial transactions processing—provision of transactions processing, reserve and liquidity services, and check clearinghouse services, including activities such as check processing, electronic funds transfer, and debit/credit card payments. New technology development and integration to provide more efficient transaction processing systems and to develop new products/services.
- Florida data centers, disaster recovery, and data management industry—provision of technology infrastructure for consolidated storage, management, and back-up of large data repositories, serving large corporations across a variety of industry sectors, and building research and consulting capabilities in disaster preparedness and recovery.

- Health information technology and bioinformatics—leverages regional capabilities across health, information technology, and financial/business services to take advantage of growing investment in and demand for electronic medical records and the use of information technology in the provision of medical/pharmaceutical services and in biomedical research and drug discovery.[47]

The University of South Florida is providing the white-collar workforce, moving the regional economy. In addition, the Port of Tampa, Florida's largest port by cargo tonnage and acreage, provides access to global markets.[48] Tampa Bay also offers the Qualified Target Industry Tax Refund incentive for high-wage jobs in targeted high value-added industries. This tax incentive includes refunds on corporate income, sales, ad valorem, intangible personal property, insurance premium, and certain other taxes.[49]

The results of Tampa Bay's strategy are impressive. Tampa Bay is home to $19,000,000,000 corporate headquarters revenue, and four of these companies are on the Fortune 500 list.[50] The result is population growth increasing by 22 percent over the last decade.[51] Close to 20 percent of residents are in the age group of 18–34, and 14 percent of the population is Hispanic.[52] One in four of Florida's business and information services is located in Tampa Bay.[53] How is Tampa Bay turning itself into a regional service industry leader? A growing economy, low cost of living, vibrant port, white-collar workforce provided by University of South Florida, targeted industry clusters, marketing and service-based tax credits are the reasons why Tampa Bay is a leader in attracting professional service firms.

Quality of Life and Professional Service Economy

Quality of life matters more for the service worker than those in any other industry cluster. The white-collar worker with higher disposable income and advanced educational attainment can choose to live in many regions of the United States. Quality of life in the region is the deciding factor. Much like their high-tech economy cousins, the service industry has a unique definition of quality-of-life factors. They range from cost of living to housing to traffic congestion to education systems. The availability and quality of higher education institutions matter more to high-wage service workers than others.

What are the specific quality-of-life factors that matter to the creative service industry worker? Traffic congestion, cultural amenities, and education institution quality are tops on the list.[54] While many quality-of-life factors impact the service industry, the dependence on central business districts and suburban office parks for work locations raise the profile on the degree of traffic congestion. Service workers in downtown and suburban locations are automobile-dependent. Traffic congestion is a serious quality-of-life issue. Congestion causes urban Americans to travel 5,500,000,000 hours more and to purchase an extra 2,900,000,000 gallons of fuel, for a congestion cost of $121,000,000.[55] It requires 60 minutes to make a trip that takes 20 minutes in light traffic.[56] Congestion levels are higher than a decade ago, even though the economy is not running at full capacity and costs the average urban American 38 hours a year.[57]

The top five regions with the most traffic congestion are Washington, DC, Los Angeles, San Francisco-Oakland, New York-Newark, and Boston.[58] Traffic congestion impacts the quality of life in a region and has a larger impact on service industry workers traveling to their office in a central business district or suburban office setting. Solutions to urban traffic congestion center on not just one response but the use of a diversified strategy, including:

- speedy removal of crashed vehicles, timing the traffic signals so that more vehicles see green lights, improving road and intersection designs, or adding a short section of roadway
- adding capacity to critical transportation corridors through additional road lanes, new street, or public transit
- changing transportation patterns through the adoption of flexible work schedules
- expanding choices such as toll roads and ride sharing lanes to provide quicker travel for those wishing to sacrifice funds or convenience
- diversifying development patterns to create more mixed uses that require less auto traffic overall[59]

Workforce and Professional Service Economy: Higher Education

As the Industrial Age transitions to the Information Age, regional access to the brain power located at world-class universities and the knowledge workers these universities produce grows in importance. No longer can a cadre of high school–educated workers be able to fuel economic development. Even workers in today's manufacturing centers are technology experts and need advanced training or an advanced degree. Higher education is an essential economic development tool for any region that wants to succeed in developing a high-wage, service-based economy. The economic benefits for a region increasing its number of college graduates are substantial. Median annual earnings of bachelor's degree recipients working full-time were $55,700, $21,900 more than high school graduates.[60] For those in the age group of 20–24, the unemployment rate for high school graduates was 2.6 times as high as that for college graduates.[61]

Massachusetts, Maryland, Colorado, Connecticut, and New Jersey lead the nation in the number of college and university graduates.[62] Unfortunately, West Virginia, Arkansas, Mississippi, Kentucky, Louisiana, and Nevada lead the nation with fewest number of college or university graduates.[63] No matter the measure, attaining a 4-year college degree is the pathway to economic success for regions looking to attract high-wage service companies. Regions such as Houston built a successful program to encourage high school students to go on to college.[64] As part of the campaign effort, the College Board purchased advertisements on 50 Houston Independent School District buses.[65] This campaign is the first to utilize advertisements on the Houston school district buses to ensure the students understand the economic benefits of gaining a 4-year college degree.[66] Many school districts across the United States focus on promoting a college degree as the next logical step in their students' road to success.

State governments are beginning to do much more than advertise to high school students on the benefits of attending college. They provide both need-based and non–need-based aid to college students. All 50 states fund undergraduate need-based programs and 30 states provide merit or non–need-based aid.[67] The amount of undergraduate aid awarded among colleges and universities across the United States in 2008–2009 through programs with a merit component increased to about $3,200,000,000 from about 3,000,000,000 in 2007–2008, but merit-based aid still lags behind spending for need-based programs.[68] In 2008–2009, need-based spending reached $4,500,000,000 for undergraduates.[69]

The development of state-based, merit college scholarship programs is a trend among growing states. These merit-based programs increase the number of students succeeding in college. The average merit-based award in 2008–2009 was $3,172.[70] Nevada offers an example of a merit-based, state-sponsored scholarship program. In 1999, Nevada was booming based upon the gaming industry and real estate–driven economy. However, state leaders realized that an overreliance on gaming and real estate would spell economic disaster. Part of their response was to create a program to increase the number of Nevada residents who graduated from college. This program, known as the Nevada Millennium Scholarship, illustrates that state-sponsored, merit-based scholarship produces the intended results. Nevada has seen double-digit increases in the number of residents attending college since it created the Millennium Scholarship program in 1999.

Building World-Class Health-Care Services

Health care is a major player in most successful regional service economies. The health-care industry, even during recent economic struggles, added an average of 28,000 jobs per month.[71] Hospitals are the major regional employer impacting local economic development. Hospitals directly employ nearly 5,500,000 people, constituting the nation's second largest source of private sector jobs, and spend over $702,000,000,000 on goods and services from other businesses.[72] Hospitals support 15,000,000 direct and indirect jobs, or one of nine jobs in America.[73]

Wages paid to health-care workers are traditionally higher than wages paid to non–health-care workers. Hospitals also provide employment for a full range of workers based upon their educational background, employing highly educated as doctors and less educated as operational staff. These businesses offer less educated workers a ladder to move up the economic opportunity chain.[74] Hospitals serve rural and urban centers from an economic development standpoint as they are the largest regional employer.[75] They are a major exporter of regional services and provide an important impact to struggling regional economies as they bring in state and federal funding for their operations.[76] The economic future is bright for health care. Health-care occupations are expected to grow by 29 percent from 2010 to 2020, the largest growth planned for any American occupation.[77] Finally, the health-care industry is more likely recession-proof than many other industries.[78]

However, health care is bigger than just the jobs they create. Research and development in the health-care industry creates jobs in biotechnology, medical devices, and many other areas. Institutions such as Johns Hopkins University in Baltimore lead the nation with nearly $2,000,000,000 in medical, science, and engineering–based research and development.[79] The Cleveland Clinic, Vanderbilt University, and others are chasing Johns Hopkins in the development of health-care research and development.

Access to high-quality health-care institutions impacts other regional employers. Healthy workers are more productive, and as life expectancy has touched nearly 80 across the United States, workers have been more productive for longer periods.[80] Health care provides an essential community infrastructure to regional workers and residents. Many states launched health-care quality programs. The top five states for health-care quality include Wisconsin, Minnesota, Massachusetts, Iowa, and Maine.[81] Cost is the other major driver companies look at when considering a region's health-care services (Table 16.4).

The shift of Ohio's economy from manufacturing to health care is an example of the new role health care plays in regional and state economies. Globalism, technology, and demographics have created a major transformation in the Ohio economy. The Buckeye state is still a national leader in manufacturing, but the number of Ohio manufacturing jobs has plummeted. In fact, no Ohio manufacturing cracks the list of current ten largest employers (Table 16.5).

Of greater interest than the decline of the Ohio manufacturing base is the enormous growth of the state's health-care sector. Five of the top ten largest Ohio's employers are hospitals. Hospitals and health care in general play a larger role in Ohio and national economy. The Cleveland Clinic alone has a $10,500,000,000 economic impact and constitutes 8 percent of the region's economy.[82] The Cleveland Clinic is only a part of Cleveland's Medical Corridor that also includes Case Western Reserve University's Hospital and others in the health care, services, research and development, and an emerging medical device industry. Catholic Health Partners, Ohio's fourth largest employer, has a total annual economic impact of $8,950,000,000, generating 30,429 jobs. [83]

Table 16.4 State health-care cost comparisons (per employee)

Georgia	$5,467
Texas	$5,924
Michigan	$6,618
Indiana	$6,666
Illinois	$6,756
Ohio	$7,076
Wisconsin	$7,233
Minnesota	$7,409
Pennsylvania	$7,730

Source: Louise Radnofsky, "Health-care Costs: A State-by-State Comparison: When It Comes to Spending, Some States May Get More Bang for their Buck," *Wall Street Journal* (April 2013).

Table 16.5 Ohio's major employers then and now

Rank	2012 Top Employers	1995 Top Employers
1	Walmart Stores, Inc.	General Motors
2	Cleveland Clinic Health System	Ford Motor Company
3	Kroger Company	Kroger Company
4	Catholic Health Partners	General Electric
5	The Ohio State University	Kmart
6	Wright Patterson Air Force Base	Walmart Stores, Inc.
7	University Hospital	AT&T
8	JP Morgan Chase & Co.	Banc One Corporation
9	Giant Eagle	Proctor & Gamble
10	Ohio Health	United Parcel Service

Source: Ohio Department of Development.

Many Ohio hospitals recognize the need for public-private partnerships to redevelop their neighborhoods as well. Mercy St. Vincent's in Toledo is leading in the redevelopment of the Cherry Street Corridor, just as Good Sam is in Dayton; Nationwide Children's Hospital, Mount Carmel, and Ohio State are in Columbus; and University Hospital and the Cleveland Clinic are in Cleveland. States like Ohio are seeing a major transformation in their economy, and health care is leading the way in this future of economic growth.

Tax Policy and Health Care

Health care, like nearly all other high-wage industries, benefits from local government tax policy, providing economic development incentives and the ability for major hospitals to act as tax-exempt, not-for-profit institutions. Again, Ohio offers an example of how hospitals gain from state and local tax policy. Both Ohio State University and Nationwide Children's Hospital launched major construction programs. Ohio state developed a $1,100,000,000 new Wexner Medical Center, agreed to retain 12,000 jobs, and create 6,000 jobs all with a $33.94-an-hour average salary. In return, the city of Columbus offered a $35,000,000 Columbus Job Creation Tax Credit, but Ohio state agreed to create Partners Achieving Community Transformation, a not-for-profit economic development corporation that would provide a $10,000,000 investment in Ohio State University east neighborhood to redevelop this struggling urban center. Nationwide Children's Hospital in Columbus offers another example of local government using tax policy to encourage growth in the health-care industry. Nationwide Children's Hospital agreed to undertake a $842,000,000 hospital expansion, retaining 5,585 jobs and creating 2,400 jobs. In exchange for this hospital expansion to remain in Columbus rather than shift to the suburbs, Nationwide Children's Hospital received a $15,000,000 Columbus Job Creation Tax Credit, priority for federal stimulus, and other infrastructure funding. Nationwide Children's Hospital further agreed to create a community development initiative, known as Healthy Neighborhoods, Healthy Families, to redevelop the housing, education, health care, and address crime in the struggling urban area surrounding the hospital. Both Ohio state and Nationwide Children's Hospital gained multimillion dollar tax incentives from the local government even though there was no threat to leaving the state. The threat was they could leave the city and take with them millions in municipal income revenue. These examples illustrates the role hospitals play in regional service economies.

Big Questions

1. Can service jobs really keep a regional economy moving?

2. What is the most important element of a successful regional service-based economy?

3. Does not every American city have a service economy?

4. How do rural areas build a successful regional service-based economy?

5. What role do airports play in building a successful regional service-based economy?

Class Writing Assignment: Mayor's Speech on Service Jobs

The mayor asked you to draft a three-minute speech outlining why Metropolis is focused on service companies as the key to their economic future. She expects you to cite the existing service industry strengths of the region, why that is so, and how that can continue into the future.

Metropolis City Council Debate: Service Company Incentive

The mayor decided the city needs a new, additional tax incentive targeted specifically at corporate headquarter companies. The proposed incentive would provide a 50 percent Job Creation Tax Credit to return half the income tax a new corporate headquarters facility would generate. Existing corporate headquarters would be excluded (and they are not happy). Recently, the *Daily Bugle* has run a series of stories about how 20 local companies failed to live up to their commitments under economic development incentives but were given a free pass by the city. A debate on this ordinance is expected to be intense.

Additional Readings

David Salvesen and Henry Renski, *The Importance of Qualify of Life in the Location Decisions of New Economy Firms*, Center for Urban and Regional Studies, University of North Carolina, January 2003, retrieved from https://curs.unc.edu/files/2013/04/neweconomyreport.pdf.

Education Pays 2010, College Board, retrieved from http://trends.collegeboard.org/education-pays.

Ellen D. Harpel, "Professional and Business Services in Regional Economies," *Economic Development Journal*, 5, 3 (Summer 2006) 50–59.

Geoffrey Booth, *Ten Principles for Reinventing Suburban Business Districts* (Washington, DC: Urban Land Institute, 2002).

Jason Potts and Tom Mandeville, "Toward an Evolutionary Theory of Innovation and Growth in the Service Economy," *Prometheus*, 25, 2 (June 2007) 147–159.

Lelsie Wimmer, "Traffic Congestion Tying up Economic Development," *Fort Worth Business Press*, 25, 35 (September 9, 2009) 19.

Matthew P. Drennan, "Gateway Cities: The Metropolitan Sources of US Producer Service Exports," *Urban Studies*, 29, 2 (1992) 217–235.

Matthias Sweet, "Does Traffic Congestion Slow the Economy?" *Journal of Planning Literature*, 26, 4 (2011) 391–404.

Richard K Green, "Airports and Economic Development," *Real Estate Economics*, 35, 1 (2007) 91–112.

Thomas Klier, "Where the Headquarters Are: Location Patterns of Large Public Companies, 1990–2000," *Economic Development Quarterly*, 20. 2 (2006) 117–128.

Chapter Seventeen
The Future of Economic Development

Chapter Goals

1. Understand how some future economic trends impact a region's growth policy
2. Recognize what changes are coming in the fundamentals of economic development and how these impact a region or state's economic development strategic plan
3. Describe the potential building block economic development strategies in the coming years
4. Describe the potential five-driver economic development strategies in the coming years

Knowing where the Puck Is Going

The future of economic development brings new ideas to the same fundamental building block and five-driver approaches to promote the creation of wealth. Future economic development trends center on emerging economic and demographic trends of a region or state. The future of economic development is not easy to predict. It requires setting public priorities and spending tax dollars more in some areas and lesser in others. It requires an acknowledgement that the old model of economic development simply may not be enough. It requires working together as a region and among states. The future is never easy, but policy makers cannot wait to make tough decisions. Global trade is creating threats and opportunities for all states and regions. China is positioning itself to become the world's largest economy by 2020. American regions and states have no choice but to think not just about what worked in the past but about what approaches will work in the future of economic development.

Economic Development Defined: New Company Target—The Middle Market

The emerging trend in economic development strategy shifts away from traditional industry cluster to support the development of existing and successful middle market companies. The US middle market's annual revenues range from $10,000,000 to $1,000,000,000, from a widely diverse industry pool. It does not matter what industry it is, or where the company is located. The focus is the size of the company and whether it is in a growth mode. The focus on middle market companies is catching the attention of economic development professionals because this category of company is growing. Middle market companies make up a surprising large percentage of the global economy, constituting one-third of all US jobs but only 3 percent of all US companies.[1] Middle market companies hold the advantage of surviving the start-up phase and reaching a great degree of stability primed for solid growth. The middle market sector actually grew during the recent recession. From 2005 to 2010, the top 20 percent of middle market companies receiving public financing grew at an average annual rate of over 26 percent. This growth is nearly ten times the rate of GDP growth.[2] Twenty-seven percent of all large companies in 2010 were reportedly middle market companies in 2005.[3] They simply grew out of the middle market status.[4] Even more enticing for economic development leaders is the fact that nearly 20 percent of the 200,000 middle market companies are in the high-wage manufacturing sector.[5] The future looks even brighter for middle market companies. Eighty percent of middle market companies expect to grow over the next 12 months.[6] Middle market companies are focused on leveraging existing talent within their organizations, the growing importance of technology (particularly business process automation, data analytics, and business intelligence), and their financials appear stronger than they were a year ago.[7]

Economic Development Organizations: Multistate Regionalism

Cities, townships, and counties regionally coordinating economic development is not new. Most states can point to a regional economic development approach. A new future economic development opportunity lies in the multistate regional economic development initiatives. State governments spend much of their time competing with each other for economic development projects. The reality is that states have much to gain from working in cooperation instead of competition. Cooperation could take the form of jointly submitting corporate site location requests, developing a common array of tax incentives, or developing innovation-based initiatives that set industry priorities for each state to ensure that cooperation wins over competition.

The widening of the Panama Canal is creating unique opportunities for multistate economic development partnerships. Like most 100-year-old transportation networks, the Panama Canal needs an update. An update it is getting. The current widening of the Panama Canal enables this invention of Teddy Roosevelt to carry larger container ships, often from Asia to the United States. The widening of the Panama Canal enables east coast American harbors to become major logistics hubs in competition with major west coast ports. The challenge is that only a few of the east coast ports were built to be deep enough to hold today's massive cargo ships. The harbors of the east coast are all in a battle to dredge their facilities to prepare for the larger cargo ships in the hopes of becoming the logistics center for the east coast, the south, and possibly the midwest. A debate going on in the state of Georgia offers an interesting opportunity for multistate cooperation to achieve economic development success. The Port of Savannah faces a $625,000,000 price tag to redevelop their harbor to ensure the larger container ships are able to pass through the Panama Canal by 2014. Savannah is competing with Norfolk (which has a port already deep enough), Charleston, Miami, and Jacksonville.[8] Some have proposed that instead of all those ports competing against each other they should join together in some way to develop a multistate, global logistics center that can effectively compete against west coast ports.[9] A multistate strategy would clearly make a stronger competitive case through the use of an effective rail and trucking network that all these ports can benefit from instead of attempting to weakly compete with west coast rivals.

Regions battling for Panama Canal business could look to regional efforts at the local level. Municipalities that once saw each other as competitors are now forming regional partnerships. Look at Louisville and Lexington. These two Kentucky cities not only are home to major college basketball rivalries but were once major economic competitors. Apart by only 60 miles, Louisville and Lexington have formed the Blue Grass Economic Advancement Movement to coordinate joint growth and economic success for both cities and their surrounding regions.[10] While this effort is in the "data collection" phase, it has the buy-in from the business and governmental leadership of both cities and is managed by 24 persons in the board of directors.[11]

Land Use: Retraction Model

Communities such as Detroit, Youngstown, and others are taking a novel approach to land use planning and growth, which may be a future trend for economic development. They are not looking for geographic expansion but are instead focused on geographic retraction. Many urban centers that exploded in growth during the Industrial Revolution have been evacuated. The population losses are staggering. The question for these urban centers is how to create a sustainable development plan. A "shrinking city" approach addresses the challenges of these diminished urban centers by promoting their retraction through a reduction of city services and land use planning. Under the "shrinking city" model, community sustainability attempts to increase long-term stability by balancing environment, economy, and equity.[12]

- Economic stability—opportunities for regeneration by rebuilding local economies, real estate values, and offering creative new business recruiting programs.[13]
- Environmental quality—reclaiming contaminated brownfields to serve environmental and economic purposes by reusing many central city sites for a new generation of uses.[14]
- Social equity—reviving neighborhoods, enhancing cultural amenities, decreasing exposure to toxins, improving quality of living through parks and open spaces, creating jobs, and teaching new skills all illustrate a renewed commitment to social equality for declining urban centers that house a large proportion of the nation's poor.[15]

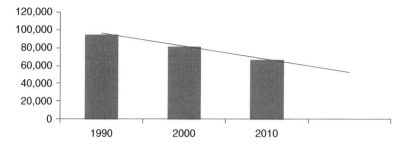

Figure 17.1   Youngstown population decline 1990–2010.
Source: Census Bureau, 2010

Economic Development Policy Case Study 17.1: Retraction Model

Youngstown and Detroit offer two recent case studies of cities planning for smaller, revitalized city boundaries as a key for future economic success. Youngstown embraces the shrinking city model. It lost half its population over the last 40 years.[16] They are not coming back. In the 1950s, Youngstown was a city on the rise, a booming industrial center that was nearly the world's center for steel production. This city of 170,000 people had plans for growth based upon the continued dominance of the American steel industry.[17] That reliance on the steel industry did not work out that well. The Youngstown steel mills closed in rapid succession in the 1970s, and the city has not recovered since (Figure 17.1).

The evacuation of Youngstown is staggering by most standards. That evacuation has exploded recently. The 2010 Census indicates that Youngstown lost nearly 20 percent of its population over just the last decade. The city is approaching the size of a suburb, not an urban center.

Forty years since this implosion of the Youngstown steel industry, municipal and civic leaders have an economic development strategy that is catching people's attention. Led by a dynamic young mayor, the community adopted Youngstown 2010 as a new land use master plan. Youngstown 2010 accepts reality. The city will not grow to 500,000 and should not have that goal. Instead, Youngstown 2010's goal was to concentrate growth and development in targeted parts of the city.

Infrastructure: Transportation Public-Private Partnerships

Economic development strategy is not the only place local and state governments are beginning to work together. Public infrastructure development presents another model for regional growth. Regions and states are struggling to finance their public infrastructure. A $170,000,000,000 infrastructure funding gap exists.[18] The American interstate highway system was built on excise taxes applied to the purchase of gasoline. Unfortunately, the gas tax is running out of gas. Congress and state governments are not showing the same zeal as in the past for the enactment of additional taxes and fees to provide the funding needed to maintain even the public roads, highways, and bridges. Future economic development is just as dependent on the provision of transportation infrastructure by the government. America's spread-out development model will not disappear overnight. Regions and states identifying new approaches to develop public infrastructure have the best chance to succeed.

Successful future economic development is dependent on the formation of transportation public-private partnerships (PPPs). A PPP is a contractual agreement formed between a public agency and private sector entity that allows for greater private sector participation in the delivery of transportation projects.[19] These projects are not just the construction of roads by the private sector, but instead they shift a larger share of the economic risk and financial rewards to the private sector. Private firms agree to construct, finance, maintain, and/or operate the project.[20] Transportation PPPs maximize the economic benefit of both existing public roads as well as create opportunities for the development of new transportation infrastructure for future development.

PPP are governed by a comprehensive lease agreement. The government leases an existing infrastructure as part of a concession agreement with a private company to operate the road. The company agrees to invest specific amounts for maintenance and accepts restrictions in tolls and operation of the road.[21] It also agrees to provide an upfront payment, discounted pricing during high-traffic times, and to accept the workforce and labor rules.[22] The company gains an unlimited rate of return and the ability to force the government to buy back the infrastructure if the government impacts the value of the infrastructure.[23] The government gains a substantial amount of money and the ability to buy back the infrastructure if the agreement is terminated.[24]

Several regions and states are leading the way with the development of transportation PPPs. Two prominent PPP projects are the long-term lease of the Chicago Skyway and the Indiana Toll Road. In the case of both, these local governments received upfront payments as part of the concession event. Chicago Skyway concession provided the city of Chicago a $1,800,000,000 upfront payment for a private concession to operate the 7.8-mile toll road south of downtown Chicago that connects two major highways.[25] The Indiana Toll Road concession provided the state of Indiana $3,800,000,000 for the private and exclusive concession of the Indiana Turnpike, which is the main northern eastwest highway that travels the entire width of the state.[26] Major tax issues exist in the structuring of these concession agreements. In short, this is a true transfer and not a "partnership."[27] The deal must be structured as a near-complete transfer of ownership and not a shame "lease."[28] The agreement illustrates the parties are engaged in a bona fide commercial transaction and not trading on the public entity's tax-exempt status.[29]

The state of Ohio is not privatizing its turnpike but instead is using the substantial revenues from turnpike drivers for transportation projects outside of the actual Ohio turnpike. This proposal provides nearly $1,500,000,000 in additional highway revenue for projects in northern Ohio and frees up additional funding for transportation projects in other parts of the state.

Workforce: Occupational Campaign

Occupational workforce marketing benefits a wide array of industries that are built around the same or similar occupations. Many cite the economic benefit the concentration of aerospace and defense industry firms provided Southern California's large pool of engineers.[30] As aerospace and defense struggled, these engineers found opportunities in innovative new companies. They built new sportsware, sports equipment, and high-tech businesses.[31] Occupational workforce marketing is a growing trend among regions and states for many reasons:

1. Cheaper transportation and instant communication kill the challenges distance once created, and regions are forced to specialize and focus on exporting goods and services as a means of economic survival.
2. Natural resources are less important in economic development as the manufacturing base goes global, and a region's workforce is the modern version of natural resources.
3. Job commitment from the employer and the employee waned in recent years, forcing government into the role of workforce developer as companies refuse to make the financial commitment in workers who are highly mobile.
4. Twenty-first-century workplace demands higher skill sets.
5. New firm creation is driven by the innovation of a highly skilled workforce.
6. Digital revolution permits workers a great flexibility in workplace location.[32]

The occupational workforce marketing campaign focuses on the strengths of traditional industry cluster of a region; thus, industry cluster analysis is the starting point for such an effort. Next, regions consider not only what companies they have but what industries are growing in related clusters. Beyond traditional industry cluster analysis, regions consider what occupations these clusters possess nationally and within their region. The target is high-wage jobs within those industry clusters and across related industries. Finally, once the region is aware of its workforce strengths and develops high-wage occupational targets, it is ready to market the region to companies likely to have a need for workers in these occupations. Marketing efforts include nonpaid media coverage, advertisements in targeted industry publications, regional marketing at industry trade shows, and social media campaigns to connect companies with the region via the Internet.

Tax Policy: Return on Investment

Challenging fiscal times pushed economic development officials to justify the use of tax incentives like never before. The response from economic development officials has not been to stop using economic development incentives. The response instead is to develop return on investment models to ensure that economic development incentives are true winners for the company and the community.

Input-output analysis is a method of measuring return on investment for a given economic development project. An economy can be divided into a number of productive industry sectors. A part of each sector's output goes to satisfy final demand for its products by consumers.[33] The rest of its output meets intermediate demand by serving as input to other sectors. Input-output analysis is a way to measure economic development success by comparing interactions among economic sectors, producers, and consumers.[34] The input-output analysis illustrates the interdependence of an economy's various productive industries both as a commodity for consumption and as a factor in the production of itself and other goods.[35] In addition, the input-output analysis measures the success of regional economies and forecasts economic growth as a result of specific actions by public or private sector partners.

Input-output analysis is used in the creation of economic impact studies and illustrates the benefits of certain "multiplier" employers. An easy-to-understand example of a "multiplier" employer is in the autoindustry. An autoassembly plant not only produces jobs but also encourages the location and expansion of a range of suppliers, such as steel, batteries, glass, and tire, near the autoassembly plant. Modern manufacturing techniques such as "just-in-time inventory" have enhanced this multiplier effect as autoassembly firms no longer hold large inventories of component parts but demand suppliers to deliver parts only when needed.

Other regions are utilizing local fiscal impact tools to measure the return on investment for an economic development deal. Return on investment as a measure for economic success uses effective tax rates for real and tangible personal property, machinery and tools taxes and local sales taxes and a multiplier effect estimated using IMPLAN employment multipliers, and an econometric model based on existing COMPAS models, to predict labor market responses.[36]

Energy-Led Economic Development: Statewide Green Build Codes and Energy Efficiency Codes

The energy-led economic development model is sweeping across the United States. Green building codes have been ongoing for a number of years at the local government level. Many communities are adopting energy efficiency codes to build more sustainable environments. California is the first state to implement a statewide green building code for new public and private developments. CalGreen requires builders to install plumbing that cuts indoor water use by as much as 20 percent, to divert 50 percent of construction waste from landfills to recycling, and to use low-pollutant paints, carpets, and floors.[37] It mandates the inspection of energy systems to ensure heaters, air-conditioners, and other mechanical equipment are working efficiently.[38] Nonresidential buildings are required to install water meters for different uses.[39] Local jurisdictions retain the ability to impose stricter green building standards.[40] The ultimate impact on construction costs is unknown at this time given the requirements are not mandatory. CalGreen follows a 2008 California Green Building Code that was voluntary but had many of the same strategies for developing green buildings.[41]

High-Tech: Crowdfunding

Capital Raising Online While Deterring Fraud and Unethical Non-Disclosure (aka Crowdfunding) is a tool used by high-tech start-up companies to skip the pitches with the venture capital community and go directly to the Internet to gain financing. Crowdfunding, or "crowdsourced funding," is a new outgrowth of social media that provides an emerging source of funding. It allows companies to pool money from individuals who have a common interest and are willing to provide small contributions toward the business. Crowdfunding can be used to raise money for charity and to gain investors in a company. However, if crowd-funding investors also can share the profits of a company, Securities and Exchange Commission (SEC) regulations apply.[42] Those crowdfunding operations not registering and complying with SEC regulations are almost certainly operating outside of the law. Crowdfunding advocates have called on the SEC to consider implementing a new exemption from registration under the federal securities laws for crowdfunding.

The Jumpstart Our Business Startups (JOBS) Act (H.R. 3606) is designed to promote crowdfunding. The JOBS Act creates a transitional "on-ramp" for emerg-ing companies (less than $1,000,000,000 in revenue) to encourage them to pursue Initial Public Offerings by phasing in compliance measures over time following their IPOs.[43] It amends the Securities Act of 1933 to permit companies to conduct offerings to raise up to $50,000,000 through a "mini-registration" and modifies the triggers for SEC reporting obligations as well as the prohibition against "gen-eral solicitation and general advertising" in connection with private placements.[44] The Act provides an exemption under the Securities Act for "crowdfunding" offer-ings less than $1,000,000.[45] Regulations from the JOBS Act are equally important as the actual legislation, but crowdfunding may move from a fundraising fad to a billion-dollar capital access business for high-tech start-up companies looking to grow.

Newly authorized crowdfunding companies may play a larger role in funding university start-ups. Crowdfunding is authorized in the federal JOBS Act and per-mits companies to raise money through the Internet with few of the Securities Act regulations impacting traditional company fundraising efforts. Georgia Tech's new crowdfunding site, Georgia Tech Starter, allows science and engineering researchers an alternative source of funding in a time of restricted government grants.[46] Unlike other crowdfunding services, online investors will not receive any tangible rewards other than a tax deduction.[47] Georgia Tech provides project review, administration, and facility upkeep, paid for by a 35 percent fee.[48] Only members of the Georgia Tech community can utilize Georgia Tech Starter, although this may expand in the future.[49] Georgia Tech may be a model for other universities to follow.

Advanced Manufacturing: Backshoring

American manufacturers regularly move production to global markets. The com-pany brand may not change, but the location of the product's manufacture does. This outsourcing of American jobs started with low-end, easy-to-produce products. However, outsourcing extends to information technology and a range of technol-ogy-dependent services. The US outsources more information technology services than established European economies.[50] Wage pressures in China are creating opportunities for low-cost states such as Mississippi, South Carolina, and Alabama to grow their manufacturing base to even larger percentages.[51] Wages in China are climbing 15 percent to 20 percent per year.[52] Many regions and states are promot-ing FDI with Chinese or American companies that invested in China to bring that investment home to the United States. China's FDI is growing globally but slowing in the United States.

The question is will Chinese companies follow the Japanese and German models. The Japanese made the first move. Beginning to succeed against their previously dominant American counterparts in the US marketplace, Toyota opened its first manufacturing plant in the United States in 1972 and assembled its first car in 1988.[53] Honda opened its first motorcycle plant in the United States in 1977 and produced its first car in 1982 in Ohio.[54] Samsung built its first American plant in 1984.[55] Today, all three companies are dominant players in the American marketplace in part because US consumers appreciate the fact that many of these companies' products are made in the United States. The Germans moved later with BMW and Mercedes opening facilities in the American south in the 1990s.

Unlike the Japanese or German economic model, China develops manufacturing and research centers based upon other country's companies. China has been satisfied with producing other countries' goods and shipping them overseas. That is beginning to change. China purchased the IBM computer-making division to create Lenovo, and Zhejiang Geely Holding Group purchased the car maker Volvo from Ford.[56] As the Chinese begin to purchase and develop more global companies, it creates an opportunity for FDI in the United States. Trade talks and public relations are only two steps that can encourage what is called "backshoring" of companies and jobs once shipped overseas. In the technology sector, federal immigration policy has high-tech companies arguing that off-shoring would be limited if more foreign high-tech workers were able to work in the United States. They point to the need to expand the number of H-1B visas, which provides temporary visas to highly skilled workers, and also, to some extent, of L-1 visas, which provides visas for intracompany transfers.[57] Quality is also driving some companies to move facilities back to the United States from markets such as China. Sleek Audio, the maker of iPod in-ear headphones, is moving production back from China to the United States because of quality concerns for the product.[58]

Regional Services Economy: The Arts

The nonprofit arts industry is a $36,800,000,000 business in the United States.[59] It is an emerging and powerful sector in many economic development initiatives built around services. Arts play a range of economic development roles by transforming struggling economies to generate new companies and jobs through tourism, crafts, and cultural attractions.[60] Arts are revitalizing once-struggling downtowns in big and small cities and attracting a new generation of workers by improving large and small communities' quality of life and tax base.[61]

Paducah (Kentucky) proves that one need not have to be a big city to create an arts-based economic development initiative. It is a river town located on the Ohio River in McCracken county. It is situated halfway between St Louis and Nashville along I-24.[62] Paducah's population is 25,024, and McCracken county's population is

65,565.[63] The median household income for Paducah is $29,275 and for McCracken county is $41,630, compared to the state of Kentucky's median household income of $41,576.[64] Of the population aged 25 years and older in Paducah, 81.7 percent has a high school degree (or equivalent) and an additional 18.6 percent earned a bachelor's degree or higher.[65]

In a global economy, Paducah has plenty to be concerned about. To address its economic challenges, in 2000, Paducah launched an artist relocation program to revitalize a historic district, LowerTown Arts District. Paducah uses dual zoning for commercial and residential use, allows residents to live and work in one building, provides 100 percent financing for purchase and renovations of existing structures or construction of new structures, and provides free lots for new construction.[66] It also grants $2,500 in city contributions for professional fees and launched a national marketing program.[67] Paducah Artist Relocation Program relocated 70 artists to the LowerTown Arts District, which is now home to over 30 studios and galleries of working artists.[68] Over 50 artists moved to Paducah to participate in the program.[69] This program is a model for other communities that wish to grow the arts as a means of economic development. The LowerTown Arts District plays host to the LowerTown Arts and Music Festival each spring and Second Saturday Gallery Walks to promote the arts studios and enhance the entertainment offerings in LowerTown.[70]

Globalism: Brazil, India, and China Inbound Investment

Succeeding in global markets is a goal for future economic development. Public policy makers illustrate little interest in moving back to economic protectionism when tariffs on foreign goods protected American manufacturing. American consumers adapted to the global economy and are accustomed to low-cost, high-quality, foreign-produced goods. Regions and states exporting more goods and services or recruiting more global companies to make US investments have higher-paid workers.

The future of global economic development is building exports and FDI with the growing, developing economies of Brazil, India, and China (BIC). By 2050, not only will the Chinese economy be substantially larger than the United States' economy, but India will be as well.[71] Brazil is estimated to be fourth behind the United States—just ahead of Japan[72] (Figure 17.2).

BIC countries gained substantially through exporting goods to higher-cost nations such as the United States. However, regions and states are now approaching these booming economies to recruit global investment and gain export-related deals. US regions and states are focusing on BIC countries because that is where all the money is.

Export and FDI campaigns geared to the BIC countries are the wave of the economic development future. Mature agricultural, mining, manufacturing, and service sectors position Brazil not only as the leading South American economy but also the sixth largest economy in the world.[73] From a macroeconomic standpoint, Brazil since the start of the twenty-first century built up foreign reserves, reduced its debt profile, and became a net external creditor.[74] Even during the current economic recession, Brazil's 2010 GDP reached 7.5 percent—the highest growth rate

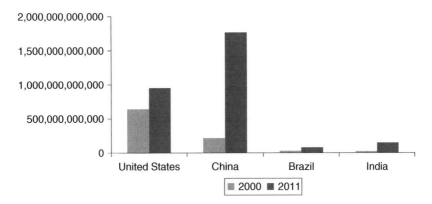

Figure 17.2 Manufacturing export growth 2000–2011.

Source: Manufacturing for Growth, Strategies for Driving Growth and Employment, World Economic Forum Report in collaboration with Deloitte Touche Tohmatsu Limited, 2013.

in the past 25 years.[75] While Brazil's 2011 GDP rate faltered to 2.8 percent, the over 100,000,000-member labor force of Brazil matched with recent financial stability made this South American country a global powerhouse and attractive global investment option.[76]

India is developing its $4,000,000,000,000-plus economy into an open-market model through industrial deregulation, privatization of state-owned enterprises, and reducing controls on foreign trade and investment.[77] The results are impressive. Beginning in the early 1990s, India's economic growth rate averaged more than 7 percent per year since 1997.[78] Diversification and sheer size is a major strength of the Indian economy. While slightly half of the country's 480,000,000 workers are still in agriculture, the English-speaking and well-educated Indian workforce is more and more shifting to higher-wage service jobs in fields such as information technology.[79] Corruption, a history of government regulation, and government-owned enterprises still act as a governor on India's economic growth, but the massive marketplace and educated workforce are still placing this emerging nation as the fourth largest economy in the world.[80]

Finally, China's transition from a closed, communist economy to a more market-oriented model starting in the 1970s produced simply amazing results just 40 years since the transformation. By 2010, China became the world's largest exporter, and the restructuring of the Chinese economy and resulting efficiency gains contributed to a more than ten-fold increase in GDP since 1978.[81] Measured on a purchasing power parity basis that adjusts for price differences, China in 2010 stood as the second largest economy in the world after the United States but has a per capita income below the world average.[82] The Chinese government faces challenges ranging from sustaining an amazing level of job growth for workers immigrating to the cities, reduction of corruption, and dealing with growing environmental challenges.[83] However, this $11,000,000,000,000 economy continues to be the economic wonder of the world with over 9 percent growth rate anticipated in 2011 and nearly half of an 800,000,000-plus workforce engaged in higher-wage industrial jobs.[84]

Big Questions

1. Can regions and states transform their economy without the help of the federal government?

2. Will states begin to work together on economic development initiatives?

3. Is the best economic development strategy to focus on successful small to mid-sized companies rather than focus on targeted industry clusters?

4. Will economic development incentives continue to be so common place in the future?

5. Is backshoring real?

Class Writing Assignment

A long list of challenges and opportunities—this is what economic development at the local and state levels is. The final assignment is to complete a White Paper at least 20 pages in length identifying what you think is the largest challenge facing local and state leaders from an economic development standpoint, identify successful and unsuccessful strategies used to address this challenge, and make final recommendations based upon academic and public policy best practice research.

Metropolis City Council Debate: Green Building Code

A junior and recently elected city council member believes the city should adopt a Green Building Code modeled after California for all new constructions including the Tech Expo. The mayor and the council president actually agree and are opposed to the ordinance, but it appears to have support in the community and on city council. A vote on the controversial ordinance is expected.

Additional Readings

Anil Lai and Ronald Clement, "Economic Development in India the Role of Individual Enterprise and Entrepreneurial Spirit," *Asia-Pacific Development*, 12, 2 (December, 2005) 81.

Bruce Katz and Jennifer Bradley, *The Metropolitan Moment* (Washington, DC: Brookings Institution Press, 2012).

Dani Rodrik, *The Future of Economic Growth*, Project Syndicate, June 25, 2011, available at project-syndicate.org.

David Shaffer and David Wright, *A New Paradigm for Economic Development: How Higher Education Institutions are Working to Revitalize their Regional and State Economies*, Nelson Rockefeller Institute of Government, SUNY at Albany, March 2010.

Economic Development Opportunities for Portland's Green Building Industry, City of Portland, Oregon, Office of Sustainable Development, October, 2007.

Eugene Trani, *The Indispensable University: Higher Education, Economic Development and the Knowledge Economy*, American Council on Education, 2010.

Mary Keeling, *Transportation and Economic Development: Why Smarter Transport is good for Jobs and Growth*, IBM Institute for Business Values, retrieved from http://www-935.ibm.com/services/us/gbs/thoughtleadership/ibv-smarter-transport.html.

Regionalism; Restructuring Local Government, Cornell University, available at cornell.edu.

Werner Baer, *Brazilian Economic Growth and Development*, 6th ed. (Boulder, CO: Lynne Reiner Publishers, 2008).

Notes

1 Defining Economic Development

1. See R. Bingham, E. W. Hill, and S. B. White, *Financing Economic Development: An Institutional Response* (Newbury Park, CA: Sage, 1990).
2. A. Johansson, et al., *"Looking to 2060: Long-Term Global Growth Prospects: A Going for Growth Report,"* OECD Economic Policy Papers, No. 3 (2012), 7.
3. Ibid.
4. Olivier Coibion, Yuriy Gorodnichenko, and Dmitri Koustas, "Amerisclerosis? The Puzzle of Rising U.S. Unemployment Persistence," *Fall 2013 Brookings Panel on Economic Activity* September 19–20, 2013.
5. Joseph A. Schumpeter, *Capitalism, Socialism, and Democracy,* 3rd ed. (New York: Harper and Brothers, 1950).
6. Kyle Fee, "Manufacturing (Still) Matters—And How It Can Endure," *Forefront* (Summer 2012).
7. William Strauss, *Is U.S. Manufacturing Disappearing* (Federal Reserve Bank of Chicago, August 19, 2010).
8. Paul Traub, *Ballard Discusses Michigan's Economy* (Federal Reserve Bank of Chicago, December 12, 2012), retrieved from http://michiganeconomy.chicagofedblogs. org/?p=52.
9. Ibid.
10. Ibid.
11. United States Census Bureau.
12. Paul A. Samuelson, "The Pure Theory of Public Expenditure," *Review of Economics and Statistics*, 36, 4 (1954) 387–389.
13. Mike E. Miles, Richard L. Haney, Jr., and Gayle Berens, *Real Estate Development, Principles and Process*, 2nd ed. (Washington, DC: Urban Land Institute, 1996).
14. United States Census, State Rankings, Statistical Abstract, retrieved from http://www.census.gov/statab/ranks/rank29.html.
15. New York City Regional Economic Development Council, New York City Strategic Plan (November, 2011), retrieved from http://regionalcouncils.ny.gov/themes/nyopenrc/rc-files/nyc/REDECFINALNYC.pdf.
16. Ibid.
17. Ibid.
18. United States Bureau of Economic Analysis, June 2013 News Release.
19. Ibid.
20. Ibid.
21. Ibid.
22. See Emilia Istrate, Jonathan Rothwell, and Bruce Katz, *Export Nation: How U.S. Metros Lead National Export Growth and Boost Competitiveness* (Washington, DC: Brookings Institution Press, July 2010).

23. See Mark Muro, Jonathan Rothwell, and Devashree Saha, *Sizing the Clean Economy: A National and Regional Green Jobs Assessment* (Washington, DC: Brookings Institution Press, July 13, 2011), and Timothy J. Considine, *The Economic Impacts of the Marcellus Shale: Implications for New York, Pennsylvania, and West Virginia*, A Report to the American Petroleum Institute (Washington, DC: Natural Resource Economics, 2010).

24. The Ten Steps to Real Estate Purchase discussion comes in large part from Ohio State University Law Professor Rick Daley's material developed for his real estate development class.

25. Retrieved from http://www.portlandonline.com/bps/index.cfm?c=30357.

26. Annual Energy Outlook 2013, U.S. Department of Energy, retrieved from http://www.eia.gov/forecasts/aeo/MT_electric.cfm.

27. Molly Ryan, "The Best is Yet to Come: Shale Boom to Boost Overall U.S. Economy, Study Says," *Houston Business Journal* (April 9, 2013), retrieved from http://www.bizjournals.com/houston/news/2013/09/04/the-best-is-yet-to-come-us.html.

28. Ibid.

29. David Roessner, Jennifer Bond, Simiye Okuba, and Mark Planting, *The Economic Impact of Licensed Commercialized Inventions Originating in University Research 1996–2007* (September 3, 2009), retrieved from http://www.bio.org/sites/default/files/BIO_final_report_9_3_09_rev_2_0.pdf.

30. Martin Grueber and Tim Studt, "Expenditure Impacts of U.S. R&D," *R&D* (December 18, 2012).

31. Jonathan Rothwell, "The Hidden STEM Economy," Brookings Institution Press, June 10, 2013.

32. Retrieved from http://trade.gov/cs/factsheet.asp.

33. Susan Helper, Timothy Krueger, and Howard Wiall, *Why Does Manufacturing Matter? Which Manufacturing Matters? A Policy Framework* (Washington, DC: Brookings Institution Press, February 2012).

34. Sophie Buhnik, "A Comparison of Urban Shrinkage in Baltimore (Maryland, USA) and Osaka (Japan): Reversed Patterns of Urban Decline ?" (Université Paris 1—Panthéon-Sorbonne, Ecole Normale Supérieure de Paris and Scirn PhD Academy, 2011).

35. Ibid.

36. See http://www.gbc.org/page/history/.

37. Bernard J. Frieden and Lynne Sagalyn, *Downtown, Inc.: How America Rebuilds Cities* (Cambridge, MA: MIT, 1991), at 259.

38. Ibid.

39. Ibid.

40. "U.S. Census Bureau Delivers Maryland's 2010 Census Population Totals," U.S. Census 2010 (February 9, 2011), retrieved from http://2010.census.gov/news/releases/operations/cb11-cn20.html.

41. Ibid.

42. 2010, U.S. Department of Labor, Bureau of Labor Statistics, Baltimore-Washington-North Virginia Wage Report, retrieved from http://www.bls.gov/ncs/ocs/sp/ncbl1604.txt.

43. Ibid.

44. See comparison at http://bber.unm.edu/econ/us-pci.htm and http://quickfacts.census.gov/qfd/states/24/24510.html.

45. Scott Thurm, Justin Scheck, and Bobby White, "Cities See Murder Slide End," *Wall Street Journal* (March 30, 2012).

46. Retrieved from http://www.baltimorecity.gov/OfficeoftheMayor/NewsMedia/tabid/66/ID/1661/City_Schools_Graduation_Rate_Continues_to_Climb.aspx.

47. City of Baltimore, Comprehensive Economic Development Strategy, 2008, retrieved from http://baltimorecity.gov/Portals/0/agencies/planning/public percent20downloads

/2008 percent20Baltimore percent20City percent20CEDS percent20executive percent20summary.pdf.
48. Ibid.

2 Strategic Economic Development Planning

1. Check-up on Portland's Economic Health, retrieved from http://www.orbusinesscouncil.org/documents/portlandregioneconcheckup.pdf.
2. Portland Economic Development Plan, retrieved from http://www.pdxeconomicdevelopment.com/.
3. Ibid.
4. Ibid.
5. Ibid.
6. Christopher A. Jarmon, James M. Vanderleeuw, Michael S. Pennington, and Thomas E. Sowers, "The Role of Economic Development Corporations in Local Economic Development: Evidence From Texas Cities," *Economic Development Quarterly*, 26, 2 (May 2012) 124–137.
7. R. M. Solow, "A Contribution to the Theory of Economic Growth," *Quarterly Journal of Economics*, 70, 1 (1956) 65–94.
8. See generally, Jacques-Francois Thisse, "Location Theory, Regional Science and Economics," *Journal of Regional Science*, 27, 4 (1987) 519–528.
9. See http://www.eda.gov/Research/ClusterBased.xml.
10. Ibid.
11. Ibid.
12. Ibid.
13. Michael E. Porter, "Location, Competition and Economic Development: Local Clusters in a Global Economy," *Economic Development Quarterly*, 14, 1 (2000) 15–34.
14. Ibid.
15. See David Birch, *The Job Generation Process* (Cambridge: MIT Program on Neighborhood and Regional Change, 1979).
16. Ibid.
17. Ibid.
18. See http://www.littletongov.org/bia/economicgardening/.
19. Ibid.
20. Ibid.
21. See Emil Malazia and John Feser, *Understanding Local Economic Development* (New Brunswick, NJ: Rutgers University Center for Urban Planning Research, 1999).
22. Technology Based Economic Development Guide (Westerville, OH: State Science and Technology Institute, 2006).
23. Ibid.
24. Retrieved from http://trade.gov/cs/factsheet.asp.
25. See generally, Richard Florida, "Cities and the Creative Class," *City and Community*, 2, 1 (March 2003) 3–19.
26. Indiana Economic Development Strategic Planning Outline, retrieved from http://www.in.gov/indot/div/projects/i69planningtoolbox/_pdf/Economic percent20Development percent20Strategic percent20Plan.pdf.
27. Ibid.
28. Economic Development Vision & Strategic Goals for the Tipton County Economic Development Corporation, Building Better Communities, Ball State University, January 2009.
29. Retrieved from http://quickfacts.census.gov/qfd/meta/long_INC910211.htm.
30. Ibid.

31. Ibid.
32. Ibid.
33. Ibid.
34. Ibid.
35. Ibid.
36. Ibid.
37. Ibid.
38. Ibid.
39. Ibid.
40. Retrieved from http://www.bls.gov/bls/empsitquickguide.htm.
41. Ibid.
42. Ibid.
43. Ibid.
44. See Tom R. Rex, *High-Wage Jobs, A Report from the Productivity and Prosperity Project (P3)* (Tempe, AZ: Arizona State University, May 2006).
45. Ibid.
46. Ibid.
47. See Using Employment Data to Better Understand Your Local Economy, Tool 4. Shift-Share Analysis Helps Identify Local Growth Engines (Penn State University, 2013), retrieved from http://pubs.cas.psu.edu/freepubs/pdfs/UA373.pdf.
48. Ibid.
49. Ibid.
50. Ibid.
51. Ibid.
52. Anjeanette Damon, "Economic Development Costs Nevada $30,000 Per Job in Tax Incentives," *Las Vegas Sun*, January 17, 2013 retrieved from http://www.lasvegassun.com/news/2013/jan/17/economic-development-costs-nevada-30000-job-tax-in/.
53. Ibid.
54. Ibid.
55. Florida Strategic Plan for Economic Development, retrieved from http://www.florida-jobs.org/office-directory/division-of-strategic-business-development/florida-strategic-plan-for-economic-development.
56. Ibid.
57. Ibid.

3   Economic Development Organizations

1. Dennis Cauchon, "Texas Wins in U.S. Economy Shift," *USA Today*, June 21, 2011.
2. Ibid.
3. See generally, John M. Bacheller, "Commentary on State-Level Economic Development in New York: A Strategy to Enhance Effectiveness," E*conomic Development Quarterly*, 14, 1 (February 2000) 5–10.
4. See generally, Jan Holtkamp, Daniel Otto, and Nuzhat Mahmood, "Economic Development Effectiveness of Multicommunity Development Organizations," *Community Development Society*, 28, 2 (September 1997) 242–256.
5. *Interview with Daniel Davis*, "New Economy, New Roles: Economic Development Organizations and Jobs," *Federal Reserve Bank of Atlanta's Economic Development podcast series, Federal Reserve Bank of St. Louis*, May 2011.
6. See Greater New Orleans, Inc, retrieved from http://gnoinc.org/initiatives/business-retention/.
7. See generally, Business Retention and Expansion Guide, Entergy, retrieved from http://www.entergy-arkansas.com/economic_development/retention_and_expansion.aspx.

8. Ibid.
9. Ibid.
10. Ibid.
11. See generally, DCI Marketing Plan Services, retrieved from http://www.aboutdci.com /economic-development/services/.
12. Eric Pages and Kenneth Poole, "Understanding Entrepreneurship Promotion as an Economic Development Strategy: A Three-state Survey" (Washington, DC: National Competitiveness Council, January 2003), retrieved from energizingentrepreneurs.org.
13. Retrieved from http://www.ncppp.org/howpart/index.shtml#keys.
14. See generally, Timothy J. Bartik, *Economic Development Strategies* (Kalamazoo, MI: Upjohn Institute Staff Working Paper 95–33, January 1995).
15. Dennis Cauchon, "Texas Wins in U.S. Economy Shift," *USA Today*, June 21, 2011.
16. Ibid.
17. Retrieved from http://www.texaswideopenforbusiness.com/about-us/.
18. Ibid.
19. 2012 Texas Economic Development Bank Annual Report (Economic Development and Tourism Division, Office of the Governor of Texas), retrieved from http://www. texaswideopenforbusiness.com/cms-assets/documents/98527-25790.bank-annual-report-2012.pdf.
20. Retrieved from http://www.pdc.us/about-the-pdc/frequently-asked-questions.aspx.
21. Ibid.
22. Portland City Charter, Section 15–102.
23. Portland City Charter, Section 15–103–107.
24. See Texas Local Government Code Sec. 501–504.
25. Ibid.
26. Ibid.
27. Ibid.
28. Ibid.
29. Ibid.
30. Ibid.
31. Economic Development Corporation Report, 2010–2011 (Texas Comptroller of Public Accounts).
32. Ibid.
33. Ibid.
34. Ibid.
35. *The 2012 Budget: Unwinding Development*, California Legislative Analysis Office, February 17, 2012.
36. Ibid.
37. Wisconsin Economic Development Corporation, 2013 Operations Plan (Wisconsin Economic Development Corporation).
38. Ibid.
39. Ibid.
40. Ibid.
41. Ibid.
42. Ibid.
43. Retrieved from http://charlotteusa.com/about-us/overview/.
44. Ibid.
45. Ibid.
46. Ibid.
47. "Annual Rankings Report," *Southern Business Development Magazine*, August 2012.
48. Joe Vardon and Jim Siegel, "JobsOhio to Refund Public Money," *Columbus Dispatch*, March 19, 2013.

49. See generally, Guy B. Adams and Danny L. Balfour, "Market-Based Government and the Decline of Organizational Ethics," *Administration and Society*, 42, 6 (2010) 615–637.

50. Andrew Stark, *Conflict of Interest in American Public Life* (Cambridge, MA: Harvard University Press, 2000).

51. Retrieved from http://www.osec.doc.gov/bmi/budget/FY12BIB/EDA.pdf.

52. Ibid.

53. Ibid.

54. Brad Watts, "What Should EDA Fund? Developing a Model for Preassessment of Economic Development Investments," *Economic Development Quarterly*, 25, 1 (2011) 65–78.

4   The Metropolis Case Study

1. City-Data, retrieved from http://www.city-data.com/city/Columbus-Ohio.html.

2. City Data, retrieved from http://www.city-data.com/us-cities/The-South/Raleigh-Economy.html.

3. Ibid.

4. Ibid.

5. "Global Rankings," *Business Facilities Magazine*, July/August 2010, retrieved from http://www.businessfacilities.com/Rankings/BFJulAug10_GLOBAL_RANKINGS.PDF.

6. City Data, retrieved from http://www.city-data.com/us-cities/The-South/Raleigh-Economy.html.

7. Ibid.

8. Ibid.

9. Retrieved from http://www.raleigh4u.com/page/major-employers.

10. City Data, retrieved from http://www.city-data.com/city/Nashville-Davidson-Tennessee.html.

11. Ibid.

12. Ibid.

13. Ibid.

14. Ibid.

15. Ibid.

16. Ibid.

17. Ibid.

18. Ibid.

19. Nashville Chamber of Commerce Report, retrieved from http://www.nashvillechamber.com/Homepage/WorkNashville/JobBoard/LargestEmployers.aspx.

20. City Data, retrieved from http://www.city-data.com/city/Nashville-Davidson-Tennessee.html.

5   Economic Development Building Block: Land Use Regulation and Zoning

1. U.S. Census Dubuque Quick Fact Sheet, 2010.

2. *Ford Zoning Site Framework, Case Study Analysis* (City of St. Paul, Minnesota, August 13, 2012), retrieved from http://www.sehinc.com/files/online/FordSitePlanningTaskForceAugust132012.pdf.

3. Ibid.

4. Ibid.

5. Ibid.

6. Candace Eudaley, *Brownfield Redevelopment in Eastern Iowa* (East Central Intergovernmental Association, January 4, 2012).

7. "Dubuque #1 in Job Creation, Greater Dubuque Development Corporation," March 10, 2011, retrieved from http://greaterdubuque.org/communication_awards.cfm.

8. See generally, Arthur Pigou, *The Economics of Welfare* (London: MacMillan, 1932).

9. See M. J. Bailey, "Note on the Economics of Residential Zoning and Urban Renewal," *Land Economics*, 35,1 (1959) 288–292.

10. See W. J. Stull, "Community Environment, Zoning and the Market Value of Single Family Homes," *Journal of Law and Economics*, 18, 2 (1975) 535–538.

11. See M. R. Correll, J. H. Lillydahl, and L. D. Singell, "The Effects of Greenbelts on Residential Property Values: Some Findings on the Political Economy of Open Space," *Land Economics*, 54, 2 (1978) 207–217.

12. See Jae Hong Kim, "Linking Land Use Planning Regulation and Economic Development: A Literature Review," *Journal of Planning Literature*, 26, 1 (2011) 35–47.

13. Ibid.

14. See Robert H. Freilich and Bruce G. Peshoff, "The Social Costs of Sprawl," *Urban Law*, 29, 2 (1997) 183, 185.

15. See B. Siegan, *Land Use Without Zoning* (Lexington, MA: Lexington Publishers ,1972).

16. The Ten Steps to Real Estate Purchase discussion comes in large part from Ohio State University Law Professor Rick Daley's class material developed for his real estate development class.

17. See Reid Ewing and Keith Bartholomew, *Pedestrian- & Transit-Oriented Design* (Washington, DC: Urban Land Institute, 2013).

18. See Kevin Lynch, *The Image of the City* (Cambridge, MA: Technology Press and Harvard University Press, 1960).

19. Ewing and Bartholomew.

20. Ibid.

21. Ibid.

22. See generally the City of Indianapolis-Marion County Comprehensive Plan, retrieved from http://www.indy.gov/eGov/City/DMD/Planning/Services/Land/Pages/comp_plan.aspx.

23. See generally http://rational-planning-model.co.tv/#Verify_Define_and_Detail_the_problem.

24. Ibid.

25. Ibid.

26. Ibid.

27. Ibid.

28. Ibid.

29. *Zoning Guide* (Washington, DC, U.S. Department of Commerce, rev. ed. 1926, §1–§2).

30. *Euclid v. Ambler Realty Corp.*, 272 U.S. 375 (1926).

31. Andres Duany, Elizabeth Plater–Zyberk, and Jeff Speck, *Suburban Nation: The Rise of Sprawl and the Decline of the American Dream* (Union Square West, NY: North Point Press, 2000), 5–7.

32. Kenneth B. Hall, Jr. and Gerald A. Porterfield, *Community by Design: New Urbanism for Suburbs and Small Communities* (New York: McGraw–Hill, 2001), 254.

33. Dallas Development Code, 51A–4 100.

34. Ibid.

35. Ibid.

36. Bob Bengford, "Planned Unit Developments—Real World Experiences," *Makers*, November 2012, retrieved from http://www.mrsc.org/focus/pladvisor/pla1112.aspx.

37. Ibid.

38. Ibid.
39. Michael Murphy and Joseph Stinson, "Planned Unit Developments," Pace University School of Law, 1996, retrieved from http://www.mrsc.org/subjects/planning/pud.aspx.
40. *Marshall v. Village of Wappingers Falls*, 28 A.D.2d, 542 (2d Dept, 1967).
41. LC-PUD Life Style Center Regulations, Grand Rapids Township, Michigan, retrieved from http://www.grandrapidstwp.org/services/planning_and_zoning/zoning_ordinance/docs/Ch__22.pdf.
42. Ibid.
43. Jim Harger, "'Village at Knapp's Crossing' in Bankruptcy Despite Landing P.F. Chang's Restaurant," *MLive*, August 28, 2013.
44. See generally, Andres Duany, *New Civic Art: Elements of Town Planning* (New York, NY: Rizzoli International Publications, 2003).
45. Ibid.
46. See http://www.cityofchesapeake.net/Assets/documents/business/development/definitions/Urban_Suburban_Rural_Overlay.pdf.
47. Ibid.
48. Ibid.
49. Retrieved from http://www.nashville.gov/Planning-Department/Rezoning-Subdivision/Urban-Design-Overlay.aspx.
50. Ibid.
51. Todd Fabbozi and Gene Bunnell, *New Centers, Case Studies of New Urbanism in the Denver and Portland Metropolitan Areas*, 2006, retrieved from http://www.cdrpc.org/New_Centers-web.pdf.
52. Ibid.
53. Ibid.
54. Ibid.
55. Ibid.
56. Peter Calthorpe, *The Next American Metropolis: Ecology, Community, and the American Dream* (New York: Princeton Architectural Press, 1993); Peter Katz, *The New Urbanism: Toward An Architecture of Community* (New York: McGraw-Hill, 1994).
57. Retrieved from http://www.mass.gov/envir/smart_growth_toolkit/pages/CS-tod-canton.html.
58. Ibid.
59. Ibid.
60. Ibid.
61. Ibid.
62. Zhu Qian, "Without Zoning: Urban Development and Land Use Controls in Houston," *Cities*, 27, 1 (2010) 31–41.
63. See Chapter 42, Houston City Code (2013).
64. Ibid.
65. Ibid.
66. Ibid.
67. Ibid at pp. 38–39.

6 Economic Development Building Block: Eminent Domain

1. *Shifting Suburbs, Reinventing Infrastructure for Compact Development* (Washington, DC: Urban Land Institute, 2012).
2. Ibid.
3. Ibid.
4. Ibid.

5. See Jeff Finkle, IEDC Presentation, Eminent Domain and Economic Development (2005), retrieved from http://law.case.edu/centers/business_law/eminent_domain/pdfs/Finkle_eminent_domain_pwrpt.pdf.
6. Todd Fabozzi, "New Centers, Case Studies in New Urbanism in the Denver and Portland Metropolitan Regions," (Capital District Regional Planning Commission, 2006).
7. Dana Berliner, *Public Power, Private Gain* (Arlington, VA: Institute for Justice, 2003).
8. Ibid.
9. See T. J. Miceli and C. F. Sirmans, "The Holdout Problem, Urban Sprawl and Land Assembly," *Foundations and Trends in Microeconomics*, 3 (2007) 286–293.
10. See R. L. Schraff, "A Common Tragedy: Condemnation and the Anticommons," *Natural Resources Journal*, 47 (2007) 165–193.
11. See L. O. Gostin, "Property Rights and the Common Good," *Hastings Center Report*, 36, 5 (2006) 10–11.
12. R.C. 163.04.
13. Ibid.
14. Ibid.
15. Ibid.
16. O.R.C. §§ 163.08 and .09.
17. Ibid.
18. *Dayton v. Keys* (1969), 21 Ohio Misc. 105.
19. *Media One v. Manor Park Apartments Limited* (2000), 2000 Ohio App. Lexis 4791.
20. R. C. 163.14; *Norwood v. Forest Converting Co.* (1984), 16 Ohio App.3d. 411, 415.
21. Ibid.; see Section 19, Article I, Ohio Constitution (stating that "where private property shall be taken for public use, compensation therefor shall first be made in money, or first secured by a deposit of money; and such compensation shall be assessed by a jury, without deduction for benefits to any property of the owner").
22. *Norwood*, at 415; see *In re Appropriation of Easement for Hwy. Purposes* (1952), 93 Ohio App. 179, 183.
23. *Hilliard v. First Industrial L.P.* ((2005), 165 Ohio App.3d 335, 345.
24. Ibid.
25. Berman v. Parker, 348 U.S. 26 (1954)
26. Hawaii Housing Authority v. Midkiff, 467 U.S. 229 (1984).
27. Kelo v. New London, 545 U.S. 469 (2005).
28. Ibid.
29. Ibid.
30. Ibid.
31. Ibid.
32. *State Eminent Domain Legislation and Ballot Measure Report*, National Conference of State Legislatures, January 1, 2012.
33. Alabama Senate Bill 68 (2008).
34. California Proposition 99 (2008).
35. Idaho House Bill 555 (2006).
36. Nebraska Legislative Bill 924 (2006).
37. Pennsylvania Senate Bill 881 (2006).
38. Delaware Senate Bill 7 (2005), Kentucky House Bill 508 (2006).
39. Arizona Proposition 207 (2006).
40. New Hampshire Senate Bill 287 (2006).
41. Mississippi Initiative 31 (2011).
42. Maine LD 1870 (2006).
43. Florida House Bill 1867 (2006).
44. Ibid.
45. Illinois Senate Bill 386 (2006).

46. Iowa HF 2351 (2006).
47. New Mexico House Bill 393 (2007).
48. Connecticut Senate Bill 167 (2007).
49. Georgia House Bill 313 (2006).
50. Missouri House Bill 1944 (2006).
51. Indiana House Bill 1010 (2006).
52. Ibid.
53. Kansas Senate Bill 323 (2006).
54. Michigan SJR E (2005).
55. Louisiana Senate Bill 1 (2006).
56. Norwood v. Horney, 110 Ohio St.3d 353 (2006).
57. Ibid.
58. Ibid.
59. Amended Substitute Senate Bill 7, 127th Ohio General Assembly (2007).
60. Ibid.
61. Ibid.
62. Ibid.
63. Ibid.
64. Ibid.
65. Ibid.
66. Ibid.
67. Ibid.
68. Ibid.
69. Ibid.
70. 2006 Tennessee Public Act 863.
71. Ibid. (amending Tennessee Code Ann. Sec. 29–17–102(a) (2005)).
72. 2006 Tennessee Public Act 863.
73. Knoxville Community Development Corporation v. Wright, 600 S.W.2d 745 (Tenn Ct. App. 1980).
74. 2006 Tennessee Public Act 863, Sec. 14 (2006).
75. Tennessee Code Annotated § 13–16–203(2).
76. Tennessee Code Annotated § 13–16–201–207.
77. Patrick Raines and LaTanya Brown, *The Economic Impact of the Music Industry in the Nashville-Davidson-Murfreesboro MSA* (Belmont University, Nashville, TN, January 2006).
78. Ibid.
79. Retrieved from www.ij.org.
80. Ibid.

7   Economic Development Building Block: Annexation

1. Retrieved from http://www.portlandonline.com/bps/index.cfm?c=30357.
2. Ibid.
3. George Embrey, "Anheuser-Busch Inc. Considers Building $50 Million Brewery in Ohio, Probably Columbus," *Columbus Dispatch*, May 28, 1965.
4. See Rana Foroohar, "How Columbus, Ohio Bounced Back from the Recession," *Time*, September 27, 2012.
5. Steve Wartenberg, "IBM Center, 500 Jobs on Way," *Columbus Dispatch*, November 29, 2012.
6. Mary M. Edwards, "Understanding the Complexities, of Annexation," *Journal of Planning Literature*, 23, 2 (November 2008) 119–135.

7. Ibid.
8. Ibid.
9. Ibid.
10. Ibid.
11. See T. Mueller and J. Dawson, *The Economic Effects of Annexation: A Second Case Study in Richmond, Virginia* (Washington, DC: The Urban Institute, 1976).
12. See David Rusk, *Cities without Suburbs* (Washington, DC: The Woodrow Wilson Center Press, 1993).
13. Mary M. Edwards, "Understanding the Complexities, of Annexation," *Journal of Planning Literature*, 23, 2, (November 2008) 119–135.
14. Ibid.
15. Zhu Qjan, "Without Zoning: Urban Development and Land Use Controls in Houston," *Cities*, 27, 1 (2010) 31–41.
16. Ibid.
17. Ibid.
18. Mary M. Edwards and Yu Xiao, "Annexation, Local Government Spending, and the Complicating Role of Density," *Urban Affairs Review*, 45, 2 (November 2009) 147–165.
19. Ibid.
20. Ibid.
21. Ibid.
22. Ibid.
23. Ibid.
24. See J. F. Norman and H. A. Green, *Annexation Issues in Tennessee: A Report to the 99th General Assembly* (Tennessee Legislative Services, Nashville, TN, 1995).
25. Rex L. Facer, II, "Annexation Activity and State Law in the United States", *Urban Affairs Review*, 41, 5 (May 2006) 697–709 at 700.
26. Ibid.
27. See Ohio Revised Code Sec. 709.03
28. See generally, Scott Houston, "Municipal Annexation in Texas, Is it Really That Complicated," *Texas Municipal League*, March 2012, retrieved from http://www.tml.org/legal_pdf/ANNEXATION.pdf.
29. Ibid.
30. Ibid.
31. Ibid.
32. Ibid.
33. Ibid.
34. Ibid.
35. Houston Quick Fact Sheet, U.S. Census Data, 2012.
36. See Olivia Pulsinelli, "Houston Leading Southern City for Population Growth," *Houston Business Journal*, August 7, 2012.
37. U.S. Census Bureau, 2012 Reports.
38. See A.R.S Sec. 9–471 (H,K).
39. Ibid.
40. Ibid.
41. Ibid.
42. Ibid.
43. Population of the 100 Largest Urban Places: 1950, U.S. Bureau of the Census, Internet Release date: June 15, 1998.
44. Carol E. Heim, "Border Wars: Tax Revenues, Annexation, and Urban Growth in Phoenix," *International Journal of Urban and Regional Research*, 36, 4 (July 2012) 831–859.
45. Ibid.

46. City of Phoenix, Community Profile, 2011, retrieved from http://phoenix.gov/citygovernment/facts/index.html.
47. Ibid.
48. See Ohio Revised Code Sec. 709.
49. Ibid.
50. Ibid.
51. Ibid.
52. Ibid.
53. Ibid.
54. Ibid.
55. Ibid.
56. See Ohio Rev. Code Sec. 709.13–709.16.
57. Ibid.
58. Ibid.
59. Ibid.
60. Ibid.
61. Ibid.
62. See Ohio Revised Code Sec. 709.022.
63. Ibid.
64. See Ohio Revised Code Sec. 709.023.
65. Ibid.
66. See Ohio Revised Code Sec. 709.024.
67. Ibid.
68. Ibid.
69. Debbie Gebolys, "Columbus Still has an Appetite for Annexation, but it's Swallowing Up Land much Slower Lately," *Columbus Dispatch*, February 4, 2008.
70. BAKIES V. PERRYSBURG, 108 Ohio St. 3d 361 (2006).
71. Ibid.
72. Ibid.
73. Mark Skidmore, David Merriman, and Russ Kashian, "The Relationship between Tax Increment Finance, and Municipal Land Annexation," *Land Economics*, 85, 4 (November 2009) 598–613.

8   Economic Development Building Block: Infrastructure

1. City of Chicago TIF Program Facts, retrieved from http://www.cityofchicago.org/city/en/depts/dcd/supp_info/tax_increment_financingprogram.htm.
2. Ibid.
3. TIF Illumination Project, http://tifreports.com/2012/07/25/chicago_tifs_2011/.
4. Mayor Emanuel Announces Reforms That Strengthen Accountability and Transparency of TIF Program, January 30, 2012, retrieved from http://www.cityofchicago.org/city/en/depts/mayor/press_room/press_releases/2012/january/mayor_emanuel_announces-reformsthatstrengthenaccountabilityandtra.html.
5. Ibid.
6. See   http://www.wbez.org/blogs/bez/2012-07/report-chicagos-economy-improving-faster-other-major-cities-101041.
7. "Chicago Best Places for Doing Business," *Forbes*, 2013, retrieved from http://www.forbes.com/places/il/chicago/.
8. City of Chicago TIF Success Stories, 2013, http://www.cityofchicago.org/city/en/depts/dcd/supp_info/tif_success_stories.html.
9. Ibid.

10. See David Aschauer, "Public Investment and Productivity in the Group of Seven," *Federal Reserve Bank of Chicago, Economic Perspectives*, Working Paper Series, Macroeconomic Issues with number 89–13 (September/October 1989a) 177–200.

11. See Alicia Munnell, "How Does Public Infrastructure Affect Regional Economic Performance," *New England Economic Review* (September/October 1990) 11–32.

12. Kevin T. Deno, "The Effect of Public Capital on U.S. Manufacturing Activity: 1970–78," *Southern Economic Journal*, 55 (October 1988) 400–411.

13. See Brian Berry and John Parr, *Market Centers and Retail Location Theory and Applications* (Engelwood Cliffs, NJ: Prentice Hall, 1988).

14. Paul F. Byrne, "Does Tax Increment Financing Deliver on Its Promise of Jobs? The Impact of Tax Increment Financing on Municipal Employment Growth," *Economic Development Quarterly*, 24, 1 (2010) 13–22.

15. Andrew Haughwout, "The Role of Infrastructure in Economic Development," Institute for Government and Public Affairs, *University of Illinois Forum* (Chicago, IL, September 27, 1994).

16. Ibid.

17. See 2013 America's Infrastructure Report Card, American Society of Civil Engineers.

18. See Rose Naccarato, "Tax Increment Financing, Opportunities and Concerns," *Staff Research Brief, Tennessee Agency on Intergovernmental Relations*, March 2007.

19. *How TIF Works: Basic Mechanics*, Minnesota House of Representatives, House Research (2013), retrieved from http://www.house.leg.state.mn.us/hrd/issinfo/tifmech.htm.

20. 70C AM. JUR. 2d Special or Local Assessments § 22 (2008).

21. See e.g., Ohio Rev. Code § 5540.031; Va. Code Ann. § 33.1–415.

22. See Ohio Rev. Code Chapter 165.

23. Ibid.

24. See Ohio Revised Code Chapter 725.

25. Ibid.

26. Ohio Rev. Code Sec. 727.01.

27. Ibid.

28. Ibid.

29. Ibid.

30. 70C AM. JUR. 2d Special or Local Assessments § 22 (2008).

31. See e.g., Ohio Rev. Code § 5540.031; Va. Code Ann. § 33.1–415.

32. Ibid.

33. See Transportation Infrastructure Finance and Innovation Act (TIFIA) of 1998.

34. Ibid.

35. Ohio Rev. Code § 5540.02.

36. See Ibid. at Ohio Rev. Code §5540.031; Ibid. at §5540.06.

37. Ibid.

38. Lawrence Budd, "Transportation Districts Tap $480M for Area Work," *Dayton Daily News*, June, 3, 2012.

39. Ibid.

40. Ibid.

41. Va. Code Ann. § 33.1–414 (2008).

42. Ibid.

43. Ibid.

44. Ibid.

45. See ibid. at § 33.1–415.

46. Ibid.

47. Retrieved from http://www.fairfaxcounty.gov/dta/realestatetax_specialtaxdis.htm.

48. Ibid.

49. See generally Gary L. Sullivan, Steve A. Johnson, and Dennis L. Soden, "Tax Increment Financing (TIF) Best Practices Study," *University of Texas at El Paso*, September 2002.

50. See Rose Naccarato, "Tax Increment Financing, Opportunities and Concerns," *Staff Research Brief, Tennessee Agency on Intergovernmental Relations*, March 2007.

51. *How TIF Works: Basic Mechanics, Minnesota House of Representatives*, House Research, http://www.house.leg.state.mn.us/hrd/issinfo/tifmech.htm.

52. Ibid.

53. See Kent D. Redfield, "Trickle Down from the Rising Tide—TIFs and Urban Development Policy in Illinois," *PRAGmatics* (Summer 2002) 3–5.

54. Ibid.

55. Ibid.

56. Pay as you Go Tax Increment Financing Districts, Ehlers Advisors, June 2006, http://www.ehlers-inc.com/downloads/newsletters/WI_Adv_Jun06.pdf.

57. Ibid.

58. Ibid.

59. Ibid.

60. *How TIF Works: Basic Mechanics* (Minnesota House of Representatives, House Research Memo), retrieved from http://www.house.leg.state.mn.us/hrd/issinfo/tifmech.htm.

61. See Craig L. Johnson, *Tax Increment Financing (TIF) Report* (Washington, DC: National Association of Realtors, November 2002).

62. Ibid.

63. Ibid.

64. Ibid.

65. Ibid.

66. Ibid.

67. Ibid.

68. Ibid.

69. Ibid.

70. Ibid.

71. Ibid.

72. Ibid.

73. Ibid.

74. Ibid.

75. Ibid.

76. Ibid.

77. See *Municipal Securities Rule Making Board, Tax Exempt Bond Status*, http://www.msrb.org/msrb1/glossary/view_def.asp?param=EXEMPTFACILITYBONDS.

78. See sec. 141 Internal Revenue Code and Testimony of Edward Klienbard to Joint Committee on Taxation of the Congress, July 24, 2008.

79. Ibid.

80. Ibid.

81. See Craig L. Johnson, *Tax Increment Financing (TIF) Report* (Washington, DC: National Association of Realtors, November 2002).

82. Ibid.

83. Ibid.

84. Or. Rev. Stat. § 457.095.

85. Or. Rev. Stat. § 457.035.

86. Or. Rev. Stat. § 457.085.

87. Or. Rev. Stat. § 457.085.

88. Or. Rev. Stat. §§ 457.095, .120.

89. Or. Rev. Stat. §§ 457.085, .190.

90. Ibid.

91. OR. REV. STAT. § 457.190.
92. OR. REV. STAT. §§ 457.420–460.
93. OR. REV. STAT. § 457.435.
94. Ibid.
95. Ibid.
96. Ibid.
97. Ibid.
98. Ibid.
99. Ibid.
100. Ibid.
101. Ibid.
102. See Greg LeRoy, "TIF, Greenfields and Sprawl: How an Incentive Created to Alleviate Slums has Come to Subsidize Upscale Malls and New Urbanist Developments," *Planning & Environmental Law*, 60, 2 (February 2008) 3–11.
103. See Craig L. Johnson, *Tax Increment Financing (TIF) Report* (Washington, DC: National Association of Realtors, November 2002).
104. See Greg LeRoy, "TIF, Greenfields and Sprawl: How an Incentive Created to Alleviate Slums has Come to Subsidize Upscale Malls and New Urbanist Developments," *Planning & Environmental Law*, 60, 2 (February 2008) 3–11.
105. Paul F. Byrne, "Does Tax Increment Financing Deliver on Its Promise of Jobs? The Impact of Tax Increment Financing on Municipal Employment Growth," *Economic Development Quarterly*, 24, 1 (2010) 13–22.
106. Ibid.
107. Retrieved from http://www.dleg.state.mi.us/mpsc/comm/broadband/broadband/broadband.htm.
108. Ibid.
109. Ibid.
110. Ibid.
111. Ivan T. Kandilov and Mitch Renkow, "Infrastructure Investment and Rural, Economic Development: An Evaluation of USDA's Broadband Loan Program," *Growth & Change*, 41, 2 (June 2010) 165–191.
112. Ibid.
113. Ibid.
114. Ibid.
115. Ibid.
116. George S. Ford and Thomas Koutsky, "Broadband and Economic Development: A Municipal Case Study from Florida," *Applied Economics Studies* (April 2005) 1–17.
117. Ibid.
118. Ibid.
119. Ibid.
120. See MI Connections 2013 Annual Report.
121. Ibid.
122. See generally, Coalition for the New Economy Report, retrieved from http://www.coalitionforthenewweconomy.org/wp-content/uploads/2012/10/10.31.12-GON-MI-Connection-Final.pdf.

9 Economic Development Building Block: Workforce Readiness

1. *2011 Skills Gap Report* (Washington, DC: Manufacturing Institute, 2011).
2. Tim Mullaney, "Want a *Job*? Look to the *Energy* Field," *USA Today*, September 30, 2012.

3. *State of the IT Skills Gap* (Downers Grove, IL: CompTIA, February 2012).
4. Peter I. Buerhaus, David I. Auerbach, Douglas O. Staiger, and Ulrike Muench, "Projections of the, Long-Term Growth of the Registered Nurse Workforce: A Regional Analysis," *Nursing Economics*, 31, 1, (January–February 2013) and "Physcian Shortage Estimate Report," (Washington, DC: *Association of American Medical Colleges*, 2012), retrieved from https://www.aamc.org/advocacy/campaigns_and_coalitions/fixdocshortage/.
5. Robert P. Giloth, "Learning From the Field: Economic Growth and Workforce Development in the 1990's," *Economic Development Quarterly*, 14, 4 (November 2000) 340–359, 345.
6. U.S. Census, 2010, Hampton-Newport News Quick Facts.
7. Kathleen McConnell, *Workforce Development for Economic Competitiveness* (Washington, DC: National League of Cities, Municipal Action Guide, 2010).
8. Ibid.
9. *Road to Success, A Virginia Peninsula Strategic Plan for Career Pathways in Advanced and Precisions Manufacturing Technologies, 2012–2016* (Peninsula Council for Workforce Development, 2012).
10. Ibid.
11. Ibid.
12. J. J. Heckman, "Policies to Foster Human Capital," *Research in Economics*, 54, 1 (March 2000) 3–56.
13. "Education Pays 2010," *Trends in Higher Education* (College Board, 2010).
14. Ibid.
15. P. A. David and D. Foray, *An Introduction to the Economy of the Knowledge Society* (University of Oxford Department of Economics Discussion Papers Series, 2001).
16. A. Bandura, "A. Self-Efficacy: Toward a Unified Theory of Behavior Change," *Psychological Review*, 84 (1977) 191–215.
17. See R. E. Lucas, "On the Mechanics of Economic Development," *Journal of Monetary Economics*, 22 (1996) 3–42.
18. See P. M. Romer, "Endogenous Technological Change," *Journal of Political Economy*, 98 (1990) S71–S102.
19. See Jeffrey J. Selingo, "The Diploma's Vanishing Value," *Wall Street Journal*, April 27–28, 2013.
20. Mitra Toossi, "Labor Force Projections to 2020: A More Slowly Growing Workforce," *Monthly Labor Review, U.S. Department of Labor*, 135, 1 (January 2012) 43–64.
21. Ibid.
22. Ibid.
23. Ibid.
24. U.S. Census Bureau, Statistical Abstract, Resident Population, percent Change, 2000 to 2009, State Ranking.
25. U.S. Census Bureau.
26. S. A. Rosenfield, *A Governor's Guide to Cluster-based Economic Development. Prepared by the National Governor's Association Center for Best Practices* (Carrboro, NC: Regional Technology Strategies, 2002).
27. Ibid.
28. Ibid.
29. *Lander County Nevada: Demographic/Economic Trends, Industrial and Occupational Targeting Analysis, and Community Business Matching Model Analysis*, Technical Report, University of Nevada Reno, Center for Economic Development, UCED 2010/11–06.
30. Ibid.
31. Ibid.
32. Ibid.
33. Ibid.

34. See T. Herr, R. Halpern, and A. Conrad, *Changing what Counts. Rethinking the Journey Out of Welfare* (Evanston, IL: Northwestern University, Center for Urban Affairs and Policy Research, 1991).
35. R. P. Giloth, "Learning from the Field: Economic Growth and Workforce Development in the 1990s," *Economic Development Quarterly*, 14, 4 (2000) 340–359.
36. Multiple Employment and Training Programs: Providing Information on Colocating Services and Consolidating Administrative Structures Could Promote Efficiencies, GAO-11–92, January 13, 2011.
37. 5 Pub. L. No. 105–220 (1998).
38. See Pub. L. No. 105–220 §134(c)(2)(A) and Pub. L. No. 105–220 §121(b)(1)(B).
39. GAO-11–92 at p. 4.
40. Ibid.
41. Ibid.
42. http://www.doleta.gov/programs/general_info.cfm.
43. Ibid.
44. GAO 11–92, Executive Summary.
45. See E. Harper-Anderson, "Measuring the Connection between Workforce Development and Economic Development," *Economic Development Quarterly*, 22, 2 (May 2008) 119–135.
46. Ibid.
47. See J. Fitzgerald, *Principles and Practices for Creating Systems Reform in Urban Workforce Development* (Chicago, IL: University of Illinois, Great Cities Initiatives, 1998).
48. Retrieved from http://www.doleta.gov/BRG/JobTrainInitiative/.
49. See N. Lowe, H. Goldstein, and M. Donegan, "Patchwork Intermediation: Challenges and Opportunities for Regionally Coordinated Workforce Development," *Economic Development Quarterly*, 25, 2 (2011) 158–171.
50. Ibid.
51. Ibid.
52. Lowe, 2011.
53. Ibid.
54. Ibid.
55. Ibid.
56. Ibid.
57. *2010 Evidence and Opportunity, Biotechnology Impacts in North Carolina* (Battelle Technology Partnership Practice, September 2010).
58. Ibid.
59. Ibid.
60. Immigration Myths and Facts: Labor, Immigration & Employee Benefits Division, U.S. Chamber of Commerce, May 1, 2011, retrieved from http://www.uschamber.com/sites/default/files/reports/16628_ImmigrationMythFacts_OPT.pdf) states.
61. Gordon F. De Jong, Deborah Roempke Graefe, Matthew Hall, and Audrey Singer, *The Geography of Immigrant Skills: Educational Profiles of Metropolitan Areas* (Washington, DC: Brookings Institute, July 2006).
62. Ibid.
63. Ibid.
64. Madeline Zavodny, *Immigration and American Jobs* (Washington, DC: American Enterprise Institute & Partnership for a New American Economy, December 2011).
65. Audrey Singer, *Immigrant Workers in the U.S. Labor Force* (Washington, DC: Brookings Institution, 2012).
66. Ibid.
67. Zavodny.
68. Zavodny, 2011.

69. Retrieved from http://www.npr.org/2012/12/09/166829186/baltimore-says-immigrants-welcome.
70. Retrieved http://blogs.edweek.org/edweek/learning-the-language/2012/07/cities_recruit_immigrants_to_r.html.
71. Elizabeth Lorente, "Dayton Ohio Considers Recruiting Immigrants to Boost Sagging Population," *Fox Latino News,* September 22, 2011, retrieved from http://latino.foxnews.com/latino/news/2011/09/22/dayton-ohio-considers-recruiting-immigrants-to-boost-sagging-population/#ixzz2RlX5ZYiW.
72. *Welcome Dayton Report,* September 2011, retrieved from http://www.welcomedayton.org/wp-content/uploads/2012/01/Welcome-Dayton-immigrant-friendly-report-final.pdf.
73. Ibid.
74. Ibid.
75. Ibid.
76. Lorente, 2011.
77. Ibid.
78. Alabama House Bill 56, 2011.
79. Ibid.
80. Ibid.
81. Ibid.
82. Samuel Addy, *A Cost Benefit Analysis of the New Alabama Immigration Law* (University of Alabama, January 2012).
83. Ibid.
84. Retrieved from http://www.grants.gov/search/search.do?mode=VIEW&oppId=227375.
85. Retrieved from http://www.doleta.gov/business/incentives/opptax/eligible.cfm.
86. Retrieved from http://www.doleta.gov/ETA_News_Releases/20100831.cfm.
87. Ibid.
88. Ibid.
89. Ibid.
90. Ibid.
91. Retrieved from http://www.raconline.org/funding/898/.
92. Ibid.
93. Retrieved from http://www.delawarepersonnel.com/training/special/blue/.
94. Retrieved from http://dedo.delaware.gov/BusinessServices/WorkforceDevelopment/WorkforceDevelopment_training.shtml.
95. Ibid.
96. Retrieved from http://www.wtg.mt.gov/default.mcpx.
97. Ibid.
98. Retrieved from https://joblink.alabama.gov/ada/works/contactus.cfm.
99. Ibid.
100. Retrieved from http://www.twc.state.tx.us/svcs/funds/sdfintro.html.
101. Ibid.
102. Ibid.
103. Ibid.
104. Retrieved from http://development.ohio.gov/files/bs/OIWTVP percent20Overview.pdf.
105. Ibid.
106. Ibid.
107. Ibid.

10   Economic Development Building Block: Tax Policy

1. Gracie Shepard, "Starbucks Plans $172 million Augusta Plant," *The Augusta Chronicle,* March 21, 2012.

2. Ibid.
3. Ibid.
4. Statement of the U.S. Chamber of Commerce, Tax Reform Working Group, April 2, 2013.
5. Barry W. Poulson and Jules Gordon Kaplan, "State Income Taxes and Economic Growth," *Cato Journal*, 28, 1 (Winter 2008) 53–71.
6. Oklahoma Council of Public Affairs Eliminating the State Income Tax in Oklahoma: An Economic Assessment, Oklahoma Council of Public Affairs, Arthur Laffer, November 2011.
7. Louise Story, "As Companies Seek Tax Deals, Governments Pay High Price," *The New York Times*, December 1, 2012.
8. GAO State and Local Government Fiscal Condition Report, 2011, retrieved from http://www.gao.gov/special.pubs/longterm/state/fiscalconditionsfaq.html.
9. Matias Busso and Patrick Kline, "Do Local Economic Development Programs Work? Evidence from the Federal Empowerment Zone Program," *Cowles Foundation Discussion Paper No. 1638*, February 2008.
10. Daniel Bondonio and Robert T. Greenbaum, "Do Local Tax Incentives Affect Economic Growth? What mean Impacts Miss in the Analysis of Enterprise Zone Policies," *Regional Science and Urban Economics*, 37, 1 (2007) 121–136.
11. See Robert T. Greenbaum and Jim Landers," Why Are State Policy Makers Still Proponents of Enterprise Zones? What Explains Their Action in the Face of a Preponderance of Research," *International Regional Science Review*, 32, 4 (October 2009) 466–479.
12. Statement of the U.S. Chamber of Commerce, Tax Reform Working Group, April 2, 2013.
13. Dmitri Koustas, Karen Li, Adam Looney and Leslie B. Samuels, "A Dozen Economic Facts About Tax Reform, Michael Greenstone," *The Hamilton Project*, Policy Memo, May 2012.
14. Tax Incentives for Economic Development: What are tax incentives for economic development, The Tax Policy Briefing Book, Tax Policy Center (Washington, DC: Brookings Institution, 2013) retrieved from http://www.taxpolicycenter.org/briefing-book/key-elements/economic-development/what-is.cfm.
15. Retrieved from http://www.esd.wa.gov/hireanemployee/resources/taxcredits/index.php.
16. Ibid.
17. Ibid.
18. U.S. Department of Housing & Urban Development, Economic Development Programs, retrieved from: http://portal.hud.gov/hudportal/HUD?src=/program_offices/comm_planning/economicdevelopment/programs/rc.
19. Ibid.
20. Ibid.
21. Ibid.
22. Ibid.
23. Retrieved from http://portal.hud.gov/hudportal/HUD?src=/program_offices/comm_planning/economicdevelopment/programs/rc/about/ezecinit.
24. Ibid.
25. Ibid.
26. 26 U.S.C. § 45D.
27. Retrieved from http://www.huduser.org/portal/datasets/lihtc.html.
28. Retrieved from http://www.chicagodevelopmentfund.org/success-stories.html.
29. Ibid.
30. Ibid.
31. Ibid.
32. 15 U.S.C. § 307 (manufacturing); 15 C.F.R. §390 et. seq. (manufacturing). For the Trade Adjustment Assistance grant, see generally, U.S. Dept. of Labor, Trade Adjustment

Assistance and Alternative Trade Adjustment Assistances Services and Benefits, http://www.doleta.gov/tradeact/benefits.cfm.

33. Ibid.
34. Ibid.
35. Ibid.
36. SBA General Small Business Loans, retrieved from http://www.sba.gov/category/navigation-structure/loans-grants/small-business-loans/sba-loan-programs/7a-loan-program.
37. Ibid.
38. Ibid.
39. Ibid.
40. See generally, http://www.sba.gov/content/cdc504-loan-program.
41. Ibid.
42. Ibid.
43. Shelli B. Rossman and Brett Theodos, *Key Findings from the Evaluation of the Small Business, Administration's Loan and Investment Programs, Executive Summary* (Washington, DC: The Urban Institute, January 2008, 38).
44. See http://www.hawaiifilmoffice.com/incentives-tax-credits.
45. See, e.g., MINNESOTA STAT. §290.0672; COLORADO REV. STAT. §39–22–122.
46. See, e.g., OHIO REV. CODE ANN. §§ 5709.65–5709.70.
47. State Incentive Guide, Business Facilities, 2011, retrieved from http://businessfacilities.com/2011-incentives-guide/.
48. See, e.g., Supplement to Federal Historic Rehabilitation Credit, WISC. STAT. §71.07(9r).
49. Estabane Dalehite, Michael Mikesell and Kurt Zorn, "Variation in Property Tax Abatement Programs Among States," *Economic Development Quarterly*, 19, 2 (May 2005) 157–173.
50. Ibid.
51. See MINN. STAT. §§469.1812–1815.
52. OHIO REV. CODE §3735.67.
53. 35 ILCS 200/18–170 (Illinois); IND. CODE §6–1.1–12.1–1 et seq.
54. Iowa Dept. of Economic Dev., High-Quality Job Creation Program, retrieved from http://www.iowalifechanging.com/business/highquality_jobs.html.
55. Ibid.
56. Ibid.
57. See e.g., http://michiganeconomicdevelopment.org/other-muskegon-incentives/.
58. See Robert T. Greenbaum and Jim Landers, "Why Are State Policy Makers Still Proponents of Enterprise Zones? What Explains Their Action in the Face of a Preponderance of Research," *International Regional Science Review*, 32, 4 (October 2009) 466–479.
59. LOUISIANA ADMIN. CODE 13:901.
60. Ibid.
61. Ian Pulsipher, *Evaluating Enterprise Zones* (Washington, DC: National Conference of State Legislatures, Feb. 26, 2008) retrieved from http://www.ncsl.org/programs/econ/evalentzones.htm.
62. See, Iowa Dept. of Economic Dev., High-Quality Job Creation Program, retrieved from http://www.iowaeconomicdevelopment.com/Finance/HQJ, for Rhode Island, see R.I. GEN. LAWS §44–3–9, and for Missouri, see MO. REV. STAT. §§ 353.010–353.190.
63. NEV. REV. STAT. §§360.750, 374.357; OR. REV. STAT §285C.
64. Retrieved from http://governor.state.tx.us/priorities/economy/investing_for_growth/texas_enterprise_fund/.
65. Ibid.

66. Ibid.
67. Ibid.
68. Ibid.
69. Retrieved from http://www.texasobserver.org/cover-story/slush-fun.
70. See generally http://www.development.ohio.gov/Business/Loans_Grants.htm.
71. Ibid.
72. "Evidence Counts: Evaluating State Tax Incentives for Jobs and Growth," *Pew Center for the States,* April 12, 2012, retrieved from http://www.pewstates.org/research/reports/ evidence-counts-85899378806.
73. Ibid.
74. Anjeanette Damon, "Economic Development Costs Nevada $30,000 per Job in Tax Incentives," *Las Vegas Sun,* January 17, 2013.
75. Evidence Counts, Pew Center for the States.
76. Ibid.
77. Ibid.
78. See generally http://www.development.ohio.gov/Business/Loans_Grants.htm.

11 Economic Development Building Block: Quality of Life

1. Retrieved from http://www.areadevelopment.com/AnnualReports/Winter2012/8th-site-selection-consultants-RE-survey-results-28282888.shtml?Page=2.
2. Mark Crawford, "When Quality of Life Closes the Location Decision Deal," *Area Development,* December/January 2010, retrieved from http://www.areadevelopment. com/siteSelection/dec09/quality-of-life-location-factors010.shtml.
3. Retrieved from http://www.nashvilleareainfo.com/homepage/research-mapping/cost-of-living.
4. See Kilungu Nzaku and James O. Bukenya, *The Influence of Amenities and Quality of Life on Regional Development in Alabama,* Paper Presented at the Southern Agricultural Economic Association Annual Meeting, Tulsa, Oklahoma, February 18, 2004.
5. See Steven C. Deller, Tsung-His Tsai, David W. Marcouiller, and Donald B. K. English, "The Role of Amenities and Quality of Life in Rural Economic Growth," *American Journal of Agricultural Economics,* 83, 2 (May 2001) 352–365.
6. See George A. O. Alleyne and Daniel Cohen, *Health, Economic Growth and Poverty Reduction, The Report of Working Group I of the Commission on Macroeconomic Health* (World Health Organization, April 2002).
7. See generally, David Salvesen and Henry Renski, "The Importance of Quality of Life in the Location Decisions of New Economy Firms," *Center for Urban and Regional Studies, University of North Carolina,* January 2003.
8. Ibid.
9. Arthur Levine, "The Suburban Education Gap," *The Wall Street Journal,* November 15, 2012.
10. Retrieved from http://www.google.com/hostednews/afp/article/ALeqM5juGFSx9LiPa ur6eO1KJAypB2ImVQ?docId=CNG.5337504e8f65acf16c57d5cac3cfe339.1c1.
11. Ibid.
12. Retrieved from http://www.edweek.org/ew/articles/2011/09/16/04pay_ep.h31.html?tk n=ZLTFXzsdy44fkSmhtr30XiweVDs12a36r0zw.
13. Susan Bodary, "Comments before the Columbus Mayoral Commission on the Schools," *The Hannah Report,* March 22, 2013.
14. Zelman v. Simmons-Harris, 122 S. Ct. 2460 (2002).
15. Ibid.
16. Ibid.

17. Ibid.
18. Ibid.
19. See Robert T. Greenbaum and George E. Tita, "The Impact of Violence Surges on Neighborhood Business Activity," *Urban Studies*, 41, 13 (December 2004) 2495–2514.
20. Retrieved from http://www.areadevelopment.com/AnnualReports/jan2011/7th-annual-consultants-survey009303.shtml?Page=4.
21. Jeff Godown, "The CompStat Process: Four Principles for Managing Crime Reduction," *The Police Chief*, LXXVI, 8 (August 2009), retrieved at http://www.policechiefmaga-zine.org/magazine/index.cfm?fuseaction=display&article_id=1859&issue_id=82009.
22. Ibid.
23. Ibid.
24. Ibid.
25. Ibid.
26. Ibid.
27. Ibid.
28. *The Impact of Times Square*, HR & A Advisors (New York, NY, March 2012).
29. Ibid.
30. Ibid.
31. Retrieved from http://www.realtor.com/data-portal/Real-Estate-Statistics.aspx.
32. Robert Carroll, John F. O'Hare, and Phillip Swagel, *Costs and Benefits of Housing Tax Subsidies* (Washington, DC: Pew Charitable Trusts, June 2011).
33. Ibid.
34. Ibid.
35. Ibid.
36. Retrieved from http://www.realtor.com/basics/buy/closepossess/taxbenefits.asp?source =web.
37. Ibid.
38. Ibid.
39. Ibid.
40. Carroll, O'Hare and Swagel.
41. James Howard Kunstler, *The Geography of Nowhere* (New York, NY: Free Press, 1993) 102.
42. Ibid.
43. Ibid.
44. Ibid.
45. Ibid.
46. Rob Alford, "What Are the Origins of Freddie Mac and Fannie Mae?" *History News Network*, September 2003.
47. Ibid.
48. Ibid.
49. Ibid.
50. Ibid.
51. Ibid.
52. Ibid.
53. Ibid.
54. Todd Greene, "Rethinking the Relationship of Health Care and Economic Development," *Community Development, Federal Reserve Bank of Atlanta*, March/April 2011.
55. Ibid.
56. See George A. O. Alleyne and Daniel Cohen, "Health, Economic Growth and Poverty Reduction," *The Report of Working Group I of the Commission on Macroeconomics and Health, World Health Organization*, April 2002.

57. Alok Bhargava, Dean T. Jamison, Lawrence Lau, and Christopher J. L. Murry, "Modeling the Effects of Health Care on Economic Growth," *GPE Discussion Paper Series, No. 33, Evidence and Information for Policy, World Health Organization* (1999).
58. Retrieved from http://www.worldlifeexpectancy.com/usa/life-expectancy.
59. Ibid.
60. Kimberly Leonard, "New Ranking Reveals Health Gaps Between and Among States Hawaii has the Best Health Care Access and Quality, Mississippi the Worst," *U.S. News & World Report*, September 18, 2013.
61. Retrieved from http://www.bellin.org/press_releases/2011/1925.
62. Crawford.
63. Ibid.
64. Ibid.
65. Salvesen and Renski.
66. See P. D. Gottlieb, "Amenities as an Economic Development Tool: Is There Enough Evidence?" *Economic Development Quarterly*, 8 (August 1994) 270–285.
67. Nzaku and Bukeyna.
68. Ibid.
69. See F. W. Porell, "Intermetropolitan Migration and Quality of Life." *Journal of Regional Science*, 22 (May 1982) 137–158.
70. Nicki Sitko, *Park City, Utah's Successful Combination of Tourism and Recreation Activities Creates Healthy Economic Development, Tourism as Economic Development*, April 18, 2005, retrieved from http://www.umich.edu/~econdev/parkcity/.
71. *Economic Impacts of Tourism, Park City Utah Report*, Wikstrom Economic Planning and Consulting, May 2009.
72. Ibid.
73. Ibid.
74. Retrieved from http://www.ksl.com/?nid=960&sid=19155597.
75. Steven C. Deller, Tsung-Hsui Tsai, David W. Marcouiller, and Donald B. K. English, "The Role of Amenities and Quality of Life in Rural Economic Growth," *American Journal of Agricultural Economics*, 83, 2 (May 2001) 352–365.
76. Ibid.
77. John C. Bergstrom, H. Ken Cordell, Gregory A. Ashley, and Alan E. Watson, "Economic Impacts of Recreational Spending on Rural Areas: A Case Study," *Economic Development Quarterly*, 4, 1 (1990) 29–39.
78. Salvesen and Renski.
79. Ibid.

12 Economic Driver: Energy-Led Economic Development

1. See Christina Williams, "Report: Oregon's green manufacturing sector looks strong," *Sustainable Business Oregon*, September 10, 2010.
2. Ibid.
3. American Natural Gas Alliance, retrieved from http://anga.us/issues-and-policy/jobs/us-shale-gas-benefits#.Uhn5UbXD-hw.
4. Ibid.
5. Jim Fitterling, "Shale Gas and American Manufacturing: Jobs, Growth and Economic Development," *Vital Speeches of the Day*, 79, 6 (June 2013) 187–190.
6. Ibid.
7. See Robert Burchell, Anthony Downs, Sahan Mukherji, and Barbara McCann, *Sprawl Costs: Economic Impacts of Unchecked Development* (Washington, DC: Island Press. 2005).

8. See David Charles Sloane, "Longer View: From Congestion to Sprawl: Planning and Health in Historical Context," *Journal of American Planning Association*, 72, 1 (November 26, 2006) 10–18.

9. See Karen Chapple, Cynthia Kroll, T. William Lester, and Sergio Montero, "Innovation in the Green Economy: An Extension of the Regional Innovation System Model?" *Economic Development Quarterly*, 25 (2011) 5–25.

10. Mark Muro, Jonathan Rothwell, and Devashree Saha, *Sizing the Clean Economy: A National and Regional Green Jobs Assessment* (Washington, DC: Brookings Institution, July 13, 2011).

11. Ibid.

12. Ibid.

13. Ibid.

14. Ibid.

15. Ibid.

16. See generally, E. R. Alexander, "A Transaction-Cost Theory of Land Use Planning and Development Control: Towards the Institutional Analysis of Public Planning," *The Town Planning Review*, 72, 1 (January 2001) 45–75.

17. Reid Ewing, Rolf Pendall, and Don Chen, *Measuring Sprawl and Its Impact* (Washington DC.: Rutgers University, Smart Growth America, 2002).

18. Mark Muro and Robert Puentes, *Investing in a Better Future: A Review of the Fiscal and Competitive Advantages of Smarter Growth Development Patters* (Washington, DC: Brookings Institution, 2004).

19. Ibid.

20. Ibid.

21. Ibid.

22. Ibid.

23. Ibid.

24. Ibid.

25. Ibid.

26. Retrieved from http://www.asce.org/Press-Releases/2011/New-Report-Shows-Failing-to-Invest-in-Transportation-Will-Cause-Job-Losses,-Shrink-Household-Incomes/.

27. Ibid.

28. American Planning Association Policy Guide on Smart Growth (Chicago, IL: American Planning Association, 2002), retrieved from http://www.planning.org/policy/guides/pdf/smartgrowth.pdf.

29. Ibid.

30. See generally, King County, Washington Definition of Development Right, retrieved from http://www.kingcounty.gov/environment/stewardship/sustainable-building/transfer-development-rights/definitions.aspx.

31. John B. Bredin, "Transfer of Development Rights: Cases, Statutes, Examples, and a *Model*," *2000 APA National Planning Conference*, April 18, 2000, retrieved from http://www.design.asu.edu/apa/proceedings00/BREDIN/bredin.htm.

32. Ibid.

33. Ibid.

34. Ibid.

35. Ibid.

36. Department of Economic Development, Montgomery County Farmland Preservation, retrieved from http://www.montgomerycountymd.gov/content/ded/agservices/pdffiles/intotoagpres2008.pdf.

37. Land Trust Alliance, retrieved from https://www.landtrustalliance.org/conservation/landowners/conservation-easements.

38. "Land Bank Buys Sundstrom Farm," *The Island Guardian,* October 7, 2008, retrieved from http://www.islandguardian.com/archives/00002238.html.

39. Ibid.
40. Ibid.
41. Ibid.
42. San Juan County Land Bank, Selection Criteria, retrieved from http://www.sjcland-bank.org/feesimple.html.
43. Ibid.
44. "Land Bank Buys Sundstrom Farm," *The Island Guardian,* October 7, 2008, retrieved from http://www.islandguardian.com/archives/00002238.html.
45. Ibid.
46. Ore. Rev. Stat. Sec. 197.005–197.860 (1991).
47. Ibid. at Sec. 197.010, 197.175.
48. Ibid. at Sec. 197.030.
49. Ibid. at Sec. 197.040.
50. Ibid. at Sec. 197.335.
51. Ibid.
52. Ibid. at Sec.197.299.
53. Ibid.
54. Ibid.
55. Ibid.
56. Stuart Meck (ed.), *American Planning Association, Growing Smart Legislation Guidebook: Model Statutes for Planning and the Management of Change, Note 6C: A Note on Existing Regional Plans* (Chicago, IL: American Planning Association, 2002).
57. Jennifer Cleary and Allison Kopicki, *Preparing the Workforce for a "Green Jobs" Economy* (John J. Heldrich Center for Workforce Development, February 2009).
58. Ibid.
59. Ibid.
60. Ibid.
61. The Pennsylvania Green Jobs Report, Part 1 (Pennsylvania Department of Labor & Industry, January 2010).
62. Building a Green Collar Workforce, October 2009, retrieved from http://greencollar-chicago.org/assets/GreenCollarWorkforce.pdf.
63. Ibid.
64. Retrieved from http://www.epa.gov/swerosps/bf/laws/2869sum.htm.
65. Ibid.
66. Retrieved from http://www.epa.gov/swerosps/bf/laws/2869sum.htm.
67. Retrieved from http://www.epa.gov/swerosps/bf/laws/liability/index.htm.
68. Ibid.
69. Retrieved from http://www.epa.gov/swerosps/bf/about.htm.
70. Retrieved from http://www.epa.gov/swerosps/bf/assessment_grants.htm
71.. Ibid.
72. Ibid.
73. Retrieved from http://www.epa.gov/swerosps/bf/cleanup_grants.htm.
74. Retrieved from http://www.epa.gov/swerosps/bf/job.htm.
75. Ibid.
76. Ibid.
77. Retrieved from http://www.epa.gov/swerosps/bf/grant_info/rlf/rlf_factsheet.pdf.
78. Ibid.
79. See http://www.epa.gov/swerosps/bf/index.html.
80. Ibid.
81. Jim Carlton, "Brownfields Bloom in Seattle," *Wall Street Journal,* July 25, 2011.
82. Retrieved from http://www.epa.gov/swerosps/bf/about.htm.
83. Ibid.
84. Ibid.

85. Retrieved from http://clean.ohio.gov/BrownfieldRevitalization/Documents/CORF _Policies_Effective06292011_Final_000.pdf.
86. See Generally, http://clean.ohio.gov/.
87. Ibid.
88. Ibid.
89. Ibid.
90. Ibid.
91. Ibid.
92. Ibid.
93. Ibid.
94. Ibid.
95. Ibid.
96. http://clean.ohio.gov/Documents/CleanOhio_Report.pdf, p. 22.
97. Ibid.
98. Ibid.
99. See U.S. Green Building Council, http://www.usgbc.org/DisplayPage.aspx?Category ID=19.
100. Ibid.
101. Ibid.
102. Ibid.
103. Ibid.
104. Ibid.
105. Ibid.
106. Ibid.
107. Ibid.
108. Ibid.
109. Ibid.
110. See the City of Oregon, Green Investment Fund, http://www.portlandonline.com /bps/index.cfm?c=42134.
111. Ibid.
112. Ibid.
113. See Peter V. Schaeffer and Cecily Ahern Millerick, "The Impact of Historic Designation on Property Values: An Empirical Study," *Economic Development Quarterly*, 5 (November 1991) 301–312.
114. Retrieved from http://www.preservationnation.org/information-center/sustainable-communities/sustainability/green-lab/valuing-building-reuse.html#.ULKA2qPpV8E.
115. Ibid.
116. See John I. Gilderbloom, Matthew J. Hanka, and Joshua D. Ambrosius, "Historic Preservation's Impact on Job Creation, Property Values and Environmental Stability," *Journal of Urbanism: International Research on Placemaking and Urban Sustainability*, 2, 2 (July 23, 2009) 83–101.
117. San Mateo City Code, Ch. 27.66, et seq, available at http://www.cityofsanmateo. org/index.asp?NID=808.
118. San Mateo City Code § 27.66.040.
119. San Mateo City Code § 27.66.060.
120. Gilderbloom, Hanka and Ambrosius.
121. Ibid.
122. Ibid.
123. Retrieved from http://www.nps.gov/tps/about.htm.
124. Retrieved from http://www.npa.gov/tps/tax-incentives.htm.
125. Retrieved from http://www.preservationnation.org/information-center/sustainable-communities/community-revitalizatin/jobs/#.ULJ9cKPpV8E.

127. *Measuring the Economics of Preservation:Recent Findings* (PlaceEconomics, June 2011).
127. Ibid.
128. See Gilderbloom, Hanka and Ambrosius.
129. Ibid.
130. Juita-Elana (Wie) Yusuf and Katharine A. Neill, "State Energy-Based Economic Development Policies and Examples," *Economic Development Quarterly*, 27, 3 (2013) 240–249.
131. Ibid.
132. "Midstream Development Key for Utica Shale Play," *Ohio Matters*, Ohio Chamber of Commerce, July/August 2013, retrieved from www.ohiochamber.com.
133. Ibid.
134. Ibid.
135. Ibid.
136. *Economic Impact Study of Ohio's Utica Shale*, sponsored by the Ohio Chamber of Commerce, retrieved from http://urban.csuohio.edu/publications/center/center_for_economic_development/Ec_Impact_Ohio_Utica_Shale_2012.pdf.

13   Economic Driver: Technology-Based Economic Development

1. See www.rtp.org/.
2. Edward B. Roberts and Charles Eesley, *Entrepreneurial Impact: The Role of MIT* (Cambridge, MA: MIT Sloan School of Management, Kauffman Foundation, 2009).
3. See Terry F. Buss, "Emerging High-Growth Firms and Economic Development Policy," *Economic Development Quarterly*, 16, 1 (February 2002) 17–19.
4. Ben Cover, John I. Jones, and Audrey Watson, "Science, Technology, Engineering, and Mathematics (STEM) Occupations: A Visual Essay," 135, 5, *Bureau of Labor Statistics, Monthly Labor Review*, May 2011.
5. Ibid.
6. Ibid.
7. Ibid.
8. Ibid.
9. *Measuring Entrepreneurship, A Collection of Indicators, 2009 Edition* (OECD-Eurostat Entrepreneurship Indicators Programme, 2009).
10. SSTI, Technology Based Economic Development Guide, 2006.
11. Ibid.
12. Ibid.
13. Ibid.
14. See generally, http://fasttrac.org/.
15. Ibid.
16. Ibid.
17. Ibid.
18. Ibid.
19. Ibid.
20. Ibid.
21. Association of University Technology Managers, *U.S. Licensing Activity Survey Highlights: FY2012*.
22. Ibid.
23. Ibid.
24. Association of University Technology Managers, *U.S. Licensing Activity Survey: FY2011*.

25. Ibid.
26. Roberts and Eesley.
27. Ibid.
28. *The STEM Workforce Challenge*, U.S. Department of Labor, 2007.
29. Ibid.
30. Ibid.
31. Bureau of Labor Statistics, 2012.
32. STEM Education: Preparing for the Jobs of the Future, Congressional Joint Economic Committee, April 2012.
33. Ibid.
34. Jonathan Rothwell, *The Hidden STEM Economy* (Washington, DC: Brookings Institution, June 2013), retrieved from http://www.brookings.edu/~/media/research /files/reports/2013/06/10 percent20stem percent20economy percent20rothwell/thehid- denstemeconomy610.pdf.
35. STEM Colorado, http://www.stemcolorado.com/about_us.html.
36. Ibid.
37. Washington STEM, http://www.washingtonstem.org/Our-Impact/Grant-Detail/?Grant DetailID=432.
38. Ibid.
39. Maryam Farhadi, Rahmah Ismail, and Masood Fooladi, "Information and Communication Technology Use and Economic Growth," *PLoS One*, 7, 11 (2012) retrieved from http://papers.ssrn.com/sol3/papers.cfm?abstract_id=2259563.
40. Retrieved from http://www.idealab.com/about_idealab/.
41. Retrieved from http://www.idealab.com/.
42. Ibid.
43. Ibid.
44. Ibid.
45. http://iedc.in.gov/entrepreneurship/venture-capital-investment-tax-credit.
46. Ibid.
47. Ibid.
48. Ibid.
49. See generally, http://www.watechcenter.org/.
50. Ibid.
51. Ibid.
52. Ibid.
53. See generally, http://capcofacts.com/capco-news.html.
54. http://www.capcoprogram.com/capco-program-locations/.
55. See generally, http://uwadmnweb.uwyo.edu/SBIR/.
56. Ibid.
57. Ibid.
58. Ibid.
59. http://uwadmnweb.uwyo.edu/SBIR/phase0winners.html.
60. See generally, http://nep.benfranklin.org/services-resources/investments-financial- support.
61. Ibid.
62. Ibid.
63. Ibid.
64. See generally, http://ocib.org/.
65. Ibid.
66. Ibid.
67. Ibid.
68. See generally, http://www.utahfof.com/.

69. Ibid.
70. Ibid.
71. Ibid.
72. Ibid.
73. Ibid.
74. Ibid.
75. Rudolf Giffinger, *Smart Cities—Ranking of European Medium-sized Cities* (Centre of Regional Science, Vienna UT, October 2007).
76. Ruthbea Yesner Clarke, Mark Yates, Mukesh Chulani, Alison Brooks, Lianfeng Wu, and Eiji Sasahara, *Worldwide Smart City 2013 Top 10 Predictions* (IDC Government Insights, February 2013).
77. http://www.fastcoexist.com/1680967/the-top-10-smartest-cities-in-north-america.
78. Gordon Falconer and Shane Mitchell, *Smart City Framework A Systematic Process for Enabling Smart+Connected Communities* (Cisco Systems, September 2012).
79. A Smarter City, IBM Solutions, http://www.ibm.com/smarterplanet/us/en/smarter_cities/article/smarter_cities_case_studies.html#ibm-sp-cs-feed=1?http percent3A percent2F percent2Fwww.ibm.com percent2Fsoftware percent2Fsuccess percent2Fcssdb.nsf percent2Fcs percent2FLSWN-943TQM percent3FOpenDocument percent26site percent3Dcorp percent26cty percent3Den_us.
80. Ibid.
81. Ibid.

14   Economic Development Driver: Globalism

1. Douglas P. Woodward and Paulo Guimarães, *BMW in South Carolina: The Economic Impact of a Leading Sustainable Enterprise*, September 2008.
2. Ibid.
3. Ibid.
4. Ibid.
5. Ibid.
6. Ibid.
7. Ibid.
8. http://trade.gov/cs/factsheet.asp.
9. Ibid.
10. Ibid.
11. http://www.uschamber.com/international/agenda/welcome-investment-abroad.
12. Ibid.
13. 2010 National Export Strategy, U.S. Department of Commerce.
14. Ibid.
15. Ibid.
16. Ibid.
17. Executive Office of the President, Council of Economic Advisors, *U.S. Inbound Foreign Direct Investment Report*, June 2011.
18. Ibid.
19. Ibid.
20. Ibid.
21. Ibid.
22. David Payne and Fenwick Yu, *Foreign Direct Investment in the United States, Executive Summary*, U.S. Department of Commerce, Economics and Statistics Administration, June 2011.
23. Ibid.
24. Executive Office of the President, Council of Economic Advisors, *U.S. Inbound Foreign Direct Investment Report* June 2011.

25. Ibid.
26. Ibid.
27. Ibid.
28. Ibid.
29. Ibid.
30. Ibid.
31. Ibid.
32. Ibid.
33. Ibid.
34. Ibid.
35. Wichita, Kansas City Profile, http://www.wichita.gov/NR/rdonlyres/E5573978-1D96-4F46-A31B-004E7D4DDDCA/0/2008CityProfile.pdf.
36. Ibid.
37. Wichita Chamber of Commerce, http://www.wichitakansas.org/economic_development-wichita_metro_profile-workforce.php.
38. See *Export Nation Report* (Washington, DC: Brookings Institution, July 2010), retrieved from http://www.brookings.edu/metro/MetroExports/GMP.aspx.
39. Wichita Chamber of Commerce Report, retrieved from http://www.wichitakansas.org/economic_development-wichita_metro_profile-workforce.php.
40. Ibid.
41. See *Export Nation Report* (Washington, DC: Brookings Institution, July 2010), retrieved from http://www.brookings.edu/metro/MetroExports/GMP.aspx.
42. Ibid.
43. Ibid.
44. Ibid.
45. Ibid.
46. *General Aviation industry makes Wichita "air capital of the world,"* FastLane, *U.S. DOT Blog,* March 21, 2011.
47. See NIAR Web Site, http://www.niar.twsu.edu/.
48. Ibid.
49. Ibid.
50. Ibid.
51. Ibid.
52. Ibid.
53. Ibid.
54. http://watc.edu/aviation/ncat/.
55. Ibid.
56. Ibid.
57. Ibid.
58. Molly McMillen, "Oklahoma Governor Signs Bill for Aerospace Tax Credit," *Wichita Eagle,* April 4, 2011.
59. Retrieved from http://www.cityofseattle.net/oir/datasheet/economy.htm.
60. See http://www.seattletradealliance.com/.
61. Ibid.
62. Bureau of Economic Analysis.
63. See Changkyu Choi, "Does the Internet Stimulate Inward Foreign Direct Investment?" *Journal of Policy Modeling,* 25 (2003) 319–326.
64. Ibid.
65. See Henry Loewendahl, *A Framework for FDI Promotion* (Transnational Corporations, vol. 10, no. 1, April 2001).
66. Payne and Yu.
67. Loewendahl.
68. Ibid.

69. Ibid.
70. Ibid.
71. Ibid.
72. Foreign Trade Zone Board Annual Report, 2012.
73. Ibid.
74. Mary Jane Bolle and Brock R. Williams, "Foreign Trade Zones: Background and Issues for Congress," *Congressional Research Service*, September 5, 2012, retrieved from http://www.fas.org/sgp/crs/misc/R42686.pdf.
75. See generally, U.S. Foreign-Trade Zones Board, Frequently Asked Questions, http://ia.ita.doc.gov/ftzpage/info/ftzstart.html (last visited November 28, 2008).
76. Ibid.
77. Ibid.
78. Ibid.
79. Ibid.
80. Ibid.
81. Ibid.
82. Pant.
83. Ibid.
84. Ibid.
85. "Alliance Foreign-Trade Zone Ranks as Top General Purpose Foreign-Trade Zone in the U.S.," Hillwood Press Release, February 28, 2012, retrieved from http://www.hillwood.com/story.aspx?ID=3918.
86. Ibid.
87. Ibid.
88. Ibid.
89. Tennessee Valley Authority, Mega Site Brief, retrieved from http://www.tvasites.com/Insite.aspx?searchArea=Properties&searchPropertiesType=Site&searchPropertiesLandType=Mega Site.
90. Ibid.
91. Ibid.
92. Ibid.
93. Ibid.
94. Richard Locker, "'Megasite' Promises Mega Impact for West Tennessee, Concept Promises Industrial Jobs—and Eco Worry," *The Commercial Appeal*, October 11, 2009.
95. Ibid.
96. Ibid.
97. Ibid.
98. TVA Mega Site Brief.
99. Locker.
100. Ibid.
101. TVA Mega Site Brief.
102. Ibid.
103. G. Scott Thomas, "Manufacturing Sector Propels Southern Economic Gains," *The Business Journals,* June 15, 2011.
104. Mali R. Schantz, "Regional Report: Southern States Receiving Their Fair Share of Foreign Direct Investment," *Area Development*, July 2011.
105. Ibid.
106. Ibid.
107. Ibid.
108. "Mitsubishi Electric Power Products Picks Memphis, Tennessee, for $200M HQ," *Area Development Online News Desk*, February 14, 2011.
109. Ibid.

110. Schantz.

111. Alabama House Bill 56, 2011.

112. Ibid.

113. Ibid.

114. Samuel Addy, *A Cost-Benefit Analysis of the New Alabama Immigration Law* (The University of Alabama, January 2012).

115. Ibid.

116. Ibid.

117. Ibid.

118. See http://www.littletongov.org/bia/economicgardening/.

119. See http://www.economicgardening.ca/.

120. Ibid.

121. *Blueprint for Propelling a New Economic Direction for Michigan*, Prepared for the Small Business Association of Michigan, Public Policy Associates, October 2010.

122. See http://www.unzco.com/basicguide/c2.html.

123. See http://www.canadabusiness.ab.ca/docs/2009 percent20Writing percent20an percent20Export percent20Plan.pdf.

124. See https://exportingpa.org/Tutorials.aspx.

125. Ibid.

126. See http://www.edwardlowe.org/ERC/?department=Defining percent20and percent20Serving percent20a percent20Market.

127. See http://www.orlandoedc.com/News/2011/01/gardening_grows_jobs.php.

128. Ibid.

129. Ibid.

130. Ibid.

15 Economic Development Driver: Advanced Manufacturing Strategy

1. William Strauss, *Is U.S. Manufacturing Disappearing* (Federal Reserve Bank of Chicago, August 19, 2010).

2. Susan Helper and Howard Wiall, *Advanced Manufacturing and New Research Centers* (Washington, DC: Brookings Institution, February 2011).

3. John W. Miller, "U.S. Steel's New $20 an hour Worker," *Wall Street Journal*, July 10, 2013.

4. Ibid.

5. Susan Helper, Timothy Krueger, and Howard Wiall, *Why Does Manufacturing Matter? Which Manufacturing Matters? A Policy Framework* (Washington, DC: Brookings Institution, February 2012).

6. Ibid.

7. Ibid.

8. Ibid.

9. Ibid.

10. Brittany M. Bond, "The Geographic Concentration of Manufacturing Across the United States," *ESA Issue Brief #01–13*, January 2013.

11. Ibid.

12. Ibid.

13. Ibid.

14. Truman A. Hartshorna, "Industrial/Office Parks: a New Look for the City," *Journal of Geography*, 72, 3 (1973) 33–45.

15. Jarmila Vidova, "Industrial Parks- History, Their Present and Influence on Employment," *Review of Economic Perspectives*, 10, 1 (2010) 41–58.

16. Ibid.
17. Ibid.
18. Ibid.
19. Ibid.
20. See R. R. Heeresa, W. J. V. Vermeulena, and F. B. de Walleb, "Eco-industrial park initiatives in the USA and the Netherlands: first lessons," *Journal of Cleaner Production*, 12, 8–10 (October–December 2004) 985–995.
21. Retrieved from http://www.dac.dk/en/dac-cities/sustainable-cities-2/all-cases/waste/kalundborg-industrial-symbiosis---waste-makes-resource/?bbredirect=true.
22. Ibid.
23. Ibid.
24. Connecticut Manufacturing Fact Sheet, Connecticut Industry and Business Association, retrieved from http://cbia.com/govaff/pdf/2011/manufacts_11.pdf.
25. Ibid.
26. Helper and Wiall, *Advanced Manufacturing and New Research Centers*.
27. Retrieved from http://www.ccat.us/initiatives.
28. Ibid.
29. Ibid.
30. Ibid.
31. Ibid.
32. Manufacturers Association of Florida, retrieved from http://www.mafmfg.com/display-common.cfm?an=2.
33. Ibid.
34. Enterprise Florida, Aerospace and Aviation Industry Facts, retrieved from http://www.eflorida.com/Aviation_Aerospace.aspx?id=306.
35. Ibid.
36. Helper and Wiall, *Advanced Manufacturing and New Research Centers*.
37. Retireved from http://www.fcaap.com/index.cfm?p=research.
38. Ibid.
39. Ibid.
40. Charles Davis, "State Environmental Regulation and Economic Development: Are They Compatible?" *Policy Studies Review*, 11, 1 (Spring 1992) 149–157.
41. F. M. Gollop and M. J. Roberts, "Environmental Regulations and Productivity Growth: The Case of Fossil-Fuelled Electric Power Generation," *Journal of Political Economy*, 91 (1983) 654–674.
42. R. Luken, "The Effect of Environmental Regulation on Industrial Competitiveness of Selected Industries in Developing Countries," *Greener Management International*, 19 (1997) 67–78.
43. Michael Porter and C. van der Linde, "Toward a New Conception of the Environment Competitiveness Relationship," *Journal of Economic Perspectives*, 9 (1995) 97–118.
44. Jean-Paul Rodrigue, *The Geography of Transport Systems*, 3rd ed. (New York, NY: Routledge, 2013).
45. Ibid.
46. Ibid.
47. Indianapolis Region: Logistics, Indy Partnership.
48. Ibid.
49. Ibid.
50. Ibid.
51. Ibid.
52. Retrieved from http://www.considerthecarolinas.com/rates/options.asp#growth.
53. Ibid.
54. Ibid.

55. Ibid.
56. Ibid.
57. Ibid.
58. Helper, Krueger, and Wiall.
59. Landon and Lehrmann, ESA Issue Brief, 2012.
60. Bureau of Labor Statistics, Annual Union Membership Survey, January 23, 2013.
61. Ibid.
62. Ibid.
63. Ibid.
64. Ibid.
65. Jeffrey M. Lacker, *Manufacturing in the New Southern Economy* (Federal Reserve Bank of Richmond, Southern Growth's 2011 Chairman's Conference, Roanoke, Virginia, June 13, 2011).
66. See generally, Michaela D. Platzer and Glennon J. Harrison, *The U.S. Automotive Industry: National and State Trends in Manufacturing Employment*, (Washington, DC: Congressional Research Service, August 3, 2009).
67. Lacker.
68. Neil Shah and Ben Casselman, "'Right-to-Work' Economics: States That Bar Mandatory Union Dues Tend Toward More Jobs but Lower Wages," *Wall Street Journal*, December 14, 2012.
69. *2012 Union Members Summary*, Bureau of Labor Statistics, U.S. Department of Labor, January 23, 2013.

16   Economic Development Driver: The Regional Service Economy

1. *Measuring Service-Sector Research and Development*, RTI International Health, Social, and Economics Research, March 2005.
2. Ibid.
3. John Ward, *The Services Sector: How Best to Measure It?* (Washington, DC: International Trade Administration, October 2010).
4. Ibid.
5. Ibid.
6. Kurt Badenhausen, "While Rest Of U.S. Economy Plods, Houston Gets Hot," *Forbes Magazine*, July 6, 2012.
7. *Global Metro Monitoring* (Washington, DC: Brookings Institution, 2011–2012).
8. Ibid.
9. Adam Bruns, "A City to Live In," *Site Selection Magazine*, September 2013, retrieved from http://siteselection.com/issues/2013/sep/texas.cfm.
10. Retrieved from http://blog.directenergy.com/2012/04/11/direct-energy-to-hire-200-people-for-key-positions/.
11. Badenhausen.
12. Ibid.
13. Ibid.
14. Retrieved from http://texasmedicalcenter.org/facts-and-figures/.
15. Ibid.
16. Ibid.
17. Ibid.
18. Ibid.
19. Ibid.
20. Ibid.

21. Ibid.
22. William B. Beyers and David P. Lindahl, *Services and the New Economic Landscape* (European Regional Science Association, August 1998).
23. Fortune 500 2012 List.
24. Ibid.
25. Ibid.
26. Vanessa Strauss-Kahn and Xavier Vives, *Why and Where do Headquarters Move?* Working Paper, IESE Business School, University of Navarra, September 2006.
27. Strauss-Kahn and Vives.
28. Indiana Relocation Headquarters Tax Credit Fact Sheet, retrieved from http://iedc.in.gov/tax-credits-exemptions/headquarters-relocation-tax-credit.
29. Ibid.
30. Retrieved from http://sccommerce.com/node/2315
31. Ibid.
32. Ibid.
33. Retrieved from http://www.tn.gov/ecd/BD_business_tax_credit.html#hq.
34. Ibid.
35. *Economic Impact of Commercial Airports, 2010*, Airports Council International- North America.
36. Ibid.
37. Ibid.
38. Geoffrey Booth, *Ten Principles for Reinventing Suburban Business Districts* (Washington, DC: Urban Land Institute, 2002).
39. Downtown Miami Economic Development Incentives, retrieved from http://www.miamidda.com/business_incentives.asp.
40. Ibid.
41. City of Columbus Downtown Development Office, retrieved from http://econdev.columbus.gov/business_services/financial_assistance.aspx.
42. See H. W. Aslesen and A. Isaksen, "New Perspectives on Knowledge-Intensive Services and Innovation," *Geografiska Annaler: Series B, Human Geography*, 89 (2007) 45–58.
43. Ellen D. Harpel, "Professional and Business Services in Regional Economies," *Economic Development Journal,* Summer 2006.
44. Ibid.
45. Ibid.
46. Ibid.
47. Ibid.
48. Ibid.
49. Tampa Bay US, http://www.tampabay.us/incentives/targeted-industry-incentives.aspx.
50. Retrieved from http://www.floridatrend.com/article/1257/tampa-bay.
51. Ibid.
52. Ibid.
53. Ibid.
54. David Salvesen and Henry Renski, *The Importance of Quality of Life in the Location Decisions of New Economy Firms* (Center for Urban and Regional Studies, University of North Carolina, January 2003).
55. *Urban Mobility Report* (Texas A&M University, 2012).
56. Ibid.
57. Ibid.
58. Ibid.
59. Ibid.
60. *Education Pays* (The College Board, 2010).
61. Ibid.

62. U.S. Census Bureau, 2007 Report.
63. Ibid.
64. Retrieved from http://advocacy.collegeboard.org/five-ways-ed-pays/campaign-materials.
65. Ibid.
66. Ibid.
67. Fortieth Annual Survey Report on State-Sponsored Student Financial Aid 2008–2009 Academic Year, National Association of State Student Grant and Aid Programs, Executive Summary.
68. Ibid.
69. Ibid.
70. Ibid. at 16.
71. "Economic Contributions of Hospitals Often Overlooked," *American Hospital Association*, 2013, retrieved from http://www.aha.org/content/13/13brief-econcontrib.pdf.
72. Ibid.
73. Ibid.
74. See Marla Nelson and Laura Wolf-Powers, "Chains and Ladders: Exploring the Opportunities for Workforce Development and Poverty Reduction in the Hospital Sector," *Economic Development Quarterly*, 24, 1 (February 2010) 33–44.
75. See Harold T. Gross, "The Role of Health Services in Metropolitan and Central City Economic Development: The Example of Dallas," *Economic Development Quarterly*, 9, 1 (February 1995) 80–86, and James O. Bukenya, Tesfa G. Gebremedhin, and Peter V. Schaeffer, "Analysis of Rural Quality of Life and Health: A Spatial Approach," *Economic Development Quarterly*, 17, 3 (August 2003) 280–293.
76. See Marla Nelson, "Are Hospitals an Export Industry?: Empirical Evidence From Five Lagging Regions," *Economic Development Quarterly*, 23, 3 (August 2009) 242–253.
77. Bureau of Labor Statistics, Occupational Outlook Handbook, 2010–2020 Projects, retrieved from http://www.bls.gov/ooh/About/Projections-Overview.htm.
78. Bureau of Labor Statistics, Growing Occupations Report, retrieved from http://www.bls.gov/ooh/About/Projections-Overview.htm.
79. Retrieved from http://web.jhu.edu/economic_stimulus/economic_impact.htm.
80. See generally, David E. Bloom and David Canning, *Health and Economic Growth: Reconciling the Micro and Macro Evidence*, Harvard School of Public Health, February 2005.
81. Retrieved from http://www.forbes.com/2009/10/09/best-states-healthcare-business-washington-reform.html.
82. A Vital Force in Ohio's Economy, *Cleveland Clinic Economic Impact Report*, 2011.
83. Economic Impact of the Investments and Operations of Catholic Health Partners on the State of Ohio, *Catholic Health Partners Economic Impact Report*, 2011.

17 The Future of Economic Development

1. See the National Center for the Middle Market, 2012 Annual Report.
2. Ibid.
3. Ibid.
4. Ibid.
5. Ibid.
6. Ibid.
7. Mid Market Perspectives, Deloitte, 2012, retrieved from http://www.deloitte.com/view/en_US/us/Services/deloitte-growth-enterprise-services/3f5c7957b2d07310VgnVCM1000001956f00aRCRD.htm.

8. See http://saportareport.com/blog/2011/11/investing-in-our-ports- percentE2 percent80 percent94-a-multi-state-regional-approach-is-needed/.
9. Ibid.
10. *Area Development*, Summer 2012, 10–11.
11. Ibid.
12. See http://shrinkingcities.ncr.vt.edu/sustainability.html.
13. Ibid.
14. Ibid.
15. Ibid.
16. Christopher Swope, "In 40 years, Youngstown has Lost more than Half its Population. Those People aren't Coming Back. But Shrinking doesn't Have to Mean Dying," *Governing Magazine*, November 2006.
17. Ibid.
18. See *Infrastructure 2008, a Competitive Advantage*, ULI and Ernst and Young (2008).
19. See www.fhwadot.gov/ppp/defined.htm.
20. See Testimony of Edward Klienbard to Joint Committee on Taxation of the Congress, July 24, 2008.
21. See Indiana Toll Road and Concession Agreement (2006), retrieved from http://www.in.gov/ifa/files/4-12-06-Concession-Lease-Agreement.pdf.
22. Ibid.
23. Ibid.
24. Ibid.
25. Klienbard.
26. Ibid.
27. Ibid.
28. Ibid.
29. Ibid.
30. See A. Markusen and E. Barbour, "California's Occupational Advantage," *Working Paper No. 12* (2003), retrieved from http://www.hhh.umn.edu/projects/prie/cal_occ_adv.pdf.
31. Ibid.
32. A. Markusen, *Targeting Occupations in Regional And Community Economic Development*, University of Minnesota, 2002.
33. John C. Leatherman, "Input-Output Analysis of the Kickapoo River Valley," *Staff Paper 94.2*, University of Wisconsin-Madison/Extension (July 1994) 14.
34. Ibid.
35. See generally Wassily W Leontief, *Input-Output Economic*, 2nd ed. (New York, NY: Oxford University Press, 1986).
36. Charles B. Kennington, *The Virginia Economic Development Partnership Local Return on Investment Model: A Tool for Analyzing the Local Fiscal Impacts of Economic Development Projects in Virginia* (Virginia Economic Development Partnership, February 2011).
37. Daniel M. Wood, "California Adopts First Statewide Green Building Code," *Christian Science Monitor*, January 15, 2010.
38. Ibid.
39. Ibid.
40. Ibid.
41. Ibid.
42. See H. R. 3606, 112th Congress, 2012.
43. Ibid.
44. Ibid.
45. Ibid.
46. Retrieved from https://starter.gatech.edu/.

47. Ibid.
48. Ibid.
49. Ibid.
50. See William Aspray1, "IT Offshoring and American Labor," *American Behavioral Scientist*, 53, 7 (2010) 962–982.
51. *Made in the USA, Again: Manufacturing Is Expected to Return to America as China's Rising Labor Costs Erase Most Savings from Offshoring* (Boston Consulting Group, May 2011).
52. Ibid.
53. Ibid.
54. Ibid.
55. See Wei He and Marjorie A. Lyles, "China's Outward Foreign Direct Investment," *Business Horizons*, 51 (2008) 485–491.
56. Ibid.
57. Aspray1.
58. Sheridan Prasso, "Why we Left Our Factories in China," *Fortune*, June 29, 2011.
59. *Arts & The Economy* (Washington, DC: National Governors Association Best Practices Report, 2009).
60. Ibid.
61. Ibid.
62. Retrieved from http://paducahky.gov/paducah/demographics.
63. Census Bureau, 2010.
64. U.S. Census Bureau American Community Survey for 2006–2010.
65. Ibid.
66. Retrieved from http://www.philaculture.org/resources/abcd/initiatives/2887/paducah-ky.
67. Ibid.
68. Retrieved from http://www.epaducah.com/why-paducah/arts/#section3.
69. Ibid.
70. Ibid.
71. PWC, World in 2050 Report, 2006, retrieved from http://www.pwc.com/world2050.
72. Ibid.
73. CIA The World Fact Book, Brazil, 2012, retrieved from https://www.cia.gov/library/publications/the-world-factbook/geos/br.html.
74. Ibid.
75. Ibid.
76. Ibid.
77. CIA The World Fact Book, India, 2012, retrieved from https://www.cia.gov/library/publications/the-world-factbook/geos/in.html.
78. Ibid.
79. Ibid.
80. Ibid.
81. CIA The World Fact Book, China, 2012, retrieved from https://www.cia.gov/library/publications/the-world-factbook/geos/ch.html.
82. Ibid.
83. Ibid.
84. Ibid.

Index

Printed in Great Britain
by Amazon